General JOHN H. WINDER, C.S.A.

General
JOHN H. WINDER
C.S.A.

Arch Fredric Blakey

University of Florida Press
Gainesville

The University of Florida Press is a member of University Presses of Florida, the scholarly publishing agency of the State University System of Florida. Books are selected for publication by faculty editorial committees at each of Florida's nine public universities: Florida A&M University (Tallahassee), Florida Atlantic University (Boca Raton), Florida International University (Miami), Florida State University (Tallahassee), University of Central Florida (Orlando), University of Florida (Gainesville), University of North Florida (Jacksonville), University of South Florida (Tampa), University of West Florida (Pensacola).

Orders for books published by all member presses should be addressed to University Presses of Florida, 15 NW 15th St., Gainesville, Fl 32603.

Library of Congress Cataloging-in-Publication Data

Blakey, Arch Fredric.
    General John H. Winder, C.S.A. / Arch Fredric Blakey.
        p.   cm.
    Includes bibliographical references.
    ISBN 0–8130–0997–9 (alk. paper)
    1. Winder, John H. (John Henry), 1800–1865.   2. Generals—Southern States—Biography.   3. Confederate States of America.   Army—Biography.   I. Title.
E467.1.W76B47   1990   90–34655
973.7′13′092—dc20   CIP
[B]

To the memory of my parents, Arch and Robina

CONTENTS

Illustrations

Illustrations follow page 144.

General William Henry Winder
Andrew Shepherd home, Washington, Georgia
Caroline Ann Cox Eagles Winder, age twenty
Caroline Ann "Carrie" Eagles, ca. 1866
William Andrew Winder, ca. 1867
John Cox Winder, college student, ca. 1850
William Sidney Winder, ca. 1866
John Henry Winder, Captain U.S.A., 1846
Field desk of John Henry Winder
Winder Building
John Henry Winder, Major, U.S.A., 1861
Winder Confederate bond
John Henry Winder, Brigadier General, C.S.A. 1862
Painting of Brigadier General John Henry Winder, C.S.A., 1862
Libby Prison, 1865
Belle Isle Prison, 1863
Andersonville Prison, 1864
Union prisoners, Winder's "victims," 1864
Colonel William Hoffman
Brigadier General Justin Dimick
Robert Ould
Prisoner of war camp, Elmira, New York
Winder Genealogical Chart
Gilbert-Hillhouse-Shepherd Genealogical Chart

ACKNOWLEDGMENTS

Many people have helped in the preparation of this study, and I now gratefully acknowledge my debts to them. My first obligation is to my good friend John Barton Lawson, formerly of the Tallahassee Police Department, who first introduced me to this subject in the mid-1960s. Bart had begun a master's thesis on Winder's role in wartime Richmond before forsaking teaching for a career in law enforcement. Several years ago, he gave me all of his research materials and has been a constant source of encouragement and help ever since.

Special thanks are due to Charles Shaughnessy and Michael Musick, Old Army Records, National Archives; Oliver Orr, Library of Congress; Richard Shrader, Southern Historical Collection, Wilson Library, University of North Carolina, Chapel Hill; Robert Willingham, Curator of Rare Books, Dillard Library, University of Georgia, Athens; Michael Winey, United States Army Military History Institute, Carlisle, Pennsylvania; Elaine Eatroff, United States Military Academy Library, West Point, New York; G. Wayne King, Francis Marion College; William Burns, Florence Museum, Florence, South Carolina; Faye Dickerson, Brunswick County Courthouse, Bolivia, North Carolina; National Park Rangers Michael Morgan and Robert Sullivan, Fort McHenry, Baltimore, Maryland; and Gary Parks, Museum and Library of Maryland History, Baltimore, Maryland.

To the efficient and courteous staffs of the following institutions and libraries, my deepest gratitude for all of your help: Hall of Records, Annapolis, Maryland; Greenmount Cemetery, Baltimore, Maryland; Photographic and Manuscript Collections, Library of Congress; North Carolina State Archives, Raleigh; New Hanover County Courthouse and New Hanover County Museum, Wilmington, North Carolina; Manuscript Collection, William R. Perkins Library, Duke University, Durham, North Carolina; North Carolina Collection and the Southern Historical Collection, Wilson Library; the Museum of the Confederacy, Valentine Museum, Virginia Historical Society, Virginia State Library, and the Association for the Preservation of Virginia Antiques, Richmond; Wilkes County Courthouse and the Mary Wills Library, Washington, Georgia; Atlanta Historical Society and the Georgia State Archives, Atlanta; Georgia Historical Society, Savannah; and the Florida State Archives, Tallahassee.

I have received excellent cooperation from the interlibrary loan personnel of many libraries, but I would be remiss if I did not give special

thanks to the staff at the University of Florida. To their counterparts
at the universities of California, Delaware, Georgia, Maryland, Pennsylvania, South Carolina, and Texas as well as those at East Carolina, Florida
State, Rice, and Tulane universities, I extend my heartfelt thanks.

In a special category, I wish to record my deep appreciation for the
help given me by the late John Winder Hughes, a great-grandson of
Winder. I spent many an enjoyable hour in the Wilmington, North Carolina, home of this amazing gentleman who celebrated his ninety-fifth
birthday in 1987. Like his mother, who also lived to be ninety-five
(1860–1955), Mr. Hughes had thoroughly studied the life and career of
his controversial ancestor. His recall and research proved to be accurate
in most instances and greatly improved my understanding of Winder's
relationship with his immediate family members. I also wish to thank
James B. "Jimmy" Hughes of Jacksonville, Florida, for introducing me
to Mr. Hughes and other Winder descendants.

Finally, I have benefited greatly from the suggestions and insights provided by the following scholars: Edward M. Coffman, University of Wis-
consin, James Lee McDonough, Auburn University, James M. McPherson,
Princeton University, William Warren Rogers, Florida State University,
Emory M. Thomas, University of Georigia, and my colleagues at the
University of Florida, David Chalmers, John Mahon, and especially
Claude Sturgill. This study is much the better for the insights and advice
given me by another colleague, Bertram Wyatt-Brown. Four readers
were invaluable in their suggestions for organizational and stylistic improvements: George D. Price, William H. Price, Deborah Cupples, and
Jeffrey Tilghman. I am especially happy to acknowledge the editorial
skills of Catherine McKenzie, Phillip Martin, and the supporting staff
at University Presses of Florida and to take this opportunity to thank
them all.

Grateful acknowledgment is made to the *Florida Historical Quarterly*
for permission to reprint previously published material and to the Wilkes
Publishing Company of Washington, Georgia, for permission to use the
photograph of the Andrew Shepherd House.

Introduction

The American Civil War has mesmerized millions of people for well over a century. Legions of scholars have expended prodigious energy examining and explaining those years, and some truly monumental studies have resulted. More books have been published on the topic than on any other in American history; the total currently exceeds fifty thousand volumes, more than one per day for each day that has passed since the war ended in 1865. Yet disagreements abound, and no responsible author will claim to have produced the definitive history of the war. New themes are pursued, new theories presented, new answers to old queries are offered, and the search for a complete understanding of the era continues.

One issue that needs to be reexamined by a modern historian is that of Civil War prisons. Quantitative history should be invaluable in this attempt, but it must be remembered that even the most sagacious combination of statistical analysis and precise mathematical modeling cannot show the vital interplay between an individual and the existing cultural institutions that often create and shape important historical events. That task is reserved for biographers or proponents of the case study, who assert that individuals do matter and can make a difference.[1]

This case study addresses the issue of Civil War prisons and prisoners from the viewpoint of the man who was ultimately placed in charge of most Confederate prisons. He was not a nonentity; his name was known throughout the Union and the Confederacy by 1863. He came from a prominent family, possessed talent and determination, held two important Confederate commands, and was tireless in the performance of his duty. Yet he failed, and his failure offers another glimpse of why the Confederacy failed.

History has not ignored Brigadier General John Henry Winder, but it has certainly been unkind to him. He lived from 1800 to 1865, but historians and other authors have written only on his Civil War career. They have focused on his controversial role as provost marshal general of Richmond and even more on his position as commissary general of prisoners east of the Mississippi River. In the former, he has been portrayed as an unpopular tyrant, and in the latter, he has been cast as the man most responsible for the sufferings and deaths of Union prisoners of war at Libby, Salisbury, Florence, Andersonville, and other Confederate prisons (see table of Confederate military prisons, chapter 10).

Although it is understandable that he has been portrayed solely in his role in that four-year conflict to the exclusion of the sixty-one years of his life that preceded it, such an image is inaccurate and incomplete. This misrepresentation began with his war contemporaries, who exaggerated his qualities, positive and negative, out of any realistic proportion. At the time of his death, he was anathema in the Union—and he remained so in the history books for decades. Southern defenders found that their attempts to exonerate Winder were neither accepted nor appreciated.[2]

Participants in the war inevitably had their judgments impaired by the psychosis of the times. For it was a bitter war, and it ended more bitterly than it began. The murder of Abraham Lincoln destroyed any hope of a national reconciliation based on his magnanimous terms. The forces of hate and vengeance, partially suppressed by Lincoln, reemerged in the mass arrests ordered by Secretary of War Edwin Stanton. Many former Confederates were incarcerated because it was believed that they had plotted to assassinate Lincoln and that they had also conspired to exterminate thousands of defenseless Union prisoners.

The charges were ludicrous. Yet Winder's subordinate, Henry Wirz, was tried and executed for the mass murder of Union prisoners. Had not Winder died of natural causes in February of 1865, he would certainly have been arrested. It is probable that he would have been tried instead of Wirz, but it is by no means certain that his fate would have been the same. He was indicted, though dead, as a co-conspirator during the Wirz trial, along with Jefferson Davis, James A. Seddon, Howell Cobb, and other Confederate leaders. Lincoln had specifically excluded, from the benefits of the pardon he had proclaimed, all officials charged with cruelty to prisoners, and President Andrew Johnson was initially hostile to the southern leadership; but it would have been extremely difficult to send a man of Winder's standing to the gallows. The only thing Winder and Wirz had in common was the color of their uniform and the cause they had served. Wirz was foreign-born, ill, poor, and without important connections. Winder would have been in an entirely different position, similar to that of Davis, Seddon, and others. To have convicted any one of them would have mandated the conviction of all. It is doubtful that this would have happened even in that highly charged atmosphere.

In the acrimonious decades following the conflict, Winder was repeatedly vilified by northern historians, politicians, and newspapers. Not until the turn of the century did historians attempt a more balanced and objective accounting of the war years, and the publication (1880–1901) of most of the official records of both Union and Confederate governments was a tremendous aid to these scholars. Even so, the bias against Winder continued. Authors such as James Ford Rhodes in his eight-volume *History of the United States from the Compromise of 1850* (1895–1917), and, to a lesser degree, editor Francis T. Miller in his ten-volume *Photographic History of the Civil War* (1912) were critical.

Rhodes relied primarily on the writings of Winder's bitter enemies John B. Jones and Edward Pollard for his assessment. Miller's staff was misled by a forged order attributed to Winder which called for the use of artillery against the helpless Andersonville prisoners if Union troops tried to free them.[3]

In 1930, William B. Hesseltine's *Civil War Prisons* was published. Even at that date, the topic was still volatile and controversial, but Hesseltine was well qualified to meet the challenge. He produced the first objective account of Winder and of the whole prison issue. Unfortunately, his book did not prevent the later publication of other, more sensational accounts. Of the latter, none had more impact than the Pulitzer prize-winning novel *Andersonville* by MacKinlay Kantor in 1955. Even though it was a work of fiction, the author stressed that his description of the central figures and events was historically accurate. In truth, the sources he used, misused, and failed to use resulted in a portrayal of Winder's character that was absolutely false. Kantor's conclusion was that "General Winder wished to kill as many prisoners as he could. It was as simple at that."[4]

An even worse exaggeration appeared in 1957. In his introduction to the reissue of John McElroy's highly inaccurate but colorful *This Was Andersonville*, Roy Meredith, obviously influenced by the horrors of the Nazi era, indicted Winder as America's Heinrich Himmler, and Andersonville as a Confederate Dachau or Auschwitz.[5]

During the 1960s and early 1970s three able historians provided needed correctives. Hesseltine compiled a series of articles by excellent scholars, again entitled *Civil War Prisons* (1962); Emory M. Thomas wrote *The Confederate State of Richmond* (1971); and Ovid Futch wrote *History of Andersonville Prison* (1968). In these works, Winder received a much more scholarly treatment than at any time previously, but Futch probably spoke for all three when he concluded that "Winder's true character was a puzzle to his contemporaries and remains an enigma to historians."[6]

This statement was an apt summation. Almost none of Winder's personal correspondence has survived, and few of his contemporaries recorded their antebellum impressions of him. Thus Winder's life from 1800 to 1861 has been virtually blank. The only author to have dealt with this period of his life, Sarah A. Duffy, in her master's thesis, devoted about forty pages to his prewar career.[7]

When I began this study, I, too, intended to focus only on Winder's Civil War career. My research left me puzzled as to what the man was actually like. The reactions to his Richmond role were too diverse and conflicting to be credible, and I sought a more comprehensive explanation by probing into his earlier career. Like others before me, I soon found that the paucity of sources precluded any definitive biography. Although no full-bodied portrait is possible, enough evidence has survived in official records, newspapers, and other primary materials to permit a detailed examination of Winder's prewar life—an examination that reveals many of his fundamental qualities and attitudes as of 1861. Obviously, an understanding of Winder's basic character is essential to any understanding of his actions during the war.

The single most important event in the formation of his character and personality occurred during the terminal stages of the War of 1812. The battle of Bladensburg was fought during the last part of August 1814, and Winder's father was in command of the American forces. At the time, Winder was fourteen years old, just beginning cadet life at West Point. When he arrived at the academy, he was justifiably proud of his father, who was supposed to command the largest army that America had fielded during the war. Victory and glory for General Winder seemed certain.

The boy's exultation lasted less than three weeks. The British invaded the Chesapeake area, marched on Washington, and were met by Winder's ill-trained and hastily assembled forces at Bladensburg on 24 August. The battle was a disaster, both for the nation and for General William Henry Winder. The Americans were routed in less than one hour, and the "Bladensburg races" became a national disgrace. The British burned the Capitol, the White House, and other public buildings and withdrew for an attack on Baltimore. There they were repulsed, but Winder was no longer in command. He had no opportunity to redeem his reputation, and he was known from then on as that "most unfortunate general" of the war.[8]

Cadet Winder's status changed abruptly. While hazing was not then a tradition at West Point, it requires little imagination to envision the harassments that were inflicted upon the cadet whose father had allowed the enemy to destroy the symbol of the young nation. Winder's reaction to this disaster is instructive. First, he determined to endure the criticisms, graduate from the academy, and make the army his career. And second, he intended to restore the Winder reputation by his own exemplary military conduct; he became inordinately defensive about any criticism that might place even the hint of censure on his military record. His determination to lead a disciplined existence was at odds with his basic makeup. Winder was impulsive, stubborn, short-tempered, profane, and aloof, but until he resigned from the United States Army in 1861, he was widely regarded as an honest, efficient, courageous, and distinguished officer. In sum, he was a typical career officer, a martinet, not fundamentally different from his Union counterpart during the war, Commissary General of Prisoners William H. Hoffman.

Hesseltine and Futch have concluded that Winder was ill suited by temperament for the positions he occupied during the war.[9] My research tends to reject this view. Loyal, somewhat innovative, and moderately flexible, he would reverse or revoke his own orders if necessary. He was certainly highly qualified by training and experience for his responsibilities, for he had served in the commissary department, was an excellent engineer, had been lieutenant governor of Vera Cruz after the Mexican War, and had demonstrated exceptional coolness and bravery under fire.

The basic problem was not with Winder. Simply put, the Confederacy did not mobilize the resources necessary to establish and maintain itself as an independent nation. Winder was caught up in the common Confederate dilemma of being responsible for a delicate and demanding situation without having the means to control it. He was vilified because his position was one of the most sensitive in the Confederacy as well as one of the most highly publicized, North and South. Given the limitations under which he labored, it is doubtful if anyone in the Confederacy could have done better. Even the most diplomatic, humane, and efficient of men would have found Winder's job impossible as conditions in the Confederacy deteriorated in 1864 and 1865.

This being so, the question must be asked, "Why did he not resign?" Military ethics did not condone either obeying or issuing orders that would lead to the death of thousands of helpless prisoners, yet Winder retained his command until death claimed him. His concept of honor would not permit him to quit. In his view, resignation would be a cowardly act that would not remedy the problem, would instead result in the burden being passed on to someone who might not possess his skills and determination. So he stayed the course, and made his name infamous in the process.

Abundant precedents for Winder's Civil War actions can be found in his old army career, but since almost nothing has ever been printed about that period of his life, I have frequently relied on direct quotations from him. While this has proved awkward at times, I would rather the reader judge him by what he said, not by what I interpret from his remarks. In some areas, the record is incomplete, and I have made what I believe are logical and credible inferences from the available data. When the record is silent, I have had to engage in speculation or be content to let the record remain mute. Where I have speculated, I hope I have made it obvious in the text and that my explanation or justification in the notes will satisfy the reader and the demands of good scholarship.

To rescue a villain from history—to overturn a historical myth—is a difficult task. Despite the efforts of Hesseltine, Thomas, Futch, and others, the popularity and critical acclaim accorded the Public Broadcasting System docudrama *The Wirz Trial* attests to the seeming permanence of Kantor's invidious portrayal of Winder. Civil War experts have, for over half a century, offered a fuller portrait of Winder than Kantor's acid depiction. Yet their efforts have been successful only in part.[10] If this work results in a more accurate image of Winder and a fuller understanding of this aspect of the Civil War in future accounts, I will have accomplished my task.

CHAPTER 1

The Last Day

6 February 1865, Florence, South Carolina

It had been about as severe a winter as most South Carolinians could remember, and Monday morning, 6 February 1865, was bitterly cold. Icy gusts of wind cut deeply into the old man and his small party at the Columbia depot as they awaited the arrival of the Wilmington and Manchester train.[1] With luck (always a factor when riding the Confederate railroads in those days), they should complete the one-hundred-mile trip to Florence before sundown.

Something about the old man set him apart from the rest of the passengers. It was not simply that he was a Confederate general, nor was it the deference shown him by the five junior officers accompanying him. There was an aura of command about him. He would have been noticed in any crowd.

Neither his size nor his stocky physique were striking. Yet his erect 5′8″ frame carried his 180-odd pounds handily, and his quick movements belied the fact that he was as old as his century—he would be sixty-five in two weeks' time. It was his face that drew one's attention. Beneath a tousled mass of snow-white hair, his craggy countenance was dominated by glacial, slate-gray eyes. He had a roman nose and a stern mouth "on which a smile seemed mockery."[2] Deep lines of worry and fatigue crisscrossed his haggard and ruddy visage. He had aged since the war began, but he still had "a striking and commanding personal appearance" that attracted one's attention at once.[3]

The general's outward appearance was largely a facade. As he boarded the train and settled into his reserved compartment for the all-day trip, he was just about used up. It was not only age and exhaustion or even the weather that had been inflicting such punishment on his constitution for the last several months. The agonizing admission that he had failed, the all-consuming chill of total defeat, made his physical ailments seem inconsequential.

His country was being destroyed, and he was going down with it. All of the sacrifices and sufferings had come to naught. The fall of Atlanta, the reelection of Lincoln, Sherman's rampage across Georgia, and Grant's incessant pounding of Lee's forces in Virginia made a Union victory inevitable. The Richmond authorities might not be willing to concede defeat, but the old man was.[4]

The Confederate government could no longer adequately feed, clothe, or provide other basic necessities for its armies in the field. The situation was far worse for the troops and prisoners under his command. Despite his best efforts, conditions in his command were atrocious. He, Brigadier General John Henry Winder, would be held accountable, but his command was an evil joke and had been since its creation.

Four months earlier he had been appointed commissary general of prisoners east of the Mississippi River. His was an imposing title, an important command, and a continuing nightmare. True, he had a few able and trustworthy junior officers, including his son Sidney at his Columbia headquarters and Lieutenant Colonel Henry Forno and Captain Phillip Cashmeyer, who were with him today; and he had finally succeeded in bringing a unified system of organization for prisoners of war into being for the first time in the history of the Confederacy, but it was far too late. His prison guards—primarily old men, convalescents, and young boys—were totally inadequate and undependable. Even worse, the commissary system and the railroad network, never effective, had almost ceased to function.

The result was that the horrors endured in the previous summer at the Andersonville prison in southwestern Georgia had been equaled or exceeded at the Florence and Salisbury prisons, and he had been powerless to prevent it. He had been accused of every atrocity imaginable by the Union press for years, and although some of the lies had cut him to the quick, he knew that the allegations were false. He knew that the official records, if they survived, would exonerate him. Yet he also knew that the northern press had not exaggerated much about the inhuman conditions of southern prisons in 1864 and 1865. Since the spring of 1864, when the Lincoln government ended the exchange of prisoners, caring for Union captives had become an insuperable problem. Food, water, clothing, shelter, and medical and other supplies became scarce, and cruelty, suffering, and death were the direct result.

The final blow to the old man's hopes had been the news in December that the exchange of prisoners would not be resumed. The existing conditions would continue. That was when he admitted to failure and advised his government to change policy. Before Christmas of 1864 and again some three weeks ago, in mid-January, Winder urged Richmond to parole the Union prisoners and send them home without exchange.[5] The Confederate leadership refused the request. Colonel Robert Ould, commissioner of exchange, informed the secretary of war that Winder's recommendation was not acceptable. The Union must agree to a resumption of the cartel or no exchange was possible. The secretary concluded that Winder's remedy was "worse than the evil" and ordered him to carry on in the best manner possible.[6]

Winder protested even as he continued to perform his duty. On 26 January he informed Richmond that the prisoners were starving and "suffering very much for want of clothing. I would be glad if the attention of the Federal Government was called to the fact." What food there was he had previously condemned as unfit for human consumption, and just two days before, on 4 February, he had warned: "The prisoners never will be properly fed until commissaries are ordered for prison duty. I never have been able to get anything from staff officers not on duty with the prisons." He asked that assistant commissaries be appointed and ordered to report "and that they be not, as heretofore, young men with no experience; the duty requires experience." There must be, at an absolute minimum, "an assistant commissary for the prisoners here," he pleaded. "Please send one."[7]

It had been a forlorn effort. Help was not forthcoming, but the enemy was. General William Tecumseh Sherman's advance threatened the security of the prisons, and General P. G. T. Beauregard informed Winder that the prisoners at Florence would have to be moved to southwestern Georgia immediately. Winder concurred, but only if troops could be assigned to guard them in transit. His command was totally insufficient for the task. Many of his men were sick, others had deserted, some were unreliable. Indeed, he was on his way to Florence today to investigate charges of cruelty and corruption in his command as well as to assess the feasibility of moving the prisoners.

The train pulled into Kingsville, and the group got off while the train changed tracks for the run into Florence. The general found a telegram from his son at headquarters awaiting him. Sidney urged his father to return to Columbia immediately. Beauregard had sent a second dispatch stating that the prisoner removal must commence at once. Sherman's forces were moving rapidly toward Columbia, and the South Carolina prisons were no longer secure.

Winder agreed that the transfer was necessary and so informed Lieutenant Colonel Forno, senior officer in his small party, but he decided to continue to Florence to determine if the allegations made against three members of his staff there were true. If so, he intended to replace them with the officers accompanying him. He informed Captain Cashmeyer, his longtime aide and current sutler of the Florence camp, that he would severely punish Captain Thomas G. Barrett and Lieutenants John Wilson and R. H. Cheatham if they had in any way cheated or been cruel to the prisoners.[8] Conditions were bad enough without behavior of that type, and there had been far too much of it already.

It was late in the day when the train reached Florence and stopped at the depot on Front Street. The Gamble Hotel, directly across the street from the station, was a welcome sight to the weary passengers, but the general departed without delay for the prison. He wanted to conclude his investigation before checking in for the night in case circumstances forced an early return to Columbia in the morning.

It did not take long to clear the town of Florence (population about 600), and the small cavalcade made good time past the farms and plantations on the two-mile ride to the prison. As they approached Stockade Road, the entrance to the compound, the prison burial ground loomed on their left. There were over 2,700 graves there. The old man had been informed when he assumed command in November that about 12,400 Union soldiers imprisoned there were dying at the rate of about two hundred per week. In the intervening months he had reduced the rate to about thirty-five per week, but the overall mortality rate was about 22 percent. This was not much better than the horrific 26 percent at Andersonville or the even higher figure at Salisbury, but it was lower than he had previously estimated and reported to Richmond.[9]

One grave, less than two weeks old and set off by itself, was the final resting place of an unusual prisoner, Florena Budwin. Winder and his men had become accustomed to widespread suffering and death after three years of it, yet hers was a sad story even to the hardened men approaching the cemetery. When her husband joined the army, she attired herself in masculine disguise and went with him. They were captured and confined at Andersonville. He died there, but she joined thousands of the survivors who were eventually sent to Florence. When she became seriously ill, a Confederate doctor discovered that she was a woman and her prison life changed dramatically. She was given a private room and the best medical attention available, and the women of Florence donated food and clothing. It was too late. The twenty-year-old lass died on 25 January of pneumonia.[10]

Winder's party turned south on Stockade Road and entered the prison outskirts. The stench of death, perhaps the most offensive smell on earth, became overpowering, more choking than the smoke drifting from the camp. The twilight revealed an eerie sight. Plainly visible were thousands of filthy, pathetic faces, desperate for news of parole or exchange. Some of the faces were devoid of all expression. They belonged to men who had fallen victim to perhaps the most cruel and incurable disease of all— homesickness. Those men had lost hope. They would die.

Death was in the air that evening and much closer to the small group of officers than anyone imagined. The old general had just entered the compound in search of the stockade commander when he clutched his chest, staggered, and fell. The heart attack was massive, total, complete —so sudden that it stunned them all. They carried the fallen general to Cashmeyer's tent and summoned the doctors, but it was a futile effort. The old man was dead. Forno took command and ordered Cashmeyer to accompany the body back to Columbia. He then sent telegrams to Richmond and Columbia. Plans had to be made not only for the funeral but for the immediate transfer of the prisoners.[11]

General James Chesnut made the funeral arrangements, and the services were held on Thursday afternoon, 9 February, in Columbia. After lying in state at city hall, the general's remains were taken to Trinity Church by an impressive escort. A detachment of cavalry was in the lead, then came the family and the pallbearers (including Generals Joseph E. Johnston, Mansfield Lovell, and Wade Hampton), followed by a regiment of infantry, various Confederate officers and officials, and several thousand citizens bringing up the rear. A newspaper reported that at "half past three o'clock the minute guns were fired and the procession moved through the principal streets to the Church, preceded by solemn music. The burial services were read by Rev. Dr. Seard, Rector of Trinity Church, and the remains were interred in the cemetery."[12] Only cemetery employees witnessed the actual burial, for Winder's body was placed in an unmarked grave. Sherman's army would reach Columbia within a week, and there was little doubt that his rampaging horde had special plans for the capital of the state where secession had begun. It seemed likely that the remains of the commissary general of prisoners would be desecrated if found, so the family decided to take no chances.

Much of Columbia was soon destroyed, but the cemetery was not pillaged and his grave was not disturbed for thirteen years. In 1878, the body was moved to the family vault at Greenmount Cemetery in Baltimore. The family erected a monument bearing the words "Blessed Are The Good And Brave."[13] The old warrior was finally home, his travels over. He had returned to the land of his heritage, the home of his ancestors, the place he had last seen in 1861, when he left to serve the Confederacy.

CHAPTER 2

The Fateful Decision

January–May 1861, Baltimore

Early in January 1861, Winder paid a visit to his brother William in Philadelphia. They discussed family and business affairs, but most of their talk focused on the crisis of the Union. By the time he returned to his Baltimore home at 55 Lexington Street on 14 March that crisis had become paramount. The city was seething with discontent. There was much boisterous derision by men in the streets that the hated Lincoln had been so fearful for his life that he had not dared enter Baltimore openly. He had sneaked through the city the night of 22 February in order to reach the Federal capital to preside over what remained of the United States. Talk of secession was everywhere, and Winder found many of his friends convinced that Maryland should and would join the Confederate States of America without delay.

Some in Baltimore were committed to the Union. They were convinced that secession was treason and were determined to follow the old flag. Others, deeply distressed by the rupture of the country, were divided in their allegiance, uncertain of their future, torn apart emotionally by the choice before them. Winder was in their ranks. He found that he had been promoted to the permanent rank of major in the United States Army during his Philadelphia visit, and he was now faced with the decision to accept the commission or resign. He accepted but made no attempt to return to his command, even though his current posting was one of the two remaining Union strongholds in the newly born Confederate States of America.[1]

Winder had been absent from his command for almost a year. When he left Pensacola, Florida, in May 1860, he had been severely ill, a rarity during his long life. General physical exhaustion and a recurrence of malaria had kept him in bed for over four months after his arrival in Baltimore. His physical health was restored, but his mental and emotional states were not.

Duty was compelling him to resume command of Fort Pickens, to rejoin his longtime comrades in Company G, Third Artillery, for on 10 January 1861 Florida had seceded and demanded that Winder's company leave the Pensacola forts. Lieutenant Adam Slemmer, then in command, refused to surrender the possessions, moved Company G from the mainland forts to Pickens on Santa Rosa Island, and successfully defied the state authorities. It appeared that war might begin then and there as troops from Florida and Alabama moved in, but a truce was soon concluded. By 28 January, tensions had subsided to the point where Slemmer could send a small detail to Barrancas Barracks, the primary garrison at Pensacola, to make arrangements for the delivery of mail and supplies. Lieutenant J. H. Gilmore received Confederate permission to recover Winder's private property and sent the items to him during the first week of February.[2]

Captain Israel Vodges arrived at that time and took temporary command. He reported that the garrison was reduced to fewer than fifty officers and men, all totally exhausted and unable to offer any significant resistance if an attack came. Clearly, Pensacola Bay was worth defending. The harbor was important as was the million-dollar dry dock and navy yard.[3] In Confederate hands this possession could cause the Union all kinds of trouble in the event of war. The situation was critical, and Winder was most definitely needed at his post.

His duty was clear. If he remained in the army, he should return to Pensacola immediately, protect and defend the Federal property there, and defy the Confederate State of Florida, with force if necessary. That was what his old friend Major Robert Anderson was doing at Fort Sumter, South Carolina. If war came, it would most probably start at either Fort Sumter or Fort Pickens, and Winder knew it. He also knew that he could not perform his duty if it went against honor and country, and therein resided the dilemma. He had now to choose between two countries: the United States, which he had served loyally for a lifetime, or the Confederate States, the nascent nation that might soon include the Upper South and thereby command his deepest loyalty. Honor demanded a terminal decision; he knew it, but he could not make it just yet, though he had postponed the decision for months.

Winder had been visiting his son John Cox Winder in New York when Lincoln was elected and South Carolina seceded, and he was with his brother William in Philadelphia when the Confederacy came into being and Lincoln was inaugurated.[4] John Cox left for North Carolina immediately to serve the South, and William made it clear that he favored secession and the formal recognition of the Confederacy. Winder's youngest son, Sidney, a practicing attorney in Baltimore, told him that he, too, intended to fight for southern independence if war came. Winder's younger brother, Charles, an attorney residing in Washington, D.C., was a prominent southern sympathizer but was not yet in favor of secession. Winder's wife, Caroline, and stepdaughter Carrie, as well as his eighty-year-old mother, Gertrude, identified with the Upper South but, like Charles, were not avid secessionists. This was also the position of his sister, Charlotte Townsend, who lived in New York. His eldest son, William Andrew, a captain in the United States Army, had also made his choice—to remain true to the Union.[5]

Winder was as divided in his basic allegiance as his sons were, but he was unable to do more than mark time and wait for some momentous event to simplify the decision for him. Another month passed and the decisive event occurred: the Confederates opened fire on Fort Sumter, and Anderson surrendered on 13 April. Lincoln declared a naval blockade of the Confederacy and summoned seventy-five thousand volunteers to end the rebellion. The war was on. The firing of the guns seemed to crystallize opinion. Millions of Americans who had been wavering indecisively now prepared to preserve the Union or fight for southern independence.

A few did not. Winder was among them, but his delay was for a matter of days only. The Upper South, including North Carolina, announced for secession. Winder had lived in the Tarheel State for a long time, had married and reared his family there, and regarded it as his adopted state. In addition, Baltimore erupted on 19 April when the first northern troops passed through on their way to Washington, D.C. Winder witnessed the Baltimore riot at first hand and concluded that Maryland would secede and the Federal capital would soon be totally isolated. He made his choice and sent the following letter on 20 April:

Col. L. Thomas
Asst General [sic]
Sir:
     The unfortunate state of the country and the circumstances under which I find myself, renders it unjust to the United States and to myself, to longer retain my commission in the Army. It is a source of great regret, that after nearly forty years service, I find it necessary to sever the ties which bind me to the Army, but situated as I am, I may find myself arrayed against my native state, against my children and kindred, this I cannot do, nor could I in future perform my duties with that alacrity which I hope has characterized my for [sic] service.
     In view of these things, I respectfully tender this as the resignation

of my commission of Major of the 3 Regt of Artillery. You will oblige me by an early answer.[6]

Now an old man of sixty-one, Winder ended his long military career with honor and distinction, but it was a wrenching decision. The choice weighed more heavily upon career military officers than on most, for they had taken the oath. Honor, duty, and country were indelibly inscribed in their being. They had fought for the flag. Could they now fight against it? Two Virginians, both noble and honorable officers, illustrate the excruciating process that many endured. Robert E. Lee sadly concluded that a union "maintained by swords and bayonets" had no charm for him. He resigned but vowed never to fight again save in defense of his native state. Conversely, George H. Thomas found that no matter how he grieved over the issue, his oath of allegiance came uppermost. For these men, and thousands like them, including Winder, neutrality was impossible. Each made his choice, and once committed, most were loyal to the end.[7]

Winder resigned "with great regret." He feared he would be arrayed against his native state, and knew that two sons and many of his kindred would become the enemy if he remained in the service. This he could not face. It would be unjust to the United States to continue in his current position, so it became "necessary to sever the ties" of a lifetime.

It is apparent from his letter of resignation that he was under great stress, but the mistakes he made—writing the word "for" when he meant "former" and addressing Thomas as "Asst. General" rather than "Asst. Adjutant General"—also indicate that he wrote in haste. Of all the thousands of his extant official letters, this is the only one in which he made those types of errors. His choice of words and his handwriting in this letter are not at variance with his usual style or penmanship; but it appears that when he finally made the decision, he impulsively wrote the message. It was almost as if he had committed himself irrevocably to end the torment of indecision, or even perhaps to ward off a change of mind. The resolution was months in the making. He acted with haste only in the actual transmission of his resignation.

Winder's reasons for ending his allegiance to the Union are clear, but his determination to enter active military service in the Confederacy is not so readily explained. Economic concerns militated against the decision, for all of his financial investments were in Maryland, Pennsylvania, and Washington, D.C., and there they remained. His age precluded a field command even if his health had permitted. He was certainly not a fire-eater or a rabid defender of slavery, yet he zealously sought and ultimately obtained an important military command in the Confederate army.

Winder never fully recorded an explanation of why he elected to serve the Confederacy, but several official letters make much of his reasoning understandable. First, he was a professional soldier. His self-image would not allow him to remain at peace in a time of war. He was proud, even arrogant, and was convinced that his abilities and experience would be valuable to the war effort even if he was too old for field command. Further, he was not content with his military reputation and rank. After a lifetime of service he was only a brevet lieutenant colonel with the permanent rank of major. He yearned to be addressed as General Winder, as his father had been. Proud of his past accomplishments, he was eager to earn new accolades.

The second reason for his decision was his empathy with the state of North Carolina. As he expressed it in May 1861, "Having been identified with North Carolina for the last thirty years, I . . . intended to cast my lot with hers and in her hour of need, to offer such service as I could render."[8] Winder believed in the principle of state sovereignty and the validity of secession, and became convinced that the attempt to restore the Union by force was unjust and unconstitutional.

That Winder was seriously ill, mentally, emotionally, and physically, for much of 1860 is a matter of record, yet his health improved dramatically once he decided where his fundamental loyalties resided. Having committed to Confederate service, he was not to miss even one day of work because of illness for the rest of his life. During the three years, seven months, and fifteen days he wore the gray, he performed his assigned tasks with zeal and alacrity, no matter how strenuous the duty. The sudden restoration of his good health strongly suggests that he exaggerated his physical ailments during the fall and winter of 1860 in order to remain in Baltimore and avoid the pain of resuming his Pensacola command. He was sympathetic to the Deep South, but he was not ready to serve the Confederacy until it included the Upper South, particularly North Carolina. When that happened, Winder's indecision vanished, and so did his health problems.

On 30 April, ten days after submitting his resignation, he was notified that it had been accepted.[9] He made ready to leave for North Carolina immediately and booked passage on the first available ship. He took leave of his wife and daughter the next day, unaware that he would not see them for more than two years and that he would never again see Baltimore or his native state of Maryland.

Winder's roots were deeply imbedded in this state. He was well aware that he bore the name of one of the most famous families in Maryland, and that it had been so since 1665 when John Winder left Cumberland, England, for a life in the New World. Already a man of some means, this first Winder prospered from the beginning. He established a large tobacco plantation on the south side of the Wicomico River in Somerset

County known as Winder's Manor and soon occupied numerous official
positions in the colony. As his standing in society changed, so, too, did
the pronunciation of his name. Originally, it was "win-der," but it became
"wine-der" some time after his arrival. When he died in 1698, the name
was one of the most influential and respected in the colony. His six children (see Winder Genealogical Chart) inherited a legacy of pride, reputation, public service, business ability, and hard work.[10]

Succeeding generations of Winders continued the tradition. Winder's
great-grandfather, William (1714–1792), became especially prominent.
He retained his portion of Winder's Manor, acquired considerably more
property, including flour mills in the Rewastico district, and was chief
judge of Somerset County for many years. He married Esther Gillis,
whose lineage was as distinguished as his own, and they had eight children, most of whom married into prominent Maryland and Virginia families or achieved distinction in their own right.[11] Two of these sons, Levin
and William, Winder remembered very well.

Levin was born 4 September 1757. He was highly intelligent, an effective speaker, and just beginning to study law when the Revolution broke
out. There were numerous Loyalists on the Eastern Shore, but the Winders were ardent patriots. Although only eighteen years old, Levin joined
the Maryland Line and was soon promoted to major of the Fourth Maryland Regiment. Able but unlucky (a Winder trait), he was held captive
for a time but attained the rank of lieutenant colonel before the war
ended. He returned to his plantation, Monie Hundred, about ten miles
south of Winder's Manor, reestablished his fortunes, and then embarked
on a successful political career. During the next twenty years he served
as an associate judge of Somerset County Court, ranking major general
of the Maryland Militia, state senator, and Speaker of the Maryland
House of Representatives. He had just been elected governor of Maryland when the War of 1812 was declared. A Federalist, he did not favor
the war.[12]

Levin's elder brother William was born in 1747 and also enjoyed a
prosperous life. A revolutionary war veteran of note, he became one
of the largest tobacco planters in Somerset County. He married Charlotte
Henry in 1773, and they had nine children. Of the six sons of this union,
Winder's own father was easily the most famous.

William Henry Winder was born 18 February 1775 on his father's
plantation, Bower Hill, in the Rewastico district near Broad Creek in
Somerset County. Educated at home during the war years and then at
nearby Washington Academy, a private school in Somerset County, he
entered the University of Pennsylvania and was graduated at age seventeen. He immediately began the study of law under his uncle, John
Henry, who had been a delegate to the Continental Congress, United
States senator, and governor of Maryland in 1797 and 1798. He com-

pleted his apprenticeship at Annapolis in the office of Gabriel Duval, a future justice of the United States Supreme Court.[13]

In January 1794 he wrote a close friend from his college days, John Rust Eaton of Greenville, North Carolina, about his future plans. He agreed to consider Eaton's invitation to practice in North Carolina as soon as he passed the bar examination. The exam was no problem for a man of his academic ability, but he decided to establish his practice in Nashville, Tennessee. It was a bad decision. A lack of clients forced the nineteen-year-old attorney to admit failure and return to his native state.[14]

Winder's career took an upward swing in 1798 when he was elected to the Maryland legislature at age twenty-three. Even more satisfying was his marriage to his first cousin Gertrude, daughter of Judge William Polk, on 7 May 1799. Winder took his eighteen-year-old bride to his new estate, Rewston (near present day Nanticoke), in Somerset County. Nine months and two weeks later their first child was born there on 21 February 1800. Winder had celebrated his twenty-fifth birthday just three days earlier, and now he had a son. The boy was named John Henry Winder, in honor of his distinguished uncle.[15]

Life was extremely pleasant—a loving wife, healthy son, six slaves, a fine house—but Winder was not satisfied. He did not want to emulate his planter father (with fifty chattels in 1800, William Winder was the county's fifth largest slaveholder), nor did he want to be an absentee owner, part-time legislator, and part-time attorney.[16] He wanted a large and lucrative law practice, and that meant living in a city. Baltimore was the logical choice.

Originally founded as one of the ports to provide an outlet for locally grown tobacco, Baltimore began its real growth in the 1750s because of the demand for flour generated by Ireland and Scotland. Although many farmers turned to wheat cultivation, the tobacco aristocracy continued to occupy the preeminent positions in Baltimore society.

The town grew rapidly during the Revolution and boomed into a full-fledged city of over 31,500 people by 1800. Freed from British restrictions, Baltimore became one of America's chief deepwater ports. Besides tobacco and wheat exports to various Hanseatic towns, iron and copper production became promising local industries. With all of the business transactions and commercial activity, it was inevitable that the Baltimore bar was soon recognized for its members of ability and prominence.[17]

It became apparent to the Winders that a permanent dwelling in the city was necessary. Not only was it cumbersome for them to live at Rewston and take the Cambridge packet across the Chesapeake Bay to Baltimore, it was dangerous. Sudden squalls frequently hit the bay and the Choptank River area, and capsizings and founderings were common.[18] Accordingly, Winder turned the plantation over to his father, purchased a large house on Albemarle Street, leased an office in Lemmon's Alley, and moved his wife, son, and slaves to the city in the fall of 1802.[19]

The next decade was eminently satisfying for the family. Winder was brilliant and magnetic, and he proved to be a talented attorney. His practice grew rapidly, and by 1812 it was one of the largest and most lucrative in Baltimore. He trained numerous students in the profession, and his office, located since 1803 next to his new house on Chatham Street, was one block from the courthouse (present-day site of the Battle Monument at Calvert and Fayette streets) and was a mecca for city officials and businessmen.[20] It was here that John Henry grew up.

Winder's mother gave birth annually from 1802 to 1809, but four children (William, William, Tasker, and Amelia) died in infancy. It was not until Aurelia was born in 1806 that Winder had a baby sister, though she died at age thirteen. He was eight when William was born, the first of his brothers to live to adulthood. His younger brother, Charles, born in 1809, was only five when Winder left home to enter the United States Military Academy at West Point. The last of the children, Gertrude, born in 1815, and Charlotte Aurelia, born in 1820, were more like daughters than sisters to their eldest brother. Gertrude was only twenty-three when she died in 1838. With death such a persistent visitor, it is understandable that the parents doted on their firstborn and denied him virtually nothing. Until he was six, there was no possibility of sibling rivalry, and his boyhood in one of the most fashionable areas of the city was one of protected, almost pampered elegance.[21]

There was much to do in Baltimore. The noise and excitement of the street vendors hawking their wares at the marketplace just four blocks from the Winder home served as an irresistible lure to the young boy. Numerous parades, mostly patriotic in nature, were especially memorable because his father marched in many of them. Public lectures on diverse subjects, performances by topflight actors at the theater on Holliday Street, and offerings by several literary clubs enriched the city's culture and the young boy's experience. The adjacent countryside provided numerous attractions. The racetrack on Whetstone Point, near Fort McHenry, opened in 1799 and rapidly became a gathering point for thousands of spectators. Riding and hunting trips were regular entertainments for the Winder family, and the bay—offering sailing, swimming, crabbing, fishing, and oystering—constantly beckoned. Visiting relatives and friends was a much-cherished southern custom, and the family traveled frequently to Bower Hill and Monie Hundred, and occasionally to Virginia and the Carolinas. His father's legal career also required trips to Annapolis and to the new capital of Washington, D.C.[22]

A visit to Belvedere, the mansion of Colonel John E. Howard, was in a special category, and the Winders were frequent and welcome guests. A local historian noted that it was a meeting place for the "best society of Baltimore" as well as "the Middletons, the Pinckneys, the Lowndeses, the Hugers and the Rutledges of the South; the Adamses, the Winthrops and the Otises of the North" and that "scarce a Senator or Representative of note from the Eastern States" failed "to visit this chosen seat."[23] As a boy and young man, Winder experienced fully the hospitality and gentility that was part of the southern aristocratic tradition.

The young gentleman was exposed to the same educational opportunities provided his father. He had the best tutors and attended the best academies in Baltimore. In addition, the Winder household sparkled with the learned and witty conversation of the leading citizens of the city. Despite enrollment in Eden School, Washington Academy, and the Old Town Academy, however, the boy was indifferent toward his studies. Although never exhibiting the flair for learning evident in his father and two younger brothers, John Henry had a sound basic education. He simply was much more at home in the out-of-doors than in a classroom and rarely turned in an academic performance that was above average.[24]

His eldest son may have been an academic disappointment to the father, but if so, he concealed it well. He did not believe in forcing his children into a career against their wishes and was inclined to indulge them. All of the children enjoyed a happy and privileged existence, but the parents made sure that they were thoroughly inculcated with the sense of duty and responsibility expected of their class. John Henry might not be a scholar, but he would be a gentleman. While he enjoyed all of the luxuries of the patrician class, he also learned that much was expected of him. How much, he found out at age twelve when his father went to war.

It appeared for some little time that the war would result in added prestige for the family, for his father was repeatedly recognized as an extremely talented officer by his superior, Brigadier General Alexander Smyth, the commander of the Niagara frontier armies charged with invading Canada and capturing York (Toronto).[25] Smyth's offensives failed dismally, as did other attempts all along the border, and America found itself on the defensive as the year 1812 came to an end. The United States Navy had success on the Great Lakes and on the high seas, but the army had little to boast about anywhere. Courts-martial were held, reputations were destroyed, and the search for competent commanders was intensified. Promotions were given to promising junior officers, and the people of Baltimore were delighted when Winder was commissioned brigadier general on 12 March 1813. The promotion was viewed favorably by local Federalist and Republican organs and by out-of-state newspapers as well, but Winfield Scott, who was ten years younger than Winder and had served with him, noted privately and prophetically, "It is a misfortune to begin a new career with too much rank, or rather, too late in life."[26]

It is doubtful that anyone was more excited by the news than thirteen-year-old John Henry Winder. The Winder tradition certainly included military service, but nothing so heady had ever happened to the family, and the boy was now fully determined to pursue a military career.[27] No record of the conversations that took place between father and son has survived, but it was at this time that Winder promised to secure an appointment to the academy at West Point for his son after he became fourteen. A condition was that young Winder continue his academic preparation in a satisfactory manner. After reaching this accord with his son, General Winder made the necessary arrangements to provide for his family in case of his death and returned to the front.[28]

The military campaigns of 1813 along the Niagara frontier were not any more successful than the previous ones. Under the command of General John Chandler, Winder's regiment moved on 4 June to Stoney Creek, about seven miles from the British forces of General John Vincent at the head of Lake Superior. Chandler posted pickets, sent out patrols, arranged his artillery properly, and gave explicit instructions to his officers on where and how to form a line of battle in case of a surprise attack.

The British attacked about three o'clock in the morning after obtaining the countersign and bayoneting the sentries and pickets. A force of some seven hundred troops charged the sleeping camp and scattered part of Chandler's army to the winds. Yet most were not routed, and a wild, pitched battle took place. In the confusion, officers of both armies lost control of the situation, and some blundered into enemy lines. Chandler and Winder both realized the need to bring the artillery to bear, and they hurried toward the center of their line. Neither knew that the position had fallen to the British, now under the command of Lieutenant Colonel John Harvey (Vincent having become lost and out of touch for the next two days), and both generals were captured within minutes of each other. Harvey realized that his troops were too scattered and cut up to do more, and he ordered a retreat, taking his notable prisoners with him.[29]

Although the Americans held the battleground and inflicted heavy casualties, the battle of Stoney Creek was a substantial victory for the British. The Americans retreated to Fort George. Forced to evacuate in December, they burned Newark on the way out. Retaliation was swift: the British torched the entire area from Fort Niagara to Buffalo and occupied Fort Niagara for the rest of the war.[30] All in all, the year 1813 was a disaster for the Americans on the Niagara frontier. A disaster of a more personal nature was the experience of Winder, Chandler, and other captured American officers.

During the early months of the War of 1812, as in the revolutionary war, there was no common agreement on, or strict observance of, rules for the treatment of prisoners. Each side tended to treat captives in the same way that it believed its own prisoners were being treated. Militia were paroled and sent home, but regulars were imprisoned until exchanged, officers and men alike. Enlisted men received harsh treatment as a general rule, and so did some officers, but many of the latter were paroled and given the freedom of the town. Some were allowed to return home before being exchanged, but they were not allowed to fight until they were declared exchanged.

An exchange meant just that: each side would "trade" a certain number of prisoners of equivalent rank, man for man, and the former captives could once again rejoin the fighting. Special exchanges also occurred with great frequency. A designated officer would be exchanged for another, or an officer of a certain rank might be exchanged for a given number of enlisted men (a colonel was the equivalent of fifteen enlisted men, for example). If a cartel of exchange could be agreed upon, then so much the better. This type of agreement provided for the immediate release of prisoners on parole until they were declared exchanged, and spared each belligerent the necessity of guarding, housing, and feeding the captives. It was obviously much easier on the prisoners as well, but such an agreement was not easy to come by.

The British took the position that twenty-three Irish-Americans in the force captured at Queenston in October 1812 were disloyal British subjects and would not be treated as prisoners of war. They would, instead, be sent to England and tried for treason. The commander of these unfortunates, Lieutenant Colonel Winfield Scott, protested vigorously and warned the British that he would urge his government to enact a policy of retaliation. After his exchange in January 1813, Scott proceeded to do just that. The Senate immediately confirmed that the president had the power to retaliate, and in May, Scott himself placed twenty-three captives of the Fort George campaign in close confinement as hostages for the Irishmen. Ironically, a cartel was agreed to on 12 May 1813, but it was not enacted because of the hostage issue. As the war grew more savage, with the burning of York and the British retaliation on the Niagara frontier, the exchange of prisoners came to a standstill.[31]

The British contacted General Henry Dearborn in June 1813 about a resumption of the exchange, but Dearborn delayed three months before sending the letter to Washington. The British informed their captives of Dearborn's negligence and also began sending them to Halifax to relieve the crowded conditions in Canada. On 19 August, Winder wrote Secretary of War John Armstrong a long report and asked that the government take action. Commissary General of Prisoners John Mason dispatched an agent to Canada to negotiate the matter, but the British government decided on a policy of retaliation while the talks were going on. A proclamation appeared in Montreal on 27 October announcing that forty-six officers and noncommissioned officers would be held in close confinement as hostages for the twenty-three men confined by Scott. The Americans responded in kind, and on 12 December the British announced that all American officers regardless of rank would be placed in close confinement.[32]

Until this time, Generals Chandler, Winchester, and Winder had been allowed a wide parole around Beauport and had not suffered unduly. Now they were under a sentence of death and confined to their boarding-houses in the small village.[33] During this period Winder contracted a mysterious lung ailment that would cause his premature death ten years later.

Winder was a captivating man and was on agreeable terms with the British commanders, but all efforts to effect his exchange had failed. The failure was largely due to the warning of his captor, Lieutenant Colonel Harvey. Harvey wrote Colonel Edward Baynes on 11 June to be "careful of exchanging *Genl. Winder.* He possesses more talent than all the rest of the Yankee Generals put together."[34]

Whether this was true or not, Winder possessed formidable legal talents, and he used those skills to break the deadlock. He persuaded the British to give him a parole for sixty days to attempt to resolve the exchange issue, and he left Quebec on 15 January 1814.

He arrived in Washington on 28 January but was unsuccessful in convincing either Congress or President James Madison to abandon the retaliation policy. In late February he departed for Baltimore for a brief visit with his worried family. He was still a hostage under sentence of death, and prospects appeared bleak. During the weeks that followed, the family received a thorough education in the complexities of prisoner exchange. Many American families suffered through the ordeal of having a loved one in captivity during the war, but the Winder experience was unique.

Winder was, by necessity, *the* authority on the matter. If his bargaining skills proved inadequate, he would probably forfeit his life. He had to find an alternative to retaliation that was acceptable to both countries, and he had about one month to do it. The advantages of enacting the cartel were obvious, but several difficult obstacles had to be overcome.

The first major problem was the lack of good faith between the belligerents. If a breakthrough came, one side would have to make concessions and then insist that the opponent respond in identical fashion. Neither side could afford to give the impression of weakness by unilaterally repealing the hostile decrees. Winder saw clearly that the policy of retaliation had to be discredited totally before an alternative could be considered. The British were ready to acknowledge this when they released Winder, and more and more Americans rapidly came to the same conclusion.

Another problem was the military impact that a total exchange would have on each side. If the number of prisoners was roughly equal, an

exchange would obviously help the weaker power. As long as former captives could be returned to the ranks, exchange was not a prudent policy
for the stronger adversary. It would be better to undergo the strain of
providing for prisoners than to free them to fight again. Each side also
had to consider what the impact would be on the soldiers in the field.
If it was known that captivity would be short and relatively punishment-
free, would substantial numbers take this opportunity to surrender and
sit out the war until they were exchanged? Conversely, it was already
apparent that the fear of a prolonged and hard captivity was detrimental
to enlistment. Would an exchange offset this so that more would enlist
than would surrender?

The military concerns were counterbalanced by humane considerations. Relatives and friends wrote petitions pleading for the release of
captives; ministers prayed for, and media representatives demanded, a
solution; and political forces could not long defend a stalemate that was
increasingly unpopular. It was obvious to Winder that public opinion
had to support, even demand, that an alternative to retaliation be attempted if the policy was to have any hope of success, but he did not
know how to accomplish it.

It soon evolved that the best way to force a change in policy was by
giving widespread publicity to the plight of a famous captive so that an
overwhelming demand for his release would be generated. When the
unsuspecting Winder returned to Baltimore, he was unaware that he
was to fill that role; but the welcome he received made it abundantly
clear that he would soon become the focal point of the whole complex
issue. Much to his surprise and delight, the city gave him a hero's recep-
tion. On the last day of February, the mayor, members of the council,
and other leading citizens gave him a testimonial dinner at Barney's Inn.
It was a great outpouring of affection and convincing proof that his capture
had not discredited him in this city at least. He was widely applauded
virtually everywhere he went, and the news coverage expanded accordingly.[35]

Winder returned to Washington and worked constantly for the next
several weeks to soften the official American position. He met with increasing success with both congressmen and members of the administration, but the time was too short. He was on his honor to return to prison
and departed in early March, his mission an apparent failure.

Upon his return to Quebec on 22 March, he was again placed in confinement, but the publicity generated by his visit home had finally convinced the administration to change course. On 19 March, Madison had
appointed him the United States representative in all negotiations for
prisoner exchange, and Secretary of State James Monroe dispatched the
document immediately.

Winder went to Montreal and began formal talks with his counterpart,

Colonel Baynes. The two made progress until another dispatch from Monroe informed them that the United States would not release the twenty-three prisoners held as hostages until the Irish-Americans held captive in England were also freed. The talks stalled, but both parties finally agreed to a convention on 15 April for a mutual exchange of all prisoners except those declared to be hostages. The Winder cartel went into effect on 15 May 1814. Winder had exceeded his instructions but correctly believed that the hostage issue would be resolved once the exchange took place. Within a short time both governments did restore their hostages to ordinary prisoner-of-war status, and in early July, the cartel for all prisoners was ratified and went into effect.[36]

Having won his release, Winder left Canada and reached Plattsburg, New York, on 20 May. He was appointed adjutant inspector general of the army but was not allowed to have a combat command until his exchange was announced. May had been an excellent month for the thirty-nine-year-old general.[37] That good fortune ended three months later. August of 1814 was the fateful month for the Winder family. The events of those four short weeks altered their lives drastically. At the beginning of the month, General Winder was the envy of his military colleagues. At the end of it, his military reputation was destroyed, and he was in disgrace.

Winder's appointment with destiny began in late June. The entire Chesapeake area had been virtually undefended since the war began, and no one had been more outraged and outspoken about it than Winder's uncle, Governor Levin Winder. Baltimore's naval defenses were adequate, but the rest of the area remained undefended and in 1813 endured many hit-and-run raids by the enemy. Influential citizens joined the governor in demanding an end to this situation, and Madison finally decided to take action.[38]

On 30 June 1814, Winder sent to Secretary Armstrong a well-considered plan of defense for the area. He suggested assembling from two thousand to three thousand regulars in Maryland, between the Patuxent River and the eastern branch of the Potomac, and concentrating ten thousand militiamen near the capital.[39] A few days previously, Armstrong had informed Winder that the president was contemplating the creation of a new military district and that Winder was being considered for the command.[40] Madison presented Winder's plan to the cabinet on 1 July, and the Tenth Military District, consisting of all of Maryland, the District of Columbia, and eastern Virginia between the Potomac and Rappahannock rivers, came into being. Winder was notified the following day that the command was his, and on 4 July the president announced a requisition for fifteen thousand militiamen to defend the vital area.[41]

Madison had good reasons for selecting Winder. He had been praised as an able, efficient, and courageous officer prior to his capture and had proved to be a resourceful and determined man during his imprisonment. He knew the area well and had presented a plan of defense endorsed by the president and approved by the cabinet. On the other hand, Winder had been out of the war for the better part of a year and had never commanded as many as one thousand men. The nonmilitary factors that Madison had to consider made Winder the logical choice. With his nephew in command, Levin Winder might be much more cooperative than in the past. At the least, he was unlikely to be as vociferous in his criticisms of the administration. In addition, Baltimore was the logical target if the British attempted an invasion, and no one was more popular in that port city than Winder. That Winder should have no difficulty in enrolling a sufficient militia was an important consideration. For both military and political reasons, he received the command.

To his dismay, Winder soon found that he had no staff, that his army existed almost totally on paper, and that Secretary Armstrong was a distinct liability. Despite repeated requests for staff officers, Winder was ignored for five weeks, and his plan for a mobile force of three thousand regulars was never implemented. He could count on no more than eight hundred. A final obstacle confronting Winder was that Armstrong believed that the best use of militia was to call them up at the moment of attack and then throw them into the fight. So, the official plan was to rely on a citizen soldiery for the defense of the area and to rely on Armstrong to assemble them.

Winder sent Armstrong a strong letter of protest on 9 July. Noting that his force of regulars would remain totally insufficient to prepare defensive works, Winder asked that he be allowed to call up at least four thousand of the militia at once. He pointed out that the British had been in the bay area for over a year and knew the rivers and terrain at least as well as the Americans. They could land in a strategic place, threaten the cities of Baltimore, Annapolis, and Washington, and conceal their intentions until the last minute. He asked Armstrong, "What possible chance will there be of collecting a force after the arrival of the enemy to interpose between either of those places?" He correctly answered his own query: "If the enemy's force should be strong—which if it come at all it will be—sufficient numbers of the militia could not be warned and run together even as a disorderly crowd without arms, ammunition, or organization—before the enemy would have given his blow."[42]

Winder wrote numerous letters to the War Department, the governors concerned, and to the militia officers in his command. He repeatedly urged that the militia be enrolled and readied to move instantly and that the men have sufficient entrenching tools. All his efforts proved disappointing. The despondent general reported on 1 August that he had fewer than one thousand regulars at his disposal and that of the four thousand militia enrolled, only about seventeen hundred of them were actually in camp.[43]

On 18 August the British sailed up the Patuxent River and landed about fifty-one hundred veteran troops under General Robert Ross at Benedict, Maryland. The strategic move made good roads available to all three cities that Winder had to defend. The alarm went up, and Winder set about gathering an army together and impressing the militia into federal service. On 20 August, he sent out cavalry units to gain intelligence, ordered troops at Baltimore to assemble at Bladensburg, and collected a force of some two thousand at the Wood Yard, about ten miles northwest of Nottingham (see map).

On 21 August the British left Benedict at dawn and arrived at Nottingham early in the evening. A flotilla of boats protected Ross's right flank, and he threw out pickets to guard against a surprise attack from his left. Winder sent a small force of dragoons to harass the enemy but did not attempt any offensive action. He had ample forces to destroy bridges and cut down trees to impede the British advance but failed to use them thus—a tactical blunder that had lethal results. The British moved from Nottingham to Upper Marlboro the next day and stayed there until late in the afternoon of 23 August. They had now moved across thirty miles of potentially dangerous, heavily wooded terrain without opposition. During those two days Winder showed convincingly that he was not up to the job. When he could have attacked or at least raided the enemy's flank, he continued to scout. On 21 August he had a fairly firm grip on things. Two days later, he had largely lost control.

The British had thoroughly confused the American command. Armstrong had long maintained, publicly and privately, that Baltimore would be the target, that the British would never attack the national capital. He was about the only one on either side whose mind was made up. Winder vacillated between Annapolis and Washington as the target; Madison, Monroe, and other officials also had their opinions. The British themselves did not make the final decision until 22 August.

Winder ordered the Baltimore forces, including the trusted Fifth Maryland Infantry under General Tobias Stansbury, to occupy a strong position east of Bladensburg and the hamlet itself. The local people volunteered to dig earthworks, and Winder sent an engineer to oversee the effort. Had the 2,350 men been allowed to occupy the strongholds, rest, and refit, they could have been the formidable force that Winder needed. Instead, they were marched and countermarched and finally placed in an unfortified position west of Bladensburg. The men were tired and hungry and in a poor position to receive an attack. Winder's orders generated confusion and mistrust among the officers, and his absence led to the rumor that he had been captured. Stansbury's wing of the army was certainly not in fighting trim.[44]

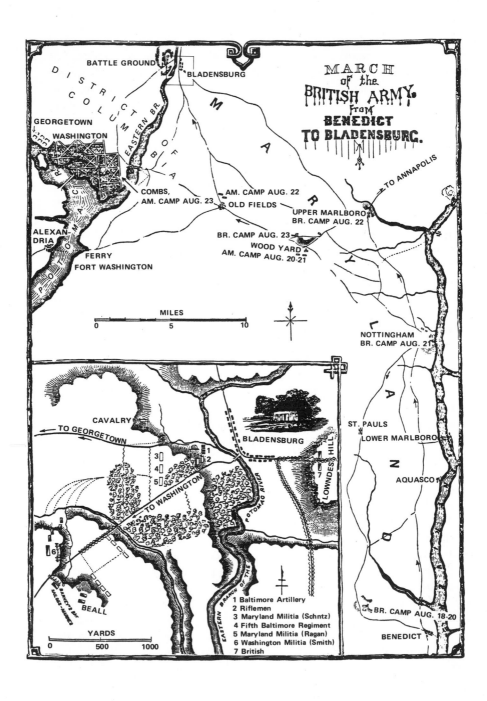

MARCH of the BRITISH ARMY From BENEDICT TO BLADENSBURG.

BATTLE GROUND
BLADENSBURG

DISTRICT OF COLUMBIA

GEORGETOWN
WASHINGTON

EASTERN BR.

M A R Y L A N D

TO ANNAPOLIS

COMBS, AM. CAMP AUG. 23
AM. CAMP AUG. 22
OLD FIELDS
UPPER MARLBORO
BR. CAMP AUG. 22

ALEXAN-DRIA

BR. CAMP AUG. 23
WOOD YARD
AM. CAMP AUG. 20-21

FERRY
FORT WASHINGTON

POTOMAC R.

MILES
0   5   10

NOTTINGHAM
BR. CAMP AUG. 21

ST. PAULS
LOWER MARLBORO

CAVALRY
TO GEORGETOWN

BLADENSBURG

LOWNDES HILL

TO WASHINGTON

3
4
5
1
2

7

AQUASCO

6

BEALL

BARNEY'S BAY
SAILORS MARINES

EASTERN BRANCH OF THE POTOMAC RIVER

BR. CAMP AUG. 18-20

BENEDICT

YARDS
0   500   1000

1 Baltimore Artillery
2 Riflemen
3 Maryland Militia (Schntz)
4 Fifth Baltimore Regiment
5 Maryland Militia (Ragan)
6 Washington Militia (Smith)
7 British

Winder's main force at the Wood Yard numbered about three thousand men, and reinforcements were arriving steadily. He could not afford to concentrate his two armies until he knew which road the British would take, so he retreated about five miles to Old Fields on 22 August. A false alarm that night resulted in the entire force being turned out and kept in formation until daylight. Winder was determined that Stoney Creek would not be repeated, but for two nights his troops received little if any sleep. Even worse, Madison, Armstrong, and other officials arrived during the night, and a presidential review was ordered for the next day.[45] It was a bleary-eyed, dispirited force that assembled in the early morning hours of 23 August, scarcely able to march, certainly not fit to fight.

Winder himself was totally exhausted. He had been in the saddle with scant rest for the better part of five days, and he still did not know exactly where the enemy would attack. Consequently, early on 23 August, he ordered Stansbury to march toward Marlboro on the Bladensburg road and sent a column of his own from Old Fields in the same direction. He then headed for Bladensburg to confer with Stansbury but soon learned that the British had finally begun an advance and were headed toward his forces at Old Fields. He ordered Stansbury to return to Bladensburg and raced back to his main wing.

When the British reached the road junction at Old Fields, they halted, a maneuver that thoroughly bewildered Winder. The enemy could now move northwest to Bladensburg, west to the capital, or southwest to Fort Washington. Ross feinted toward Fort Washington. Winder and Secretary of State Monroe, who had taken on the self-appointed role of scout, strategist, and advisor, were convinced that the attack was on. Winder ordered a retreat across the Eastern Branch Bridge and set up headquarters at Combs. The retreat was the final dissolution for much of his command, officers and men alike. They were tired, hungry, and dispirited. The retreat was virtually a run toward the false security of the city by the demoralized Americans.[46]

It was apparent to everyone during the night of 23 August that the commanding general was at the end of his resources. Winder met with Madison and Armstrong in the early hours of the morning and made his final error. He asked for formal guidance from Armstrong and the government.[47] This appeal for a "democracy of command" was hardly likely to inspire confidence in anyone and proved that the general had lost confidence in himself.

Shortly after daylight on 24 August, Madison, Armstrong, Secretary of the Navy William Jones, Attorney General Richard Rush, Secretary of the Treasury George Campbell, and several subordinates met with Winder at the Navy Yard. News spread that a council was being held, and a number of prominent citizens strolled into the meeting and gave their considered opinions about the proper course to follow. About ten o'clock Monroe rode up, and shortly thereafter a dispatcher informed the group that the British were definitely on the move to Bladensburg. Monroe galloped off to give his unsolicited and unwelcome assistance to General Stansbury, but the meeting continued another hour before Winder ordered his army to Bladensburg and set off himself. He never explained why he delayed at this critical juncture, but this lost sixty minutes could not be made up and contributed mightily to the dismal spectacle that followed.

Stansbury initially had things fairly well in hand at Bladensburg. He posted two companies of artillery and five companies of riflemen to cover the bridge approach and formed his main force—the Fifth Maryland and two smaller regiments—about two hundred fifty yards behind them in an orchard. This was a fairly strong position that afforded protection from British fire and would enable the second line to support the first.

Just as Stansbury got his men into position, Colonel William Beall and about eight hundred militiamen arrived from Annapolis and reported that the British were in hot pursuit. Beall's men passed through Stansbury's lines and took position in the rear.[48] Brigadier General Walter Smith arrived simultaneously with the Washington militia and sought out Stansbury. Since they were of identical rank and Winder was nowhere around, there was a dispute over command. Smith's forces finally fell in beside Beall's, but Monroe arrived in the meantime and ordered Stansbury's troops out of the orchard and positioned them about two hundred fifty yards in the rear. Stansbury returned from his argument with Smith to find his main force out in the open, in clear view of the enemy, devoid of any protection, and totally unable to give support to his first line. He was understandably upset when Winder finally rode up and belatedly assumed command.

Winder believed that it was too late to order the men back into the orchard without creating even more confusion, so he left Stansbury's two lines as he found them and ordered Smith and Beall to form a third line on a hill about five hundred yards to the rear. This was a strong position, but it was also too far away to support the more advanced lines. More important, the troops in the first lines did not even know there was a third line of defense (see map inset).

So, about ten minutes before the British attack got underway, Winder had finally united his army, but it was scattered about in a dangerous fashion. It was positioned so that each line could not support the others, most of the men were in the open, and the concentrated might of the enemy would have an overwhelming advantage in numbers as they attacked each line separately. Winder's observation to Armstrong on 9 July that it would prove impossible to assemble the militia effectively was about to come true.

The British ran into heavy fire from the artillery and riflemen when they forced the bridge, but they soon crossed and fanned out on the other side. The first American line was outflanked in a matter of minutes and forced to retreat. The enemy then advanced against Stansbury's main force without reinforcements. Winder saw the weakness and ordered the Fifth Maryland to attack. The Americans hit the British hard and forced them back to the river to await reinforcements.

Just when it appeared to Winder that the battle was going well, the British opened up with Congreve rockets, and Stansbury's militia panicked. The men threw down their weapons and ran. The officers were powerless to stop them. Winder saw to his horror that Stansbury's right and center were disappearing "in universal flight." He ordered the Fifth to stand firm and personally attempted to rally the mob but was unable to do so. The Fifth was then open to a flank attack, and Winder ordered a retreat. The men followed orders in good fashion until Winder changed his mind and ordered them to reform. They complied only to be ordered once again to retreat. Demoralized by indecisive orders, infected by the panic-stricken militia, cowed by the rockets and the steady advance of the nerveless British infantry, they, too, broke and ran. The second line ceased to exist.

The British were astonished. They had not yet begun to fight, and it appeared that all resistance was at an end. Not so. Commodore Joshua Barney with some five hundred sailors and marines, "the precious few fighting men in the whole damned army," according to their commander, had arrived at the third line. Disregarding the fleeing militia, Barney positioned five large naval guns in the middle of the road and prepared to fire. Smith's troops were on his left and Beall's were on his right. If they would protect his flanks, he would provide an opportunity to rally the American forces.[49] When the British got close, Barney's heavy guns scored with devastating effect. The militia also fired with dispatch. The British, in trouble for the first time, reformed and came on again. Beall's militia broke and joined the race toward Washington. Winder joined Smith and, even though the District militia was fighting well, ordered a retreat. He told Smith to reform closer to the capital while he raced ahead to try to reassemble such troops as he could. Now only Barney's men remained, and five hundred could not hold off forty-five hundred for long, no matter how valiantly they fought. Barney surrendered at four o'clock, and the British continued their march to Washington.[50]

Winder was not able to rally his forces before the city. The "Bladensburg races," as the rout was instantly labeled, were over. The enemy entered without opposition, burned the public buildings, and departed the next day. Ross withdrew to his transports on 26 August and proceeded to his next objective. By then, Winder had collected what forces he could and headed for Baltimore. He correctly anticipated that the British would attack as soon as possible, but he was appalled to learn upon his arrival that the commander of the militia, Major General Samuel Smith, refused to relinquish command and that his uncle, Levin Winder, backed Smith.

In the battle for Baltimore, Winder played an unimportant role. The British attack came close to success on land, but the fleet could not bombard Fort McHenry into submission. Winder was present at the battle of North Point, where his Bladensburg opponent, General Ross, was killed. He had previously helped erect the defensive works about the city, which proved invaluable in the American victory, but his sun had set. The defeat of the British, which so inspired Francis Scott Key "by dawn's early light" on 14 September, certainly compensated to some degree for the national humiliation at Bladensburg, but it was not Winder's victory. In mid-October, General Winfield Scott replaced him as commander of the Tenth Military District, and Winder finished the war in unimportant commands on the northern frontier.[51]

An angry public demanded an explanation for the defeat at Bladensburg. The most serious charges were levied against Armstrong, who was forced to resign in disgrace. Monroe was also severely criticized, and the Federalist newspapers had a field day with Madison. As commanding general, Winder received less public criticism than one would expect, but it was more than enough to destroy his military reputation forever. In his own defense, Winder described all of the difficulties under which he had labored. He blamed the rout on the lack of experience and skill of the militia and the extreme fatigue of all of the troops. He admitted that, given another chance, he would make a few changes in the disposition of his army but concluded that "no advantage of position is proof against groundless panic and want of discipline, skill, and experience."[52]

The congressional committee assigned to investigate the disaster reported in great detail to the House of Representatives in late November. In Winder's favor, every officer who witnessed his performance, including those who thought he had botched the whole thing, testified to his coolness, daring, and personal bravery during the battle; and all agreed that no commanding officer could have stemmed the panic-stricken troops.[53] In addition, the finding of the court-martial headed by Winfield Scott was released on 25 February 1815, and Winder was again exonerated. The court declared that Winder's conduct was commendable. "Before the action he exhibited industry, zeal and talent, and during its continuance a coolness, a promptitude and a personal valor, highly honorable to himself and worthy of a better fate."[54] It was later reported that even the hero of New Orleans, Andrew Jackson, defended Winder. He was quoted as saying that had "all the men on that field been such as Winder, there was force and numbers enough to have gone into the woods, *cut clubs* and driven the British forces back."[55]

All of the commentary was true, but it did not go far enough. Armstrong's conduct and Monroe's interference certainly hampered Winder before the battle, and the militia performed worse than at any other time during the war. Ultimately, however, Winder allowed an army inferior in numbers to rout his forces in less than thirty minutes. He could have prevented Monroe's actions and the altercation between Smith and Stansbury if he had left for the battlefield when he first learned that the British were on the move, and he could certainly have impeded the British advance from the time they first landed at Benedict. No matter what Winder's defenders might have said, any competent commander should have prevented the enemy from seizing the capital in such leisurely fashion. The public knew it, and the official exonerations did not prevent anonymous doggerels from appearing in print. The Bladensburg races entered the national vocabulary almost overnight, and wags soon announced that the only Americans who died at the battle had run themselves to death. From then on, the name Winder was inevitably connected with military humiliation. Even his closest friends felt it necessary to refer to Winder as "that most unfortunate general" of the War of 1812.[56]

Being "damned by faint praise" and aware of sub rosa ridicule at one's expense is hard to endure, but Winder stood it. He returned to his legal practice with zest and thoroughly enjoyed his remaining years. His family had more difficulty in coming to terms with their changed position in society. His three sons found it especially irksome and humiliating to cope with the snide remarks and innuendos they encountered. It became almost an obsession with them to restore the family honor in the public eye, each in his own way.

The youngest son, Charles Henry, followed his father's positive example and became a noted attorney. Although he never attained the legal reputation of his father, he was a widely respected Washington lawyer when the Civil War broke out. The second son, William Henry, engaged in a lifelong correspondence attempting to restore his father's reputation. He contacted everyone of prominence, from Madison on, who had been connected with the battle and never hesitated to chastise authors whose depiction of his father was not to his liking. As late as March 1860, he wrote to Henry B. Dawson that Dawson's recent work on the War of 1812 was inaccurate as far as General Winder was concerned, and he enclosed numerous testimonials from high-ranking participants in support of his claim.[57]

The eldest son chose a different response. He intended to restore the Winder name to a position of prominence in American military history. The son would redeem what the father had lost. History would not irrevocably bind the name Winder to Bladensburg. He had made that vow, if not in those exact words, shortly after he began cadet life at West Point in August 1814, and he tried valiantly to keep it thereafter.

If the conclusion of the Winder cartel in May 1814 had also been the conclusion of Winder's military career, or even if he had remained in captivity for the remainder of the war, it is doubtful that his son would have been on his way to serve the Confederacy the first day of May 1861. In normal times John Henry Winder would have "taken the cars" (to use the expression of the times) of the Washington branch of the Baltimore and Ohio Railroad and changed lines at the Federal capital. He had made the forty-five-mile, three-hour trip frequently and knew the whole area intimately.[58]

After passing the Relay House, about nine miles west of Baltimore, the traveler soon passed into Prince Georges County, the great tobacco-producing section of Maryland. Numerous farms and plantations were visible, and one could catch a distant view of the Maryland Agricultural College amid the pine thickets and scrub forests. The stations were mere hamlets, except for Laurel Factory, until one approached within a few miles of the District of Columbia and entered Bladensburg.[59]

Bladensburg. Until mid-April 1861, it had been a peaceful village, located in the hilly country on the eastern branch of the Potomac. It was now becoming a military camp, essential for the defense of the capital, just as it had been during the War of 1812. But Winder could not allow the memories of what had happened to his father there on that hellish August day forty-seven years ago to command his attention. He knew that the stigma of Bladensburg had not been removed by his wearing the uniform of the United States for over thirty-six years, for excelling in almost every command he had been entrusted with, not even for his courageous and meritorious conduct in the war with Mexico fifteen years previously.

He did not know, could not have guessed, that he had already missed the opportunity of his lifetime. Had he remained true to the Union and returned to duty at Fort Pickens, he might have become a national hero, just as Anderson did after the defense of Fort Sumter. It was the one chance he had to erase the disgrace of Bladensburg. He hoped that service in the army of the Confederate States of America would finally witness the fruition of his goal. He boarded ship, sailed to Norfolk, Virginia, crossed over to Portsmouth by ferry, and took the Seaboard and Roanoke line to Raleigh. About 2 May he arrived and offered his services to the Confederate State of North Carolina.[60]

CHAPTER 3

A Rebel in the Making

May–June 1861

Winder met with Governor John W. Ellis and other North Carolina officials early in May, and Ellis asked Winder to organize an advisory board
for the state and to serve on it "as the Military element." Winder agreed
and Ellis advised him to proceed to the Confederate capital of Montgomery, Alabama, to secure the appointment. The governor provided a letter
of introduction and issued a pass entitling Winder to free passage on
the railroads as an officer on special duty for the state of North Carolina.[1]

Winder left on 10 May and arrived at Montgomery two days later.
He found the small city inundated with hundreds of office seekers, newspaper correspondents, newly elected officials, and all manner of curious
hangers-on.[2] He also found that his mission was a waste of time. In the
excitement and confusion inherent in creating a new nation, many mistakes and misunderstandings occurred, and Winder was informed that
the position he sought had been filled before he left North Carolina.
He returned to Raleigh in a state of high indignation and vented his
frustrations in a long letter to Ellis on 21 May. He noted that:

> The position offered was filled within a day or two of my departure
> and after some delay and hesitation, I was offered the commission
> of colonel of the 1st Infantry coupled with an inferior command [Fort
> Caswell] not at all connected with the appointment. It will certainly
> be thought at Montgomery that there was some reason, not very
> flattering to myself, for this sudden and entire change of purpose.
> I am desirous of rendering what Service I can to the State and shall
> do so, but the circumstances connected with the offer of the appoint-
> ment, are such, that self respect forbids my acceptance, under other
> circumstances it would have been different.[3]

Winder had cause to be irate. He had subjected himself to more than a week of physical discomfort and fatigue only to be insulted when he finally had a meeting with Confederate officials. None of the commanders of North Carolina during 1861 and 1862 possessed credentials equal to his, and none had his wide-ranging experience in all aspects of military affairs. Even his own son, John Cox Winder, had been commissioned major and placed in charge of preparing the defenses of Fort Fisher and other important North Carolina coastal fortifications.[4] John was a capable engineer but had no prior military experience. The idea that his son would have a more important command and only slightly less rank was intolerable to the old warrior, and he haughtily rejected the offer. Still, Winder very much wanted to serve his adopted state. He was more at home in North Carolina than anywhere else, even Baltimore, for it was here that he had spent his most fruitful years.

The year 1828, when he was first posted to the state, marked the end of a difficult period for Winder. In 1823 he had resigned his commission in order to marry his first wife, Elizabeth Shepherd, of Washington, Georgia, and become a gentleman planter. One year later, his father died and left the family in severe economic straits. His mother was forced to turn her home into a boardinghouse in 1825 because he could offer her no help, having failed to manage his father-in-law's Georgia plantation successfully. Then, in 1826, Elizabeth died. Winder abandoned his attempt at a civilian career and returned to the service in 1827.

He had a three-year-old son, William Andrew, to provide for, as well as the continuing obligation to try to relieve the economic distress of the rest of his family. He had ruined a promising career as an instructor at West Point when he lost his temper with a cadet, and was replaced after only one year. September of 1828 was the nadir of his life, and he had no idea that when he took up his duties in the Fort Johnston commissary department at Smithville (now Southport), North Carolina, he had arrived at the place that would be his home for the next twenty years.[5]

Fort Johnston, a "delightful, high, and healthy" site, was located on a bluff along the Cape Fear River some twenty miles south of Wilmington. The fort was the mainstay of the small town of Smithville, and life at the garrison was "filled with musters, drills, formations, card playing, drinking, marble-shooting, hunting, fishing, and occasional trips into Wilmington."[6]

The number of year-round residents not connected with the army was exceedingly small, but the population swelled noticeably during the summer months. Planters and residents in and around Wilmington believed that fevers were caused by miasmas emitted from the rice fields, and many spent the "sickly season," August through October, in Smithville for health reasons. Some of the summer residents built small frame cottages near the fort, and others stayed at boardinghouses. There was much interaction between these people and the army because the fort was the center of many social activities and community endeavors. Picnics and oyster roasts were frequent, and the army band was much in demand both in town and on nearby plantations.[7] Associations between local women and soldiers posted at the fort sometimes led to marriage, and that was to be Winder's happy fate shortly after he met Caroline Ann Cox Eagles.

Caroline Ann Cox was born on 25 May 1800, and lived in Edenton, North Carolina. Born into upper middle-class society, she was the only surviving child of Thomas and Peggy Cheshire Cox. Her mother died when Caroline was young, and her father remained a widower until his death in 1819. She was living with an uncle, John Cox, when she met Joseph Eagles in 1819. They married at Edenton on 1 February 1820 and returned to Eagles's plantation near Wilmington after a brief honeymoon.[8]

Joseph Eagles was descended from one of the most respected families in the Cape Fear region. Family roots went back to 1737, when Richard Eagles received a grant of 540 acres on an island formed by the two branches of the Cape Fear River directly opposite the town of Wilmington. The island was known from then on as Eagles Island, and the rice plantation was appropriately christened "The Forks."[9]

Richard left one-third of his land to his daughter Susannah, wife of Alfred Moore, and the rest to his son Joseph in 1777, and the descendants of the two families shared the island for the next seventy-five years.[10] Joseph, who died in 1791, also left two surviving children: Sarah Isabella, who married Thomas F. Davis, Jr., and Joseph, who married Caroline Cox.

Caroline's new home was on the eastern side of the island (a few hundred yards south of where the battleship USS *North Carolina* is presently moored), and Wilmington was easily accessible by boat. A steam-powered rice mill was conveniently located on the east bank, and Eagles augmented his income by offering its use to neighboring growers.[11] The plantation exceeded 300 acres, but not all of the land was in cultivation. Eagles owned twenty-seven slaves in 1820, four of whom were too young for field work and two of whom were house servants. Eleven men and nine women cultivated the rice fields under the direction of the overseer, a slave named Mingo. This slave, about thirty years old in 1820, managed the plantation for Joseph and later for Caroline and Winder until the estate was sold in 1849. He was paid sixty dollars per year for his labors.[12]

Life was pleasant enough on the island but became less so as the family increased. Caroline Ann Eagles, known as Carrie, was born on 23 October 1822, the only child destined to reach maturity and the only one born on the plantation. The second daughter, Olivia Cox, arrived on

15 August 1824. She was born in a large two-story house located on Walnut and Second streets in Wilmington which Eagles had purchased three months earlier. The last of the children, Sarah Josephine, was also born there during the month of March two years later.[13]

Living in town enabled the Eagles to entertain more frequently and provided more opportunities for the children. They had a wide circle of friends and maintained a close relationship with relatives on both sides of the family. They saw John Cox in distant Edenton on occasion and were in frequent contact with Thomas and Sarah Davis. Caroline was especially fond of her nephew, George Davis (who would become the Confederate attorney general), and he would be of considerable help to her in the future.[14]

It was fortunate that Caroline had relatives who were prosperous and in eminent social positions, for she soon needed their support. Joseph became ill and died quite suddenly on the night of 19 June 1827. He bequeathed his house, house servants, and Mingo to Caroline and the remainder of his estate to his daughters. Under the Sixth Rule of Descents in force in antebellum North Carolina, his youngest daughter was his direct heir. Olivia and Carrie were the heirs of Josephine, and Carrie was the heir of Olivia. Caroline would become residual heir only upon the death of the last surviving daughter, Carrie.[15]

Thomas F. Davis, Thomas F. Davis, Jr., and John Cox were the executors, and Cox was designated guardian for the children. Eagles specified that Mingo should continue as overseer and that if he became unable or unwilling to discharge his duties, he should be paid thirty dollars per year for the rest of his life. Thomas F. Davis, Jr., was authorized to direct the overseer's activities whenever necessary.[16]

The next two years were not prosperous for Caroline and the girls. Rice birds hit the crop with unusual severity in the fall of 1828, storms battered the area a year later and caused further extensive damage, and prices were low for both years.[17] The settlement of Eagles's estate created additional concerns for the young widow. There were several large debts outstanding, and loans from the Bank of Cape Fear alone exceeded $4,900. A further complication arose when two of Eagles's cousins contested the will, claimed one-third of the plantation as their right, and filed for a partition.[18] Caroline's financial condition was not perilous when she departed for Smithville in 1829, but she was not free of economic worries when she met Lieutenant Winder in the summer of that year.

Winder had arrived in Smithville in November 1828 and had begun learning his duties as assistant commissary of subsistence.[19] Caroline had departed Smithville for Wilmington by that time, and Winder was too busy with army business and personal concerns to have had time for extensive socializing in any case. His father-in-law, Andrew Shepherd, had just died, and Winder's son was one of the heirs of his considerable estate. Winder made several trips to Georgia during the subsequent months, but he was free to engage in the usual social activities in 1829.

It cannot be determined when or where they were first introduced, but the courtship was in full flower before the year ended. They were well matched, being the same age, having similar backgrounds, and sharing similar needs. He needed a mother for his son and she a father for her daughters. He knew that he would soon acquire twelve slaves from the Shepherd estate but had no land; she had a plantation in need of additional labor. That they fell deeply in love was simply the final bond.

Since each would bring both property and familial obligations to the marriage, a contract was drawn up in November 1830. The agreement specified that each was solely responsible for individual debts and that each retained sole ownership or control of property then in their possession.[20] With the legal niceties behind them, they were married by the Reverend William D. Cairns on the evening of 10 November 1830 at Saint James Episcopal Church in Wilmington.[21]

Winder was obviously attractive to women. For the second time, he had married a beautiful, aristocratic lady. No portrait of Elizabeth Shepherd has been found, but she was described as a woman of "classic beauty." Caroline, a petite figure barely five feet tall in heels, was certainly striking in appearance. Her porcelain-complexioned face was dominated by dark blue eyes and capped by a luxuriant growth of wavy, dark auburn hair. She had an engaging personality, a mischievous grin, and a smile that Winder must have found devastating. She also had a resolute and independent character. Although she would endure much hardship in her life, her marriage to Winder was strong and unwavering. This was one of those nineteenth-century "companionate" marriages, based on love and mutual respect, that worked wonderfully well. The vows they exchanged that November evening were honored to the full for the rest of their lives.[22]

Although Caroline was a strong individual, she deferred to her husband in all important matters. The Old South was a bastion of white male supremacy, and the women usually accepted this dominance without question. It was Winder who made most of the decisions, whether they concerned christening the children or selling the plantation. He no doubt consulted with her on most decisions—certainly about anything concerning the plantation— but he was clearly the dominant partner during their long life together.

At the time of his second marriage, Winder was in a solvent financial position for the first time in six years, and it was due exclusively to the death of Andrew Shepherd. Seven heirs were entitled to an equal share of Shepherd's holdings, and it took over two years for the final settlement to be made. The division and disposal of the land, equipment, and cotton went smoothly, but the presence of eighty-seven slaves was a complicating factor.

Shepherd had willed his house and town lots to his wife, Mary, and specified that she was also to inherit a slave family of ten members.[23] His children and grandson were to inherit the other slaves. Slave owners did not lightly break up slave families, for both humane and practical reasons; but it did happen fairly frequently when estates were settled, and to some extent it happened here. The final disbursement took place on 22 December 1830, and Winder received twelve slaves valued at $4,225 as his son's share of the estate.[24]

Winder sent ten of the slaves to the rice fields under Mingo's supervision. Since Caroline had house servants, he had no need to train new ones, so he sent two teenage females to help his mother operate her Baltimore boardinghouse.[25] He also acquired "a Negro boy called Jack or John" for $170 in March 1832, and Jack apparently became his orderly for most of the next two decades.[26]

The Eagles estate was in some dispute in 1830, but it was clear that Caroline and her daughters owned twenty-five slaves outright.[27] There was fear of a slave revolt in Wilmington that year, and the garrison at Fort Johnston was reinforced. The rumors proved false, but the Nat Turner rebellion in 1831 sent a shiver of fear throughout the white South and renewed fears of an uprising in North Carolina.[28] Again, no revolt took place, and in neither year was there any trouble on Eagles Island, before or after Winder's slaves arrived, probably because Mingo was an excellent overseer. The plantation was reduced to slightly more than one hundred acres in February 1833, the result of the partition obtained by Eagles's two cousins. Caroline sold her house in Wilmington one year later for $1,700 and liquidated the last of her late husband's debts.[29] Thereafter, the family lived in Winder's quarters in Smithville.

Winder immediately made plans to relieve the financial condition of his Baltimore family. The additional slave force would permit both of his brothers to leave the operation of the boardinghouse to their mother and join Winder in a venture that he felt would dramatically improve the family fortunes. As assistant commissary of subsistence, he was in charge of procuring large amounts of food and other goods for Fort Johnston, almost all of which came through Wilmington merchants. He proposed that his brothers go into the mercantile business and obtain the army account by underselling the local merchants.

William remained in Baltimore and made arrangements with a New York firm while Charles journeyed to Wilmington to establish a local outlet. He arrived in 1831 and was soon active in various community affairs. Charles was training for the law, and his advice was welcomed at town meetings whenever legal topics appeared on the agenda. He served as secretary at these meetings on more than one occasion and received a cordial welcome in Wilmington society.[30]

Charles had a lot of time for community activities because he was spectacularly unsuccessful in competing with the established mercantile firms of Wilmington. An advertisement for a going-out-of-business sale appeared in February 1832, and a notice in the local newspaper in April recorded the outcome of the venture: "Charles H. Winder being about to leave this town, requests all persons indebted to him to make immediate payment; and persons to whom he is indebted, are requested to present their demands."[31]

This experience with Winder's business acumen was enough to last both brothers for the rest of their lives. Charles returned to Washington to resume his legal studies, and William moved to Philadelphia and became a very successful building contractor and real estate developer. From then on, Winder invested in William's projects, not vice versa, and Charles handled the legal affairs for the family.[32]

Shortly after his ill-fated mercantile venture, Winder engaged in another vain attempt to improve his financial position. Caroline's share of the plantation did not include the rice mill, and this gave Winder an idea. He would buy a tract of land containing a large pond and build his own mill. He thought so highly of the idea that he decided to take a six-month leave in November 1833 to pursue his plan on a full-time basis.[33] The Eagles Mill Pond became available late in 1833 for $2,500, and Winder hastened to acquire it. He scraped together $773 and applied for a loan of $1,727. The Bank of Cape Fear directors were not impressed with his plans and refused the loan until he could provide additional guarantees. He talked two local planters into cosigning the note and gave them a mortgage on the property equal to the amount of the loan.[34]

Having secured the cherished property, Winder attempted to obtain the necessary capital to build the mill. Apparently, no one but Winder believed that another mill was necessary. Time passed, his note became due, and his cosigners and the bank brought suit against him for $1,955.55 in September 1834.[35] Winder was forced to sell his mill pond for $1,500 in March 1835.[36] He had managed to lose slightly more than $1,228 in a period of fifteen months. This sum was more than double his salary for those months. Properly chastened, he was content to leave plantation affairs to the competent Mingo and Robert H. Browne, a Wilmington merchant and property manager, from then on.[37]

Caroline soon realized that she had not married a financial wizard, but he was a loving husband and devoted father. William Andrew got on well with his new family, and Winder apparently doted on his daughters. The whole family was grief-stricken when Sarah Josephine died at age six in April 1832. Winder asked for emergency leave and was granted thirty days.[38]

The family visited Edenton in April and then sailed for Baltimore in May. This may have been the first time Winder's mother and sisters met Caroline and the girls as well as the new addition to the family.[39] Caroline had given birth to a son on 1 October 1831, and he was christened John Cox Winder. Shortly after the family returned to Smithville, Caroline again became pregnant, and another son, William Sidney, was born on 14 July 1833. Winder and Caroline lost two other children in infancy, a son in 1838 and a daughter two years later.[40]

Winder's professional career proceeded in the customary manner, and he was promoted to first lieutenant in November 1834.[41] From 1829 to 1836 he performed double duty at Fort Johnston, continuing as commissary officer and also serving as an engineer on the Cape Fear Improvement Project. In the latter capacity he directed slaves hired by the army and provided their rations. As many as two hundred and fifty slaves at a time were hired to work on fortifications and to clear obstacles from the river, and their owners received fifty cents per day per slave. It was a demanding position, and Winder filled it well.[42]

During the winter of 1835, Winder's company was notified that it would soon depart for Florida to assist in the Indian removal.[43] The Seminoles had been assigned to a reservation in south central Florida by the Treaty of Moultrie Creek in 1823, but white Floridians never accepted their continued presence and pressed for their removal. The Floridians' efforts were rewarded in 1830 when Congress announced that all Indians would be moved to reservations west of the Mississippi River.

Many of the eastern tribes resisted this policy, and none were more recalcitrant than the Seminoles. The army began the process of deportation in earnest in 1832 and 1833 and encountered increasing resistance during the next two years. Defiance erupted into war in December 1835 with the massacre of Major Francis Dade and over one hundred enlisted men.[44] It would be seven years before the army could claim victory over its outnumbered opponents.[45]

The army was woefully unprepared for this war, and nearly every soldier soon regarded duty in Florida as the least desirable imaginable. Winder wanted the opportunity for promotion that combat would provide, but he did not want to serve in Florida. He had been there in 1821 and 1822, knew the Indians, the terrain, and the climate, and had no desire to return. At this time he was more concerned with providing for his family than with his career and asked if he could remain at Fort Johnston by transferring to another company. He opted for continuing in the dual role of engineering officer and commissary assistant if he could stay and "attend to army business as well as my own."[46]

The request was denied, and he departed in February 1836, not to return to his family until August of the next year. His homecoming was ruined within days of his return when he came down with malaria. He was bedridden for over a month and was unable to return to duty until late November.[47] This brief visit established a pattern that became the rule for Winder during the next decade. He was ordered to distant frontier posts, making it increasingly difficult for him to be with his family. For example, he had to request emergency leave in December 1838 when several members of his family became seriously ill. His infant son died before he arrived, and so did his sister Gertrude in Baltimore.

For the next two years he served in Arkansas and on the Maine frontier, posts unsuitable for his family. Finally, in 1840 he was assigned to Fort Preble in Portland, Maine, but he received word in July that yellow fever was raging in Smithville and that his whole family was seriously ill. On 15 July he asked for and obtained emergency leave for ninety days and hurried to North Carolina.[48] He wrote his commanding officer on 3 August from Hickory Springs in Chatham County to request additional leave and to report on what had happened:

> I found when I got home a very distressed family, one child [infant daughter] had been buried two days before my arrival and another Daughter [Olivia] had just left to travel with little expectation of returning alive—her mother could not go with her on account of the illness of another member of the family. She was therefore obliged to go with her sister but little older than herself [Carrie]. . . . I overtook them at this place—my daughter although a little revived by travelling, is not I think materially better—as travelling seems to be the only hope for her, I urgently request my leave of absence be extended.[49]

Olivia lingered for several weeks but died at her Smithville home on 26 September 1840.[50]

A full year passed before Winder was able to send for his family, and their reunion was of short duration. The move to Fort Preble, overlooking the harbor at Portland, Maine, was expensive, for it required fifteen oak chests just for the family linens, clothing, and collection of seventeenth-century silver. Winder's aristocratic taste for quality possessions is evidenced by the fashionable field desk that he carried from assignment to assignment. This portable desk contained shaving and stationery compartments, and the drawers were lined with velvet. He and his family were exceedingly well-dressed, and his house was handsomely furnished as well.[51]

Winder was named adjutant quartermaster of Fort Preble in April 1842 and was promoted to captain six months later. The promotion meant that Winder now had his own company, but it also entailed another separation from his family. He was ordered to take command of remote Fort Sullivan in Eastport, Maine, the first of several postings that lacked the facilities necessary for the needs of his family. They were forced to return to Smithville in November 1842, after being together for only thirteen months.

It was at this time that the decision was taken to send eighteen-year-old William Andrew to Philadelphia. He had wanted to enroll at West Point and enter his father's profession, but Winder had twice tried unsuccessfully to secure the appointment. William Andrew therefore went to stay with Winder's brother William and attend the same university that his grandfather had, the University of Pennsylvania. It was probably at this time that he began the study of medicine, although he did not become a physician until after the Civil War.[52]

Winder found it increasingly difficult to obtain leave when plantation affairs demanded his presence. He asked for leave in September 1845, shortly before departing for a new assignment in Florida, and stressed the urgency of his request. He stated that he had received a leave of absence in 1843 but "was turned back at Washington and failed to accomplish anything." He also noted that he had been denied leave in 1844 and during the spring of 1845 because he was "the only officer at the post." He continued: "I have not been able to attend to my affairs for nearly five years and my agent is urging me to come and do so. If I am not able to do it now it will be ruinous to me on my own account and still more to an account of an unsettled estate of which I have control. I can do all that I have to do and be at Tampa as soon as the company arrives."[53]

The administration of the plantation was a rather complicated legal affair. The deaths of Sarah and Olivia meant that Carrie was the heir to the Eagles's share of the estate. Winder was the administrator for William Andrew's portion, but not for Carrie's, and John Cox, as the eldest son of John and Caroline, also had legal rights. The land remained solely in Carrie's name, but the slave forces were merged and operated as a unit. Disbursements and profits had to be divided and percentages of other investments determined, and administrators had to be appointed for the deceased daughters—all of which necessitated several appearances before a magistrate. Winder obtained leave and reached Smithville in October.

The most pressing item at this time concerned an investment that Winder's brother William wanted to make in Washington, D.C. Not only had Winder used his own money in William's ventures, he had also consigned much of the plantation returns to them. An accounting in 1849 revealed the following breakdown of expenses, profits, and investments:

The Estate of Joseph Eagles in account current
with J. H. Winder 1830–48

For use of the estate	$ 8,886.11
For use of Caroline Eagles	4,112.70
For use of Olivia Eagles	1,917.07
For use of Sarah Josephine Eagles	77.39
For use of Mrs. Winder	1,342.75
	16,336.02
Amt. paid to R. H. Browne	9,417.06
Cash on hand, R. H. Browne	249.10
Investment with W. H. Winder, Phil.	10,207.37
	36,209.55
Sold rice crop in Jan. '49 for	6,128.91
Sold house in Wilmington for	1,700.00
Balance as of 31 December 1848	$ 9,896.94

It can be seen from this account that more money had been invested with William in the decade 1839–1849 than was reinvested in the plantation from 1830 to 1849. The number of slaves increased from thirty-seven in 1830 to fifty-three in 1853; part of this accretion may have resulted from additional purchases. Natural increase alone could have resulted in this number, but it is possible that at least part of the $8,886.11 expenditure was used to acquire slaves. Of the $10,200 invested with William, $1,000 was made as a result of Winder's trip home in October 1845.[54]

William had several ongoing projects in Philadelphia, New York, and Washington, D.C. He would soon rebuild the National Theater on Pennsylvania Avenue near Willard's Hotel in the national capital, but in 1845 he was convinced that there was a pressing need for a new government building. Congress was unwilling to authorize federal funds for building projects, so the various departments had to rent from the private sector. William realized that many of these rented rooms were inconveniently located and not fireproof. Accordingly, the brothers purchased property at the corner of F and 17th streets, and William began construction after obtaining assurances from Secretary of War William Marcy that the government would enter into a five-year lease for some or all of the rooms in the building. William's foresight was immediately confirmed; the Navy and War departments moved into the building even before it was finished.

The Winder Building was the tallest and largest office building in the capital when it was completed in 1848. It rose five stories above a dry cellar, contained 60,000 square feet, and was divided into one hundred thirty offices, all leased by the government. The brothers received

$22,750 in rent annually until 1854, when they decided to sell. William and Secretary of War Jefferson Davis agreed on a price, but Congress refused to allot the money until William threatened to double the rent. The government acquired it in June 1854 for $200,000.[55] The records do not reveal what percentage of this sale was Winder's, but it must have been substantial. All in all, his decision to invest the $1,000 in 1845 proved to be the best business decision he ever made.

Winder left for Florida in November 1845 and sent for his family to join him at Pensacola, but again they were together for less than a year. War with Mexico was declared, and Winder was ordered to Vera Cruz. He would not see his family again for almost two years. He wrote regularly, but of the thousands of letters penned in his lifetime, only one has survived intact. Dated 12 May 1847, it was sent from Jalapa, Mexico, to his son John Cox at Pensacola.

Tell your mother I have been delighted at the receipt of her last two letters of the 23rd and 28th of April and you can't think how much pleasure it gave me to find that you and Sid gave your mother no trouble and that you are improving in your learning. Since I last wrote, I have been to church. It is very handsomely ornamented, the face of the Virgin Mary over the altar is very handsome and her face, as she stands by Christ on the Cross, with her hands clasped and eyes raised, had an extremely mournful expression. There are a great many other figures all as large as life—there are no pews or seats—there are three aisles separated by pillars and arches. The people all kneel on the floor and during sermon sit down. It looks right funny.

Yesterday I was interrupted to go and witness the punishment of some man who broke into a Mexican house and robbed it of money and trinkets. A part of the punishment was flogging and Watson of the band was detailed to do it. He said his conscience was too tender; he struck so softly that Col. Childs ordered him to strike harder but he did not do it, so he got himself into the guard house and will probably be very severely punished for his folly—it is at last determined that our Regiment stays here this summer as part of the Garrison. It is a very healthy place and pleasant if I could talk Spanish. I shall learn I think before the summer is out. I have moved my quarters next to the Barracks, the yard has the greatest profusion of flowers and the old man is very clever. He told me that any of the furniture I wanted I was welcome to the use of, so that I think I shall find my situation quite pleasant, or at least as pleasant as any would be away from home. We seem to know as little about what is going on as you do. I never see any part of the Army but our own. I hear nothing. Very often we get the

news of things about us by the New Orleans papers. Dr. Steiner
is very sick with typhus fever. I have not been able to get to see
him, but shall try to do so today. I am afraid poor Sgt. Thompson
is not long for this world. He has not been well since he had the
measles at Tampico. I went to see him yesterday at the hospital,
and he looks as badly as a man can look and be alive.

Ask that scamp Sid why he didn't write to me; I shall expect a
letter from him very soon. . . . None of you ever say anything about
Sarah, how she behaves—I am sorry that Jenny has lost her things.

Tell your mother I shall send by the same mail that comes with
this letter a check of $90.00 to Major Van Nep and ask him to send
her the money. This is for April. I send a flower for your mother—it
is a blue flower on a large bush that appears to be a jasmine. The
bunch I send is small. The whole bush is covered with them. You
must all write often. I write by every mail that I know of. Some
times they slip off without my knowing it. Kiss your mother and
sister for me and tell them to kiss Sid.[56]

If this letter is typical, then one must suppose that Winder was an
affectionate father and a loving and considerate husband. His reference
to Sarah and Jenny indicates that he had at least some cursory concern
for the house slaves. Although he mentions adding Spanish to his foreign
language skills (he had taken French at West Point), it is doubtful that
he ever became proficient in that language. Winder's reference to the
Catholic congregation's actions as being "right funny" suggests that he
attended out of curiosity rather than religious need. He was apparently
at home in various Protestant denominations, for he had been christened
and brought up in the Presbyterian faith and became a practicing Episco-
palian at West Point, since that was the "established church" of the Academy and attendance was compulsory. He had married his first wife in
a Baptist ceremony, and William Andrew had been baptized in that faith,
but Winder returned to the Episcopal fold when he was posted in North
Carolina in 1828 and remained a member for the rest of his life.[57]

Caroline, Carrie, and Sidney were active in the Episcopal Church for
most of their lives, and William Andrew converted at a young age, but
John Cox did not become a member until 1864.[58] Religion was important
to the family (with the possible exception of John Cox), but only the
women were especially pious or devout. Winder attended church when
he could, but in neither his personal correspondence nor official communications is there any reference to a deity or anything remotely religious.
None of his contemporaries recorded anything about his religious beliefs,
and the records indicate that he was not a man of deep religious conviction.

Winder returned from Mexico in time to spend Christmas of 1848 with his family at Fort Johnston. This Yuletide was a bittersweet occasion. Even though the whole family was together for the first time in six years, it was the last time they would celebrate the holidays in Smithville. William Andrew, recently commissioned a second lieutenant, obtained leave; and John Cox and Sidney, students at Columbiad College near Washington, D.C., were also able to attend.[59]

Winder knew that he would not again be posted at Fort Johnston, and William Andrew had orders to report to New Hampshire. Seventeen-year-old John Cox was determined to become an engineer, and Sidney wanted to enter the legal profession. The necessity of attending to plantation business with the family dispersed was an ever-increasing nuisance; therefore, while they were all assembled and thereby able to conduct legal affairs as a unit, the family decided to sell The Forks and the fifty-three slave "members of the family."

This must have been a traumatic time for the Winders, especially Caroline and Carrie, for many of the slaves had indeed been like family to them. But they bowed to Winder in this matter, perhaps because the family found a buyer for the whole force and thus avoided separating any of the slaves from each other. At any rate, the Wilmington and Manchester Railroad had just been formed, and the company needed both the land and the labor force. Carrie sold the land for $2,500 on 1 January 1849.[60] George Davis, Caroline's nephew and an influential attorney, handled the transaction but soon reported that there was an obstacle regarding the sale of the slaves. Winder had never been legally appointed administrator for Sarah Josephine, and this was not accomplished until 1853. The slaves, house servants and field hands alike, were leased to the railroad company from 1849 to 1853 and were sold to the company in June for $28,000. The total estate (plantation, improvements, slaves, and rice crop) came to $37,396.94. The money was divided equally among Carrie, William Andrew, John Cox, and Caroline and Winder.[61] When Sidney attained his majority in July 1854, Winder instructed Davis to divide his and Caroline's share between John Cox and Sidney, but the record does not indicate what percentage went to each son.[62]

Winder's attitude toward slavery in 1850 was most uncommon for a man of his heritage. He was born into a slave society and had a long affiliation with chattels. His family had owned slaves for two hundred years, and he twice married into slaveholding families. He had willingly attempted to manage the plantation for his father-in-law, readily claimed twelve slaves as his son's share of Shepherd's estate, and purchased his orderly, Jack, in 1832.[63] When he was lieutenant governor of Vera Cruz following the Mexican War, he had no hesitation in seeking out and returning runaway slaves to their owners. Finally, in actuality if not legally, he was the absentee owner of the North Carolina plantation for twenty years. Winder obviously regarded slavery as part of the natural order, but he was atypical of many if not most slaveholders, including his parents, in that he never formed a strong personal attachment to any of his bondsmen, including Jack. His parents freed several slaves and refused to sell black family members even in times of financial distress.[64] They cared for their servants as individuals. Winder did not. He came to regard his plantation holdings as an encumbrance that was not particularly profitable. Nothing indicates that he was ever intentionally cruel to any of his chattels, but his treatment of the slave Mingo illustrates his indifference to the emotions, intellect, and psychology of his charges.

As noted, Mingo was the overseer of the Eagles/Winder rice plantation for approximately thirty years. He had been promised a modest financial stipend and physical leisure in his old age. Implicit in this understanding was that he would never be sold and might even be freed. He had labored loyally for Winder and his family and was clearly entitled to Winder's gratitude if not his affection. He received neither. When Winder sold the slaves, the name "Old Mingo" headed the list.[65]

Like most white Americans of his time, Winder believed that blacks were racially inferior; like most southerners, he felt that slavery was the only way the two races could peacefully coexist. Yet he never developed the paternalism so characteristic of the planter mentality, never felt that the peculiar institution was a panacea for all ills afflicting civilization, and never espoused the radical view that slavery must become national in character. Winder was not overly concerned about the morality or immorality of the system. He was, essentially, an amoral pragmatist—and a rather cold-blooded one. He believed that slavery was necessary but viewed slaves primarily as property, to be acquired or discarded with little regard for humanity. When it appeared more lucrative to invest in real estate than to improve or expand the plantation, he sold the slaves. His action was based on economic considerations and personal convenience, not on deeply held moral, religious, political, or social convictions.[66]

To some extent, Winder regarded his slaves as he did his Federal captives during the Civil War. He wanted the material needs of both satisfied and would not condone physical cruelty at any time, yet he never concerned himself in either case with their nonmaterial requirements. Curiously enough, this view worked to the advantage of black Union soldiers in captivity. To Winder, a Federal prisoner was just that, regardless of race, and deserved equal treatment. He may have been the only top Confederate official who felt that way.

Given his attitude, it is not surprising that he was not personally caught up in the national controversy surrounding the slavery issue at the time he decided to sell. When he made that decision, the nation was in the worst political crisis of its brief history. The great debate in and out of Congress, on whether to permit slavery in the territory acquired from

Mexico, was reaching a climax. Initiated when the House passed the
Wilmot Proviso in 1846 and the Senate blocked it, the issue created
so much turmoil that tensions seemed at the breaking point in 1849.
Sectional rivalry was at a height never before witnessed. Whereas southern spokesmen, goaded by the rising tide of critics inveighing against
the evils of slavery, threatened secession if the peculiar institution was
barred from the new possessions, many northerners held that it would
be monstrous to allow slavery to expand into areas where it had not
previously existed. The attention of the nation was riveted on Washington. It was up to Congress and the administration of Zachary Taylor to
reach a compromise and preserve the Union.

For the better part of a year, from December 1849 to September 1850,
Congress grappled with the fundamental questions of what the United
States was and would be in the future. Could the country continue half-
slave and half-free? Was sectional pride, prestige, and honor stronger
than the ties of Union? Were the differences between North and South
primal, elemental, and irreconcilable, or was compromise, the essence
of the creation and preservation of the nation thus far, still attainable?
As it turned out, compromise was possible, just barely, but for the last
time.

The passage of the Compromise of 1850 required skilled manipulation
by pragmatic political leaders. Building on the spirit of reconciliation
urged by Henry Clay and Daniel Webster, Stephen A. Douglas and other
moderates maneuvered the bills through Congress by resorting to temporary and shifting political coalitions. If the compromise was not destined
to achieve permanent peace, it at least postponed the national disruption
for a decade.[67] Tensions soon diminished to what passed for normal during
that troubled time. Still, sectionalism was in the ascendant, in the nation
and in the army. More ominously, sectionalism was yielding to southern
nationalism in much of Dixie, particularly in the Lower South.

Like the majority of his countrymen, Winder followed the great debate. Like them, he was gratified that the Union would endure. Whether
he believed the measures to be a fair adjustment, a permanent settlement, or merely a temporary evasion cannot be completely determined.
Having decided to sell the slaves, and never to own another chattel,
he was not susceptible to the extreme southern rhetoric that proclaimed
slavery a positive good, a Christian duty, a national necessity. As a southerner, he believed that his section had legitimate grievances as expressed
by John C. Calhoun during the debate, but he did not favor secession
then or a decade later. Conversely, he was outraged by abolitionist demands to destroy the harlot, slavery, and had no sympathy with any
antislavery movement.[68]

In all probability, Winder did not truly care whether slavery followed
the flag or not. He doubtless approved of the Compromise of 1850 if

only because it allowed him to return to business as usual. His life was the army. Honor, duty, his life if necessary, he had pledged to the service. For him, slavery was primarily a means of economic improvement, but he did become more entrenched in the southern camp as the tumultuous years of the 1850s unfolded. He served from 1852 to 1860 in South Carolina and Florida, the two most radical states in the South, and this no doubt influenced his attitude and ultimate actions; but in 1850, when he left North Carolina, he was content with the status quo.

Now, eleven years later, in June 1861, he again left North Carolina. Chagrined and angry that he had not secured a position commensurate with his rank and experience, he joined the horde of office seekers descending on Richmond, the new Confederate capital. Winder checked into the Spotswood Hotel in mid-June and talked with President Jefferson Davis soon after. On 21 June his old friend Adjutant General Samuel Cooper told him he could expect some important news momentarily. Late that evening or early on 22 June, Cooper forwarded a commission signed by Secretary of War Leroy Pope Walker offering Winder the rank of brigadier general in the provisional army and appointing him inspector general of the military camps in the Richmond area. He accepted immediately.[69]

Winder had finally attained the rank and position he had so ardently pursued. He did not know Richmond well, but he soon became extremely knowledgeable about every facet of life in the city. Before a year had passed, he was widely known by the inhabitants, many of whom roundly cursed him, and by late 1862 he was routinely referred to as the dictator of the Confederate capital. The Winder name was soon associated not only with the ineptitude of the father at Bladensburg but with the misrule of Richmond and the mistreatment of prisoners by his son, Brigadier General John Henry Winder, Confederate States Army.

CHAPTER 4

Confederate Brigadier

1861

The Richmond of mid-1861 was markedly different than it had been before secession. Located at the falls of the James River and nestled among the hills of southeastern Virginia, the state capital in 1860 was a cultural and social center in the southern tradition. The population approached 38,000 and the city was home to five colleges and literary institutions, seventeen journals and periodicals, and some thirty churches. Richmond was also the terminus for five railroads and housed forty-three tobacco factories, several iron foundries, and numerous flour and cotton mills. It was described as a city where few people bothered to lock their doors.[1]

When the Confederate Congress voted to make Richmond the capital of the new nation on 27 April 1861, the tranquillity of the antebellum era ended abruptly. The population more than doubled within a few months as some 40,000 disorganized and ill-equipped volunteers from Dixie poured into the area to defend the capital. Not all of these troops constituted the flower of southern chivalry, and Richmond citizens underwent a rapid disillusionment as soldiers engaged in drunken brawls and made general nuisances of themselves. Deserters, stragglers, and the riffraff that are part of even the best of armies infested Richmond. Regiments became hopelessly disorganized in the suburbs, and enterprising businessmen further aggravated the situation by setting up saloons adjacent to the military camps. For many civilians, the heroes of the spring of 1861 became the "brass buttoned loafers" of the fall.[2]

The population was swelled not only by members of Confederate officialdom but by speculators, gamblers, and criminals of every description. Sallie Brock Putnam reported that by 1862 "thieving, garrotting, and murdering were the nightly employment of the villains who prowled around the city, until, by the increased vigilance of the police under the newly-appointed Provost Marshal, this alarming state of affairs was in a manner rectified."[3]

Winder was the newly appointed provost marshal, but earlier, in 1861, his duties were not so all-encompassing. As inspector general of the camps, he was primarily responsible for overseeing the fitting-out of soldiers for field duty. He also handled discharges, returned deserters, and secured medical care for sick or wounded soldiers. His staff consisted of only six officers, and the turnover was rapid, since his assistants transferred to field duty as soon as possible. He soon notified Adjutant General Cooper that he needed permanent staff if he was to be effective, and he received authorization to employ three civilians for clerical work.[4] This was Winder's first encounter with the fundamental problem that would haunt him the rest of his life: insufficient resources to accomplish the assigned task.

Early in July, Winder came to the attention of John Beauchamp Jones, a clerk in the War Department. Jones soon regarded Winder as his nemesis and vilified him at every opportunity. Since so many later writers relied on Jones's *Rebel War Clerk's Diary* for their assessment of Winder, it is well to note that Jones voiced his prejudice from the beginning. His first entry, dated 8 July, reveals his bias.

> There is a stout, gray-haired old man here from Maryland applying to be made a general. It is Major (U.S.A.) J. H. Winder, a graduate of West Point, I believe; and I think he will be successful. He is the son, I believe, of the General Winder whose command in the last war with England unfortunately permitted the City of Washington to fall into the hands of the enemy. I have almost a superstitious faith in lucky generals, and a corresponding prejudice against unlucky ones, and their progeny. . . . He may take the prisoners into his custody—and do other jobs as a sort of head of military police; and this is what I learn he proposes.[5]

Jones was a man of overpowering prejudices. He was also Winder's most constant and severe critic. Biased from the beginning, his dislike turned to hatred within a short time, and his remarks must be considered in that light.

Jones's observation also reveals the confusion and inaccuracies that surrounded the War Department at that time. As mentioned, Winder had been commissioned on 21 June and had been on the job for almost three weeks before Jones became aware of him. Not only was Winder inspector general during July, he was also listed as a brigadier general in the Maryland Flying Artillery, better known as the First Maryland Battery.[6] On 16 July, General Robert E. Lee ordered him also to take command of the camp of instruction located at the fairgrounds, but he rescinded the order two days later.[7] His association with the Maryland Flying Artillery must have been about as brief as his tenure at the fairgrounds, but his duties as inspector general remained constant.

Beginning in July, the remaining months of 1861 were hectic for Winder. He faced increasing personal pressures, and his professional duties and responsibilities expanded enormously. Beset by worries concerning his family, he was ordered to deal with unruly Confederate soldiers and deserters, Union sympathizers in the Confederacy, and Union soldiers and civilians captured at the battle of Bull Run, or first Manassas.

Winder's family was widely scattered when he commenced his duties. His mother was in Columbia, South Carolina, and "very, very ill," according to Mary S. Stark, erstwhile correspondent of Mary Boykin Chesnut.[8] Unlike Edmund Ruffin and other out-of-state fire-eaters who had hurried to the Palmetto State to observe the secession attempt from the beginning, Gertrude Winder was merely visiting family and friends when she contracted a severe bronchial infection. Fortunately, her grandson John Cox was able to go to Columbia and help her return to Baltimore after she recovered. He had been in Richmond on a recruiting mission for the state of North Carolina when the firing on Fort Sumter occurred. Having seen his grandmother safely home, he returned immediately and was placed in command of Company A, Second Engineers, at Fort Fisher, North Carolina, for the duration of the conflict.[9] Gertrude lived with Winder's wife and daughter until December 1863. At that time, Caroline and Carrie crossed the lines and stayed with Winder in Richmond for a brief time, but they soon departed for Hillsborough, North Carolina, where they spent the rest of the war years with Caroline's relatives. Gertrude then moved into a Baltimore boardinghouse operated by a close friend, Mary Louisa Hughes, on North Charles Street.[10]

William Sidney Winder began the practice of law in Keokuk, Iowa, in 1858 but returned to Baltimore late in 1860. He was eager to join the Confederacy but was unable to do so until October of 1861. When his father left in May, it fell to him to look after the affairs of the family. When his grandmother's health improved and he was sure that his mother and sister could cope with the situation, he, too, headed for Richmond. Commissioned first lieutenant on 29 October, he was ordered to report to his father and served with him throughout the war.[11]

William Andrew Winder was a captain in the Union's Third Artillery. He served at Fort Alcatraz until July 1864 and finished the war at Point San Jose, California. Although he had no contact with his father after the war began, he suffered because of his name. In August 1864, General Henry Halleck ordered an investigation to determine whether Captain Winder had ordered photographs of the interior and exterior of Alcatraz published in an attempt to aid the Confederacy. William Andrew's commander, Brigadier General George Wright, reported that he had never doubted Winder's loyalty and that he was an intelligent, efficient officer who had performed excellently at Alcatraz. Wright noted: "In the summer of 1862 there was considerable talk in the city of San Francisco in relation to Captain Winder, growing out of the fact, I apprehend, that the captain's father was in the rebel army; and as I wished to increase the force on the island, I sent Captain Black with his company of the Ninth Infantry as Captain Black ranked Captain Winder."[12]

Halleck was not satisfied until informed in December 1864 by General Irwin McDowell that Winder's character and record were outstanding and that he was an excellent and extremely patriotic Union officer.[13] No further investigation occurred, but William Andrew's career obviously suffered because of his father's position in the Confederacy.[14]

Winder's brothers also experienced discomfort and some humiliation because of his allegiance to the Confederacy, but it is fair to assume that they would have had difficulties in any case. Although Charles Henry Winder was a respected attorney in Washington, D.C., he was a strong advocate of the right of secession. He was not a slave owner in 1860, but he employed two slave women in his household.[15] He was arrested as a disloyal citizen on 9 September 1861 but was placed on parole and released during the second week of October. For the rest of the war he remained free, even though several northern newspapers continued to label his attitude as "treasonable" from time to time.[16]

William Henry Winder was a prominent man in Philadelphia, but he refused to take the required oath of allegiance as a captain in the Reserve Grays of that city. He publicly denounced Lincoln's actions and notified Secretary of War Simon Cameron in August that the Union could not be "preserved by bloody war." He wrote Secretary of State William Seward the following month and denounced abolitionists as the sole reason for all the trouble.[17] Cameron ordered William arrested on 10 September and his correspondence confiscated. Letters to and from Clement Vallandigham, John C. Breckinridge, and other well-known rebel sympathizers were seized, as well as property deeds, photographs, and all personal papers.[18]

All of the letters in William's possession were written before the firing on Fort Sumter, and he had not been in contact with any Confederate official, including his brother, since that time. Nevertheless, he was imprisoned at Fort Lafayette in New York until October and then sent to Fort Warren in Boston Harbor. He would remain there, without being formally charged, for the next fifteen months.

His mother made several attempts to secure his release. She wrote General Winfield Scott on 22 October to ask that he intervene, but she received no response. She next asked her minister, the Reverend John C. Backus of Baltimore, to use his influence. Backus wrote Cameron that the general's widow had been totally dependent upon her three sons but that one was now in the Confederate Army, and the "other two sons have been recently arrested."[19] After his release, Charles also made an appeal in behalf of his brother. On 5 December 1861, he informed the War Department that William was the "Sole support of a mother now past eighty years of age" and in late January 1862 he asked Seward to release William because his presence was vital to the family security "due to certain real estate holdings in D.C. in his name."[20]

William's retention was not as arbitrary as the family thought. He was offered his freedom on 14 January if he would take the oath. He refused, continued to protest his arrest, and insisted on an unconditional release. His warden, Colonel Justin Dimick, was an old and intimate friend of John Henry Winder's. They had served together in the old army and had been fast friends since they entered West Point in 1814. Dimick saw to it that William did not suffer physical discomfort but could do little else, and William was not released until 27 November 1862. Still defiant, indignant, and unrepentant, he publicly branded the Emancipation Proclamation, declaring, "It will attach an inextinguishable odor of infamy to itself."[21]

William remained free for the duration, but none of his personal possessions were ever returned. Since he was the "custodian" of the Winder correspondence, including letters to and from his brother, almost all of the Winder letters were lost. A few survived because William had forwarded them to other family members (a common custom of the times), and thus they were not confiscated.[22]

Winder followed the plight of his brother through the newspapers and also in his family's letters as he continued to perform his official duties.[23] He rented a house on the corner of Third and Leigh streets, a short walk from his official headquarters at Broad and Ninth. His responsibilities increased sharply after the mayor's court of Richmond forwarded all cases subject to military authority to his office. Beginning in September 1861, all soldiers arrested by civil authorities, as well as civilians and aliens accused of disloyalty, were assigned to Winder. In addition, he was still responsible for maintaining law and order in the camps around Richmond and remained in charge of the increasingly difficult job of dealing with Union prisoners.[24]

With regard to the Confederate soldiers, drunkenness was by far the major problem confronting Winder and the Richmond police. Mayor Joseph Mayo had fewer than one hundred policemen, a force totally inadequate for the job. Even after the city council closed all drinking establishments on Sundays and at ten o'clock on weeknights, drunks inundated Richmond. This ordinance, passed on 8 July, proved very difficult to enforce.[25] By September, however, even with the limited force under Mayo's command, the jails were packed and the court docket hopelessly overcrowded. Mayo appealed to Winder for aid, and the general took

immediate, effective action. He rented a large tenement to accommodate
the prisoners and removed them from the city jails without ceremony.
The soldiers remained in his custody until they could be tried and returned to their units.[26]

Winder also took a more active interest in deserters. On Sunday morning, 23 November, Richmond citizens noticed a company of Winder's
men marching briskly out of town. Hoping to see some captive Yankees,
a small crowd gathered and followed the troops. Their ambition was
thwarted when the soldiers stopped a train, apprehended six miserable
deserters, and confined them in the same tenement with the drunk and
disorderly.[27]

Winder's actions removed the strain on the jails and the court docket,
a popular move endorsed by the press, but his attempts to deal with
citizens accused of disloyalty resulted in criticism. The Confederate government faced the same type of internal dissent that confronted the Federal government, but it attempted to handle the problem in a less rigorous fashion. The suspected presence of Union spies and sympathizers,
enemy aliens, and untrustworthy residents who followed the old flag soon
seized the imagination of Richmond citizens. Some, in and out of government, became increasingly fearful and demanded drastic action to halt
treasonable activities.[28] The War clerk Jones, about as paranoid on this
subject as anyone in the city, noted on 7 August that there was

> a tremendous excitement! The New York *Herald* has been received,
> containing a pretty accurate list of our military forces. . . . Who
> is the traitor? Is he in the Adjutant-General's office? Many suppose
> so; and some accuse Gen. Cooper, simply because he is a Northern
> man by birth. . . . For my part, I have no doubt there are many
> Federal spies in the departments. Too many clerks were imported
> from Washington. And yet I doubt if any one in a subordinate posi-
> tion, without assistance from higher authority, could have prepared
> the list published in the *Herald*.[29]

Subversion and espionage fell generally within Winder's jurisdiction,
but the chain of command was not explicitly clear, even after the Alien
Enemies Act of August 1861 was proclaimed. This legislation required
all males over fourteen years of age to swear allegiance to the Confederacy or leave within forty days; if they did not swear, they would be declared enemy aliens. Winder handled the cases of disloyal soldiers by
courts-martial, but civilians accused of betrayal had to be tried by local
or state civil courts. He used both methods when dealing with aliens.[30]

To investigate charges of disloyalty, Winder had to create a force of
civilian detectives. This proved to be one of the most unpopular actions
that he ever took. The men he hired were soon referred to in print
as "alien plug-uglies" and were widely hated by the citizens of Richmond

in 1861 and 1862. The term *plug-ugly* had received national attention during the Baltimore elections of 1854 and 1856. Composed primarily of labor union members and newly arrived, non-English-speaking immigrants, the "plugs" attempted by force and guile to liberalize Maryland's strict state constitution. They specialized in illegal campaign tactics and were not averse to violence. The city police were sympathetic, or at least inefficient in controlling them, and elections in Baltimore were tumultuous until 1860. At that time, the state assembly ejected many Baltimore members as illegally elected, and placed the city police under direct state control.[31]

Richmonders believed that many of the corrupt former policemen of Baltimore were in Winder's employ after the fall of 1861. Since fourteen out of the thirty men constituting Winder's force were from Maryland, and six were from New York and Philadelphia (both foreign and unsavory cities in the minds of southerners), the appellation "alien plug-uglies" seemed a fitting description of the detectives charged with investigating disloyal southerners in Richmond. The term was soon used exclusively to describe Winder's detectives.[32]

One cause of the widespread hostility was the presence of several German Jews on the force. Winder was not anti-Semitic, but many in Richmond were.[33] Another cause was that the detectives were all able-bodied, and many believed that they should therefore be in Confederate uniforms. Finally, a few detectives were indeed the dregs of society and some of the others were, at best, a pretty disreputable bunch. Their consumption of alcohol, willingness to engage in illegal and unsavory acts, and arbitrary and abrasive manners became legend. Several were honest and efficient policemen, but taken as a whole, they were not a charming group. Still, they were all that Winder had to work with. This became his lot throughout the war; from detectives to prison guards, he was forced to utilize the lowest elements of southern society.

The Richmond jails, recently emptied of drunken soldiers by Winder, were soon filled with people accused of disloyalty. A few were arrested by Winder's force, but the great majority were sent by Generals Joseph Johnston, John B. Floyd, and Henry A. Wise. Overwhelmed by the number of suspects, Winder suggested to Secretary of War Walker on 25 August that a special commission be created. He advised Walker that the commission should be directed to investigate each case, prepare a summary, and present its conclusions to the secretary and to the local authorities.[34]

Walker approved of the suggestion and appointed two respected Virginians, John Randolph Turner and James Lyon. The commissioners worked diligently and saved the government both time and expense, but Winder's work load was not significantly reduced. He continued to investigate and confine suspects and to forward information, and quite often disposed of these cases. His task was eased dramatically in late September when the new acting secretary of war, Judah P. Benjamin, discharged virtually all of the suspects and sent them home. However, criticism of Winder and his detectives remained on the increase as 1861 came to an end.[35]

Winder made an unfavorable impression on most if not all of the political prisoners. He confined them in Castles Godwin and Thunder, the two tobacco warehouses with glorified and misleading names that he had converted into prisons. One female suspect flatly told him to mind his own business when he attempted to interrogate her. Another southern woman, Mrs. C. V. Baxley, was arrested in Baltimore by Union agents on 30 December 1861. She admitted that she had carried "innocent" letters to and from Davis, Winder, Benjamin, and others to relatives and friends in the North, but denied she was a Confederate spy. She told of her experiences with the "unpolished" Winder during her initial run as mail courier as follows: "General Winder . . . conducted me (for which I owe him a grudge) somewhat unceremoniously into the presence of His Honor [Davis]." She concluded that while Winder was courteous toward her, he was certainly not gallant.[36]

Winder may not have been especially chivalrous around Mrs. Baxley, but he was not immune to feminine charms, if Elizabeth Van Lew can be believed. Van Lew was not physically attractive and was in her forties when she met Winder in 1863, but she was a charming woman. She was also a Union spy who planned to penetrate Libby and other Richmond prisons to foment escapes. She requested then Secretary of the Treasury C. G. Memminger to recommend her to Winder and he did so. She then asked Winder for a pass and he granted it. She later told a friend, "I can flatter almost anything out of old Winder; his personal vanity is so great." She told Winder, "Your hair would adorn the Temple of Janus. It looks out of place here." A few more such remarks and she got her pass.[37]

If Winder was susceptible to flattery on that occasion, hundreds would soon claim that he was as unfeeling as stone. At no time was this claim more prevalent than after the passport system was enacted on 8 August 1861. The system, soon to become odious to administrators and applicants alike, was necessary to implement the proclamation respecting aliens invoked by Davis at the same time. Everyone having legitimate business in the United States had to obtain a passport, and Winder was ordered to oversee the operation.[38]

The issuance of passports was an irksome, time-consuming, thankless task from the beginning. Some applicants were aliens or alleged aliens attempting to avoid military service. Others were profiteers and spies, and some had legitimate reasons for crossing the lines. Decisions were difficult, mistakes were frequent, and each mistake or refusal made Winder a new enemy. An overriding factor was the inconsistency in the passport system, as responsibility shifted back and forth between Winder's office and the War Department. Corruption was inevitable under the circumstances, and some of Winder's detectives were accused of selling passports from the start. It was soon apparent that this was true.[39] The War clerk Jones claimed that Winder personally denied passports to former political enemies. The records refute this charge, but there is no doubt that his association with the system angered many residents from the beginning, and his reputation suffered accordingly.[40]

Some clarification of Winder's responsibilities came in October, when the Military Department of Henrico was created and he was placed in command. The department encompassed Henrico County, of which Richmond was the county seat. It was expanded in 1862, but after 21 October 1861, Winder was responsible for all intercourse in the department between the Union and the Confederacy, in addition to his other duties in and around Richmond.[41]

The Confederacy experienced shortages of every description from the beginning, but the situation worsened in Richmond with the approach of the first winter of the war. Coffee was so scarce that newspapers featured recipes for substitutes. Coal profiteering appeared, leather became virtually impossible to obtain, and the women of Richmond were urged to make soap. Conditions were ripe for profiteering blockade runners to enrich themselves. Gold, necessary for the economic life of the Confederacy, was siphoned north by illegal runners for their own profit. Information injurious to Confederate military plans was carried north also. Meat supplies were inadequate, subversives continued to chalk Unionist slogans on the walls of buildings, the passport system caused much discontent, and the people grew restive under Winder's alien police force. Richmond was a rather grim place as the year 1861 ended, and Winder was blamed for some of the despair.[42]

Part of the gloom was due to the presence of large numbers of sick and wounded soldiers, Confederate and Union alike. Hundreds of incapacitated Confederate soldiers waited hours and sometimes days at Winder's office for their discharge papers. The snarl of red tape generated by Winder's office, the Surgical Board, and the Quartermaster's Office caused grievous delays. Maimed and ill men experienced extreme discomfort, and this caused much anger and discontent among the Richmond population, the great majority of whom had never seen or even imagined anything like it in their lives.[43] In addition, the Richmond *Examiner* charged in October that Confederate dead were not receiving a decent burial and that Winder was directly responsible for this outrage. The paper's editor, Edward Pollard, was hostile to the Davis administration and had been hostile to Winder personally from the beginning of the war, and the paper rapidly degenerated into a nonobjective "hate sheet." Although there was no truth to the charge, the attack hurt Winder's reputation in some quarters and gave additional ammunition to his enemies.[44]

Winder, though immediately responsive to any official criticism, never responded to this or subsequent attacks from the press, no matter how offensive or even outrageous the charge might be. He told Alfred Ely, a Union congressman who had been captured while sightseeing at Bull Run, that his policy was to ignore censure from the newspapers.[45] He believed, perhaps wrongly, that the best course was to remain silent and do his duty.

Most of the Richmond press also accused Winder of excessive leniency in his treatment of Union prisoners of war. The Richmond *Dispatch* reported on 2 July that the prison depot located on Main Street about two blocks from the county courthouse then contained "from seventy-five to one hundred of old Abe's disciples." The paper ridiculed northern claims that Confederate authorities were cruel to their captives and complained instead that "a large number of them" were "wandering around freely on parole." Three weeks later, the *Examiner* charged that Winder virtually pampered his charges while Confederate prisoners suffered barbarous treatment in the North. The paper lamented the many courtesies granted by Winder and sarcastically praised him as "an oasis in a moral desert" who furnished refreshment in the middle of a war.[46]

Winder was subjected to this type of unfounded criticism throughout the war. The Richmond organs accused him of undue harshness in dealing with southerners and of superfluous leniency in providing for the needs of Union prisoners. Conversely, the northern press accused him from the beginning of inhumane treatment of prisoners of war, and the vilification intensified to an incredible level within a short time.

Winder's decision to ignore the criticism was probably the correct one, but he might possibly have improved his image in Richmond if he had taken a different attitude toward the press. He realized that any attempt to suppress the southern journals was impossible and would invite even more serious attacks. His only recourse was to remain silent or to actively court press members, explain his actions in detail, perhaps solicit their opinions (whether he heeded their advice or not), and grant extensive interviews. There were some reporters who admired and defended Winder throughout his Richmond career, and he might have gained more adherents if he had been more accessible. Conversely, any such attempt could have misfired. Winder was no diplomat. His abrupt manner and curt speech, coupled with the disdain he felt toward civilians who questioned military policy, might have resulted in an even more unfavorable projection of his image.

He, of course, had no control over northern commentaries. Several of his famous captives during the early part of the war did exonerate him, but by 1862 their accounts were discounted in favor of more sensational renditions.[47] His character would have been blackened even if his personality had been more attractive and his actions more diplomatic. He was damned no matter what he did. His reputation in the North as a cruel tormentor of helpless Union prisoners was firmly entrenched during the first year of the war, and he could do absolutely nothing about it but ignore the slander and go about his business.

Winder and other officials were required by Confederate law to confine prisoners of war and to issue them the same rations provided Confederate soldiers. The secretary of war oversaw the operation. Confederate policy dictated that captives be disarmed and a report made of the number, rank, and corps of each. Although personal property was to be respected, all horses were to be confiscated for Confederate use. Sick and wounded prisoners were entitled to the same care given to Confederate soldiers.[48]

The actions taken by both governments regarding prisoners were inconsistent and ill defined during 1861—and indicative of the complexity surrounding this sensitive issue. The capture of Union troops in Texas in February 1861 resulted in the confinement of the enlisted men and the release of the officers on parole. In May, Union soldiers forced the surrender of a brigade of Missouri volunteers, even though Missouri remained in the Union, and released them on parole only after they took an oath not to fight against the United States.

Lincoln's position was that secession was illegal, that he was contending with a rebellion, that the rebels were traitors, and that England and other countries erred when they gave the Confederacy the rights of a belligerent nation. He therefore refused to recognize southern captives as prisoners of war. He ordered that they were to be tried for treason and that all Confederate seamen acting under letters of marque be tried as pirates. Davis demanded official recognition of his country and would not settle for less.

The test came when the Union captured Captain Walter Smith and his crew of the brigantine *Jeff Davis* in June. They were placed in irons in Philadelphia and the prosecution of these privateers as pirates proceeded. In July, Davis informed Lincoln that he would retaliate in kind if any harm came to the captives. After the Union defeat at Bull Run, over one thousand Federal soldiers in Confederate prisons gave instant credibility to Davis's threat. Even so, Lincoln refused to change his course.[49] It was at this point that Winder was placed in charge of the Union captives in Richmond and assumed an ill-defined supervision of prisons in the Carolinas and other states.

Winder immediately learned that the Confederacy was unprepared to confine, much less to house, feed, and clothe, his charges. There were no large prisons in Richmond or anywhere else in the South, and no effective system was ever created to establish them. Prisons came into existence without an overall plan, almost as a series of accidents, and temporary structures became inadequate prisons for the duration. Southern governors and other officials actively opposed the establishment of prisons in their sphere of influence. Very few able-bodied men would serve as prison guards, and the civilian population denounced the presence of prisoners as an onerous burden. There was no clear-cut chain of command, and Winder discovered to his dismay that the care and supervision of prisoners ranked at the absolute bottom of Confederate priorities.[50]

Winder was hampered by the lack of skill and experience in administrative matters on the part of prison officials, and virtually crippled in that the Confederacy never established an efficient system of prison organization. Despite these liabilities, he did an excellent job in 1861 and 1862. Indeed, given the conditions under which he labored, his performance was much superior to that of his Union counterpart, Colonel William Hoffman.[51]

Prior to Winder's appointment, Secretary of War Walker had contacted the governor of North Carolina and asked that the state establish a prison and furnish guards at Confederate expense. Henry T. Clark answered that Salisbury would be the best location but that providing sufficient guards would be very difficult. It proved to be impossible, and he notified Walker in July not to send any more prisoners because he could not handle them.[52] This meant that the Bull Run captives would have to be confined in Richmond, at least temporarily, and that was the situation when Walker ordered Winder to take charge.

Winder was forced to confine the first arrivals on 29 July in the city almshouse. This "salubrious location" was a new building, and an *Enquirer* reporter noted, "An air of neatness pervades the whole establishment." Perhaps this was so but it was a makeshift operation and everyone knew it. Since hospital space was not available, Winder had no choice but to place the wounded Federals in this structure. He put them in the south end of the second story until Surgeon General Samuel Moore could house them, and he began the search for more permanent quarters for the rest.

The first prison in Richmond, called Liggons, or No. 1, was in the Rocketts district near Twenty-fifth and Main. Formerly a tobacco warehouse, the three-story building measured thirty by seventy feet, and iron bars covered the windows of the first two floors. The Richmond authorities intended to use the structure in case of a slave insurrection.[53] It was the nearest thing to a prison in the city, inadequate as it was, and it was about as close as the Confederacy would ever come to providing one anywhere.

Winder separated the officers from the enlisted men and made a favorable impression on the former even though they had expected to be paroled and were understandably upset when they were placed in confine-

ment. Congressman Ely, confined with the officers, praised Winder from
the start. He recorded in his journal, which he published after his release,
that Winder immediately visited the officers and apologized for the un-
comfortable quarters. He told them that their "arrival was unexpected,
and therefore he was unprepared." Two weeks later he noted that Winder
"seemed unusually pleasant" and asked how they "were getting along."
And on 3 September Ely wrote, "I desire to say here, that Brigadier
General John H. Winder has treated me with the utmost kindness and
respect, and his demeanor and gentle courtesy of manner, when he visits
the officers, indicate a disciplinarian it is true; but a person at the same
time of humane feelings and not disposed to exercise his power beyond
its proper limits."[54]

Colonel Michael Corcoran of the Sixty-ninth Regiment, New York State
Militia, testified that "General Winder always did all in his power, as
far as consistent with existing rules and orders, to make the prisoners
under his charge as comfortable as possible." An unidentified wounded
officer wrote "of the tenderness with which General Winder carried [him]
in his arms," and in January 1862, Captain J. T. Drew, Company G,
Second Vermont, wrote Winder expressing his gratitude for Winder's
kindness toward him when he was ill.[55]

A Union physician, Charles Carroll Gray, offered a slightly different
opinion, and his report is probably a more accurate reflection of what
most captive officers felt toward their warden. He praised Winder in
the beginning but became more critical with the passage of time. Gray
was caught up in the chaos of Bull Run and arrived in Richmond on
2 August. Winder met him at the depot and "seemed much surprised"
when Gray told him he was not on parole. Winder found lodging for
Gray in the home of one of his subordinates and told him to report to
his office the following day. Gray was then paroled and assigned to work
in the two hospitals on Main Street. His parole allowed him to move
freely anywhere in the Department of Henrico.

Gray's pleasant sojourn ended on 31 August when Winder revoked
all paroles and ordered an end to all communications with the North.
Unaware that Davis had ordered Winder to take this action, Gray won-
dered if some Confederate defeat was responsible for this "sour temper."
He was soon mollified when Winder exempted physicians from his de-
cree. They were given a badge signifying their medical status and permitted to move freely within the city limits of Richmond.

Gray was transferred to Castle Pinckney in Charleston on 10 September but was back in Richmond within a month. He recorded that Winder
and his staff treated him well but that prison life was becoming impossible
as month after interminable month passed with no sign of release in sight.
When he was informed in mid-1862 that his eleven-month confinement
was over, his opinion of Winder had changed. On 9 July Winder told

the physicians that the orders had been issued for their general exchange "but that he had *no time to forward it*. Upon the whims of such an old dotard we are held in this vile imprisonment. There will come a day, perhaps."[56]

Gray revised and transcribed his diary for his family in 1877 and added a number of critical comments about Winder that did not appear in the original. Instead of the passage quoted above, the revision of the same event is as follows: "Winder says that for medical officers, the order has been issued for our general exchange but that he had *no time to forward it*. Was there ever so sickly a statement as this? It is so like the old dotard, that it may be said so. 'When this cruel war is over,' if we have anything to say about the condition of peace, the hanging of old Winder should be made a *sine qua non*."[57] Gray's revision reflected the postwar image of Winder, and other former captives also changed their remarks to adhere to the temper of the times.

There was some criticism of Winder by the prisoners from the beginning. No captive loves his captor, and most prisoners disliked and resented Winder even while they admitted that he was merely doing his job. Some, like Lieutenant William C. Harris, recorded that Winder was a "martinet of forty years' standing, abrupt, profane, and coarse in speech." Harris believed that Winder's visits inevitably resulted in rougher treatment for the inmates, since the guards feared him "as if the shadow of his presence surrounded them."[58] Harris never conversed with Winder. He based his comments on hearsay and the limited observations of Winder accorded him, but they were at least partially accurate. Winder was a martinet, gruff and abrupt, and it is highly probable that his speech was profane on occasion. Winder apparently never visited the enlisted men, and none of them recorded their impressions of him at this time.

In addition to the criticism leveled at him by the Union prisoners and the Richmond press, Winder was berated by other Confederate officials from time to time, but he never failed to respond when this happened. He never intentionally initiated a dispute with his fellow officers during his long career in the old army or while in Confederate service, but he was quick to defend his actions and to attack his opponent in turn when anyone questioned his military activities.

For example, although he and Surgeon General Moore were on good terms and cooperated in good fashion, they did have occasional conflicts. Moore visited the prisons on 1 August and reported to Secretary Walker that the warehouses were overcrowded, unclean, and not well policed. Walker reprimanded Winder, and the general replied that the overcrowding was Moore's fault because he had confiscated one of Winder's prisons and converted it into a hospital. He concluded by informing Walker that he was currently negotiating for another building that should relieve the overcrowding, but he did not deny that the guard was deficient and that Moore's observations were essentially correct.[59]

He also warned that conditions would worsen unless he received additional guards, and that is precisely what happened before the month of August ended. The constant arrival of new prisoners rendered Winder's facilities inadequate even after he had acquired another warehouse and after Adjutant General Cooper had admitted that Richmond could not cope with the situation and asked all generals in the field to hold their captives until better arrangements could be made.

Efforts to relieve the pressure on Richmond commenced in September. Several hundred captives were sent to Charleston; New Orleans; Tuscaloosa, Alabama; and Salisbury, North Carolina. Winder oversaw the removal and continued to attempt to upgrade the Richmond facilities. In spite of numerous visits and unceasing orders to prison commanders, he accomplished little in his efforts to improve the guard details at the prisons, and this liability made all other attempts at improvement futile. Major J. T. W. Hairston, commander of Castles Godwin and Thunder from October 1861 to March 1862, reported: "The guard was relieved every morning at nine o'clock, a new regiment being furnished every day at that hour. This regiment was always composed of raw recruits who were sent thither to learn the duties of a soldier . . . there was seldom a day when I was in charge . . . when the whole crowd of federal soldiers—save those who were sick abed in hospital—might not have marched away with impunity."[60]

Hairston exaggerated the situation, but there was a rapid turnover of guards and they were almost without exception raw recruits. As such, they were lax at times, but many were overzealous and some were simply trigger-happy. In August, a guard killed a prisoner for putting his head out of a window, and Corcoran protested to Winder. Winder assured the Union colonel that he would stop this immediately, but he was unable to command universal obedience from the guards. A total of three prisoners were shot during 1861 for no reason.[61] One of the few guards who impressed Winder was a private from Louisiana, Henry Wirz. Wirz was assigned to Winder's command on 26 August and began the work that would ultimately cost him his reputation and his life.

Despite Hairston's observations, there were few successful escapes in 1861. On 6 September, two prisoners escaped from Liggons, but the guards wounded one and recaptured both in a matter of minutes. The following day eleven escaped, but all were caught within the week. Captain George C. Gibbs, commander of the guard detachment, reported to Winder that the latter escape occurred because the guards were drunk, and asked him to close the grogshops near the prison. Winder promptly endorsed the request and asked Mayor Mayo to issue the order.[62]

Overcrowding and inadequate police remained fundamental problems but the lack of food and other necessities soon became Winder's major concern. Ely noted in early September that wounded men were not treated because of the shortage of plaster and lint. He frequently heard the southern remark "Tell your master, Lincoln, to raise the blockade, and then we will tend to you."[63]

Prison rations were meager from the beginning, and sugar and coffee were not issued after September 1861. Prisoners who could afford to supplement their rations by purchasing additional food did so, but most of the captives had nothing more than the standard issue of bread and boiled beef. In addition, the Confederacy was never able to provide clothing for soldiers, either their own or the Federal captives, and the prisoners were soon dressed in rags.

The Confederate official charged with providing food for the Confederate Army and the Union prisoners was one of Winder's former students at West Point, Colonel Lucius B. Northrop, commissary general of subsistence. Northrop was one of the most vilified men in the Confederacy even in 1861, and the criticism never abated. A contemporary maintained that the commissary system "was badly managed from its very inception. Murmurs loud and deep arose from every quarter against its numerous errors and abuses. . . . Colonel Northrop had been an officer of cavalry, but for many years had been on quasi-leave, away from all connection with any branch of the army—save, perhaps, the paymaster's office."[64] Most historians agree that Northrop was not the incompetent that his contemporaries thought, but he was definitely not an easy man to work with. Abrasive, eccentric, stubborn, and quarrelsome, he nonetheless performed about as effectively as anyone could have in his position. Northrop and Winder had much in common, both professionally and personally, and it is not surprising that they were soon at odds with each other.

Winder began what became a long-running dispute in August when he informed Walker that Northrop refused to pay for the food consumed by five Federal prisoners confined in the county jail. Winder offered to handle the matter by paying the bill personally in order to avoid any unnecessary delay. Walker ordered an inquiry, and Northrop replied in a blunt, abusive letter that the problem was due solely to Winder's ignorance of where to apply for the payment of such bills. Northrop stated that while his office was in charge of subsistence, payment of such bills was the responsibility of the quartermaster's department. Winder was not the type to back down to anyone when it came to his knowledge of proper procedure, and he sent a blistering reply. The bickering between these two key officials ended only with Winder's death almost four years later. Northrop usually provided prison rations, but there were occasions when the quartermaster's office paid for provisions, and in several instances Winder paid for the necessities out of his own pocket.[65]

The inability of the disputing officials to cooperate caused some unnecessary hardships for the prisoners, but it was never the root cause for the widespread suffering that ultimately occurred. That happened only after the commissary system virtually collapsed in 1864 and Federal captives died by the thousands. As in so many other areas, the Confederacy never developed the skills necessary to utilize the available resources effectively. The demands were too great and would have been so, even if Northrop and Winder had worked together in perfect harmony.

Winder continued to acquire new buildings in Richmond to relieve the overcrowding and made strenuous efforts to improve the guard details. But in 1861 his attention became increasingly focused on the heart of the problem: the inability of the two governments to agree to a general exchange or to enter into a formal cartel guaranteeing the automatic exchange of prisoners. Davis pressed Lincoln for a general exchange before the battle of Bull Run occurred. Lincoln ignored him, and the trial of the captured privateers charged with piracy proceeded. Acting through Secretary of the Navy Stephen R. Mallory, Davis reacted on 15 August. Winder was ordered to place two Federal navy officers in close confinement in retaliation for the same actions taken against two Confederate midshipmen. Two weeks later, Winder was ordered to revoke all paroles and to establish a much more stringent system of confinement for all prisoners. At the same time, 30 August, the Confederate Congress formally authorized Davis to act in reprisal against the Union if any Confederate prisoners were mistreated.[66]

Some Confederate officials and most of the Richmond newspaper editors asserted that Federal prisoners were better off in Confederate custody than they had been in the Union army or even at their homes, and urged Davis to cut off all food and medicine to the captives until Lincoln agreed to a cartel. Winder opposed this extreme policy and, fortunately for all concerned, Davis did not "raise the black flag." Instead, he ordered the release of fifty-seven wounded Federals on 7 October. They were placed on parole and sent north under a flag of truce. Lincoln reacted to this humanitarian move by releasing an identical number of wounded Confederates, but he refused to change his basic position.[67]

The matter came to a head in November when Captain Walter Smith and three crew members were found guilty of piracy by a Philadelphia jury. Acting Secretary of War Benjamin ordered Winder to select by lot from the highest ranking captives one officer to be held in the felon's cage as a criminal awaiting execution and thirteen others to be held as criminals pending the outcome of the trial for the rest of Smith's crew.[68]

Winder and his staff appeared in full dress uniform on 10 November and assembled the seventy-five captured officers. Winder stated that he had an unpleasant duty to perform and read Benjamin's order. He placed six slips of paper containing the names of the captured colonels in a tin, shook it, and asked Congressman Ely to select one. Ely picked the ballot with Colonel Corcoran's name on it. Corcoran's fate would be the same as Smith's. Thirteen other officers were selected in the same manner, and the hostages were sent to the county jails in Richmond and Charleston.[69]

This Confederate action soon had the desired effect. Northern attention and public concern immediately focused on Corcoran's plight.[70] Winder had anticipated a northern outcry for an exchange of prisoners, and it was most probably he who had advised Davis to take this action. Winder was with Davis frequently at this time and told him of the resolution of the prisoner issue by his father during the War of 1812. He could also attest to the concerns family members felt when one of their own was in captivity, as both of his brothers were then in prison. Winder knew from the mail coming into the prisons that a great deal of pressure was building up in the North for an exchange. Northern newspapers confirmed what he already knew, and he almost certainly told Davis that the best policy for the Confederacy was to wait for public opinion to force Lincoln to change his policy.[71]

Lincoln is justly remembered for his humanity, but equally important, perhaps more important, was the toughness and resolution in the man. He was for a hard war and an easy peace; the killing would stop anytime the South ended the rebellion and returned to the Union. In the meantime, even though he knew that Union prisoners were suffering somewhat, he was determined not to recognize the Confederacy in any way. He feared that a cartel for prisoner exchange would do just that, and he resisted it for as long as he could. Helping Lincoln to some extent was the exchange of prisoners in the field by opposing generals and also the continuation of special exchanges permitted by Davis. He could favor these exchanges without the danger of recognition and could hope to destroy the Confederacy before public opinion forced him to change course.

Congressman Ely was one of the special exchanges that took place in December, and he recorded that the "kind-hearted General Winder" had said that "he would now be happy" to see Ely "at his own home."[72] Other exchanges of this nature continued, but the Confederacy lost no opportunity to blame Lincoln for rejecting a cartel as the autumn months of 1861 yielded to the coming of winter.

Winder's workload continued to be heavy and tedious because of the lack of a cartel, and he found it necessary to secure a larger command center. The *Enquirer* reported in mid-September, "Inspector General Winder will this morning remove his headquarters to the commodious hall on the first floor of the building on the Southeast corner of Broad and 9th Streets." The paper noted that Winder's former "contracted and illy arranged quarters" were not adequate for his "multifarious duties." Three days later, the journal stated that the health of the prisoners was excellent and that the privates were being fed better than they had been while in the Union army, but it lamented the weekly expense of over $11,000 for the needs of the 1,700 prisoners. Although sugar and coffee had been eliminated from their rations and their morale was low because there was no cartel, the reporter concluded that "discipline and vigilance" was quite good at the prisons and that this was due to Winder's good work.[73]

Contrary to this optimistic report, Winder knew that conditions were bad and that they would worsen when winter arrived. Prison accommodations were so inadequate in Richmond that beginning in November increasing numbers of captives were sent south for the winter. The clothes they were captured in had deteriorated, and they presented a "pitiably tattered and shivering appearance." In October prisoners coming into Richmond were packed into freight cars with standing room only, and the civilian crowds in the streets became increasingly rude. The prisoners responded in like manner, and the situation was ugly by the end of November.[74]

Winder sent about one thousand of his captives to New Orleans, Charleston, Columbia, Salisbury, and Tuscaloosa, but the prisons in these places were generally worse than the Richmond facilities. For example, Captain Elias Griswold, assistant quartermaster in charge of the Tuscaloosa prison, informed Winder on 10 December that the former paper mill was totally useless as a prison. There were no floors, windows, or fireplaces in the building, and the immediate vicinity was not well suited for waste disposal. Winder obtained permission from the War Department for Griswold to rent the insane asylum in town and confine the prisoners there.[75] Reports such as Griswold's convinced Winder that his November plan to use Richmond as a receiving station only and to send all prisoners to other states was not feasible.[76] Significant numbers of them would have to remain in Richmond no matter how heavy a burden they became.

It was also obvious to Winder that he had to have more authority and more resources if he was to carry out his responsibilities adequately. He was convinced by year's end that the time was long since past when the makeshift policies so far utilized would suffice. The problems were too vast to be solved without a fundamental change in attitude and policy. If the Confederacy was to survive, many cherished beliefs would have to be altered.

The Confederate leadership shared Winder's views and implemented a thoroughgoing restructuring of the southern way of life early in 1862. Winder was given more power and responsibility in the Richmond area than anyone could have foreseen when the Confederacy was born. On 27 February 1862, a week after his birthday, the sixty-two-year-old general was appointed provost marshal general of Richmond and charged with enforcing martial law in Henrico County. Thousands of citizens were soon asking themselves and each other what type of man had entered their lives so abruptly and with such devastating effect. Their answers varied widely, but none of them really knew the answer: the man in question remained an enigma. In order to understand Winder fully, they would have had to go back in time, to have witnessed his life as a West Point cadet, for it was during those years that the basic formation of his character and personality took place.

CHAPTER 5

The Formative Years

1814–1828

The United States Military Academy that Winder entered in 1814 was not a happy place. Captain Alden Partridge, acting superintendent, strongly suspected that certain faculty members were out to sabotage his leadership. The cadets appeared to be a rowdy and indifferent lot, and the physical facilities were painfully inadequate. Partridge's assessment of conditions at West Point at that time was an accurate one.

The academy was created by Congress on 16 March 1802 as a part of the corps of engineers. In its first year it housed five officers and ten cadets. For the next decade it was, in effect, an apprentice school for military engineers. There was no set academic year, no definite or consistent system of instruction or examination, and no class ranking of cadets. The curriculum comprised courses in mathematics, engineering, natural philosophy, astronomy, and geography.[1]

Faced with the possibility of war with England or France or both, Congress reorganized the academy on 24 April 1812. The number of cadets was increased to two hundred and fifty, the staff was expanded, and a four-year curriculum was ordered. Cadets had to pass an entrance examination in reading, writing, and arithmetic and be at least fourteen years old and in good physical condition. Funds were authorized to build barracks and other needed structures. Brigadier General Joseph Swift, the first graduate of the academy, was named superintendent, but he elected to remain in Washington and designated Partridge as acting commander.[2]

The academy under Partridge failed to accomplish the legislative goal. The entrance exam remained oral, a curious means of determining proficiency in writing. Further, the age requirement was not enforced, and regular classes and exams were not held. Even worse, Partridge showed favoritism toward both faculty and cadets. Military drill was at his convenience, and overall discipline was poor. Neither staff nor students strictly observed the vacation period, 15 December to 15 March, and absenteeism was a major problem. About the only accomplishments made during the war years were the erection of South Barracks and the expansion of the curriculum to include experimental philosophy, drawing, and French. Military training was limited to fencing, drill, and camping out during the summer months. During the encampment period the cadets studied fortifications in various cities, but Partridge discontinued this practice in 1815 even though Congress had enacted it into law three years earlier.[3]

On 12 May 1814, Secretary of War Armstrong notified Winder of his appointment as a cadet and the boy immediately dispatched his acceptance: "I hasten to inform you that I accept [the appointment] and accordingly I will repair as speedily as possible to the military school at West Point and report myself to the commanding officer at that place."[4] This was an exciting time for the fourteen-year-old boy. President Madison placed his father in command of the Chesapeake defenses in July, and young Winder was almost certainly the envy of the 147 other cadets of his class when he reported on 5 August.[5] Winder and the others were housed in dilapidated buildings and issued blue summer and winter uniforms, the last class to receive that color. Beginning in 1815, the cadet gray of today was issued in honor of Winfield Scott's gray-clad victors at the battle of Chippewa in July 1814.[6]

The first matter of business facing the new cadets was to meet the faculty. Partridge, "Old Pewter" to the students, taught engineering, and William Eveleth was his assistant. Jared Mansfield arrived in 1814 to teach natural and experimental philosophy but was frequently on leave; his assistant, Captain David B. Douglass, bore the brunt of the work. Douglass was popular neither with the cadets nor with Partridge, but he was married to the daughter of Andrew Ellicott, professor of mathematics. Ellicott was sixty years old when he joined the staff in 1813. He was a noted astronomer but had no prior teaching experience. John Wright was Ellicott's assistant until 1816, when Charles Davies assumed the position. Claudius B. Thacker taught French in 1814 but was replaced by Claudius Berand the next year. Christian Zoeller taught drawing, Pierre Thomas was the assistant swordmaster, and Adam Empie was the chaplain and professor of ethics.[7]

They were a mixed group in terms of ability, and the lack of textbooks hampered them all; but their major problem was a disagreement about the basic role of the academy. Mansfield and Ellicott wanted the cadets to receive a more classical education, but Partridge envisioned another École Polytechnique whose mission was to turn out engineers. The dispute soon became public, and the result was that very little if anything of academic importance was presented to the cadets in 1814. Despite this conflict, most of the cadets found life fairly enjoyable, and many of them liked and respected Old Pewter.[8] Winder was one of them, and he relished academy life until news of the disaster at Bladensburg arrived.

Winder most probably learned of his father's defeat through the 27 August issue of the New York *Commercial Advertiser.* This was the first New York newspaper to print the news, and it was terribly inaccurate. It placed the British army at 13,000 strong and reported that Stansbury was dead, the Fifth Baltimore almost totally destroyed, and the commanding general missing. Winder could not have learned his father's true fate until early September when more correct accounts became available.[9]

Cadet Winder's dreams and hopes for his father's career disappeared when the outcome of "the races" became known and his status among the cadets fell. He must have been sorely troubled for the remainder of 1814, but details are unknown; a fire in 1838 destroyed most of the records for that term. At least some of the cadets probably subjected him to taunts, and he may have been involved in the "occasional pugilistic encounters" later recorded by one of his friends, George Ramsey. He probably received sympathetic understanding from Ramsey, Thomas Noel, James A. Chambers, William S. Maitland, Justin Dimick, and others of his class. His conduct certainly impressed upperclassman Samuel Cooper, who graduated in 1815. Cooper, destined to become the ranking Confederate general, knew Winder at West Point from August 1814 to December 1815 and became one of his major defenders during and after the Civil War. Winder may have suffered intensely or weathered the ordeal well. About all that can be said is that he looked forward to seeing his father during the long break beginning in mid-December.[10]

The early months of 1815 were decisive in molding Winder's character. The question facing him was whether to return to West Point. He had enrolled in a burst of patriotic enthusiasm generated in large part by his father's military commitment. Now, the war was over, the family name was tarnished, and his father had every intention of resuming his legal career as soon as possible.

The fifteen-year-old had a wide choice of opportunities open to him. A career in law or medicine had long been a family tradition, and meager academic talent was not a barrier to either vocation. Winder had many kinsmen on both sides of the family who would have helped him enter these professions; he had twelve close relatives, including his father, who were either lawyers or doctors in the Baltimore region in 1815. Plantation management was also an option; most of these relatives owned farms or plantations, and three more were full-time Maryland planters. In addition, his two great-uncles, Levin in Wicomico County, Maryland, and John in Northampton County, Virginia, would have welcomed him at this time. After his apprenticeship, he could have become a gentleman planter and operated Rewston.[11]

Exactly why he rejected these opportunities must remain a matter of conjecture, but one primary consideration must have influenced his decision. Winder was a proud, headstrong youth, but even at fifteen he knew some of his limitations. His father was a witty, gregarious, and attractive personality, a brilliant lawyer, and an outstanding orator, equally at home before the United States Supreme Court or addressing throngs of Baltimoreans numbering in the thousands. The son could not compete with him intellectually or in force of personality. In virtually every civilian career open to him he was bound to be less successful than his sire.[12]

Conversely, he was much larger and stronger physically. He was fitted for and enjoyed the strenuous outdoor life; he liked "Old Pewter" at West Point and the routine. He had probably already weathered the worst of the hazing now that peace had been announced and the nation was pompously congratulating itself for standing up to the best the British had to offer. If he returned to the academy and made a career in the army, he might have the opportunity to redeem his family's honor and military reputation. In this one vital area he might prove superior to his father. It is very likely for these reasons that he chose to continue his military career.[13]

The regimen that he returned to in March 1815 was physically demanding but not necessarily intellectually challenging. The cadets were divided by physical size into two companies and governed by officers elected in rotation from the ranks. Following reveille at 6:00 A.M., the companies mustered for roll call. They then returned to South Barracks to police their rooms and attend to personal hygiene. At 7:00 they marched to the mess hall for breakfast. Within the hour, they marched back to their quarters and either studied on their own or recited to their professors. The bugle sounded at 12:30 for lunch, and the morning ritual was repeated. From 2:00 P.M. until dusk they were again supposed to study before assembling for sunset parade. After that drill and the chaplain's evening prayers, they were dismissed. The bugle sounded tattoo at 8:00 P.M., and they returned to their rooms for the night.[14]

There were a few breaks in this routine. On Sundays, after morning and afternoon services, the cadets could spend the rest of their time as they pleased. Athletics furnished a popular release from monotony, and the cadets participated in a wide range of summer and winter sports. Summer encampment, during which time the professors did not teach, was resumed in June 1816. The cadets visited fortifications, held public reviews, and enjoyed "a short relaxation from their usual studies."[15]

There were obvious defects in this system, the most critical being the lack of regular classes, exams, and overall discipline. Cadets could study in their rooms and use their time wisely, or they could remain intellectually idle. All types of boys and young men were in attendance, and they ranged from the high-minded to the roguish, from boys of twelve to married men with families. Many flouted the rules and some committed serious crimes. Neighboring farmers accused the cadets of stealing sheep and chickens, and about everything else they could get their hands on. Drunkenness and absenteeism were all too common, and the elected officers and noncoms were sometimes the ringleaders in the unsavory escapades. Cadet indebtedness was another problem. They were paid at several stations other than the academy, and it was impossible for the academy officials to settle their debts on payday. Many owed money to tailors, shoemakers, stewards, washerwomen, and saloonkeepers in the area and in New York City.[16]

Little improvement resulted from a reorganization of the chain of command in January 1815. Partridge was designated superintendent and Swift became inspector of the academy, but the problems continued. The deplorable conditions worsened during the latter part of 1815. Partridge took leave in October and turned the command over to Captain Douglass, Ellicott's son-in-law. The two men decided to change established policy and discredit Partridge by inviting a board of visitors, previously authorized by Congress but not utilized by Partridge, to conduct unscheduled examinations in December. Headed by Governor DeWitt Clinton and General Jacob Brown, the board examined the cadets and was not impressed.[17]

When Partridge returned in January 1816, he brought charges against his rebellious faculty. Douglass and Ellicott filed countercharges, and the quarrel became official. A court of inquiry supported Partridge in March, but backbiting and rumormongering continued. Partridge admitted to Secretary of War William H. Crawford in July that discipline was virtually nonexistent.[18]

Winder was one of the cadets in disciplinary trouble. Douglass reported to Swift in late June that he had arrested Winder for disobeying orders. The exact offense and the punishment were not recorded, but it is probable that Winder lost his temper with the unpopular Douglass and was confined to quarters for a short time. At any rate, Winder felt he had been wronged and took leave for the rest of the year.[19]

Conditions were so bad that there were no graduates in 1816, and the deterioration continued the next year. When President Monroe arrived in June 1817 for a brief inspection, five faculty members handed him a written protest against Partridge. Monroe ordered Swift to find a new superintendent and to court-martial Partridge. Swift notified Major Sylvanus Thayer on 17 July that he had been appointed superintendent and ordered him to relieve Partridge and bring order to the academy.

Thayer arrived on 28 July and found that the institution had virtually ceased to function. Partridge had arrested the protesting faculty members and refused to relinquish his post. Most of the cadets were on unlimited vacation or at camp and were not to return until ordered to by Partridge. The only positive news was that North Barracks was completed and could now house cadets, if indeed there was going to be a fall term. The situation called for firmness and tact, and Thayer was equal to the task. He refused to debate the argumentative Partridge, ignored his insults, and simply showed him Swift's orders. Partridge finally relented and reluctantly departed, muttering threats. Thayer assembled the faculty and informed them of the new standards that would take effect immediately. He next ordered the cadets to return in August and set about completely reorganizing and reforming the academy. It was a rude awakening for staff and students alike.

Thayer imposed an iron discipline and began discharging cadets and faculty who were unqualified. He instituted regular classes, exams, and drill, and classified the cadets according to academic ability. He broadened the curriculum and ordered that a board of visitors monitor the exams, which were extremely rigorous, in January and June of each year. His impact on the academy's pedagogical method, curriculum, library, and physical facilities was such that he was soon recognized as the "father" of that institution.[20]

Thayer encountered resistance from several quarters. Perhaps the most surprising was Partridge's dramatic return one month later. On 29 August 1817, he informed the astonished Thayer that he was resuming command and that Thayer could leave. Some of the cadets welcomed Old Pewter's return and demonstrated in his behalf. They had not enjoyed their brief association under Thayer's new order. Thayer went to see Swift, and the outraged inspector ordered Partridge's immediate arrest and court-martial. The trial, headed by Winfield Scott, occurred in October. Rider Henry Winder, Cadet Winder's uncle, was the trial judge advocate who compiled the charges and specifications. He performed his task objectively, dismissed some complaints that were obviously unworthy and without merit, and insured that Partridge received a fair hearing. He was found guilty of flagrant disobedience of orders and ordered cashiered from the service.[21]

The dismissal of Partridge did not end Thayer's problems. The majority of cadets remained loyal to the former superintendent and engaged in a major mutiny against Thayer in November 1818. Cadet discontent focused on the person of Captain John Bliss, Thayer's appointment to the newly created position, commandant of cadets. The duties of this officer included the teaching of tactics but were primarily concerned with imposing discipline and assigning demerits to unruly, unwary, or unlucky cadets. The position would have been highly unpopular regardless of the personality of the incumbent, but Bliss was a fiery disciplinarian whom the students hated. The mutiny occurred after Bliss manhandled a cadet on 22 November. Almost every cadet in residence, including Winder, signed a petition of protest and demanded that Thayer take action. He did, but it was the opposite of what the cadets wanted and expected. Thayer dismissed the complaint and the most vocal complainers as well. He supported Bliss, crushed the uprising, and actually increased discipline by ordering that the commandant would in the future have two assistants who would live in the barracks with the cadets and constantly monitor their activities day and night. These men were to be junior army officers who would also teach tactics, but their primary duty would be to enforce discipline. They would have the authority to issue demerits on the spot and the knowledge that any infractions they reported would be favorably acted on by the superintendent.[22]

The failure of the revolt convinced the cadets that Thayer could not be resisted. They might not like him, indeed they might hate him, but they feared him and came to respect him as well. His standards were high and his rules puritanical and inflexible, but he was consistently fair in his treatment of everyone at the post.

The position of assistant instructor of infantry tactics was never a popular posting with either the officers or the cadets. These junior lieutenants usually occupied the berth for only one or two years, but it was a demanding and an important posting for the incumbent and the academy. Personality traits were soon revealed to all, and Thayer would not retain anyone who did not measure up. Bliss was replaced as being too hotheaded—not the last to suffer this treatment. Almost precisely ten years later, Second Lieutenant John Henry Winder would also be dismissed from this position and for exactly the same reason.

Thayer's implementation of a rigorous testing program based on meritorious conduct in and out of the classroom resulted in the establishment of four classes of cadets in September 1817. Each class was divided into two sections and Winder was placed in the third class, first section. He had been enrolled at West Point for three years and was ranked only as a sophomore. Obviously, he had not applied himself during the Partridge years. His determination to become a professional soldier was negated by his inability to challenge himself intellectually. He was lacking in self-discipline. He conformed to Partridge's standards, which stressed "obedience, regularity of conduct, and strict attention to duty," but did not attempt to further his education beyond the minimum academy standards. He had survived the purge and had at least not been reduced to freshman or plebe status, but he had clearly come to a standstill during the Partridge regime.

Thayer's arrival proved a godsend to Winder. He needed the discipline and thrived under the rigid system. Although he had great difficulty with certain courses, he did not miss a term, take leave, or get into trouble during his three remaining years at West Point. This was unusual, even a rarity, at the time. The commandant of cadets recorded in December 1817 that several cadets were absent without leave, and noted that a considerable number were on furlough or had resigned. As of May 1818, there were twenty-four in the first class, forty in the second, forty-nine (including Winder) in the third, and sixty in the fourth, a total of one hundred and seventy-three. More than seventy-five cadets had either resigned or been dismissed during Thayer's first year. Fewer than half of Winder's class (sixty-six out of one hundred and forty-eight) eventually graduated, and he was the only one who made it through Thayer's system without a single demerit.[23]

When the grades were posted from the December 1817 examinations, Winder found that he was sixth out of twenty in his section in French and mathematics, the core courses of the curriculum for the first two years. His instructor, Lieutenant Charles Davies, was an excellent and demanding teacher and would eventually become the most famous mathematician in America. When the term ended in June 1818, Winder had dropped to eleventh out of twenty-three in his section but had been promoted to second class.[24]

Upon his return from summer encampment near New York City in 1818, Winder began that portion of the curriculum for which he was least well equipped and soon found himself in academic difficulty. In January 1819, he ranked thirteenth out of thirty-nine in experimental philosophy (the course stressed physics and chemistry and constituted the heart of the academic requirements for second classmen), but he ranked twentieth in elementary drawing, which was concerned with topography and mapmaking. He was thus listed as "deficient" in the latter course, the only such grade he ever received. When the term ended in June, he had fallen to twenty-first overall, ranking eighteenth in descriptive geometry, twentieth in philosophy, and thirty-first in drawing.[25] Winder's draftsmanship, like his penmanship, remained extremely poor for all of his life.

Winder was promoted to the first class in September 1819 and finally found his stride. The consolidated weekly class reports frequently listed Winder as "best" in engineering, the core of the entire four-year curriculum, and also in the second category, encompassing geography, history, ethics, and national law. Another indication of his improvement was his selection in January 1820 as captain of the First Company. When he graduated in July, he ranked eleventh out of thirty in the class of 1820.[26]

Winder's long stay at West Point marked him for life. It took courage for him to return to the academy after his father's military disgrace. Thayer did not permit hazing but there is little doubt that Winder experienced some humiliating moments during the Partridge regime. Before his education commenced in earnest in 1817, he had learned to discipline his temper and had no more trouble with Douglass or any other faculty member. His impetuous temperament would occasionally cause problems in the future, but he was not as excitable as he would have been without the disciplined life of West Point.

After Thayer's arrival, Winder applied himself diligently and eventually won the respect of his peers and superiors, but he was not intellectually gifted. In fact, he was a very slow learner. Of the sixty-six cadets who entered with him and completed the program, fifty-five graduated earlier than he did.[27] As a student and throughout his life he was not intellectually curious. In this respect he failed at West Point, for the education he received at the academy was not designed to be an end unto itself, but a beginning. Thayer adhered to the ideals of the Enlightenment (as did Thomas Jefferson, when he asked Congress to create the institution); and his purpose was to build men—men who would improve their society through force of character as professional soldiers, civil engineers, math professors, and architects.[28]

The first three years of cadet training did not provide an education in war or even in the techniques of war. Some of the professors included a generalized history of war in their offerings, and the assistant instructors drilled the cadets in elementary military tactics. But the assumption was that Napoleon's career represented the apogee of the military art as a technical specialty and that France was the source of military wisdom. Supposedly, since nothing else could be learned in this area, it made no sense to devote precious time to its study when the student could more properly be exposed to the greater challenges of expanding the American frontier and improving the technology of the times.[29]

Winder was an avid and excellent student during his final year, which did focus on the military profession, and probably would have excelled earlier with a curriculum more oriented toward military preparation. He was finally engaged in training for his life's work. He had always wanted to be a soldier. Now he was finally learning how to go about it.

The change in his academic standing was immediately noticed by the superintendent. Without this improvement it is doubtful that Thayer would have asked Winder to become an assistant instructor of tactics seven years later. Winder would not have been an able assistant in any other area of the curriculum, but he had the drive and the talent to do exceptionally well in his narrow field of interest.

The conclusion seems inescapable that Winder was more fitted for the type of education offered at the Prussian War Academy by Gerhard Scharnhorst and Carl von Clausewitz than at the United States Military Academy of Thayer. He was not truly the type of student that Thayer attempted to create. Winder's experiences at the academy certainly exposed him to the wider horizons of American life that many academy graduates would partake of, but his inclination for a military career remained paramount. Unlike many graduates (Jefferson Davis, for instance), who recorded that the academy had rendered them "unfit for civilian life" but who later resigned their commissions for successful civilian careers, Winder, when he made that self-judgment, was correct in his appraisal.[30]

One of the more obvious residues of his six-year stay at the academy was Winder's erect bearing and spit-and-polish image, which marked him as a military man even when he appeared in civilian attire. The experience also made him more reserved and formal in manner. His mode of speech became crisper and his vocal intonations more abrupt as he lost his drawl but not his accent.[31] It does not appear that he used tobacco as a cadet or at any time afterward, and he apparently did not consume alcohol while at the academy. It is most improbable that he could have indulged either vice for long, without being caught. In later life he did drink moderately on occasion, and he did not believe in prohibition even when he was attempting to enforce it in Richmond during the Civil War.[32] He grew up physically, mentally, and, to some extent, emotionally at the academy. He had entered as a pampered youth barely in his teens and with only the vaguest idea of what it meant to become a soldier. He emerged as a disciplined and determined young man, an officer who could be counted on to perform his assignment to the limit of his abilities.

Winder was enjoying a brief vacation in New York City when his commission as second lieutenant in the army arrived on 1 July 1820. Of the four branches of the army, only the corps of engineers (the most prestigious) was closed to him. Service in that echelon was reserved for the top two or three cadets of each class; but the artillery was only slightly less desirable (the cavalry and infantry were next in descending order), and he was ordered to report by 23 July for garrison duty in the artillery corps at Fort McHenry near his Baltimore home.[33]

Winder visited his family that July for the first time in three years. His sister Aurelia had died the previous summer, but he had not been able to attend the funeral. He had been closer to her than to his much younger brothers, but the loss was partially compensated for by the birth of Charlotte Aurelia on 14 May 1820. The last of the children born to William and Gertrude, this baby sister became the special favorite of her older brothers. They were a tightly knit family for the rest of their lives and worked diligently to help and support each other in peace and in war.[34]

The population of Baltimore approached 63,000 in 1820, and the young lieutenant found that his father was again one of the most respected and popular figures in the city. General Winder had largely overcome the stigma of Bladensburg; he was powerful in local and state politics and was recognized as being among the preeminent attorneys in the region. He was narrowly defeated in 1816 for the office of United States senator and was elected to the Maryland senate the next year, a position he held until his death in 1824. His closest friend was Roger Brooke Taney, future chief justice of the United States Supreme Court, and they often worked together. Presidential aspirants, including John C. Calhoun, courted him and asked for his support in 1824. An extraordinarily resilient man, "the swift-footed General" had made an incredible comeback.[35]

In spite of the general's prominence and happy home life, the year 1820 was a time of mixed blessings for him. He was forcibly reminded of the war years when he was notified on 29 March that he owed the government $4,485.85 for unauthorized expenditures during 1812 and 1813. This was a staggering amount even for one of his earning capacity. He appealed but was formally notified in September 1821 that he would be sued if the payment was not forthcoming.[36] He liquidated almost all of his holdings and paid the debt the following year, but this action meant that his family would face virtual bankruptcy if he died in the near future, and that is exactly what occurred.

Duty at Fort McHenry gave Second Lieutenant Winder the luxury of visiting his family regularly after his prolonged absence, but it was not the place for an ambitious officer to further his career.[37] Early promotion was probable only for those stationed where combat was a possibility, and in 1820 the frontier between Georgia and Spanish Florida offered definite promise. Andrew Jackson's invasion of Florida in 1818 induced the Spanish to negotiate the Adams-Onís Treaty with the United States, but the treaty was not yet ratified and the Indians of the area might prove hostile. In order to obtain frontier duty, Winder asked to transfer from the artillery corps to rifles in October 1820. The rifles were phased out the following year, but in 1820 there were several companies stationed in Georgia. Winder secured the appointment, and before the year ended he reported for duty to Colonel Frederick Hindman on the Georgia border.[38]

Field duty on the frontier proved uneventful. There was very little for Winder and the others to do except patrol the border during the winter of 1820–1821 and read about congressional intentions toward the army. Intensive debates in and out of Congress about the necessity of the United States Military Academy and the size of the army took place constantly. Antimilitarism intensified when America was at peace, and this was especially true when the nation was in economic distress like that following the Panic of 1819. Secretary of War John C. Calhoun energetically defended the academy, and it survived, but on 2 March 1821, Congress ordered a reduction and reorganization of the army. Under the direction of Generals Winfield Scott, Edmund Gaines, and Jacob Brown, the army was reduced to six thousand men. Within a year there were 541 commissioned officers and 5,642 noncoms and privates in the ranks. As Sam Houston later recorded, the regular army was a "fine little thing, kept more for show than for any useful purpose." Two inspector generals visited every post and reported in November 1822 that everything was in good order, but in reality the reduction had thoroughly demoralized the army.[39]

Winder certainly did not feel that everything was in good order. The rifles were abolished, and in May 1821 he was ordered to report to Colonel John Fenwick of the Fourth Artillery for ordnance duty. He immediately asked for a transfer to the Third Artillery in order to serve in the new American territory of Florida. He believed that war with the Seminoles was probable and reported to Lieutenant Colonel William Lindsay at Fort St. Marks in August of 1821. This was the first of seven tours of duty for Winder in the "land of sunshine."[40]

Few Americans in or out of the military knew the realities of living in frontier Florida, and Winder was totally ignorant of the true conditions or he would never have volunteered for duty at Fort St. Marks. The area was nearly uninhabited except for the small garrison at the fort, and Fort San Marcos, renamed Fort St. Marks, was in a deplorable condition. Located close to the Gulf of Mexico at the junction of the St. Marks and Wakulla rivers, the old Spanish structure had never been maintained and had been used primarily as an Indian trading post during the centuries of Spanish occupation. Spanish soldiers had battled stinging insects and other vermin there for decades, and this role now passed to the Americans.

Winder soon discovered that the summer months were almost unbearable and that the potentially hostile Indians in the region were the least of the problems. Except for settled areas along the St. Johns River, St. Augustine in East Florida, and the enclave around Pensacola in West Florida, the territory was a forbidding wilderness abounding in all manner of inhospitalities. The "dog days" of August were hot and humid without a breath of air stirring, broken only by the violence of frequent thunderstorms and occasional hurricanes. The sultry, muggy nights made it difficult to sleep even without the ubiquitous presence of vermin. Mosquitoes vied with sand flies for stinging supremacy, and chiggers, lice, fleas, ticks, ants, wasps, rats, and roaches were determined to share the soldiers' quarters. Sandspurs were plentiful along the coast, and the interior was replete with poison oak, poison ivy, and vines harboring vicious barbs. Poisonous snakes and alligators were also well represented.[41]

The "sickly season," which began in June, usually ended in October, and the following months were pleasant, although some Decembers were quite cold. Winter usually commenced in January, and February was inevitably dark, dismal, and chilly. At least the short winter was seldom severe, and the weather began to change for the better in March.

Winder was not impressed with the weather or Fort St. Marks, but he reported that the area around the Indian village of Tallahassee, about twenty miles northeast of the fort, was beautiful. When Tallahassee became the territorial capital in 1824, Winder told a Maryland newspaper reporter that the hills in and around the site were very similar to those of the Baltimore countryside.[42]

Winder was in contact with the Seminoles at various times during his first posting but did not really come to know them until his subsequent tours of duty during and after the Second Seminole War. They were excellent farmers and ranchers and were equally adept as hunters and fishermen. Their knowledge of medicine, especially in treating fevers and snakebite, was superior to that of the white man. They were, however, easily corrupted by the white man's whiskey, and there was plenty of it around. Whiskey, highly regarded for its medicinal value, was standard issue in the army until 1838. Winder eventually became sympathetic to the plight of the Indians, in Florida and elsewhere—an attitude that was to have an enormous influence on his firstborn son—but he never developed any tolerance for the presence of alcohol on army posts. He came to view liquor as a major problem, whether in the possession of Indians or enlisted men under his command.[43]

Duty at this remote post was boring, and it soon became obvious that there would be no Indian war in the near future. Winder asked for a furlough and departed on 19 January 1822 for Augusta, Georgia.[44] Why he chose that place remains a mystery. But the decision altered his life in dramatic fashion, for he either met or renewed his acquaintanceship with a seventeen-year-old schoolgirl from Washington, Georgia, in Wilkes County. Before the month was over, the young romantic was convinced that he was in love. The lady of his fancy, Elizabeth Shepherd, was taken with the young lieutenant, but there was a major obstacle to their courtship. Andrew Shepherd was determined that his daughter would not marry a soldier, and his opposition was understandable. Winder's monthly pay was only $25, and he was allowed an additional $28.50 for subsistence. The latter sum was used to pay rent for his quarters and forage for his horse and to provide for the needs of his servant.[45] Shepherd did not want Elizabeth subjected to the harsh, barren life that she would inevitably encounter in remote frontier posts like Fort St. Marks. On the other hand, Winder was of the elite, and Shepherd had nothing against him personally. He would be welcome to visit when he could.

Winder returned to his post in February but became more and more lonely as the months passed. He was clearly smitten by Elizabeth and asked for additional leave at the beginning of summer. On 22 August 1822, he set off for the Shepherd plantation, little realizing that his departure from Florida on that day was the first step leading to a four and one-half year absence from the military life.[46]

Winder arrived in Augusta by boat and from there made the two-day journey to Washington on horseback. The rich, deep-loamed, and well-watered hills still teemed with game, but the steady advance of the ax and plow had changed this trapper's paradise to a land dominated by cotton. The colony of Georgia opened the area to settlement in 1773, and hundreds of Virginians, Carolinians, and other colonials rushed to acquire the cheap, fertile land. Cognizant of the increased population and the patriotic aura of the area, the Executive Council of Georgia decreed in 1780 that a town be laid out south of the capital of Fort Heard and that it be named for George Washington.

Two Virginia families that rapidly attained prominence in the new town were the Gilberts and the Shepherds. Felix Gilbert and his sons were the leading merchants in Washington by 1785 and also owned several thousand acres of land in the county. James Shepherd and his son Andrew were planters of note by that time and very active in county affairs. Equally respected and even more influential was a couple from Massachusetts, David and Sarah Hillhouse.[47] Intermarriage among these three families occurred fairly regularly, and one of the progeny was the young woman that Winder set his heart on marrying (see Shepherd Genealogical Chart).

Felix Gilbert, who died in 1801, left his business to his sons; the rest of his estate was divided among his four daughters.[48] One of these daughters was Mariah Gilbert Christmas, a recent widow with a young son. Two years after the death of her father, she married Andrew Shepherd, but her son died within a year and Mariah died during or shortly after the birth of Elizabeth on 11 October 1805.[49]

Shepherd was fortunate in that Mariah's brother Felix H. Gilbert and his wife Sarah also had a daughter born that year and were quite willing to help care for Elizabeth.[50] The close family ties became even closer on 20 April 1807, when Shepherd married Mary Hillhouse, Sarah Gilbert's younger sister.[51] The union was a happy one, and Elizabeth soon had a number of sisters and a brother for playmates. Two daughters and a son were born within three years, and the Shepherds ultimately had six children, including Elizabeth, who attained adulthood.[52]

Mary Shepherd treated Elizabeth as if she were her own child. A loving, gentle woman, she was also strong willed, well educated, and independent, a proper tribute to her own mother, Sarah Porter Hillhouse. Sarah and her husband David had moved to Washington from Hadley, Massachusetts, in 1787, acquired a local newspaper, and published it as the Washington *Monitor* from 1791 to 1815. Sarah became the editor in 1803 when David died, the first woman in Georgia and one of the first in the country to enter this profession. She proved to be an astute businesswoman, and her daughter Mary helped make the venture a success.[53]

Sarah sold the paper in 1815, and she and Mary turned their considerable skills to the improvement of Washington. They both wanted to increase the educational opportunities and facilities for the young women of Washington, and in 1820 they convinced the town council to purchase an old theater and turn it into the Washington Female Academy. One of the commissioners at that time was Andrew Shepherd, whose daughter Elizabeth became one of the first students.[54] Shepherd had an excellent relationship with his mother-in-law, and she lived in his home from the early 1820s until her death in 1831. Shepherd purchased the two-story frame structure in 1816, and eventually it became home to John Henry Winder, the only extant structure that he ever lived in.[55]

When Winder went courting in 1822, he found that privacy was hard to come by in the Shepherd home. The household included Andrew and Mary, Elizabeth, four of her half-brothers and half-sisters, and Sarah Hillhouse. Eight house slaves were in attendance and lived in quarters on the ten and one-half acres containing the house.[56] In addition, Shepherd was a Virginian and practiced the Old Dominion's creed of excessive hospitality and generosity to a fault; the house was usually crammed with visitors and overnight guests.[57]

Winder enjoyed and appreciated the munificence of his host, and he and Shepherd apparently got along rather well. Shepherd was a major in the Georgia militia and had seen limited action during the War of 1812. He was very much aware of General Winder's role during that conflict and, more importantly, of the reputation he had since attained.[58] Quite possibly the two discussed Winder's West Point years, the Indian problems still confronting Georgia and Florida, and other topics of the day. They also discussed Winder's future with Elizabeth, and the talk was not at all to Winder's liking. To his dismay, Winder found that Shepherd would not consent to the marriage as long as he remained in the military, and Elizabeth would not marry without her father's consent. One solution was to turn the young soldier into a gentleman planter. Shepherd was in poor health, his sons were too young to manage the plantation, and reliable overseers were expensive and hard to find.

The problem was that Winder very much wanted to remain in the army. His thirst for military glory remained unabated; he yearned for an opportunity to distinguish himself. Besides, he knew nothing of cotton cultivation. He had some experience in tobacco culture, and Shepherd raised a small crop of tobacco, but Winder lacked the training and the temperament to oversee the work of almost ninety slaves and to attend to the myriad duties of successful plantation management.[59]

On the other hand, Winder was young enough to learn under Shepherd's guidance, and his future with Elizabeth was at stake. He could never hope to inherit the entire plantation, but any children that he and Elizabeth might have would share the estate on an equal basis with Shepherd's other offspring.[60] In addition, he could earn more money than the army offered and could live as befitted a gentleman planter. Elizabeth was the great passion of Winder's life, and he agreed to give cotton culture a try.

In this manner Winder's six-month courtship came to a successful conclusion: on 12 February 1823, he and Elizabeth were married at the New Ford Baptist Church by the Reverend Guy Smith. Elizabeth brought a sizable dowry to the marriage, including a two-thousand-dollar inheritance she had received in 1814 upon the death of her uncle, Felix H. Gilbert.[61] Winder brought only himself, fully committed to Elizabeth but not totally convinced that plantation management was the life for him.

Winder's actions before and shortly after the marriage indicate that he was uneasy about his decision. He submitted his resignation on 19 January 1823 but apparently stipulated that it not become effective until September. Either that, or he sent a subsequent letter retracting his withdrawal. Unfortunately, few of his messages to the adjutant general's office that year were placed *in toto* in the official record, but a summary was made of all his official correspondence as a matter of course. At any rate, he did not resign until 31 August, more than seven months after his marriage. Winder confirmed in 1827 that this date was correct and stated that he had resigned because of ill health "and some other circumstances which no longer exist."[62]

One of the circumstances that Winder alluded to was that Elizabeth became pregnant during the late summer or fall of 1823. The pressure on him to manage the plantation successfully thereby increased, since the child would be an heir of the estate. Still, even though the young couple could afford a home of their own at that time, they stayed with the Shepherds.[63] This may have been part of the understanding between Winder and Shepherd, or it may indicate that Winder was not certain that he was destined to live permanently in Washington. In either case, Winder soon regretted his decision to resign, for the next three years were sad and traumatic for the former lieutenant and his wife.

Early in 1824, Winder and Elizabeth visited his family in Baltimore. They were there in May when his father became fatally ill. The general struggled for eleven days before succumbing to "Bilious Catarrh" on 24 May. He had contracted the lung ailment in 1814 in his Canadian prison cell and had suffered periodic bouts with it ever since. It was not an easy death. Racked by chills and fever, and unable to sleep, he required constant fanning by family members and friends. The slightest noise caused intense pain. Chatham Street was chained off to prevent street noise, and such was the respect for the man that no one crossed the barrier when the reason for its existence became known. The general rallied briefly but died "without a sign or an agitation of body or mind."[64]

Roger B. Taney and other close friends were at the deathbed and took charge of the arrangements, but it was immediately apparent that virtually every high official in civil, military, and Masonic organizations was determined to participate in the funeral. As one of his sons later recorded, "The public took the funeral out of the family's hands."[65] *Niles Weekly Register* reported that "no man, perhaps, ever died in Baltimore who was more generally esteemed—and, though not a *fortunate general*, a more honest or more zealous soldier never was in the 'tented field.' His departure is regarded as a *public loss*, and may fairly be said to have put our city into mourning."[66]

Services were held at his home on Chatham Street, and the funeral procession was immense and unprecedented. Troops of cavalry and infantry were followed by Masonic lodges, clergy of all denominations, and the pallbearers. The family members were next and then came more soldiers, as well as judges and other members of the bar, the mayor, city and county officials, the regents and professors of the University Maryland, and fully 15,000 citizens of Baltimore. It was by far the rgest funeral procession in the history of the city and was to remain o until well after the Civil War. Everyone in the procession wore black crepe on their left arms, and the flags of the city hung at half-mast. The eulogy was delivered by William Wirt, attorney general of the United States.[67]

Wirt wrote Secretary of War Calhoun on the day of Winder's death.

Winder has left a widow and four children in extreme distress and without a relation on either side able to help them. Two of his children are boys, the eldest sixteen years of age [William], the younger about fourteen [Charles]. They are both at college here; and are both said to be very fine youths. The Bar of Baltimore, who were devotedly attached to poor Winder, have determined to take the elder under their patronage and to educate him at their own expense in his father's profession. The younger it is hoped may be admitted at West Point and educated for the Army.[68]

Calhoun replied that he was "deeply distressed at the death of Gen'l Winder. In virtue and honor he has left none superior behind him." He noted that there was no vacancy at West Point for Maryland at the time but that he would make an exception due to the circumstances. A further exception had to be made because Charles was blind in one eye. Despite this liability, Charles was appointed to the academy on 1 July 1824.[69]

There was little for John Henry to do except give some much-needed advice to Charles as the youth prepared to enroll at the academy. Whatever counsel Winder gave his youngest brother was in vain. Charles completed his first term but soon fell into bad habits. He was not destined to become the second Winder to graduate from West Point.[70]

General Winder left everything to his wife Gertrude and appointed her sole executrix, but attorney John Morris actually settled the estate and became guardian for the children. Morris had been Winder's student and had also served on his staff during the war. In 1824, he was president of the Mechanics Bank of Baltimore and a member of the first branch of the city council.[71] Morris moved diligently to settle the family's affairs during the remainder of 1824 and early 1825. He rented Winder's two law offices, attempted to recover the many books that were on loan, and engaged in a wide-ranging correspondence to secure commissions that Winder was entitled to. For example, he notified Henry Clay that Winder's share of a case involving Florida land claims came to $117.33, and Clay promptly sent the money.[72]

While the estate was being settled, Elizabeth gave birth to a son sometime in June or July of 1824. They named the boy William Andrew, in honor of both of his grandfathers.[73] The birth may have been the only happy event the family experienced during the next several years, despite being one more responsibility that Winder could ill afford. The decline of the family fortunes following the death of the patriarch was rapid and embarrassing for all concerned, but it was most humiliating for the eldest son.

The settlement of the estate confirmed what many must have suspected; General Winder had been a spendthrift. His earnings were large but so were his debts. He had entertained frequently and lavishly and had been extremely generous to unfortunate kinsmen and friends, even after he had liquidated his investments to pay the unauthorized war expenses demanded by the government.[74] Gertrude learned early in 1825 that she owned the house, three slaves, and very little else. Her situation worsened on 30 June when she was notified that Charles had been expelled from West Point. Finally, William proved lacking in forensic skills, dropped his legal studies, and became an additional burden on his beleaguered mother.[75]

Gertrude had led a sheltered life and was ill prepared to head the household. The forty-three-year-old widow had the responsibility for four children ranging in age from four to sixteen, two female relatives (one of whom was over fifty), one male slave, aged eighteen, two female slaves, aged eighteen and about twenty, and one Free Negro woman, the mother of the slaves.[76] By 1826, Gertrude's financial situation was desperate, but she refused to sell any of the slaves. She intended to provide for her family, black and white, even if it meant a substantial decline in social status. She took that step by turning her lovely home into a boarding-house. A family friend, John C. Breckinridge, informed Henry Clay of her plight and asked if her son William might be appointed to a minor clerkship in Washington. He stated that William was a moral young man of "exceptional talents" but the position was not forthcoming.[77]

William and Charles were too young and inexperienced to contribute much toward financial security, but this did not apply to the eldest son. John Henry Winder was twenty-four years of age, well educated, employed, and in excellent health when his father died. One might expect that he could have prevented or at least ameliorated this mortifying situation. It was his responsibility, and he did try, but he failed his family when they most needed him. During the next two years, he demonstrated conclusively that he was by training, talent, temperament, and inclination, not suited for civilian life.

Winder was deeply ashamed of this period of his life. He never revealed for the public record what he did during that time, although he had many opportunities to do so. In the 1840s, Captain George Cullum was selected to compile a complete biographical register of West Point graduates. He revised it constantly prior to publication in 1868, utilizing all available records and information furnished by the graduates. Winder repeatedly and meticulously updated his military accomplishments for the work, but he never responded to Cullum's queries for the years 1823 through 1827. Regarding that span of time in Winder's life, Cullum wrote "Civil History Unknown."[78] Winder obviously wanted this interval expunged from memory and history, and he very largely succeeded.

The few extant records indicate that Winder and his family returned to the Shepherd plantation during the latter part of 1824. Within a year, he found himself and his in-laws in a financial condition similar to that of his Baltimore family and for much the same reason. Andrew Shepherd's health degenerated, and by October 1825 he was incapacitated.[79] Winder attempted to manage the plantation alone but did not possess the necessary skills. He labored until 1826 when Elizabeth died, apparently a victim of yellow fever.[80] This was the final blow for Winder, and he decided to reenter the army. An overseer, Zachariah Colly, was hired to oversee the plantation from 1827 until 1830, when the estate was divided following Shepherd's death.[81]

Winder returned to Baltimore either in late 1826 or early the following year. He could have followed the usual course of academy graduates who resigned from the army and become a civil engineer, surveyor, or even an architect. His West Point training provided him with skills much in demand. Most of his colleagues who resigned from the military during the 1820s secured positions that paid well and carried much prestige in society, though not as much as that enjoyed by later graduates after the railroad era began.[82]

Winder may have considered these civilian options and may have even worked as an engineer for a short time, but he had otherwise failed in civilian life and admitted it. He informed Adjutant General Roger Jones on 22 February 1827, "I find I am qualified to do little after being so long accustomed to a military life," and asked to be reinstated "with such rank so as to interfere with nobody."[83] Jones was an old family friend, and he had known Winder since he was a small boy. He immediately informed Secretary of War James Barbour that the former lieutenant was "intelligent, moral, and regularly qualified." He noted that Winder did not want his rank to offend anyone and suggested that he be given credit only for his two years of active service so that the class of 1825, including brevets, would be senior to him. In effect, Winder's career would resume as if he had graduated on 1 July 1825 instead of five years previously. Barbour agreed, forwarded Winder's commission on 2 April, and ordered him to report for temporary assignment to the First Artillery Regiment at Fort Washington.[84]

Winder's return to the military enabled him to provide for himself and give some limited financial assistance to his mother, but it did not end the insolvency that had plagued his family since the death of his father. Moreover, he was forced to add to his mother's burdens by leaving his son in her care. He attempted to rectify the situation somewhat by gaining additional favors from Jones. In a letter posted 23 April he made the following appeal:

> I have already troubled you so much that I really feel ashamed to make any fresh application but my *Brothers* wish very much to go to West Point. One of them has been there but youth (being age 14) led him into many follies, he was dismissed, but I have hope his experience will induce him to do better. The other is nineteen years old of studious habits and well calculated to go through with some credit to himself. My object in writing is to ask if it is possible for one or both of them to succeed in getting appointments. I am afraid you will think me troublesome. My excuse is the situation of the two boys.[85]

Winder was unsuccessful in his efforts. His simultaneous request to be stationed permanently at Fort Washington so as to be near his family was also denied. Instead, he was assigned to garrison duty in Connecticut until Superintendent Thayer requested that he come to West Point as an assistant instructor of infantry tactics in September 1827.[86] Thayer had been having considerable problems with the high-spirited cadets. The Christmas party of 1826 got completely out of hand, and some seventy cadets engaged in a riot against the officers. Thayer ordered all concerned to be tried by court-martial, and nineteen cadets were expelled. Captain Ethan Allen Hitchcock, assistant instructor of tactics since 1824, opposed the expulsions. He was removed and replaced by Winder.[87]

The superintendent's policy was to staff his faculty with West Point graduates. He knew that these officers had the necessary professional qualifications, and he also knew them as individuals. He maintained an exhaustive file on every cadet and was an excellent judge of character.

He remembered that Winder had shown great promise during his final year.

The physical facilities had expanded during Winder's seven-year absence, but life at the academy was about as it had been during his student days. Duty for the assistant instructors was time-consuming, solitary, and somewhat monotonous. They did not receive extra pay for teaching, and the turnover was rapid. Some officers felt that there was not much of a future for faculty at West Point; but early promotion was possible for exceptional instructors, and the assignment provided an excellent opportunity to make valuable contacts.[88]

Two of the cadets Winder met were Jefferson Davis and Robert E. Lee. He did not have either as students, but he did know them rather well. He lived in the student barracks, and part of his job was to monitor the activities of all the cadets. Davis later wrote that he "had no particular knowledge" of Winder "as an instructor of tactics" when he was a cadet but he served in several details under Winder's command.[89] Lee and many others who later served the Confederacy knew Winder as a firm but fair disciplinarian and heard that he was a good instructor, but that was about all. One of Winder's students that year was none other than Cadet Lucius B. Northrop, but there is no indication that their later feud had any roots leading back to this time.

Winder performed his duties with zest and efficiency, and he was an effective teacher. The board of visitors in June 1828 made special mention of the cadets' knowledge of tactics, and Winder could claim a great deal of the credit for this praise.[90] It appeared that he would be a success in his first assignment after his return to the military life, but that was not to be. His tour came to an abrupt end during the early weeks of the annual summer encampment.

On 16 July Winder told Cadet Thomas Avery of the academy band that he was confined to camp, and the young man protested the order. They were in Winder's tent, and Avery became obstreperous when Winder ordered him to keep silence and to leave his quarters. Avery refused and Winder's temper flared. He threatened to remove Avery physically—a threat that provoked Avery to a physical assault. Winder subdued the cadet, placed him under arrest, and immediately brought charges against him.

Avery's court-martial was held during the first two weeks of August. The board found him innocent of all charges except his refusal to be silent and his failure to leave Winder's tent. He was sentenced to a short confinement and loss of pay for his digressions.[91] Winder's punishment was more severe. Thayer would not tolerate an officer who could not control his temper. As he had done with John Bliss earlier, Thayer backed his appointee during the controversy but relieved him shortly thereafter. Thayer notified Winder before the month was out that his posting at the academy was over. Winder wrote to General George Gibson, commissary general of subsistence, asking for a position in his command. He was soon notified that he was to report to Fort Johnston at Smithville, North Carolina.[92]

September of 1828 was a bleak time for Winder. He had failed in civilian life and done little better at West Point. His family was still in economic distress, and he was not sanguine about prospects for an end to this condition. It must have been difficult for the high-strung aristocrat to admit that he alone was responsible for his failures, but he finally realized that self-control was indispensable to his career. He was determined to overcome this fault and his efforts were successful; but it is doubtful that he ever imagined that his luck would turn for the better within two short years. Instead, as he gazed at the immense stone buildings of the quadrangle for the last time, his spirits were probably as gray as his surroundings. He had spent seven years at the academy and would never return, but he was inescapably a part of it. It had molded him and matured him, and although it had now rejected him, he was finally ready to become a professional, an officer and a gentleman of distinction and courage, a graduate the academy could be proud of.

CHAPTER 6

The Emergence of a Professional

1828–1860

Winder served in nearly all parts of the United States during his long tenure in the army, from Key West, Florida, to Fort Kent in northernmost Maine, to Fort Gibson in Arkansas. He endured every variation of climate and was exposed to about every killer disease of his time, but he managed to enjoy good health almost all of his life. Most career officers took frequent sick leave; many died from yellow fever, malaria, cholera, measles, and other diseases; and significant numbers were incapacitated for life. It took an especially rugged constitution and a good amount of luck to serve on the frontier and emerge healthy. Except for occasional recurrences of malaria, Winder enjoyed better health on the frontier than his family did in supposedly safer areas. He was thus able to learn and perform the duties of his profession without any significant interruption.

As a junior officer, Lieutenant Winder learned the routine duties of his rank while serving as assistant commissary, assistant adjutant, assistant quartermaster, and, after attaining the rank of captain, company commander. He learned to manage men—soldiers and civilians alike—and to exercise authority properly. He also faced the possibility of death or disablement in combat, first in the Indian wars and then in Mexico.

Winder's second tour in Florida commenced in 1836 after the outbreak of the Second Seminole War. He left his Smithville home in January of that year and soon realized that Florida had not changed much since he had first served there fourteen years earlier. Duty there was tough enough during peacetime, and almost impossible during war. For the next two years his experiences, which mirrored those of almost every soldier engaged in the conflict, consisted of one trying and exhausting mission after another with very little to show for it most of the time. Still, if the tour was tiresome and vexing, it provided him the valuable opportunity of coming to the attention of the top commanders of the army.

His first command in Florida signaled the type of fatiguing and frustrating assignments he could expect during the rest of the posting. He took command of Fort Drane, some ten miles south of Micanopy, and made the following report on 30 November:

> Two squaw prisoners made their escape on the night of the 28th—in a review of all the circumstances I cannot attach any blame to myself. I am the only officer at the post and have only one Sergeant for duty and am necessarily obliged to trust the guard to a corporal though in this instance I think the blame rests with the sentinels. I myself had that night visited the guard and the tent of the squaws three times and found them present at the last inspection. I did not lay down until after midnight sometime. Being then fatigued from the labors of the day and from being obliged to be up more or less every night I thought I might trust the sentinels—but it seems I was mistaken—they escaped . . . [and] I am almost disposed to think they had some help.[1]

Winder was ordered to Fort Heileman on Black Creek (present-day Middleburg) in January 1837 as commissary officer and post treasurer. This was his first important assignment; the fort was the main depot for the whole Florida army. Winder was thus in constant contact with the top commander in Florida, General Thomas Jesup, and other officers of influence. He encountered unexpected difficulties during the next several months but handled the assignment in excellent fashion.[2]

One of the responsibilities of the commissary officer was to supplement regular rations with fresh beef at reasonable rates whenever possible. Winder found that the local ranchers recognized their opportunity for economic gain. Their cattle were range, or "scrub," stock and not very tasty, but they demanded and obtained exorbitant prices for the animals. In addition, the cattle were not always branded or otherwise marked, and it was frequently impossible for Winder to determine which animals had been paid for before he had them slaughtered.

Winder demonstrated an ability at this time to cooperate effectively with civilians, an unusual trait among army officers, but the effectiveness did not endure for long. He procured an adequate beef supply without any trouble until July 1837, when Robert Rollins and John Wiggins swore "that the cow killed by Lieutenant Winder was the property of Nathaniel Jones" and Jones demanded $12.50 in compensation. The price was outrageous but Winder could not risk alienating the locals and was forced to pay. He resented it and hired Benjamin Frisbee, a longtime resident of the area, as his assistant at $50 per month to prevent future claims of this type. This salary was in excess of that permitted by regulations, but Winder believed that the money was well spent. Frisbee performed well, and Winder had no more problems in obtaining the necessary supplies.[3]

Fort Heileman's population increased enormously during 1836 and 1837 as civilians sought security from the Indian menace, militia units were mobilized into service, and army units arrived in ever increasing numbers. The results were disastrous. A major epidemic broke out because of fundamental ignorance of proper hygiene in a congested area. Hundreds sickened, many died, and there was a continual flow of men invalided out of the service.[4]

Winder took a short leave in August and returned late in November of 1837. Fort Heileman had lost much of its strategic importance by that time, as the war had moved into central and south Florida, and he spent the next six months in command of various interior forts. He came under fire several times but returned to Fort Heileman in March 1838 evidently convinced that he would not see combat in his commissary role and that early promotion was therefore most unlikely.

During the next several months Winder made a determined attempt to secure a promotion by transferring to ordnance. Hearing that Congress would soon expand the Ordnance Corps and create several vacancies with the rank of captain, he contacted several high military and civilian officials and solicited their support. He had no difficulty in gaining a recommendation from Generals Gibson and Jesup based on his own merit, but the appeal to others was largely based on their memory of his father.[5] For instance, in requesting that Adjutant General Jones use his "great influence" on his behalf, Winder wrote, "I do not ask it from any claim I could have on you, but knowing the great friendship my Father entertained for you I am encouraged to request your assistance."[6] He wrote in similar fashion to J. M. Stewart, who was an influential Baltimorean, and Chief Justice of the Supreme Court Roger B. Taney.

Stewart was friendly with Secretary of War Joel Poinsett and was quick to ask a favor. "I have every reason to believe that his [Winder's] conduct is and always has been exemplary. I do not know exactly what it is desirable to ask for Winder, but we shall be thankful if he can be promoted, and I assure you that whilst this notice of the son will be nothing more than a just tribute to the memory of his gallant father it will be most acceptable to the people of Baltimore."[7]

Chief Justice Taney couched his appeal to Poinsett almost totally in memory of Winder's father. "[Winder] has been in the army many years and . . . is an officer of merit. He is the son of the late Gen'l W. H. Winder . . . and although his career was not a fortunate one . . . he was always activated by the highest and best motives and made sacrifices in the public's service which few men would have been willing to encounter. He was one of my most intimate and beloved friends and the deep interest I feel for his family must be my apology for troubling you on the subject."[8]

While he awaited the outcome of these efforts, Winder's tour in Florida ended, but his dealings with the Indians did not. May of 1838 found him adjutant of the First Artillery posted in the Cherokee country at Fort Butler, North Carolina. Preparations were being made to ship the Cherokees to western reservations that summer and in August, Winder was sent to Clarksville, Georgia, to take part in the planned deportation. He was not a participant in the Cherokees' "trail of tears" that winter, but this duty in the Indian removal did have an influence on him.[9] Winder's postings during the next twenty years frequently brought him in contact with the remaining Seminoles as well as the tribes on the western reservations.

During Winder's leave late in 1838, he must have talked with his family a great deal about the plight of the Indians, for his fourteen-year-old son William Andrew became convinced that America's official policy was wrong. He became more sympathetic to the Indian cause with the passage of years and, as an army officer himself during the 1850s, worked hard to obtain better treatment for the Indians of the Pacific coast. After the Civil War, he devoted the rest of his life to improving reservation policy.[10]

In the summer of 1839 Winder learned that he would be sent to Arkansas as soon as his commissary books were audited. He was ordered to bring all documents, vouchers, and official records dealing with his position as assistant commissary for the years 1834 through 1838 to Washington for an official audit before departing for the West.[11] He reported to that "dirty shabby village" in September, and the experience his father had undergone was much on his mind.[12]

The audit took two months and he stayed there even though his services were "much needed with his Regiment." He was informed on 1 November that the government refused to honor $32.65 of the $4,355.34 dispersed during his tenure. The news was gall and wormwood to Winder and he protested. His records were meticulous if not neat, and he asked Quartermaster General Jesup for help. Pointing out that Jesup knew first-hand the conditions under which he had labored in Florida and the amounts he had been obliged to pay civilian assistants, Winder asked that the $32.65 expenditures be accepted. Jesup was sympathetic and supported Winder, but the auditor's report stood and Winder was forced to pay. Among the expenses disallowed was the payment for Nathaniel Jones's cow.[13]

Winder left the capital in November for Fort Gibson, Arkansas, and assumed the position of bearer of dispatches for General Matthew Arbuckle. His humor was not improved by the difficulty of the trip. He did not reach his post until mid-December, being much delayed "by the lowness of the rivers." The fort was bleak and primitive, and there was much pneumonia during the winter months, but officers and enlisted men alike enjoyed hunting deer, pheasants, buffalo, and wolves. There was little else to do but observe the various cultures of the different Indian tribes when they came to the fort to trade.[14]

Winder was promoted to captain in October 1842 and ordered to take command of Fort Sullivan in Eastport, Maine. This remote post, which he reached on 7 November, was so near the international boundary that artillery practice was impossible. Any target placed on the water would endanger British property, as the shot would inevitably land in British Canada and might set off a war.[15] Winder was displeased with the assignment, since it again precluded any possibility of sending for his family, and he was appalled at the state of affairs existing in Company G, First Artillery. This was now his company, and he would command it until he resigned in 1861. It consisted of three noncoms and sixty-three privates when Winder arrived. Discipline was slack, and drunkenness and desertion were commonplace. He immediately instituted a stern policy to remedy the problems and soon got results. The men of Company G found that their new commander was a no-nonsense martinet who had no hesitation in purging his command of undesirable elements.[16]

Winder reported in May 1843 that his post account for the previous month would have to be altered because Private William Moulton had deserted and "thus injured the United States" to the extent of $6.61, the value of the clothes he was wearing. He also reported that a Private O'Brien had been arrested "for assaulting a man and a woman in East Port" and urged that he be discharged. In addition to O'Brien, "a drunkard and very riotous," Winder moved against Private John Thompson, "a confirmed drunkard and worthless at his very best" and six other enlisted men. With the discharge of these eight soldiers, Company G was reduced to fifty-five men, the number prescribed by law by the winter of 1843.[17]

In April of the next year he was ordered to take his company to Fort Kent, the northernmost possession of the army and the most desolate and isolated post in the East. He found no medical officer at the post and urged that one be sent immediately: "As soon as the snow disappears which will be in about ten days, our communication will be cut off from the interior for waggons and a part of the season I am told even for horses."[18]

Even with O'Brien, Thompson, and the others out of the company, Winder found that drunkenness was even more of a problem at Fort Kent than it had been at Eastport, and he no longer had his top sergeant to help maintain discipline. He had recommended Henry Smith for ordnance sergeant the previous January, although he could "ill afford to lose such an able man" and no doubt missed his presence keenly during the months to come.[19] The availability of alcohol in this remote post was due to the actions of anonymous customs officers, who had recently confiscated a large supply of whiskey and sold it to the soldiers at cut-rate prices. Winder was under orders to cooperate with the British people of New Brunswick and to prevent any possible conflict between them and his command. The mission was jeopardized when drunken soldiers inevitably got into fights with British civilians.

Winder did not have the authority to override customs officials, but he stopped the sale of whiskey in an unusual and highly effective manner. He bought the entire stock for $105 with his own money and placed the liquor under lock and key at the fort. He reported his action to the adjutant general Roger Jones and asked if the government would refund his money. Jones approved Winder's action as "highly praiseworthy" and recommended that the government honor his request. Winfield Scott also endorsed the idea, but Secretary of War William Marcy returned the letter with a note stating, "I do not see how this request can be complied with."[20]

Winder next wrote the secretary of the treasury and explained his actions. "There is no civil authority here to enforce the laws of Maine against the sale of spiritous liquors, which leaves us entirely at the mercy of the miscreants who are destroying the health as well as the discipline of the troops at this fort." He also enclosed a letter from the post surgeon who testified to the vileness of the whiskey. The surgeon, who had arrived in late April, stated that over two-thirds of the sickness at the post was due to the alcohol and that he had never seen worse whiskey. The liquor was bad enough to begin with, but the customs officers had adulterated it even more. "Among the articles used in this process are black pepper, salveratus, soap, tobacco. Indeed the common name of *rot gut* given it by the lumbermen and others is sufficient indication of their opinion of its noxious qualities."[21]

Secretary R. J. Walker was no more impressed than Marcy had been, and Winder received no reimbursement. The loss of the money rankled, but it did not prevent him from similar undertakings in the future. Several times during the Civil War he used his own money to buy food for Union prisoners and asked Confederate officials, who proved to be more generous than the United States government had been, to honor the debts. Winder normally went by the book, but he would take unorthodox measures if he felt the occasion warranted it.

When one considers the lot of the enlisted men at these isolated garrisons, it becomes much easier to understand their attitudes toward drink and desertion. There was an immense distance between officers and men. The duty was monotonous and demanding, and discipline was draconian. Training and drill were daily events and the soldier began each day at sunrise. Within thirty minutes after reveille was sounded, his room or tent was inspected and he was then allowed breakfast. After the morning meal the soldier cleaned his firearm, polished his breastplate, buttons, and cartridge box, brushed his clothing, and washed himself preparatory to parade at 9:00.

After the raising of the colors, the men passed in review before the commanding officer. They were then dismissed from ranks and allowed to change to fatigues unless they were detailed to guard duty, in which case they remained in dress uniform. The rest of the day was occupied by artillery practice, military drill, and various assignments on the post. Civilian help was not usually available, so soldiers shod the horses, repaired boots and clothing, mowed the grass, constructed or repaired buildings, and did anything else that was necessary. Dinner was usually at 1:00, and the troops reassembled at sunset for retreat, when the national colors were lowered. The roll was called then and again at 9:00, and the soldier was expected to be in bed at 9:30, when taps was sounded by the drum.

This routine in lonely and remote areas was hard to bear. Leave was difficult to obtain and pay was low—eight dollars a month for privates and only seventeen dollars a month for a sergeant major—and sometimes late in arriving. Punishments included confinement in the guardhouse with loss of pay, performing heavy work under guard, and floggings for serious violations.[22] Small wonder that drink, even vile whiskey, was a welcome solace to the enlisted men. But Winder would not permit it. Even though several months of his pay was literally poured in the ground, he ordered the whiskey destroyed.

The policy of enforced sobriety was not popular with the men of Company G, and though it was not uncommon for commanders to lose control of their men under these conditions in remote areas, it never happened to Winder. He was a stern disciplinarian but he was fair, and his company soon learned to respect him. He never demanded anything of the men that he did not also endure, and he played no favorites. He intended to have his command well worked up all of the time, even if this meant that he had to suffer financially by personally destroying their whiskey supply. Discipline could never be instilled or maintained if he condoned drunkenness, so he instantly punished those who violated his order to abstain.[23]

September of 1845 brought a transfer of Company G to the other end of America, to Fort Brooke at Tampa, Florida. Problems with the remaining Seminoles had renewed, and the army sent reinforcements to the troubled area. Transport problems delayed the departure, but Winder took command of the fort on 2 November. He reported that Captain John Sprague had also arrived and would depart immediately for Charlotte Harbor to council with the Indians.

He also conducted his own investigation of the intentions of the Seminoles and soon concluded that the native whites were causing the problems. Specifically, he asserted that an Indian agent, Thomas P. Kennedy, was the ringleader. Kennedy's trading post dispensed liquor to Indians and whites alike, and the results were all too familiar to Winder. He informed the adjutant general on 20 December, "The Indians are and have been disposed to remain quiet and peaceful." He blamed Kennedy for submitting "an absurd and baseless report" about Indian spoliations and concluded: "I have sent a message to the chiefs, by the Indians who come here to trade, not to listen to anything calculated to give them uneasiness [and] should any of the whites molest them in their territory not to take action themselves but to apply at this post for protection. The force at this post is more than sufficient for any and every purpose short of actual hostilities."[24] Adjutant General Jones forwarded Winder's report to the secretary of war and noted: "This is quite satisfactory. Capt. Winder is a discrete officer of good judgment and what he says about the Indians is just what we all supposed to be the real state of the case, notwithstanding other vicious, onerous reports."[25]

Winder's assessment of the Indians' situation was correct. They caused him no problems, but that was not true of the agent Kennedy and other local whites. Most of Winder's troubles were minor, even trivial, but his actions once again demonstrate the type of officer he was. For example, on 26 January 1846, he reported that he had issued standing orders to kill any hogs encroaching on the post. He continued, "And now Kennedy has had a soldier arrested on a warrant for killing a hog which was depracating [sic] on the public property. There appears to be an understanding among certain persons here, that they will defy the orders of the Post and let their hogs run at large, and if killed, to prosecute and annoy as much as possible." One solution was to fence out the hogs, which would cost about $1,000, but he felt it would be better if he had the authority "to kick out Thomas P. Kennedy, M. C. Brown, J. T. Magbee, and such others as from time to time may be found troublesome" and to close the Fort Brooke trading post.

After his friend Captain Sprague established a trading post at Charlotte Harbor, Winder did close the Fort Brooke post and remove Kennedy and company from the payroll.[26] Winder also faced difficulties in his own command. He spent part of New Year's Day reporting on the case of Sergeant A. Long, who had deserted and was in confinement. Winder believed that the "poor man" was "deranged," and he was not inclined to press charges.

Winder received orders the following month to proceed to Pensacola and assume command of Fort Pickens. He reported that his company was far below strength because of transfers and expiration of enlistments. Including officers, he had only forty-one men, but part of his company was on detached duty, and he had just twenty-nine men to complete the armament of Fort Pickens. He asked for replacements; but in May 1846 the United States declared war on Mexico, and mustering in volunteer units took priority. Thus Winder's company remained sadly understrength.[27]

A number of regular army units were already with General Zachary Taylor in Mexico when war was declared, and reinforcements were immediately dispatched to him; but Winder was ordered to complete the work on Fort Pickens. The work progressed slowly under the blazing July sun. Winder was not in a happy frame of mind as he supervised the work and got his family settled into his quarters at Barrancas Barracks that summer of 1846. His temperament was not improved when he learned that Colonel B. H. Pierce, his commanding officer, had reported the previous December that Company G was not properly worked up. Pierce had reviewed Winder's company shortly after their arrival at Fort Brooke and found them lacking in discipline and a "soldier-like" appearance, but he pointed out that the company was far understrength and contained a number of new recruits.

Pierce's report was really not that critical, but Winder wrote a long letter of protest and made some intemperate remarks. He pointed out that Pierce had prevented him from drilling his eleven recruits as a unit and stated that he was not surprised that the company was in bad shape. He also took exception to Pierce's remarks about discipline being laggard and then took him to task in the following manner: "How far Col. Pierce is qualified to judge of the proficiency of troops in their exercises, is questionable, as he made two distinct attempts to carry the troops through the manual [of arms] exercise, and failed signally both times."[28]

Pierce was not the only recipient of Winder's wrath that month. At a party hosted by the Winders, Caroline mentioned to the wife of Captain Lucien Webster, who was on detached duty, that she supposed the Websters would soon be vacating their quarters. A misunderstanding resulted, and Mrs. Webster wrote her husband that she would not be allowed to retain their quarters. Webster immediately wrote the adjutant general and complained vehemently about Winder's conduct in ordering his wife out of her house. Winder was initially dumbfounded when he learned of Webster's charges, but this soon turned to anger. He confronted Mrs. Webster with her false statements, and she immediately notified her husband and the adjutant general that she was at fault. She stated that Winder had shown her every courtesy and had never intimated that she would be required to move. She accepted full responsibility and apologized for the entire episode, but her husband did not follow her example. Predictably, Webster soon received a blunt message from Winder. He told Webster that he would be far better served in the future to ascertain the facts before attempting to sully anyone's reputation, and concluded: "You may rest satisfied that Mrs. Webster shall not be troubled and that everything will be done for her comfort that I can do—this I would have done both as a pleasure and a duty—now I do it as duty."[29] Clearly, his was not an irenic nature.

The foregoing passages provide some insight into Winder's attitudes and character at that date. He had little use for civilians who complicated his mission, especially those who dispensed alcohol in the area of his command. And he wanted his orders obeyed, even somewhat trivial ones such as his standing order regarding hogs depredating public property. His professional judgment of Pierce's report was sound and accurate; but his personal attack was totally unnecessary and illustrative of how sensitive he was to any criticism that might damage his professional image and reputation. His explanation of the Webster affair was satisfactory, and the matter was unimportant anyway. Webster clearly erred in the course he took, and his failure to apologize is inexplicable. In that instance, Winder's reaction is perhaps more understandable, if not commendable, and clearly indicates that he would not take the initiative in resolving a dispute when he was the injured party. Many if not most professional soldiers were vain and irascible, and their temperaments were not improved by the strains of living together in enforced intimacy at stultifying, isolated, and unimportant peacetime postings. Petty problems could become major disputes, and this happened to Winder on more than one occasion.

Perhaps the most important reason for Winder's acerbity that summer was that there was a war on, he was not in it, and his company continued to decline in strength and numbers. He reported in September that over one-third of his men were ill and that he had been forced to hire a civilian to lacquer some of the ordnance to protect it from the salt air. He reported that his convalescents were unable to perform even light duty. "I almost despair of seeing them well this winter." By the first of September he had only thirteen men present for duty.[30]

While his men struggled to regain their health and to finish the work on the fort, Winder was ordered to Mobile to muster in a company of Alabama volunteers for duty in Mexico. He remained there for most of December and disgustedly reported that red tape had snarled the procedures to such an extent that many of the men either returned home or enlisted in a Louisiana unit; the Alabama company could not be mustered. He had wasted a month and was not in a festive mood when he returned on 23 December to celebrate Christmas with his family.

If anything more was needed to increase his frustrations, it was a letter from his brother William informing him that their sister was married. William was disturbed that Charlotte Aurelia had been seeing James Townsend of New York, a man fifteen years older than she. His means were "abundant for a single man but small for a family," and his character was not quite up to William's standards. He opposed the marriage, but Charlotte prevailed and the marriage was performed at his house in Philadelphia. On the positive side, Winder learned that his mother was healthy and wintering in Washington with Charles, whose law practice was booming, and that his son William Andrew was seeking a commission in the army after successfully completing his collegiate career.[31]

Winder's attitude toward his son's decision to enter the army is not recorded in any of the correspondence that has survived, but he was almost certainly proud and enthusiastic about it. He had attempted to secure an appointment for William Andrew at West Point, had personally taught all of his sons the basics of engineering, and had certainly instilled in them his own deeply held concepts of honor and duty to country— concepts that he tried to exemplify throughout his career. He ardently believed that all true patriots should rally around the flag during a time of crisis. Later on, he was proud that all of his sons served during the Civil War, each according to his beliefs, and he almost certainly supported William Andrew's decision to enter the military at this time.

If his exact reaction toward his son's decision is unknown, his own attitude toward the Mexican War is a matter of record. He received the welcome news in January 1847 that he would finally be allowed to go to Mexico. Only by distinguishing himself in war could he acquire the reputation he so ardently desired, and perhaps restore the Winder name to one of respect in military history. To some extent, he shared the outlook of his friend and fellow officer, Captain Robert Anderson, that "no more absurd scheme could be invented for settling national difficulties . . . killing each other to find out who is in the right." But, like Anderson, he knew that war was the one way to rapid promotion and military distinction.[32] Winder was ordered to take his company to Tampico, then under American siege and soon to become the headquarters for Winfield Scott's advance to Mexico City. For both military and political reasons, President James K. Polk relegated Taylor's offensive in northern Mexico to a secondary role. The major thrust would be directed by Scott, who decided to follow the same route taken by Cortez in 1519. Winder worked diligently to ready his company for action, but he still found time to make a personal purchase: a small United States flag which he vowed would be the first flag to fly over the capital of a conquered Mexico.[33]

Shortly after bidding his family farewell, Winder must have feared that he was not destined to even reach Tampico, much less raise his flag over Mexico City. On 12 February 1847 he reported from the Chandeleur Islands that Company G, on board the schooner *Elizabeth*, had "sailed on the morning of the 11th and went ashore at 12 o'clock same night on this island and is totally wrecked; with much difficulty we saved the troops and guns." A storm caused the boat to founder, and it took them over nine hours to make it to the island. The sea was cold and the pounding of the waves severe, but "not a murmur was heard from the men, not a breach of discipline even the most minute and I say with pleasure that the behavior of the company during the whole time was such to make me feel proud of their discipline."[34]

A fishing boat rescued the company, and they reached New Orleans on 13 February. The men had salvaged their guns and anything that would float, but much necessary materiel was lost and it would take time to refit. While Winder was delayed, Scott took Tampico and then occupied Vera Cruz in late March. His next objective was Jalapa, about seventy-five miles in the interior, and elements of his army moved toward that city on 8 April. Winder arrived in Vera Cruz three days later. Captain Anderson noted that Winder arrived with only twenty-eight men on that Sunday evening but that he had not seen him. "Indeed our Army covers so much ground that I do not attempt visiting anyone."[35]

Winder and Anderson met the next day, when Company G was ordered to escort a siege train to Jalapa under Anderson's command. Winder remained in Vera Cruz to take charge of some five hundred recruits and departed for Jalapa after a week. The country was low and sandy for the first fifty miles, and the march was hot and dusty. There was much straggling because of heat prostration, and Anderson reported that about one-half the company fell out.

The first range of hills was near Cerro Gordo, and it was at this strong point that the Mexican army made a stand. The Americans attacked and secured the place on 19 April, but only after a fierce engagement. Anderson's command was not in the battle—"by some mismanagement we were delayed"—and the march continued. Scott's forces occupied Jalapa that same day, and Puebla, which was about eighty miles from Mexico City, fell to them on 15 May. The army paused for the next three months to regroup and await replacements for men whose twelve-month enlistment had expired. Winder reached Jalapa with the recruits in late April. He had come under sporadic fire during the march but suffered no casualties. He resumed command of Company G and set about whipping it into shape.[36]

Winder's unit was assigned to Colonel Thomas Childs, commander of the Second Brigade in the Second Division of General David Twiggs. Childs and Winder came to dislike each other intensely before the war was over, and this hampered Winder's career to some extent, but both worked diligently to drill their men into an effective fighting force during the next six weeks.

Childs's brigade was ordered to join the rest of the division at Puebla to begin the drive to Mexico City on 18 June. The enemy occupied the mountain pass at La Hoya when the American offensive halted, and the brigade had to overcome it before the command could unite. Childs placed Winder in charge of the advance guard, consisting of two companies, and he experienced his first combat command on 19 June. Childs succinctly reported that the "cautious approach of Capt. Winder enabled him to fire with effect" and that after his attack had secured the heights, the brigade reached Puebla without further incident.

There was more to the skirmish at La Hoya than Childs reported. Although the engagement was brief and rather insignificant, Winder showed his fitness as a battlefield commander. As Childs noted, Winder approached the enemy cautiously. He personally scouted their position and concluded that an immediate flank attack would surprise the enemy and clear the pass. He realized that speed was essential and did not wait for the brigade to come up, much to Childs's annoyance. But, he also knew the difference between speed and haste. He positioned his untested troops with care before launching an all-out attack. Realizing that it was vital for his men to see their commander in action, he led the assault. The men responded to his aggressive leadership, took the high ground, and routed the enemy. They killed four Mexican soldiers, captured three, and suffered no casualties.[37]

The arrival of reinforcements at Puebla permitted Scott to reorganize the army, and he attached the First Artillery to the First Brigade, Twiggs's division. The division moved out in early August, and Winder's company was again in the vanguard. He had honed Company G to a fine edge, and the results were soon evident. Winder set a brutal pace and permitted no straggling. He pushed forward across the continental divide and reached Ayola, seventy miles from Puebla, in only three days. His company again saw action on 16 October at Ocalaca, where he caught up with the Mexican rear guard as they retreated toward Contreras. Winder again attacked immediately, killed five of the enemy, and incurred no casualties.[38]

The fight at Ocalaca was limited and not sufficiently noteworthy to call Winder's performance to the attention of senior commanders. As Captain Anderson recorded in some detail, all officers of his rank faced great difficulty in gaining recognition for meritorious accomplishments.

A Capt. of the line of the Army has the least possible chance of being mentioned among the *distinguished*, however distinguished his conduct may be. The reason why, is a very simple one. As he is *part* of a Command, whether Regt. or Battalion, whatever is done by the *Regt.* or *Battalion*, is placed to the credit of *its* commander. It is only by a captain's being detached with his Compy. on some special service that he has a chance to distinguish himself. Hence the advantage of an officer's commanding a Battery. . . . If I should be brevetted, it will be *luck*. Genl. Scott, though my best friend, cannot designate me, unless I am reported to him—the ill-will or ill-temper of the Regt. Commander might not, even under a highly favorable case, give him an opportunity of so doing.[39]

The future hero of Fort Sumter was generally correct in his appraisal but too pessimistic in his predictions. Although neither he nor Winder commanded a battery, both achieved recognition and promotion. Anderson was wounded at Molino del Rey and finished the war as a brevet major. Winder would go him one better; he was brevetted twice and attained the rank of brevet lieutenant colonel.

The first real opportunity for Winder to distinguish himself in exceptional fashion came on 20 August 1847. Scott decided to attack Mexico City from the south and planned a flanking movement to secure the Acapulco road. The Mexicans anticipated this action and placed four thousand men on the fortified hill of Padierna, just north of Contreras. The position was strong, but the Americans executed a night march on 19 August and attacked the defenders from the rear at daybreak. The enemy was routed within twenty minutes.

Childs did not mention Winder in his report, but he should have. He reported that as the First Brigade moved toward the fort, he observed a large body of the enemy on its left flank and ordered "Maj. Dimick to face the brigade to the left and, advancing in line, attack this force in flank. This was done in the finest style, and the 1st artillery . . . met the enemy outside the work . . . and the whole gave way. Cavalry, formed in line for the charge, yielding [sic] to the bayonets of our foot, the rout was complete."[40]

Major Justin Dimick, Winder's old friend and immediate commander, had reported to Childs that of the twelve officers and two hundred-plus men in the First Brigade's attack, Winder merited special mention. He stated that Winder's company "was on the hill and in pursuit of the enemy a little in advance of the other portions of the regiment. He . . . came within half musket range, and poured a destructive fire upon them in their flight."[41] Winder's performance was easily the most impressive turned in by the regiment, but it was merely a warm-up for what followed before the day was done.

The Americans pressed on after their victory at Contreras but soon encountered stiff resistance at nearby Churubusco. After a series of skirmishes, the battle concentrated before a massive stone convent. The structure, built by the Franciscans in 1768 on the site of an Aztec temple, was partially concealed by tall cornfields. The Americans seriously underestimated the extent of the works and the strength of the defenders. The result was a three-hour bloodbath, and Winder was in the thick of it.

As Twiggs's division approached Churubusco, the First Artillery was

detached to support a contingent of rifles in an attack on the western
bastion of the convent. The officer in charge of the reconnaissance erroneously reported that the enemy had only one piece of artillery in place
and that the position should fall rather easily. Misled by this report, Dimick deployed his five companies for the attack. Lieutenant G. W. Smith
of the engineers later reported, "[Dimick's command] filed by and soon
encountered, at the distance of one hundred and fifty yards from the
enemy, the heaviest fire of artillery and musketry that I ever heard."[42]

The report of the brigade commander, General Persifor F. Smith, revealed the extent of the miscalculation and the disastrous consequences
it held for the First Artillery.

> At this time, the tremendous fire from the neighborhood of the
> church showed clearly, not only that there was a strong force sta-
> tioned there, but that there was also a more considerable work there
> than was at first supposed . . . the place was regularly fortified.
> The church buildings formed a large square; the lower front toward
> us was chiefly a wall scaffolded for infantry. Behind it rose a higher
> building also covered with infantry; behind it the church and a high
> steeple . . . also filled with men. In front [of the whole] was a curtain
> [wall] connecting two salient angles . . . garrisoned by about two
> thousand men and . . . seven [artillery] pieces. What was supposed
> to be the one-gun battery was the salient angle which enfiladed the
> road, so that when the 1st artillery attempted to turn it, they found
> themselves . . . exposed to all the musketry of the walls beyond.
> They, however, stood their ground with great loss, getting such cover
> as the ground afforded, and firing at the embrasures when opportu-
> nity offered.[43]

Major Dimick stated in his report that the attack had pushed off at
noon. "Almost immediately a shower of musketry, grape, and round shot,
poured upon us under which the battalion advanced" and encountered
"a regular bastion front, the curtain of which had four pieces in embra-
sure, besides nearly a thousand infantry, both of which kept up such
a constant stream of fire that I could not advance . . . and ordered the
men to cover themselves as well as possible."

For over two hours the regiment moved slowly toward the bastion.
Casualties mounted, but there was no panic. The extreme right of the
American line advanced to within one hundred yards of the objective,
but Winder moved under ferocious fire "to within seventy yards of the
works, being exposed to the fire of two pieces of artillery *en barbette*,
in addition to the fire of a considerable force of infantry." Winder's men
maintained a terrific fire "on the cannoniers and infantry" so that "the
enemy were driven from their guns and bastion . . . and surrendered."
Elements of the Third Infantry joined Winder's final assault. The two

regiments became intermingled and poured into the fort together. Winder became tangled up in the mass, and an infantry captain was the first officer to enter the bastion and accept the surrender; but Winder's role was decisive and Dimick gave him full credit. His report resulted in Winder being brevetted major for "gallant and meritorious conduct in the battles of Contreras and Churubusco."[44]

Casualties were heavy for the First Artillery, as they were for all units engaged. The army as a whole suffered over one thousand men killed, wounded, or missing in action, or about one in seven; but the enemy was completely overwhelmed. Some three thousand Mexican prisoners were taken, and the way was finally open for an assault on Mexico City if that proved necessary. Regimental losses were 21 killed out of 228 engaged, and 7 were from Company G. Winder's unit had finally been bloodied.[45]

General Antonio López de Santa Anna asked Scott for an armistice the day after the battle, but the peace talks were not productive. The final campaign for the conquest of the capital pushed off in early September, and there was a sharp fight at Molino del Rey on 8 September. Five days later the Americans attacked Chapultepec, the last barrier between them and Mexico City proper. The two main gates or causeways into the city were San Cosme and Garrista de Belen (a garrista, or garita, was a fortified stone building normally used as a police or customs station). Winder was ordered to take the Belen causeway. He succeeded after a hard fight and came within inches of being killed. "A round that knocked off the head of one of my men who stood close to me scattered his brains in my face & a piece of the bone of the scull cut me in the face."[46] Wiping away the gore, Winder continued the attack without faltering. His coolness and bravery commanded the respect of the entire regiment.[47]

The Americans entered Mexico City on 14 September, and Winder was ordered to take two companies to silence an artillery force positioned on a bridge. He reported in the early afternoon that he had driven "the enemy off . . . & put an end to the fire from that Quarter."[48] For his conduct at Chapultepec and Mexico City he was made brevet lieutenant colonel. Winder basked in the recognition of his military valor, but at Belen he had obtained his victory at a high price. Among the forces opposing him were the young boys from the Mexican Military Academy. These cadets were decimated by Winder's attack.[49] If he ever felt remorse, it went unrecorded, but this calamity left bitter memories in Mexico for a long time. The wound was not healed until a century later, when President Harry S. Truman paid homage to the memory of "Los Niños."

Winder was apparently successful in attaining another of his goals, the raising of the first flag over the capital, but he did not receive the credit.

The Marines were nationally depicted unfurling the stars and stripes over the "halls of Montezuma," but Winder was first. An officer who witnessed the event recorded that the initial flag raised "was a small one which [Captain] Winder had long carried on his person. It was the size of a very large pocket handkerchief."[50] Had he been hailed in the national press for his accomplishment, it would have gone a long way toward restoring the Winder military reputation, but that was not to be.

The conquest of Mexico City virtually ended the fighting, and the military occupation began while the diplomats tried once again to effect a treaty of peace. Twelve cities were placed under martial law and garrisoned with American troops until August 1848. Winder was ordered to Vera Cruz on 9 December and designated lieutenant governor of that city. He arrived on the 22nd of the month with the remnants of his company and took up his official duties. He was charged with keeping the peace and was given adequate authority and resources to do so. Besides Company G, he also had Company H directly under his command and three other companies on standby if needed.[51] In addition to being chief of police, he presided over military courts and dispensed the punishments ordered, attended to the needs of prisoners, arranged for guards, and established day and night watches for civilian and military jails. It was a demanding position, but he was well paid for his efforts. His salary as lieutenant governor was $200 per month, and his treasurer's fees exceeded $775 for the seven months he was in Vera Cruz.[52]

There was need for disciplinary actions in the occupied city almost daily. Fights between civilians and enlisted men were common and sometimes ended in death. Stiff sentences were the rule for enlisted men. The culprits were fined, jailed, confined to hard labor with ball and chain, or flogged. The court ordered Winder in June to "cause Charles Vernon to receive fifty lashes, well laid on his back, with a raw hide." Capital punishment was also in evidence. On 23 March, Private Henry Clark was found guilty of murder, and Winder hanged him that same day.[53]

Winder spent much of his time serving on courts-martial and dealing with prisoners, but among his many other duties he had to approve the issue of all gambling licenses, return all captured runaway slaves, and censor the press. He ordered the editor of the *Arco Iris* to report to him and explain his remarks about the conduct of American officers at Castle San Juan de Ulloa. After his meeting with Winder, the editor decided his remarks were not true and repudiated his earlier statements in the next issue.[54]

Winder gained much experience in Vera Cruz that he would later need in governing Richmond, but not all of that experience was transferable to another situation. He was firm but fair, and his rule was effective. He was not squeamish when an iron hand was needed, and though he instantly complied with orders that mandated executions, he did not act in a cruel or arbitrary manner. The Mexican people under his control certainly resented the American presence but were generally docile. Most of Winder's troubles came from within the army, and he handled them with dispatch. All in all, he was an excellent administrator, but he was operating in a conquered country with the full force of the military behind him, not in his own homeland and not against his own countrymen. He excelled in administering martial law in Vera Cruz because he had few limits placed on his actions. If the press aroused his ire, he censored the offending material or closed the publication down. If the peace was broken, he had the troops at hand to quell any disturbance. He proved conclusively that he could control a captive people and unruly soldiers, but this was not the situation he faced during the Civil War. He learned then, probably to his great dismay, that he could not treat Richmonders as defeated subjects or trample their cherished freedoms with impunity, as he was able to do in Vera Cruz.

Winder's stint as lieutenant governor came to an end with the signing of a peace treaty on 29 July 1848. Two days later he was ordered to join his regiment aboard the *Iowa* bound for New York. He was to go to Pensacola and pick up all regimental and company property there before rejoining his command at Fort Columbus, New York. His unit sailed on 1 August, the last to leave Mexico.[55]

Winder obtained leave in mid-September and joined his family at Smithville for the last time. It was at this time that they decided to sell the plantation, and the family dispersed to various parts of the country, never again to be united as a group. Second Lieutenant William Andrew Winder, sworn in on 17 March 1848, departed for duty in California, John Cox and Sidney returned to Columbiad College near the national capital, and Winder took his wife and daughter with him to New York.[56]

Brevet Lieutenant Colonel Winder assumed command of Fort Columbus on Governors Island in New York Harbor in March 1849 and did not depart until December of the next year. It was an extremely pleasant twenty-one-month assignment for the whole family. Duty was light and the Winders had ample opportunity to sample the sights and excitement of New York City. It was the first time that Caroline and Carrie were not attended by slaves, their first experience—and probably a novel one—with free labor. Winder hired an English-born mulatto, William Day, as his personal steward and engaged two young Irish women as household servants.[57] It can be assumed that the Irish temperament was considerably different from what Caroline and Carrie were accustomed to, but even if angry outbursts occurred, it was far better than the ordeal they soon endured in Florida.

Winder was ordered in December 1850 to take command of Fort

Myers in southern Florida, deep in the troubled area known as the Seminole reservation. Although the Seminole War was declared at an end in 1842 and the remnants of "the nation" confined to the Everglades region, the situation remained volatile. Whites advanced into the Seminole domain and sporadic conflicts occurred in 1849. The army was again dispatched to garrison existing forts, construct new ones, and resume the attempt to relocate the Seminoles in the western reservations.[58]

General David Twiggs, placed in command of the army in Florida in 1849, began the task of reestablishing the army's presence in the area. Fort Brooke, headquarters for the army, and the adjacent village of Tampa had been completely destroyed by a hurricane in 1848. Within two years, Twiggs had rebuilt the fort and Tampa had a population of 441 people.[59]

Twiggs next determined to erect a major fort in the Indian country. The location for this post was largely determined by the matter of supply. All army supplies were shipped to Tampa, off-loaded, then transshipped where possible or carried overland to interior forts. Overland travel was onerous and would become dangerous if hostilities were resumed. Twiggs wanted the post to be on or near a navigable body of water, and he chose the location in February 1850. Fort Myers, built on the site of old Fort Harvie and named for Twiggs's son-in-law, was on the Caloosahatchee River about fifteen miles inland from the gulf. Twiggs further determined that only the finest materials and workmanship would suffice, and he mobilized a substantial labor force of military and civilian, skilled and unskilled, free and slave workers and began the assault on the wilderness in August 1850. The work continued for several years, and almost sixty impressive structures were ultimately built.

When Winder and his family arrived on 10 December 1850, some of the officers' homes were in place, a 1,000-foot wharf extended into the river, and plans had been made for the barracks, administration building, blockhouse, guardhouse, bakery, blacksmith shop, sutler's store, warehouse, and stables. The Indians were peaceful and visited the fort regularly, and whites frequently sat at Indian campfires near the compound. Seafood of all description was plentiful and the climate was pleasant, but the idyllic ambience of the post was negated by the remoteness of the location. It was an oasis in the middle of the wilderness. "There was not a single settler or trace of civilization in the surrounding country," and the nearest town was Tampa, one hundred miles away by boat.[60]

Duty at Fort Myers proved to be hard on the women. Nearly cut off from civilization and dependent upon the garrison for companionship, Caroline and Carrie must have felt that they had entered a new and forlorn world. Fishing, swimming, sailing, even extended visits with the Seminoles, soon paled into a deadly monotony. Life at the post was far removed from the bustle of New York City or the quiet civility of Wilmington. Few of the officers had their families with them, and some of the women in residence were not socially acceptable. As Sidney soon recorded, his mother and sister were "burned up, as it were, shut out from all society."[61]

The posting also took its toll on Winder. It was the most trying tour of his career, and the Indians constituted only a minor part of his troubles. Winder was under the overall command of Brevet Brigadier General Thomas Childs, his superior during the Mexican War, who took over from Twiggs on 12 November 1850. The two men did not like each other personally, and Childs had slighted Winder professionally during the war. Their relationship, initially at least, was correct if not cordial, but they became bitter enemies before Winder's tour was over.

Childs sailed from Fort Brooke early in 1851 and inspected Winder's Fort Myers command on 11 January. Accompanying Childs was Brevet Colonel Samuel Cooper. Cooper became adjutant general of the army the next year and assumed the same position in the Confederacy in 1861. If Childs was hostile, Cooper was anything but. He knew Winder better and for a longer period than anyone except Winder's family. Their relationship went back to 1814 at West Point, and they remained close friends for over fifty years. Cooper's respect for Winder increased over the years, and he was one of Winder's strongest defenders during and after the Civil War.[62]

Present at Fort Myers was the veteran Indian agent, Captain John Casey. Casey was more knowledgeable about the Seminoles than any white in or out of the army. He and Winder had served together during the Second Seminole War, and Winder had a high regard for Casey's abilities. They were in agreement as to what had to be done, and Casey acted as spokesman when Childs and Cooper arrived. In their estimation, the task facing the army was formidable. A plan to police the area effectively while simultaneously enacting the long-range policy of Indian removal had to be devised. Casey believed, correctly as it turned out, that another war would ultimately be necessary to achieve the goal of eliminating the Seminole presence in Florida. In the meantime, a series of roads and forts should be built in strategic areas of the Indian country, and that would be no mean task.

The Seminole reservation in 1851 was ill defined but covered a vast area west of Lake Okeechobee and south of present-day Sebring. The logical location for a string of forts was along the Peace River, from present day Bartow south to Punta Gorda. They could be supplied overland from Fort Brooke when necessary and by the Peace when conditions permitted. The Peace was as capricious a waterway as there was in the state. Navigable for only part of the year, the river ranged from a raging torrent flooding its banks to a trickle that could easily be waded by a small child.[63]

Childs gave tentative approval to the proposal, but no comprehensive plan had been developed when he received orders to report to California and relinquished command to Winder on 10 April 1851. Winder was now in charge of the whole operation, and before a year passed, he found himself at odds with the secretary of the interior, the paymaster for the southeastern states, and ultimately, Thomas Childs.

Winder increased the number and scope of scouting missions and military patrols in an attempt to gain a more accurate overview of the situation. He strongly backed Casey's efforts to assemble the chiefs at Fort Myers for a decisive conference, and he continued to construct roads and forts in the interior. But his plans were hampered by bureaucratic interference from the newly created Department of the Interior before a month had passed.

Secretary of the Interior Alexander Stuart removed Casey from his position in May 1851 and appointed Luther Blake special Indian agent. Blake had performed well during the Creek removal in Georgia, and Stuart had full confidence in him. Blake reached Fort Myers on 8 May, and Winder and Casey cordially welcomed him. Blake soon concluded that a delegation of western Indians to serve as go-betweens with the Seminoles was an absolute necessity, and he told Winder on 20 May that he would leave for the West immediately. He asked Winder to serve as Indian agent in his absence.

In the meantime Winder wrote Adjutant General Roger Jones on 8 June to ask for guidance on another matter. He informed Jones that a small band of Indians led by Chief Itchu Emathla had been living "north of the reservation line" but that they "had moved down into the nation" as per his orders. However, the chief wanted permission to round up his hogs, which were spread out in the area bounded by Lakes Okeechobee, Kissimmee, and Istokpoga. He asked Jones to contact the proper department to see if permission could be granted, and added that he had opened the Fort Myers trading post and that the Seminoles were not content with their ammunition allotment. "Captain Casey says one-half [keg of] powder and from 4 to 6 pounds [of shot] for each man per annum is enough. Bowlegs and other chiefs think not. Will the Department please instruct me on this point and at what age [Indian] boys are to be entitled to the privilege of purchasing ammunition."[64]

Jones passed Winder's request to the War Department, which forwarded it to Interior. Over a month passed before Winder received an answer, and it was not what he had expected. Secretary Stuart bluntly informed him in July that he had no authority to do anything without special orders from Interior, that there was a Department of Indian Affairs for Florida, that Blake was the only authorized Indian agent, and that Interior would welcome Winder's assistance only if it became necessary.[65] For once, Winder did not respond in characteristic fashion, but this did not mean that he had mellowed over the years. He was crustier than ever, as the next several months would prove. He was simply too busy with his myriad duties at that time to lodge a protest. Also, he may have consoled himself with the knowledge that Blake's widely publicized mission for the Interior Department was anything but a success.

Blake planned to assemble the leading chiefs at Fort Myers and then take them to the White House for a personal meeting with the president. Winder assisted in gathering the chiefs but studiously stayed clear of the rest of the operation. Billy Bowlegs and other leaders left Fort Myers for Washington, D.C., in July 1852 to meet with President Millard Fillmore. Interior officials in the capital and other cities feted the Indians in an attempt to induce them to move to the western reservations. They gave gifts and promises, but it was all in vain. Fewer than forty Seminoles emigrated, and the Indian problem was transferred from Interior to the War Department the following year. Blake was removed in June 1853, and Casey resumed his position. Blake billed the government almost $48,000 for his efforts and eventually collected over $20,000. Even the reduced figure meant that it cost over $500 for each Indian who left, hardly a bargain rate.[66]

It was fortunate for one of Winder's men that all Seminoles had not departed. He reported in February 1852 that the drummer boy, Theodore Rogers, wandered from the post, "got lost in Big Cypress Swamp, and stayed that way for eight days." Winder hired several Indians to find Rogers, and it required nine days to restore his health. Winder paid them ninety dollars for their efforts.[67]

The remoteness of Fort Myers added to Winder's command problems. He reported in March 1852 that no paymaster had been to the post for over six months. Major G. H. Ringold was the paymaster, but he remained in Charleston and employed an agent to provide the service. This arrangement was clearly not effective, and Winder and the paymaster were soon engaged in a minor altercation. Winder initiated the dispute in innocent enough fashion on 9 August 1851, when he informed Ringold that he had no authority to turn over the muster rolls to two Tampa men who claimed to be the paymaster's agents. He asked Ringold if he should send the rolls to him or to the paymaster in New Orleans. It was a cordial letter and deserved a more civil answer. Ringold replied:

> it has been the custom time out of mind, as I have no doubt you are fully aware, for Pay Masters to make use of the agency of Sutlers in the payment of such troops . . . as may be remote. . . . But as your letter unavoidably leads me to conclude that you feel disposed to set aside this time honored custom I take occasion to inform you that I have full authority from the Pay Master General to use the services of sutlers in making payments to troops. . . . It is not my desire to raise any disagreeable issue between yourself & myself officially or in any other way. . . . I write this in the very best

spirit imaginable to show you in the first place, that I do not act without authority, and in the next that I have the interest & convenience of yourself & those under your command as much at heart as yourself. . . . I would be glad to hear from you in the same friendly spirit in which I have written this.

Winder promptly honored the request. Employing the same thinly veiled sarcastic tone utilized by Ringold, he informed the paymaster that during nearly thirty years' service he had never seen payment by proxy but had heard of an occasional case. He continued:

I have no disposition to set aside any custom or to give any body inconvenience & I do not think my letter . . . will evidence any such disposition, if any such custom did exist, the late order in relation to pay Rolls would put an end to it.

. . . As you seem to lay great store upon his [a certain Ferris from Tampa] being Sutler I will state for your information, that he is not sutler, he was removed before my arrival. . . .

Pay Masters have other duties which cannot be done by proxy, one is the receipt from officers of money belonging to . . . deceased officers and soldiers . . . [and] there are several at the post now.
. . .

P.S. There is one point I have omitted, you say it is not your desire to make any disagreeable issue with me officially or otherwise, if such is made it will be your doing, for I make no issue at all, I simply pursue such course as I think plainly marked out by the orders & regulations.

After this exchange, each man having satisfied his ego by informing the other of how he should correctly perform his duty, Ringold became conciliatory and indicated a willingness to end the dispute. Winder agreed, but only after notifying Assistant Adjutant General W. W. Bliss in March 1852 that Ringold's designated agent had attempted to reach the fort in December but lost the payroll when he was attacked by Indians. He concluded: "I hope some remedy will be applied to correct the evil—it is unjust to the men to keep them six months without pay—and now it will be eight months before they can be paid."[68]

It was at this time that General Childs returned to Florida. He relieved Winder of command on 4 March 1852, and established his headquarters at Fort Brooke. On 30 April he issued Special Order No. 4, stating that since most of the forts would be abandoned as soon as the Indian removal was complete, they should be built as inexpensively as possible. To that end, no skilled workmen should be hired and soldiers should not receive extra pay for "constant duty" for a period exceeding ten days without his permission. On 5 May he decreed that the special order applied to

Fort Myers.[69] It took more than two weeks for news to travel from Tampa to Fort Myers. Meanwhile, Winder had written Childs, on 4 May, that he would need skilled labor and that extra duty for the men would be required to complete the barracks at Fort Myers and to build an interior fort on the Peace River. Unaware of the special order, he left his post in early May and built Fort Winder, about two miles from present-day Fort Ogden.[70] He kept the men on constant duty until both projects were finished and sent a bill for $96.45 on 21 August. He stated that the extra pay was necessary, since the climate and hard work had ruined his men's clothing, and that he had been forced to hire skilled carpenters and masons to complete the barracks at Fort Myers.

Childs not only refused to authorize the expenditure, he brought charges against Winder on 8 September 1852. He charged Winder with willful disobedience of orders and neglect of duty. He stated that this was not the first time that Winder had been guilty of disobedience and that "no matter how distinguished an officer's record is he *must* obey his superior's orders."[71] This was the only serious charge ever made against Winder and he was, in turn, incredulous, outraged, and ultimately convinced that he was the victim of a conspiracy whose root cause was embodied in the sectionalism present in the army. His defense was meticulously compiled and convincingly professional, but he could not conceal his hostility and ended with a scathing personal attack on Childs.

He responded to the accusal in November and included ten "exhibits" from various officers and offices proving that he had been neither disobedient nor neglectful in any manner. He informed Adjutant General Cooper of the specific charges and dealt with them in order. To the first charge, willful disobedience of a posted order, Winder responded that (1) he was not aware of the order when he began the projects; (2) he had informed Childs on 4 May, before the special order included Fort Myers, that the projects would require the additional expenses associated with extra duty and that Childs had acquiesced for over four months, thus indicating tacit approval; and (3) Special Order No. 4 was illegal in that it violated the 1819 congressional act regarding constant duty. Winder admitted that Childs could have "an opinion" about the legality of his order but that it did "not make it binding."

The neglect of duty charge concerned Winder's estimate of the number of men required for extra duty and his failure to clear the details with Childs before issuing the vouchers for the additional money. This dealt exclusively with the Fort Myers project, and Winder was fully aware of Childs's order before the barracks were finished. Winder's explanation was that (1) the timber had to be cut and hauled in from the cypress swamp and the lime burned from the oyster shells while the weather permitted; (2) the building had to be finished before the rainy season began in June, since "you cannot lath and plaster in the rain"; and

(3) the four men permitted extra duty by Childs were too few to complete the task. Winder then offered his explanation of why Childs brought the charges.

He stated that he "was much surprised as was every officer at the post" that the accusations had been made but that this was only one of many examples of Childs's personal hostility toward him. He stressed that Childs had returned after an eleven-month absence "completely ignorant of what was needed or planned" and brought charges simply to get them on his file "to my prejudice." Further, "[Childs] returned and relieved me from the command of the troops in Florida [on] 4 March 1852, and established his Head Quarters at Tampa on 14 March. Before notifying me that he had or was to assume command, he fired orders to the subordinates of the command and thereby, I think showed want of consideration and courtesy."[72]

Winder next referred to Childs's statement that he had been guilty of disobedience before. He asked, "If that was so, why wait eleven months to file charges, why not when I supposedly disobeyed orders then?" He concluded by charging that Childs "never went to California but ran around Washington for several months, in that time there was nothing on earth to prevent his preparing the charge to trial."[73]

Cooper forwarded the materials to the secretary of war on 13 October 1852. Winder's case was convincing, and the charges were dismissed. It was clear that Winder was correct when he charged that Childs was ignorant of what had transpired during his absence. The War Department did not judge Fort Myers to be a temporary post, and spending on a lavish scale continued for the rest of the decade. By 1859, there were fifty-seven large structures on the post, including a $30,000 hospital.[74] It was also true that the work on the barracks had to be completed before the rainy season began. Winder knew the climate and the local conditions, and he also knew that a major troop buildup was planned for Fort Myers. Childs had not seen the post for almost a year, but he, too, knew that troop strength was scheduled to increase, and it is difficult to see why he included Fort Myers in his special order.

Winder was at least partially correct when he stated that Childs had long been hostile toward him and brought charges simply to have them in his file. He failed to add that the animosity was mutual, though anyone reading his countercharges could come to no other conclusion. Personality clashes between army martinets occurred fairly frequently, but the enmity between Childs and Winder went deeper than mere personal dislike. Childs was an antislavery Massachusetts man of deep religious convictions, and Winder was, at that time, still a slave owner. Although the decision to sell the slaves had been made, he was not at all apologetic about his affiliation with the institution and was intensely proud of his southern heritage.

It is not surprising that sectional differences surfaced and intensified between Childs and Winder. This problem became increasingly prevalent in the army during the 1850s. Even the diplomatic Robert E. Lee, superintendent at West Point, found it impossible to preserve the "band of brothers" camaraderie, the esprit de corps for which the institution was famous. Winder and Childs were career professionals. They were supposed to be neutral toward national policies and priorities, above sectional disputes. They were not. In this case, it appears that Childs allowed his personal feelings to cloud his professional judgment. When Winder's actions were first brought to his attention by Major W. H. French, Childs preferred charges without conducting a thorough investigation.[75] He was apparently influenced by northern-born officers in his command, including Colonel Ira B. Crane. Crane, also from Massachusetts, made no secret of his dislike of the South and of Winder. In 1848, he had requested that the "First Regiment of Artillery be stationed in the northern states at the end of the [Mexican] war," and he was quick to vilify Winder during the Civil War.[76]

Winder's antipathy toward both Childs and Crane is well documented. Although he never hesitated to launch a written attack against his superiors when he felt he had been wronged, in no other instance did he react so venomously. He was normally content to dismiss the competence of his accuser with a sarcastic phrase or two, but not this time; his pernicious charges against Childs as a man and an officer consumed the better part of three pages.[77]

The intensity of his response also indicates that he was aware that a part of the charges was valid, for he was guilty of disobedience of orders. His explanation delineating the mitigating circumstances was sufficiently convincing to merit the dismissal of the charges, but he clearly violated standing orders when he placed the men on constant duty and hired skilled workmen to complete the barracks at Fort Myers. The truth seems to be that Winder had been in command and refused to change his plans when Childs returned. He remained convinced that only he knew the proper course of action for the whole area. The special order was, in his opinion, not only an obstacle to be ignored but proof that Childs did not know what he was doing. His later charge that the order was illegal because it violated an act of Congress was flimsy at best, but the rest of his defense was valid. The monetary sum in question was insignificant, the equivalent of one month's pay for a major, and the money had been well spent. But Childs was within his rights to bring charges.[78] An oral reprimand might have been more appropriate and if the two men had been on amicable terms, it is doubtful that the episode would have happened. Winder and Childs never reconciled. Childs had no more official trouble with Winder, but the malice each harbored ended only with Childs's death in 1853 of yellow fever.[79] The malevolence Crane felt for Winder, which was fully reciprocated, was ended only by Winder's death.

Winder had several close friends in the army who were northern-born and who stayed with the Union after the war began. Justin Dimick, for example, was from Connecticut. They had been fast friends since their cadet days, and their close relationship survived the turbulent 1850s and even the Civil War. Dimick was promoted to colonel in 1861 and placed in command of the prisoner-of-war camp at Fort Warren, Massachusetts.[80] In this capacity, he was aware of the problems Winder faced in the opposite camp. He knew, better than most contemporaries, how volatile the prisoner-of-war situation was, and he never criticized or censured Winder's actions toward Union prisoners during or after the war. Winder and Dimick were fundamentally opposed in their ultimate loyalty, but they respected each other's position and retained their mutual esteem. That was not true of Winder and Childs, and Winder became anxious to leave Fort Myers.

In January 1853, Winder asked for a six-month leave of absence. He was informed that he could not relinquish command of Fort Myers until the Indian delegation returned from its Washington visit. The dismal outcome of the Department of Interior's attempt to achieve a peaceful Indian emigration became public when two Jacksonville newspaper reporters interviewed Winder in April of that year. According to the *Florida Republican*, Winder stated that the Indians were "perfectly tranquil—bringing in the fruits of their nomadic exploits, game, including wild turkeys, which they are selling at twenty-five cents apiece."[81] More important, a reporter from the *Florida Mirror* announced: "We came through [Florida] in the stage with Col. Winder of the U.S. Army, commander of Fort Myers. He says the delegation which went . . . to Washington, left most of their presents at Fort Myers . . . and have since declined receiving them, as they have failed to comply with their promises of emigration. He says also be [*sic*] a careful estimate made by John Jumper, one of the western delegation, that there are only 286 Indians remaining in Florida, and only 86 of these are men and boys able to bear arms."[82] Winder concluded the interview by stating that the army hoped that peace would be preserved even though the Seminoles would not go to the western reservations.

Winder left Jacksonville in mid-April and went to Washington to furnish additional information regarding the audit of his Vera Cruz command. While there, he finalized the sale of the slaves. He and his family were finally financially secure, and they spent the rest of the year visiting relatives and friends. He was in Montpelier, Vermont, in August as a witness for Dimick in a lawsuit, and visited his eldest son in Rutland, Vermont, the following month. Among other things, he and Dimick wit-

nessed William Andrew's application for bounty land. The family spent
the rest of the year in the vicinity of Baltimore.[83]

Winder asked for six months' additional leave in September 1853, and
the request was granted. This was the first time he had taken such extensive leave, but it does not appear that he considered resigning from the
service, even though he was now financially independent. There was
no denying that the years had taken their toll on the Winder family.
Winder's hair was rapidly turning from iron gray to white, and his sturdy
physique was becoming decidedly portly. Carrie was thirty years old and
destined to remain unmarried, and Caroline was increasingly reluctant
to endure any more hardships in remote postings such as Fort Myers.
In addition, both of his brothers were prospering, his mother was in
good health, and Charlotte and her husband were enjoying a pleasant
life in Oyster Bay, New York. His son John Cox was a successful engineer
engaged in the construction of the Pennsylvania railroad system, and
Sidney was well on his way to becoming an attorney. All in all, Winder
had no pressing financial need to remain in the military.

While the frequency and extent of his absences increased markedly
after 1853, it is probable that he remained in the service simply because
he enjoyed the habit of command and could not envision a life of relative
leisure. Another explanation could be that he was still not content with
his military reputation. Or, he may just have followed the path of least
resistance, believing himself still unfit for anything but the military life
and still desirous of serving his country.

Winder's leave ended in April 1854, and he assumed command of Fort
Moultrie in the floral city of Charleston.[84] The next two years were personally felicitous, although sectional animosities were on the increase.
He and his family found Charleston a welcome change from Fort Myers,
and even though Winder never deeply imbibed South Carolina politics,
he was increasingly sympathetic to the radical position. The national situation deteriorated during his two years at Fort Moultrie. The passage
of the Kansas-Nebraska Act, the emergence of the Republican party,
"Bleeding Kansas," the Sumner-Brooks affair— all increased the probability that the nation would not endure. Dissolution and secession were
espoused by radicals in both the North and the South, but Winder
avoided the extremists. It was during this time that he most probably
came to feel that secession was a legitimate means of addressing injustices
inflicted on the South, but he never became actively involved in the
controversy. He kept his attention focused on his duty and on the men
under his command.

Winder was close to the men of Company G, and he was proud of
the veterans who stayed in the military after seeing duty in Mexico.
He sent several letters to the adjutant general in 1854 requesting that

certificates of merit be issued to three deserving soldiers in his command. These certificates were, in effect, the enlisted man's brevet and entitled the holder to an additional two dollars per month. In September, he stated: "I cannot but feel it a great injustice that these certificates have been withheld. Company G was in the actions of Cerro Gordo, La Hoya— the two days of Contreras, Churubusco, Chapultepec— Garrista De Belen & the city of Mexico & I think the records will show as many killed and wounded as any company in the Regt. I trust that certificates will be forwarded to the three men above mentioned."[85]

Not only did Winder treat his men generously, but he quickly offered their services and all the facilities of his command to the needy people of Charleston when a hurricane severely battered that city in September. His actions were remembered over a decade later when the Charleston press notified friends and foes alike that he had died in the service of the Confederacy.[86]

In July, Winder's brother William attempted to secure Winder's appointment as governor of the soldiers' asylum in Baltimore, apparently at the request of his mother. This was a lucrative position, and the post would enable him to finish his military career in his native city and spend the remaining years with his mother. The appeal was made to Secretary of War Jefferson Davis. William had a wide circle of acquaintances and considerable influence in Washington at that time. He had just sold the Winder Building to the government and was well known to Davis and others in prominent official positions. He was the regular Philadelphia correspondent for that city's *Daily News* as well as for the *Norfolk Day Book* and the Baltimore *Sun*.[87] Despite William's influence, Davis did not support the petition. This instance effectively refutes those later critics who maintained that Winder's position in the Confederacy was due solely to being Davis's "pet."

Winder's stay in Charleston ended in October 1856. He was ordered to Florida again, and he served in that state for the rest of his active career. On Christmas Day he arrived at Key West very much alone. It is very doubtful he could have attended the wedding of his son John Cox to Octavia Bryan in Raleigh on 20 December. Caroline and Carrie were at the Winder home in Baltimore, attending to the needs of his mother.[88]

Duty in the "southernmost city" was not as arduous as it had been at Fort Myers, but it was well that the women remained in Baltimore. Winder reported the following from Indian Key in September 1857:

The yellow fever having broken out at Key West of a very malignant type & every man in my company without exception is subject to the disease, I have deemed it prudent, after consulting with the medical officer at the post, to remove the command to this place.

I have employed a reliable citizen to take charge of the barracks at $75 per month and a ration & I have left the only man of my company not subject to the yellow fever to assist him. So far there are no symptoms of the fever among the men. My own health is so much impaired (not from fever) that I find a great difficulty in writing this communication.[89]

Winder was ordered to Fort Dallas (Miami) early in 1858 and took a leave of sixty days beginning in May. He rejoined his family in Baltimore, and they journeyed to New York City for a brief visit with John Cox and Octavia. This was Winder's first opportunity to meet his new daughter-in-law, whose engineer husband was then employed by the Croton Aqueduct Department of New York City. Winder returned to Florida in June and was ordered to abandon Fort Dallas and take his command to Pensacola. He sent for his family and moved into his old barracks in mid-June. At that time, Company G was eighty-nine strong, including the officers, and they had to garrison the three forts protecting Pensacola Bay.

The Third Seminole War (1855–58) was over when Winder assumed command in Pensacola. Garrison duty was not demanding, and the years were uneventful as far as his command was concerned, yet he grew increasingly lachrymose and frequently took leave in 1858 and 1859. His official reports grew more lackluster, and he made mistakes, something he had never previously done.[90] He was clearly worried about the future.

Having spent most of the 1850s in Florida and South Carolina, the two states where the secessionist impulse was strongest, he knew that sectional tensions were at the breaking point. Even the Dred Scott case, in which his old sponsor Chief Justice Taney proclaimed that slavery was national and could not be curtailed, was insufficient to ward off the fear and anger of the Lower South that resulted when the North condemned this view. Worse, several northern states passed personal liberty laws that nullified the fugitive slave provision in the Compromise of 1850, and the Republican victory in the 1858 off-year elections guaranteed that slavery would not expand into any territory without a fight, Supreme Court opinion notwithstanding.

Finally, there was John Brown. When the northern public cheered his goal of emancipation and made him an instant martyr, southerners felt threatened to the extent that they refused to believe the condemnations of Brown expressed by Lincoln, Seward, and other northern leaders. Southerners felt that the northern public approval of Brown was tantamount to a declaration of war. Southern honor would take little more. If a Republican president were elected, the last cord would be severed.

Winder was repeatedly subjected to the rising tide of southern emotion during these years, and it left him emotionally depressed. When he became physically ill in May 1860, he took leave and returned to Baltimore. He turned Company G over to Lieutenant Slemmer, and never saw it again. Eight months later, Florida seceded from the Union and demanded the surrender of the Pensacola forts. Winder was needed at his command, but, as has been related, he never went.

After enduring the torture of indecision for several months, he committed himself wholeheartedly to the Confederacy. Full of his old vigor and determination, he was again ready to do his duty. When the war began in earnest during the early months of 1862, the people of Richmond found out what it was like to come under the sway of this stern professional. He demanded much of himself and much from those under his command. They would not enjoy it, but many would agree that about everything he did and tried to do was necessary. Few would argue with the goals he espoused, but many would disagree with the means he employed to that end. Some would come to know him well and praise his actions; others would come to despise his very name; almost no one truly comprehended the type of man he actually was.

CHAPTER 7

"Dictator" of Richmond

1862–1864

By the spring of 1862, it appeared that Lincoln would soon restore the Union on his terms. After the defeat at Bull Run, Union forces made significant progress on every front. The rebels were forced out of Missouri, New Mexico, much of Tennessee, and the western part of Kentucky. New Orleans was in Union hands by May, and victory in the West seemed certain.

In the East, Port Royal, South Carolina, and part of eastern North Carolina fell to Union arms, and Richmond was in extreme peril. General George B. McClellan had finally embarked on his peninsular campaign to pierce the heart of the Confederacy. His magnificent Army of the Potomac, 110,000 strong, stood poised to conquer the Confederate capital, government, and principal army at one stroke. Victory for the Federal forces and the Union seemed assured.

President Davis conceded in his inaugural address on 22 February 1862 that the permanent government was replacing the provisional one at a critical hour. He addressed the issue of Confederate defeats and disasters, admitted that mistakes had been made in the conduct of the war, but expressed his firm conviction that the young nation would endure. There was little to justify Davis's optimistic assertion that a reversal of fortune would soon occur, but he was correct. Union blunders, coupled with an amazing rebel resurgence on both military and home fronts, resulted in the Confederacy coming very close to victory before the year ended. Union forces under McClellan were horribly misused, and General Ulysses S. Grant's victories were frittered away in the West. Rebel armies under able leadership went on the offensive.

Before 1862 was over, both sides realized that they were involved in a barbarous fight to the finish and that the whole tenor of the war had changed in a revolutionary manner. Lee's invasion of the Union was bloodily repulsed at Antietam. Lincoln issued his preliminary Emancipation Proclamation, and the war to restore the Union also became a crusade to abolish slavery in the Confederacy. This had a tremendous impact in Europe. It ended Confederate hopes that Britain and France would recognize their nation and force a quick end to the war by mediation.

The Confederacy would have to gain independence on the battlefield, and the leadership understood this. Every effort was made to attain victory in 1863. More men went into the armies than at any other time, and those on the home front had to sacrifice even more. Confidence was high, but the nascent nation almost broke under the burdens of total warfare.[1] The price of Confederate survival was dearly bought, not only with battlefield casualties but with the southern way of life. The most basic civil liberties—freedom of speech and assembly, protection from unreasonable search and seizure, trial by jury, the writ of habeas corpus—were frequently violated. Freedom of the press and the sanctity of private property were abused. Southerners suffered from attempts to impose wage and price controls, prohibit alcohol, impress goods, and abolish private ownership of firearms. Ultimately, the beliefs in state sovereignty, the right of secession, even the legitimacy of slavery, were destroyed by the demands of war. The conduct of the war went a long way toward killing the civilization southerners were trying to preserve and protect.

Americans, North and South, chafed under governmental restrictions, but southerners especially resisted the attempt to limit their personal liberties. Individual freedom, after all, was the reason white southerners seceded in the first place, and they did not surrender this belief easily. All attempts by the Richmond government to centralize the war effort at the expense of individualism were unpopular sooner or later, and the agents charged with implementing the hostile actions were intensely disliked. It was Winder's lot to be the unwelcome instrument of Confederate policy in the Richmond area from 1862 to 1864, which virtually revolutionized the antebellum way of life.

In his inaugural address, Davis boasted that southern civil liberties had not been constrained as they had in the North. That luxury ended immediately. On 27 February, Davis suspended the writ of habeas corpus in Norfolk and Portsmouth, Virginia. Two days later, he declared martial law in Richmond, appointed Winder provost marshal general, and ordered him to establish an efficient military police system within a ten-mile radius of the city.[2]

The Richmond press initially welcomed the proclamation of martial law. The *Examiner* urged that it be "rigidly and sternly enforced," as did the *Enquirer*, but the latter warned that the suspension of civil rights

"might become a fatal weakness" if the powers were abused. The *Whig*
editorial position was that martial law should have been imposed earlier
and that "King Alcohol" should be dethroned.[3] These editorials suggest
just how chaotic life had become in Richmond. Many residents feared
to walk the streets, some agonized that starvation would be their fate,
and all were terrified that McClellan would soon capture the city. As
the peninsular campaign unfolded, from March to July 1862, and the
Federal threat increased, Petersburg and its environs were also placed
under Winder's version of martial law. Even then, his command was
small in comparison to other military regimes in the Confederacy.

The Confederacy imposed martial law on parts of North Carolina and
South Carolina in 1862, and General Mansfield Lovell imposed it on
New Orleans even before Congress granted authorization. Lovell's stern
policy was resented and opposed by the inhabitants of the Crescent City
until the Federals' stunning capture of the place in April. Four generals
in the field also took draconian measures: P. O. Herbert placed Texas
under martial law in May; Earl Van Dorn did the same to Louisiana
and Mississippi, and Thomas Hingman to Arkansas, in July; and Braxton
Bragg imposed military rule on Atlanta in August.[4]

In every instance, martial law was eventually actively opposed by the
citizens. All martial law commanders were unpopular, but Winder received more notoriety than the others, for his command was the focal
point of the Confederacy. Richmond was the capital, the seat of the war
effort; as such, it made the news every day. In addition, Winder held
power longer than other commanders, and his rule was therefore more
thorough. Finally, Winder made little attempt to placate prominent people or cultivate the press. He felt that the times demanded drastic action,
and he took it. Even Winder's ardent critics, then and later, conceded
that he cleaned out Richmond in 1862 "from center to circumference.
Spies, traitors, loafers, slackers, all were swept out, saloons and gambling
dens closed . . . in short, order was brought out of chaos."[5]

Winder began the assault upon the "evils" in his command on 4 March.
He created a provost guard from troops at his disposal, appointed Captain
A. C. Godwin provost marshal, and told him to restore law and order
in Henrico County. Godwin, a Virginia native and previous commander
of Rocketts prison, moved with alacrity. He made several hundred arrests
within two days, and the crime rate fell to manageable proportions.

Despite this early success, Winder realized that the area was too large
and unwieldy for Godwin's forces and reorganized the command on 9
March. He divided the district into two sections and assigned the eastern
half to Godwin, now an assistant provost marshal. Captain John C. Maynard, a Richmond native, was given equal rank and responsibility for
the west. Supervising both officers was a new provost marshal, Colonel
John Porter, but Winder changed the occupants of this position fre-

quently in the coming months. Finally, Winder designated Samuel B. Maccubbin, a fellow Baltimorean, chief of detectives and assigned him the civilian section. Unfortunately for Maccubbin, his force consisted almost exclusively of Winder's "plug-ugly" detectives.[6]

The Richmond newspapers praised Winder's military appointments but all were hostile to the police force from the beginning. Godwin and Maynard were repeatedly lauded, and Maccubbin was characterized as "an experienced, efficient, and courteous officer," but the detectives were routinely labeled "plug-uglies," "rowdies in uniform," and "blood tubs."[7]

Winder had broad powers under martial law, but he was not a dictator. The mayor's court remained open, and the Richmond police still functioned under martial law. Winder's provost guard was used primarily against military offenders, though he also had the authority to try civilians accused of crimes against the Confederacy, and his detectives worked exclusively on civilian cases. Winder's orders had a direct impact on all residents, civilian and military, but local and state governments continued to exercise their respective powers.[8] Residents of Richmond soon found out how comprehensive Winder's powers were. The Richmond *Examiner* summed up his responsibilities on 26 March. The paper noted that he was to suppress marauding, brawls, and drunkenness among civilians and soldiers alike, control the passport system, and regulate even the most minute affairs of everyday life.[9] With responsibilities so broad, reliable men so scarce, and only "plug-uglies" to contend with civilian offenses, it was not surprising that Winder gained a reputation in some quarters for arbitrariness, partiality, and insolent despotism.

Winder knew that many problems besetting Richmond were caused by armed men consuming alcohol. He had dealt with this problem during his old army days and attacked it with all the authority of his office. His first general order established outright prohibition and required all citizens to surrender their firearms to the Confederacy. No alcohol was to be distilled or distributed, and all swords, side arms, shotguns, were to be turned in to Captain Charles Dimmock at the state arsenal. Dimmock would compensate everyone for their loss.[10]

The attack on "King Alcohol" commenced with vigor. Provost guards closed and boarded up all saloons and combed the city for violators. The press complimented Winder's actions, executed "with sound discretion and characteristic vigor." There was no protest from the population, and it appeared that prohibition might work. Disillusionment followed in a matter of days. The front doors might have been barred, but the back ones were not. Confirmed reports reached Winder that liquor was being sold in a "business as usual" manner, and the press reported that the "cheerful clinking" of glasses could be heard behind the boarded facades.[11]

Winder soon concluded that total prohibition was not the solution. Some residents defied the law simply for their own pleasure, but many had medical prescriptions for alcohol. Physicians of the 1860s valued the medicinal qualities of spirits. Winder found that some druggists had issued prescriptions for alcohol during the ban and had charged exorbitant fees for their illegal services. He modified his prohibition order on 14 March. Forced to concede that a provision governing the legitimate use of alcohol was necessary, he ordered all druggists to report to his office. If they could furnish prescriptions signed by a reputable doctor, they received permission to dispense alcohol. At the same time, he attempted to curtail their supply by ending the importation of alcohol into Richmond. He threatened conductors of trains and canal packets with court-martial if they continued to supply the whiskey merchants.[12]

It was soon apparent that not even the modified policy was being obeyed. Winder concluded that mendacious apothecaries accepted prescriptions they knew were fraudulent and then claimed, when arrested, that they had been hoodwinked by a scoundrel. As measures for obtaining liquor became more devious, some of Winder's men instituted a policy of entrapment. They forged prescriptions, presented them to unwary druggists, and arrested them if the forgeries were honored. Quite often, Winder's men consumed the evidence. Several witnesses heard one of the provost marshals tell a druggist whom he had just arrested, "Your brandy was as fine as any I ever drank in my life."[13]

Inevitably, entrapment charges were made almost daily against some of the detectives. Winder bristled at the accusations. He attributed them to rumormongers, malcontents, and friends of the accused, and arraigned the druggists at a general court-martial on 17 April. He was vexed when all of them were acquitted, and wrote on the release for their discharge, "Not approved, and you may congratulate yourselves upon escaping a merited punishment."[14] Despite the acquittal, Winder remained convinced that his men were innocent of entrapment. Even his enemies conceded that he was honest and sincere in his convictions. The hostile editor of the *Examiner* concluded, correctly as it turned out, that Winder was "completely innocent" but "unaware of the evils going on behind his back."[15]

The entrapment controversy revealed one of Winder's shortcomings, which became increasingly obvious during the rest of his life. He acted as if he were an unfailing judge of men, and he was not. He placed total confidence in his appointees and defended them against all criticisms. He never ordered Maccubbin or the provost marshal to investigate the charges made against their forces or undertook any inquiry of his own. Instead, he concluded that his ranks had been infiltrated with impostors and announced in June that each detective would have a certificate of authorization from his office. It would serve as an identity card and would be shown to anyone who questioned the validity of the arresting officer. He ordered the detectives to execute their duties with firmness and decision and assured the public that his men would act with courtesy. This stance made him appear to be a naive bungler when, four months later, he fired the detective force for, in his words, "malfeasance, corruption, bribery, and incompetence."[16]

The press supported Winder's war on alcohol for three months before a reversal of position took place and their criticism became as vociferous as their earlier approbation. The *Enquirer* proclaimed in June that Winder's policy had "increased private debauchery and stimulated rascality to an extent unparalleled before in this community. The heartless speculation, the low subterfuges, the distribution of the vilest alcoholic concoctions, and the multiplication of misery and dissipation which are now apparent to the eyes of everyone who will see, are due alone to this 'prohibition law' from the 'war authorities.'"[17]

Winder relented somewhat in the autumn by permitting certain individuals to import specified amounts of whiskey but canceled the policy on 28 October, stating "Too many have cheated."[18] He returned to a modified version of his plan in December and allowed up to six thousand gallons of liquor per month into Richmond with the proviso that it not be sold to soldiers. He hoped that his plan, coupled with a recent ban on the manufacture of alcohol except for medicinal purposes enacted by the Virginia legislature, would form a workable policy. About the only effect was to drive up the price of liquor. By the end of 1862, whiskey sold for nearly $23 per gallon.

Winder warned the public that some unscrupulous dealers had adulterated their product and that much illness had resulted, and he reminded everyone that alcoholic consumption was strictly regulated. To protect public health and to insure adherence to legal limits, he ordered all who desired to sell alcohol to register with his office before 5 December 1862. He also established a board to investigate all appeals concerning seizure of liquor by his forces. This gave protection to legitimate dealers, and over 100 applicants registered during the first month.[19]

Winder never found a means to eliminate whiskey from Henrico County. The general public refused to support prohibition, and enforcement proved as futile in the 1860s as it did in the 1920s. Drunkenness and physical violence were common in Richmond before, during, and after the period of martial law. Yet Winder indisputably made Henrico County a much safer place than it would have been otherwise. He was correct in recognizing that alcohol was at the root of much social unrest, but the consumption of whiskey was one basic right that southerners refused to give up.

Another problem that defied solution was the passport system. This matter caused more discontent than any other difficulty Winder addressed. All of his other actions, initially at least, had some support in some section of the population, but the passport system was unpopular even with Winder and the men charged with enforcement.[20] There was resistance to the edict from the date of issuance in August 1861, and the protest increased after Winder intensified his efforts the following year.[21] On 17 March he issued a special order making the conductors of trains and canal packets directly responsible for examining passports, and he warned that miscreants would face court-martial if violations occurred.[22] He conducted a sweep on 19 March, and eighty-nine operators were arrested.[23] The violations continued and criticism mounted. The frustrations of the system were summed up by Senator David W. Lewis of Georgia in an address to the Confederate Congress.

> I must get someone who can identify me to go along with me to the Provost Marshal's office to enable me to get a pass. At the Provost's I shall be met at the door by a soldier with a bayonet. After getting the pass, I shall be again met at the cars by other soldiers with bayonets, who will demand to see my pass. The conductor must see my pass. At other times along my route I must be confronted by other armed men, and be obliged to obtain other passes, and undergo other examinations. This system will be kept up until I arrive home with a pocket full of Provost Marshal's passes.[24]

A further complication of the system was that there was still no general passport office. Winder's office was supposed to have sole authority, but the War Department continued to intervene. The War clerk Jones reported on 5 June that he had been ordered to reopen his office, "as the major-generals in the field refused to permit the relatives of the sick and wounded in the camps to pass with orders from Brig.-Gen. Winder or his Provost Marshal."[25]

Winder protested to Secretary of War George W. Randolph that all the confusion experienced in 1861 would return if this order was not revoked and insisted that there must be a clearly recognized chain of command. He was only partially successful, and friction developed immediately. The War Department bypassed Winder on several occasions, and he visited Jones's office on 22 July "boiling over with rage." He told the clerk that if he issued another pass he would experience "the terrors of Castle Godwin." He then saw Randolph, and they reached an understanding. The following day the secretary ordered Jones to confine his passes to people going to camps in or near Richmond. All other passports would be issued under Winder's direction.[26]

The situation continued to deteriorate during the fall and winter months, and public discontent swelled. Winder was perplexed by the dilemma and ordered his provost marshal to examine the possibility of eliminating the system. Major Elias Griswold, who had replaced Godwin on 25 April, reported at length to Winder on 15 January 1863. In a well-considered report, Griswold concluded that the system was obnoxious to the people. It limited their liberties, resulted in delays and frustrations, and injured their self-respect. All attempts at eliminating or ameliorating the system had failed, he concluded, and injured dignity was the price for retaining it.

If passports were abolished, Griswold believed that the rate of desertions would increase. Most soldiers deserted because of the boredom and privation of camp life, not cowardice, and they were fairly easy to apprehend under the system. He also feared that uncontrolled swarms of visitors to the camps would wreck army discipline. Spies and disloyal persons would also benefit from the abolition and Griswold recommended that the system be retained despite its unpopularity.[27]

Winder concurred but was well aware that many in Richmond opposed his decision. The prevailing opinion of the residents was probably best expressed by Randolph Abbott Shotwell, who condemned the passport system, martial law, and the detectives. After a visit to Richmond in October 1862, Shotwell recorded that Winder was "a man of arbitrary ideas joined to a perfect pliability of character" and that he had "become plastic as wax in the hands of the Richmond Cabinet while greatly influenced, also, by a gang of ex-'Plugs' of Baltimore, whom he . . . enrolled in his detective force, and who virtually rule Richmond."[28] Over a month later, Shotwell wrote, "General Winder rules Richmond like a military Camp; nay, not like a well-disciplined camp, for his rule gives annoyance merely to honest men and faithful soldiers, while permitting the city to be over-run by rogues, spies, speculators, foreigners, blockade runners, and fellows of that ilk." He concluded that Winder was honest and patriotic but was too much under the influence of his "none-too-honest subordinates."[29]

Criticism of this type was not new and had preceded Winder's Richmond command. As early as 1 July 1861, there were reports that Davis, Lee, and others had instituted a reign of terror. A reporter at Fort Monroe questioned refugees from Richmond, one of whom stated that "a worse than Roman inquisition prevails in Virginia. There is a standing order that no one shall be permitted to leave the country." He concluded that "Governor Letcher is completely overruled by Jefferson Davis and Beauregard, and even his patriotism is called into question by many of the rebels."[30]

Still, there can be no doubt that Winder's wide-ranging proclamations caused discontent. As early as May 1862, the *Enquirer* reported that there were rumors that Winder would soon resign as provost marshal general for service in the field and that his replacement would be Brigadier General Henry A. Wise. "The rumor may be premature, but the fact is patent that such a change as far as the District of Henrico is concerned is eminently desirable." The paper concluded with the hope that his conduct in the field would render him "less liable to censure."[31]

Winder's relationship with the Richmond press was complicated and varied. He was lavishly praised, criticized without mercy, and occasionally referred to in humorous fashion. Although editors and publishers of all the papers usually gave initial approval to his actions, they sometimes simply printed his orders without comment. This soon led to charges that Winder had threatened to censor the news or even end the freedom of the press.

The fear that Winder might arrest the publishers and close the papers was well grounded, if an account by the War Department clerk Jones is accurate. Jones noted that in March 1862 Secretary of War Benjamin penciled an order to the press to abstain from any mention of the arrival of arms and other materiel from abroad. Winder signed the order, and Maccubbin's detectives showed it to the editors. (It was never formally copied or distributed and thus was not included in the *Official Records*.) Jones gave the following account of Winder's actions as of 23 March 1862, subsequent to Benjamin's order.

> General Winder was in this morning listening to something Maccubbin was telling him about the Richmond *Whig*. It appears that, in the course of a leading article, enthusiastic for the cause, the editor remarked, "We have arms and ammunition now." The policemen, one and all, interpreted this as a violation of the order to the press to abstain from speaking of the arrivals of arms, etc., from abroad. General Winder, without looking at the paper, said in a loud voice, "Go and arrest the editor and close his office." Two or three of the policemen started off on this errand. But I interposed, and asked them to wait a moment, until I could examine the paper. I found no infraction of the order in the truly patriotic article, and said so to General Winder. "Well," said he, "If he has not violated the order, he must not be arrested." He took the paper, and read for himself; and then, without saying anything more, departed. . . . The policemen threatened to stop the *Examiner* soon, for that paper has been somewhat offensive to the aliens who now have the rule here.[32]

Jones also noted on 17 April that several publishers had expressed fears that Winder would close them down if they dared utter their true sentiments. He concluded, "It is, indeed a reign of terror!"[33]

In support of Jones's allegations, an unsigned letter from Albemarle County appeared in the 20 March issue of the *Whig*. It stated, "I hear the 'Pressmaster' is again in our midst, and if he calls on me it will be the third time—and perhaps as often on you."[34] Also, Congressman Muscoe Garnett of Virginia requested an investigation to determine if anyone had attempted to "muzzle" the press.[35] Winder was not named in either instance, but no one had any doubts about the identity of the "Pressmaster."

Conversely, if Winder ever attempted to intimidate the press, it was an uncharacteristically weak effort, because the *Whig* had no apparent apprehensions about addressing the incident recorded by Jones. The editorial of 25 March declared: "We have been informed that General Winder was going to close this journal if it does not quit printing falsehoods. If he made such a statement it must have been in fun or jest . . . [as] we had not imagined that Lincoln's Provost Marshal had come among us."[36]

The editorial concluded that the *Whig* had offered constructive criticisms for over nine months and that Winder and the administration had heeded them and acted with vigor, and the Cause was the better for it. Two days later, the paper attacked the war powers of President Davis, because he might place any city "under the absolute despotism of a General from beyond the Potomac, with a gang of detectives from still further North."[37]

Criticism of this type occurred far too frequently for there to be any substance to the charge that Winder controlled the press, but he was lauded at times. On 12 March the *Dispatch* asked its readers to "behold the wonders" that martial law had accomplished. The next month the paper noted that Winder had ended the "vile rows of drunken soldiery," that the streets were quiet, that brawls were rare, and that "peace, serenity, security, [and] respect for life and property" had returned to Richmond.[38] In mid-July, the *Whig* reported the following:

> Persons who have not had occasion to visit General Winder's office during business hours, have scarcely any idea of the extent of business which the General and his associates have to perform. The space allotted to outsiders is crowded all the time, and it really is curious to observe how rapidly the General is plied with interrogatories, and with what equanimity and definitiveness he answers them. At times, he apparently carries on conversations with two or three persons simultaneously, while examining or signing papers, yet there is no confusion, and as far as we have seen, no exhibition of ill-temper or official self-importance. The duties of the office appear manifold, and it is obvious that the position is anything but a sinecure.[39]

In a lighter vein, the *Enquirer* stated that dogs were becoming quite a nuisance and that a fox terrier going through the lines with a letter containing treasonous language had been arrested and brought before Winder for trial. "The prisoner had such a dogged look that he was immediately judged guilty and sent to Castle Thunder. . . . No attention whatever was paid to the wretched health of the cur, but he was ordered to be fed on bones."[40]

The press coverage of Winder during 1862 varied widely. There was an occasional report designed to cause a chuckle at his expense, but most of his actions resulted in either lavish praise or total condemnation. There may have been a few people who believed that he intended to end the freedom of the press and who agreed with Jones that they were under a "reign of terror," but their fears were false. The Confederacy never suffered the suppression of the press or of other basic rights to the degree imposed by Lincoln on the Union. Over 13,000 people were arbitrarily arrested and some 300 newspapers suppressed, at least temporarily, in the North. Compared to these numbers, Winder's actions at his worst constituted only a minor irritant.[41]

A reign of terror never existed in Richmond, but terror is perhaps an apt description of the state of mind of many residents in March 1862. The prospect of starvation suddenly confronted the city when Federal gunboats sealed off the James River and McClellan's army arrived on the peninsula. Overland transportation became the only means of furnishing foodstuffs for the booming civil and military population, and it proved deficient. The comparative prosperity that had existed during the winter's military lull disappeared almost overnight, and Richmond faced shortages of every description.[42]

The Richmond marketplace was widely perceived to be monopolized by hucksters who charged outrageous prices for their goods. The public outcry could not be ignored, and Winder made an ill-fated attempt to improve the situation. On 31 March he embarked on a policy of price controls. He established a maximum price for most commodities, restricted the purchase of these goods to a ten-mile radius of the city, and promised not to interfere with country farmers coming into Richmond. He followed this order with another that harked back to the days of the late Roman Empire. If violations occurred, both buyer and seller would be court-martialed and the informer would be given the produce.[43]

Both orders became effective on 7 April, and the result was immediate and disastrous. Hucksters avoided Richmond and convinced honest country folk to do the same. Food supplies almost disappeared, and many citizens fled Richmond in search of a full stomach. Winder modified his position on informers and directed instead that military authorities confiscate all produce sold at higher rates and distribute it to the hospitals.[44] The situation worsened, and the public demanded relief.

The *Whig* announced on 12 April that price controls on commodities would not work but advocated that Winder establish maximum prices for restaurants. "We do not know if the venerable General is prepared to administer a remedy to all of the evils which afflict us, but it certainly seems legitimate to restrain somewhat the avarice of those who require exorbitant prices for cooked food."[45]

The Richmond City Council asked Winder to revoke his edict on 25

April and even considered ways to remove "our despotic friend."[46] Winder complied on 30 April and temporarily lifted all price controls. Farmers returned to the market, but prices soared to such outlandish levels that the French consul noted, "Richmond has become a hell for all those who are forced to live here."[47] Public excoriation of huckstering intensified to such an extent that the press called for a return to price controls in mid-July. Winder refused to repeat the April experience but did set limits on the price of corn on 12 July. He expanded the edict to include livestock fodder and straw before the month was over. The press reported a temporary improvement, but the supply of produce began to dwindle during the first week of August. Winder was saved from further experiments when the War Department declared on 6 August that martial law did not include price fixing.[48]

Shortages of food and the resulting inflation of prices served notice that a nation of farmers could experience starvation. Production of supplies was not the problem; distribution was. Competition at the marketplace was eliminated because of inadequate means of transportation, not a failure of crops. The situation became critical during the winter months of 1862–1863. Commissary General Northrop informed Randolph on 3 November that not only was food not in adequate supply in Richmond, it was not reaching Lee's army in sufficient quantities. He reported that unless something was done "to afford transportation for all the wheat" that could be purchased, he did "not see anything but failure and ruin" for the army. "I am powerless to remedy the evil."[49] Northrup's lament became common throughout the Confederacy: "I am powerless to remedy the evil." Winder and others would use these words countless times in the future.

The failure to provide armies in the field with food supplies was cause for alarm, and the government resorted to impressment. This was a desperate policy in that the impressed goods were paid for at prices fixed consistently lower than those of the marketplace. Producers suffered and so did consumers when army agents impressed goods bound for local markets. Some cities and towns experienced severe food shortages as a result, and this was true of Richmond in 1862 and 1863.[50] Impressed goods were paid for in depreciated currency, and inflation became a problem the Confederacy never solved. Inflation was not limited to food supplies, of course, and Winder had also attempted to set prices in areas other than the markets. On 12 March he required hack owners to post the legal rates for their service and to adhere to them rigidly. Rather than submit to price controls, many hack owners imitated the hucksters and withdrew from the streets. They waited in vain for Winder to retreat as he had done with the hucksters. When the *Enquirer* suggested that the horses be impounded and sent to Confederate forces on the peninsula, many owners remembered how often Winder had followed similar suggestions, and they resumed business at the reduced rates.[51] The situation improved temporarily, but problems with hack owners recurred regularly.

Inflation in all areas of life was intensified by the appearance of "shinplaster" money. This was paper money having a stated value of less than one dollar. It was issued in the best tradition of the "saddle bag banks" by almost any organization having access to a printing press. Richmond residents were confronted with the necessity of examining each shinplaster individually and arriving at a decision as to which issuing institution might possibly be solvent. Richmond's markets were inundated with spurious shinplasters, and Winder once again heeded the public outcry. On 16 April he forbade the issuance and circulation of individual notes, provided for their redemption, and threatened violators with court-martial. The shinplasters disappeared overnight, and the press praised Winder for this admirable "stunner," this "commendable act."[52]

Winder continued to intervene in the most minute details of Richmond life. He broke a strike by disgruntled lithographers in short order. Declaring that these exempted men had no right to strike during time of war, he confined them in Castle Godwin. He also decided that paperboys were too greedy and fixed the price of newspapers at five cents per copy. The reaction was predictable. The editors approved of some price-fixing, but not when it involved their product.[53]

If the editors chafed under some of Winder's restrictions and criticized him unduly in 1862, they reserved their harshest attacks for Davis and Congress when it appeared that they were not going to defend Richmond from McClellan's army. Winder had reported in February that the field fortifications around Richmond were worthless, and Davis informed Congress in March that he would not allow the army to be trapped within a besieged city even if it was the Confederate capital. Davis ordered General Johnston to move down the peninsula and attack McClellan as far away from Richmond as possible. He also asked Congress to pass the first draft in American history. The conscription act of 16 April proclaimed that all men between the ages of eighteen and thirty-five had to serve in the army for three years. Although this struck at the heart of states' rights, Richmonders hoped that it might save their city.

Johnston delayed McClellan but continued to retreat, and by May both armies were within sight of Richmond. Plans were made for evacuating the government archives, and many prominent people left the capital. Congress did little to inspire confidence. On the contrary, that body voted itself a raise on 22 April, adjourned, and joined the crowd at Winder's office asking for passports to leave the city.[54] Richmonders were outraged at this less than admirable act. The *Whig* captured the public mood when it printed the following on the day after Congress adjourned.

For fear of accidents on the railroad, the stampeded Congress left yesterday in a number of the strongest and lowest canal boats. These boats are drawn by mules of approved sweetness of temper. To protect the stampeders from the snakes and bullfrogs that abound along the line of the canal, General Winder has detailed a regiment of ladies to march in advance of the ranks, and clear the tow-path of the pirates. The regiment is armed with pop guns of the longest range. The ladies will accompany the stampeders to a selected cave in the mountains of Hepsidam, and leave them there in charge of the children . . . until McClellan thinks proper to let them come forth. The ladies return to the defense of their country.[55]

As the military situation worsened, nascent Unionism appeared in the form of slogans chalked on fences and walls in the city. Union sympathizers, suspected spies, and untrustworthy aliens came under Winder's jurisdiction, and he pursued them with zeal. All foreigners were registered by his agents and he and his staff received all inquiries and correspondence concerning spies that came into the government's possession.

Because it was the Confederate capital, Richmond was the center for spy rings, and hundreds of arrests occurred in Henrico County. The most dangerous spies usually escaped, but Winder enjoyed some success in capturing them. In April 1862, his forces arrested Timothy Webster, a key agent in Allan Pinkerton's force, which acted as the secret service for McClellan. Webster was a letter carrier, and he had been issued numerous passports during 1861 and early 1862. Winder and other top officials used him to deliver personal correspondence to family and friends in the Union and were mortified when he was exposed as a spy. He was convicted and hanged on 24 April 1862. More successful spies were Lafayette C. Baker, later Lincoln's chief secret service agent; S. Emma E. Edmonds, who apparently entered Confederate lines frequently; and Elizabeth Van Lew, previously mentioned. Even when Winder's forces arrested a known spy, Mrs. Patterson Allan, for example, justice did not always prevail. Mrs. Allan was clearly guilty, but her attorney, former Secretary of War Randolph, succeeded in postponing her trial for the duration of the war.[56]

Winder's "plugs" had been active in 1862 and made several arrests before martial law was declared, but there was little public attention until Captain Godwin arrested John Minor Botts and eight other prominent citizens on 2 March. The suspects were confined in McDaniels Negro jail in Lumpkins Alley. This building was promptly christened Castle Godwin and recognized by the press as the "official" Confederate prison in Richmond.

Winder had thirty suspects in custody by 15 March. Botts was easily the most conspicuous, and the government decided to frighten all Unionists by charging him with treason. Winder suggested that Botts be granted a parole of honor and confined to house arrest. Botts received decent treatment and later recorded that Winder had been prompt and courteous in handling his case, but the old Whig nationalist was understandably incensed by the whole affair. Although he stoutly maintained that he was a neutral, not a Unionist, he was detained for almost two months. Not until 28 April was he allowed to return to his farm, and only on condition that he say nothing hostile about the Confederacy in the future.[57]

Winder's campaign against suspected Unionists was generally popular with the press, although the *Whig* reported that some arrests were made without sufficient cause. There were quite a number of accusations forwarded to Winder about "traitors in our midst," but few were valid.[58] Many of the accused were citizens of other states, and Winder was soon engaged in a dispute with Governor Zebulon Vance of North Carolina as a result of his arrest of the Reverend Robert J. Graves.

Graves had gone to New York for a throat operation and observed that the Federals were engaged in massive preparations for a prolonged struggle. He feared that the South was not, and when he returned, he expressed this view to William J. Bingham, a prominent North Carolina educator. Bingham urged Graves to write up his observations and send the account to the press. The result was "A Long War," published by the *Enquirer* on 6 November. It appeared to some that Graves was trying to encourage Confederate war weariness, and two letters accusing Graves of disloyalty were forwarded to Winder. Captain T. E. Upshaw wrote that he overheard Graves tell Federal soldiers at Harrison's Landing "everything he knew about Richmond," and another citizen claimed that Graves was "a Yankee and a spy."[59] The investigation revealed that Graves had lied when obtaining his passport to return to North Carolina from Richmond, and Winder ordered his arrest. He sent Maccubbin to Orange County, North Carolina, in early December with orders to return Graves to Richmond.

Maccubbin arrived in Orange County on 14 December, a Sunday morning. Graves was preaching at Bethlehem Church near The Oaks. After listening to the sermon, Maccubbin arrested him, took him to Richmond, and confined him in Castle Thunder. The news caused an uproar in North Carolina. Governor Vance demanded that Graves be returned. He reported that he had attempted to stop the train transporting Graves but failed, and stated that if any trial took place, it would be in North Carolina. The Fayetteville *Observer* denounced the action on 15 December and proclaimed that even if Graves was guilty, the military had no right to remove him from the state. Senator William A. Graham, long a power in Tarheel politics, issued a resolution for Graves's return, and on 20 December the Senate approved it.

Secretary of War James A. Seddon, who replaced Randolph on 19 November, responded to Vance on 27 December. He informed the governor that Graves's case was being reviewed but that Winder acted "with overzeal in not first fully satisfying himself that the party charged was not a citizen of North Carolina. As such, while amenable to arrest on sufficient grounds as a Spy, or even as a traitor, he could with no propriety or legality be removed from the State."[60] Seddon concluded that the trial should be conducted in North Carolina and promised to send Graves home. In the meantime, Winder questioned Graves and, in the process, managed to insult the entire state of North Carolina. The North Carolina press reported in January 1863 that Winder had proclaimed their state a "nest of damned traitors" and urged all citizens to execrate him and work for his removal.[61]

Senator George Davis of North Carolina, Winder's nephew by marriage and soon to become the Confederate attorney general, worked behind the scenes to quell the uproar. He wrote Edward J. Hale, editor of the Fayetteville *Observer*, several long letters explaining what had happened. On 16 January Davis stated:

I have known Gen. Winder well and intimately for a great many years. He is quick and impulsive, sometimes hasty, but eminently truthful and upright. Such characters are never deliberate slanderers. He married in North Carolina, and was a citizen there for many years; and I *know* that he has always entertained, and *expressed* the highest respect, and no little affection for our good old State. So much as to the probability of the story which misled you. Now as to the fact. He never said that "North Carolina was a d——d nest of traitors," nor anything equivalent to it, nor anything at all like it. What he really said was this. When Mr. Graves was brought before him, in the course of the examination he was asked what was his motive in writing the discouraging letter published in the Richmond papers (which, as I am informed, was a part of the offence for which he was arrested) and his reply was this singular one "There are a good many quakers in the region of No. Ca. where I live, and I wrote it for their benefit." Then the General broke out—"You wrote it to encourage the Quakers, when you know they have been against us from the first, and that they are a set of d——d traitors?" I do not defend the justice, the dignity, nor the good taste of such language. I simply state the fact.[62]

Davis wanted Winder exonerated, but he told Hale that his letter was not intended for publication. He refused to vindicate Winder publicly but no doubt hoped that Hale would share the news with other editors and stop the attacks on Winder. Hale responded that he respected Davis's viewpoint but that Winder should deny the charge if false or admit that he was guilty. Davis replied that Winder, like George Washington, submitted to obloquy in silence, believing that the calmer judgment of men in the future would vindicate him. Hale harbored reservations, but his respect for Davis was such that he printed no more about Winder.[63]

While the Davis-Hale correspondence was going on, Winder informed Bingham concerning the Graves case. Bingham recorded on 27 January, "Gen. Winder, in a letter to me under date 19th inst., very kindly written, states that 'Mr. G's' trial is going on, and the witnesses have been sent for." Winder concluded that it was not the "discouraging letter" to the *Enquirer* that was the reason for the trial, but instead, "numerous communications alleging disloyal practices while in the enemy's lines."[64]

Graves was removed to North Carolina in January. Winder was probably not surprised when the state court in Hillsborough returned him to Richmond for trial. In the meantime, he made a successful attempt to placate Vance. In June and July of 1863, Winder and Vance cooperated in a cordial manner concerning North Carolina deserters John Medlin and Miles Dobbins. Vance requested Winder's help in locating Dobbins, and Winder's detectives finally found him hiding in the mountains in Yadkin County. In these and other cases, Winder kept Vance fully informed and left the final resolution to the governor. For example, he wrote the governor, with regard to the Medlin case, "I will hold the man subject to your order—or, should you decide it best, will have him tried in court martial upon the charge of desertion."[65]

Winder was more diplomatic with state officials after the Graves case, but he continued to inspire fear in Unionist hearts. J. J. Marks, a captured Federal officer and a surgeon, recorded that Winder took a "malignant satisfaction in ruining every man who was suspected of any lingering regard for the Union." Marks continued that, when he was granted parole, Winder ordered him to leave Libby prison and proceed to Petersburg. Marks wanted to ask for permission to remain, but a Confederate officer told him: "I know nothing about the intention of General Winder in ordering you off, but this I will say for your good, what he commands you to do, obey instantly; send no petition to him, ask no favor of him; and let me tell you, if you are not off tomorrow morning, it will be a long time before you will have another opportunity; there will be something hatched up against you, and you will be treated as a dangerous man, or a spy."[66] Winder was not the fiend Marks described, but his book, published in 1864, was well received in the North.

At about the same time Marks met Winder, Commodore Samuel Francis DuPont recorded his impression of the general. In a letter to his wife on 15 November 1862, DuPont wrote that "General Winder, the provost marshal, who belonged to General Brannan and Dr. Crane's regiment (they) told me only on Sunday last that a man more fitted for his place as a *borreau* [sic] could not be conceived."[67] *Bourreau* can be translated as "hangman," "tormentor," or "executioner." Winder would be described in even more chilling fashion in the Union press.

Winder was overzealous at times, but his reputation was not such that any prisoner feared to ask a favor. William Scholfield, for example, was confined to Richmond on parole and had asked District Attorney P. H. Aylett if he might be permitted to go to Goldsboro, North Carolina, to attend to personal business. Hearing nothing from Aylett for two months, he went to Winder. Although three separate departments had to be consulted, Winder sent Scholfield on his way the same day.[68]

If the civilians resented the application of martial law to themselves, they were overwhelmingly supportive of it when Winder used his powers to curb military offenders. After the imposition of martial law, Winder had ordered all officers not on duty in the city to report to his office at once. If they were assigned duty in Henrico County, they were to remain at their posts or face imprisonment. All other military personnel—recruits, convalescents, officers, and enlisted men—were to report to Camp Winder. The camp was located on Cary Street in the western outskirts of Richmond. When the peninsula campaign unfolded, it was converted into a vast hospital complex. By 1864, it was second only to Chimborazo Hospital in size. There were about 100 buildings and several thousand tents covering 125 acres, and the patient capacity exceeded 5,000. It was probably the only hospital where for brief periods the majority of nurses were disabled soldiers and blacks.[69] However, in March 1862, when Winder ordered the military to assemble there, it was a camp of instruction.

Winder's orders eliminated almost any excuse given by idle soldiers when they were approached by the provost guard. Offenders were either sent to Castle Godwin or placed in irons and returned to their units. Winder also ordered that the military be more considerate of civilian safety and welfare. He stopped teamsters from galloping through the crowded streets, restricted horses and light carriages to a speed of five miles per hour, and reduced freight haulers to a walk.[70]

On 21 March, Winder moved against the substitute agencies. These enterprising operators hired men to serve in the army in place of any civilian who could pay for the substitute. Operating out of saloons and other places, they conducted a brisk business until Winder outlawed the activity. He warned that he would conscript both the principal and the substitute and confiscate the money if the practice continued. He reissued the edict in August and ordered the provost guard to strictly enforce the ordinance.[71]

When McClellan approached within sight of Richmond in May, Confederate field commanders asked that Winder help curb the problem of desertion. General D. H. Hill was convinced that thousands of his men had deserted to Richmond under pretext of illness. On 10 May he requested Secretary of War Randolph to order Winder "to hunt up all those who have not surgeon's certificates" and return them to their regiments.[72] Winder complied promptly; he posted guards at the depot, combed the hospitals for malingerers, and ordered the guard to carefully examine all discharge papers. Several thousand stragglers and deserters were quickly apprehended, but Winder's force was not large enough to return them to their units under guard. The delay caused dissension between Winder and both Hill and Johnston. Hill complained to Lee and the War Department that Winder was not returning the stragglers to their outfits but was assigning them to other units or keeping them in Richmond under his own command. Johnston objected to Winder's role and asked Lee for complete authority over the Department of Henrico. Davis and Lee denied Johnston's request, but on 23 May, Lee ordered Winder to return to their units all soldiers detailed to guard and transport stragglers.[73]

Winder notified Randolph five days later that his force had been inadequate for most of the month but that for three days he had been able to return stragglers to their units at the rate of 1,000 per day. Then his force had been depleted by Lee's order to return the detailed soldiers. The result was that his guardhouses were overflowing and he lacked the manpower to send the malingerers back. He also complained that Hill had invaded Camp Winder with surgeons and an armed guard and had taken patients away over the protests of the camp surgeons. He reminded Randolph that he had informed him on 22 May that the existing policy required him to send written discharges to the commanders of sick soldiers before they could be released and that these notifications were not always delivered promptly or were neglected by the officers in the field. This meant that "many a brave soldier, who should be at home tenderly cared for, loses his life in the crowded hospitals." Winder's conclusion was that the regulation should not be enforced. Davis agreed on 31 May and told Winder to discharge the patients and then notify their commanders.[74]

Despite the difficulties, Winder returned over 4,000 men to the ranks by the end of May. This was a considerable feat because Winder never had more than 2,000 men under his command; yet he was expected to return deserters, enforce martial law in all of its ramifications, guard Federal prisoners, oversee the camps of instruction, and discharge disabled or ill soldiers from the hospitals. Desertion from 1862 on remained a constant problem, and Winder issued public appeals for help. He asked all citizens to help identify and report deserters and was especially pleased when fourteen-year-old Thomas Murphy apprehended one and brought him to the general's office. Winder gave him a $30 reward and also a job as his messenger boy.[75]

Winder was less pleased with several surgeons in charge of military hospitals. In June, Winder and Alexander Lane, commanding surgeon at Camp Winder, almost came to blows. Winder inspected the camp and found it in "a deplorable condition." He also found that Lane had diverted prisoners from work details ordered by Winder and that he had defied regulations by reporting directly to the War Department instead of to Winder. When taken to task, Lane responded in an "abusive, improper, and insubordinate" way, and Winder informed Randolph that he intended to press charges.[76] Disputes of this type were common but seldom resulted in formal charges being filed. Top officials, especially Lee, usually delayed or ignored such matters and waited for them to fade away.[77] Shortly after Winder quarreled with Lane on 14 June, both men were too busy to pursue the argument. Confederate forces attacked McClellan, and Richmond was deluged with wounded soldiers.

The initial effort to defeat McClellan at the battle of Seven Pines occurred on 31 May. Thousands of Richmonders observed the battle at a distance, but Winder and his aide-de-camp, Robert Brown, "rode down to the battlefield" and beheld "scenes of Carnage" far beyond what either had ever experienced. They remained at General James Longstreet's headquarters until wounded Confederates and captured Federals began streaming into Richmond.[78] Winder left immediately to attend to these problems.

Over 5,000 Confederate wounded, among them General Johnston, filled all hospitals and overflowed into private homes. Winder placed appeals for help in the newspapers and warned that although he personally regarded impressment as a great evil, he would take that action if it became necessary. Richmonders rallied, but they were overwhelmed with more casualties in July, after Lee, who replaced Johnston, took the offensive. For seven days during the last week of June, some of the worst fighting of the war took place. By 1 July, McClellan was driven off and Richmond was safe, but the number of Confederate casualties was awesome.

The month of July 1862 was an unforgettable time for Richmonders. Sallie Putnam recorded that "death had a carnival in our city." Residents "lived in one immense hospital, and breathed the vapors of the charnel house."[79] Homes, barns, hotels, warehouses, stores, churches, courthouses—all available buildings were converted to temporary hospitals, yet thousands suffered and died in the July heat. The grotesque was everywhere. Gravediggers could not bury the dead quickly enough, and swollen bodies burst the confines of their coffins. Small mountains of amputated limbs rose behind all of the hospitals.[80]

Richmond staggered under the sudden increase in population. Thousands of relatives arrived in the city to attend their suffering kin or to claim their remains. The addition of almost 8,000 captured Federals compounded the problem.[81] Even before the July crisis, available housing was almost nonexistent. Burton Harrison, who arrived in March to become a secretary to President Davis, noted then that every house in the city was full, "from cellar to roof" and that it was "almost impossible to get any room at all, even at rates varying from forty to sixty dollars per month."[82]

Richmond met the challenge somehow, and the worst was over by August, yet many problems persisted. Winder's schedule remained overwhelming, and his ordeal continued and even worsened as summer yielded to autumn. Scarcity of all necessities resulted in another round of skyrocketing inflation. Housing was critical and food was so expensive that Winder again imposed price controls on some products.[83] The temperament of the city was not improved by the economic hardships, and Winder found that more residents than ever before were willing to defy his edicts. The protest against passports and criticism of his detectives grew in volume. Winder was soon aware that with the threat from McClellan removed, Richmonders wanted an end to martial law.

In August, the War clerk Jones gleefully recorded that both houses of Congress were "thundering away" at Winder's "plug-uglies" and that the adjutant general was "annulling, one after the other, all Gen. Winder's despotic orders." He added that Senator Brown was "very bitter" and would oppose any extension of martial law after it expired in mid-September.[84] Senator Albert G. Brown of Mississippi was indeed critical. He said that Winder's men seemed "imbued with a desire to do small things in a great way, while matters of tenfold importance . . . escape their attention." He noted that people wishing to enter the provost marshal's office were cursed and abused, that the passport system aided only spies, and that he joined with other senators in the belief that Confederate law did not permit the position of provost marshal.[85]

Congress debated the issue of martial law from August through October of 1862. The original congressional authorization of February 1862 was ambiguous in that it implied that the suspension of habeas corpus and martial law were identical. Congress restricted the suspension of habeas corpus to those who violated Confederate law in April, but the issue continued to simmer and the legality of martial law remained a disputed point.[86]

Vice-President Alexander Stephens made his position clear in September. Already alienated from Davis, Stephens concluded that the position of provost marshal, or military governor, was "unknown to the law." In answer to James M. Calhoun, who had been appointed military governor of Atlanta by Braxton Bragg and who wanted to know what powers he had, Stephens responded that "Gen. Bragg had no more authority" for making the appointment "than any streetwalker" in Atlanta.[87] Presumably, the same lack of power applied to Winder.

Davis disagreed and informed Congress in September that provost marshals "were employed, not appointed," and that they had jurisdiction over army personnel only, "unless martial law was in effect." He conceded, however, that price-fixing was not legitimate and that he had forbidden the practice on 26 August.

Congress was not placated and directed the Judiciary Committee to determine if martial law could be abolished. The committee reported on 19 September that Davis had authority to suspend habeas corpus but that, unless the violation was against Confederate law, all civilians were entitled to a jury trial and that no state or municipal civil court could be bypassed. Davis notified Congress in October that the law suspending habeas corpus had expired and that it was no longer in effect anywhere in the Confederacy. He also declared that, when it was in effect, the basic freedoms of the people and the power of the civil courts had not been hampered. He ignored the issue of martial law, and the congressional debate continued.[88] The Senate passed a resolution stating that the powers of any provost marshal extended only to the military population, but a joint resolution abolishing martial law failed. Finally, on 14 October, Congress again gave Davis the authority to suspend habeas corpus anywhere until thirty days after the Congress reassembled in May.

Martial law remained in effect in Richmond, but Winder was occasionally overruled by Davis or Randolph. He arrested a man for hiring a substitute and confiscated the money on 30 September, but Randolph told him that he had no justification for his actions. He was authorized to suppress the substitute system, but he could not impress the offender into the army or confiscate the money.[89] Randolph and his successor, James A. Seddon, occasionally found that Winder was overzealous, and it is doubtful if Davis ever intended that martial law be so pervasive in application, but all supported Winder's methods as well as his intentions. After being overruled on the substitute issue, Winder asked Randolph for clarification of his authority. "This state of affairs causes me great embarrassment and renders it expedient that my future conduct should be in strict accordance with the view of the War Department, of which I am not yet advised."[90] Reassured that vigorous enforcement of martial law was necessary, Winder resumed his efforts.

Richmond in the fall of 1862 began to resemble the Richmond prior to martial law. According to the *Enquirer*, "The prevalence of every variety of villainy in Richmond should be sufficient to cause the citizens to guard themselves well. . . . Pickpockets, garroters, burglars, and thugs infest the city." Drunkenness was again on the increase, and "improper women," daily "flirting and flaunting" their wares, filled the city.[91] Camp followers and prostitutes caused many problems for Winder, and he also

faced unusual situations caused by affronts to "respectable" women. On
1 October, Winder was ordered to investigate the conduct of Colonel
John Hunt Morgan. This intrepid cavalry commander, already famous
for his raids into Kentucky and Ohio, was accused of threatening to rape
Richmond women if they did not cook for his men. He reportedly told
the women that if they refused his request they had "better sew up their
petticoat bottoms."[92] Winder was satisfied that Morgan had not behaved
improperly, and the colonel was soon back in the war.

Castle Godwin was packed with civilian offenders, yet the newspapers
reported at the end of October that the crime rate "exceeded the bloodi-
est days of Baltimore and the worst rascality of New York." Criticism
of the "plug-uglies" reached massive proportions. They were accused of
accepting bribes for issuing passports to spies and of engaging in all manner of illegalities while subjecting Richmond to "bayonet rule."[93] Winder
was no longer able to ignore the criticisms or dismiss them as unfounded.
On 9 October the *Dispatch*, quoting the Philadelphia *Enquirer*, carried
an account of a disloyal southerner arrested on Winder's orders. He had
purchased a passport for $100 from one of the detectives. Once behind
Union lines he joined the Federal army and the South had one more
foe to contend with. Winder's investigation convinced him that some
of his men had taken bribes, and on 24 October he fired the whole force
with the exception of Phillip Cashmeyer and Samuel Maccubbin.[94]

Curiously, the press reaction to the wholesale dismissal was mixed.
The *Enquirer*, hostile to the detective force for months, nevertheless
concluded that "much good was accomplished by the more energetic of
the corps, and special commendation is deserved by . . . Maccubbin."
The *Whig* approved the action but praised Maccubbin as an "efficient
and attentive" officer, as did the *Examiner* and *Dispatch*. Jones was more
consistent; he wholeheartedly approved of the firing but lamented that
Winder and his provost marshal were not included.[95]

Winder increased the numbers of provost guards in the city and organized a new system of police under Maccubbin. He had guards posted
at "virtually every corner," and the number of both military and civilian
arrests increased markedly. In the reorganization, Winder moved with
more deliberation and moderation than he had previously exhibited. He
consulted with Mayor Mayo and Major General Gustavus W. Smith, the
interim secretary of war, and carefully screened all applicants. He rehired
some of the old staff who had served ably and drew the new officials
almost exclusively from natives of Virginia. The reconstituted detective
force met with favor from the press and the citizens of Richmond.[96]

Winder was extremely busy but took time to pose for an "official" portrait. He had been photographed on 2 October and was probably unhappy
with the result. He intended to convey a stern, martial image, but in
the photograph he appeared instead to be a figure of menace. His hair

was in some disarray, his piercing eyes were partially hooded, and his mouth appeared cruel rather than firm. The portrait, completed on 22 November, projected a totally different image.[97] Seated in full-dress uniform, sword in hand, his countenance was that of a dignified warrior; the malevolent, even sinister depiction of the photograph had vanished. He would have been dismayed to learn that the photograph, not the portrait, became his official image; for nearly a century an engraving of it was the only image of Winder as a Confederate general in circulation. A phrenologist, and there were many, could not help but conclude that here was a man who looked as though he were capable of committing all the crimes he was accused of, a man quite capable of conducting a reign of terror and of causing untold suffering and deaths among Union prisoners.

Winder was not benign in physical appearance or official actions. The times were hard and produced hard men. It was a truism that it took iron men to sail wooden ships, and the same applied to other branches of the military. For most of 1862, Winder's actions made him one of the most controversial figures in Richmond. He attempted to limit the rights of the citizens in ways that inevitably caused resentment. He made mistakes, defended a group of detectives of whom some were unworthy of his trust, and rarely appeared tactful or diplomatic. There is little doubt that he had more critics than admirers at that time. After the reorganization of his staff in November 1862, his remaining years in Richmond were calm by comparison. He would earn increased respect and admiration from Richmonders before he was through, but he never completely overcame his image as the "formidable dictator" of the capital of the Confederacy in 1862.

Winder's reconstituted force returned to the streets and once again launched offensives against lawbreakers. One of the first "dens of iniquity" closed by his new force was a saloon operated by some of his former detectives. The "plugs" bought a saloon on the outskirts of town and offered drinking, gambling, dancing, and prostitution for entertainment. They celebrated opening night by killing one of their members, and Winder put an instant end to their operation. The press reported that only "respectable Baltimoreans" remained in Richmond by the end of November 1862.[98]

The winter of 1862–1863 witnessed increasing hardships and an escalating crime rate. Some of the "plugs" had been replaced by others with criminal propensities, and the situation deteriorated. Winder launched raid after raid against saloons, gambling establishments, and houses of prostitution, but the gain was negligible. Petty theft rose rapidly when shortages became critical, and burglars had an easy time during January and February when the streets were not lighted because gas was unavailable.[99]

The press commended the efforts of Winder's force and implied that some of the credit for the reorganization should go to Mayor Mayo. That popular official declined the honor and said that while he had the greatest respect for Winder, he had nothing to do with his police force. Mayo had troubles enough with his city police without accepting responsibility for any of Winder's men. The press severely criticized Mayo's force in May 1863 and concluded that thieves were virtually exempt from arrest. Conditions worsened and Mayo told his men in November that if night burglaries were not substantially reduced, he would recommend to the city council that the force be abolished.[100]

Mayo and Winder were both frustrated in their war on crime, but Winder received most of the public attention. The crowning indignity came on 18 November 1863. The *Enquirer* reported that "the dwelling house . . . occupied by Brigadier General John H. Winder, was ingloriously entered on Wednesday night . . . and robbed of a number of articles of clothing and domestic use." While the incident was extremely embarrassing to the chief law officer of Richmond, Winder was fortunate in that nothing of real value was taken. The burglar was after food and clothing only and did not take Winder's custom-made gold watch or his handsome field desk.[101]

A few months before the break-in at his own home, Winder had recovered a valuable portrait of George Washington. He received notes of gratitude from G. Washington and R. B. Washington (grandnephews of Washington) in April "for the interest" he had "evinced in recovering this relic, so valuable in its associations" to their family.[102] This particular recovery was an unusual success, however, and the robbery rate remained high in 1863 and worsened after Winder left Richmond in 1864. The *Whig* declared in March 1864, "Sending even the worst criminals to the prison is now only a farce," but admitted in July that since Winder's departure, the night force had become "utterly worthless."[103]

Winder's new force did not receive the level of criticism accorded the "plugs," but some of his men were an embarrassment. Augustus Simcoe of Norfolk joined the force in August 1863, and Winder proudly asserted that the Virginian would be a good detective. Two months later Simcoe was arraigned on charges of shooting a prostitute, Ella Johnson. She swore that while in bed with her he became too rough, and when she told him to leave, he shot her. Simcoe was found guilty but was later pardoned by Governor Billy Smith.[104]

Winder was mortified when the *Whig* announced on 9 March 1864, "Gen. Winder's Special and Confidential Detective Arrested for Treason." Captain Phillip Cashmeyer, Winder's "most special detective" gave an exchanged Federal prisoner several letters addressed to northern officials. He was placed in Castle Thunder until the letters, written in German, could be translated and examined. The letters revealed that Cashmeyer had only been attempting to impress some of his former friends by revealing the number of passports he had used in his duties. The investigating officer informed Winder that Cashmeyer had made "a contemptible ass" of himself but that he was no traitor. The letters were in German because that was the only language he could write. He was released and returned to Winder's office on 12 March, duly repentant.[105] He served Winder faithfully for the rest of the general's life.

Prior to his arrest, Cashmeyer was one of the few former "plugs" who had an excellent reputation with the press. He had been praised for his part in the battle of Seven Pines when the *Whig* erroneously reported that he had killed two Federals in battle. He was also commended for breaking up a Union spy ring in March 1862. His relative popularity with the press was due to his practice of furnishing it with copies of Union newspapers throughout the war. He obtained the Federal organs when he delivered the mail by flag-of-truce boat to City Point. After his arrest, he was usually referred to as "Winder's pet."[106]

An even more controversial case involved the conduct of Captain George Washington Alexander, superintendent of Castle Thunder. Alexander resigned from the Federal navy in 1861 and became a blockade runner. He was captured in July 1861, charged with treason and piracy, and confined in Fort McHenry. His wife helped him escape in September 1861, and Winder appointed him provost marshal the following June. He was promoted to captain on 12 June, and appointed assistant adjutant general the same month, and Winder placed him in charge of all Confederate state prisons in Richmond until October 1862. He was relieved by Thomas P. Turner on 27 October and became the superintendent of Castle Thunder at that time.[107]

Alexander found Castle Thunder to be a severe trial. The 3 1/2-story tobacco warehouse contained political prisoners of all descriptions: disloyal citizens, suspected spies, captured blacks, Confederate soldiers undergoing punishment, and all prisoners awaiting execution. Alexander found that many of the inmates would go to any lengths to escape and that some of his guards were unreliable. On 19 November 1862, seven prisoners escaped by bribing the guard detail. Each escapee told the two guards that the last man had the money and fled before it was discovered that there was no money. They were recaptured the same day, and Winder ordered the guards shot after they were pronounced guilty. One prisoner escaped after obtaining "fine clothes" from a visitor and "strolling past the unsuspecting guard." A deserter, R. C. Webster, attempted to flee the prison hospital even though he was in irons. Both were apprehended the same day. William Campbell was a different story. Charged with desertion and condemned to death, Campbell escaped from Castle Thunder four times before facing the firing squad.[108]

The increased vigilance of Winder's new force resulted in some five

Gen.ʳ W.ᵐ H.ʸ Winder.

General William Henry Winder, commander at the Battle of Bladensburg. From the St. Memins Collection, Library of Congress Historical Collection no. 393.

Andrew Shepherd house, Washington, Georgia, Winder's home during his first marriage. From Robert Willingham, Jr., *We Have This Heritage: The History of Wilkes County, Georgia, Beginnings to 1860.*

Caroline Ann Eagles, Winder's stepdaughter, circa 1866. This illustration and those that follow, unless otherwise indicated, were furnished by Carol Winder of Raleigh, North Carolina.

Caroline Ann Cox Eagles Winder. In the possession of Caroline D. Ashford of New Bern, North Carolina. This portrait could not be photographed without the occurrence of distortions resulting from attempts at restoration. The image here is a composite that comes close to what one sees when viewing the restored portrait.

William Andrew Winder, Winder's son by his first wife, Elizabeth Shepherd, circa 1867.

John Cox Winder, Winder's first son by his second wife, Caroline Ann Cox Eagles Winder, circa 1850.

William Sidney Winder, Winder's second son by his second wife, Caroline, circa 1866.

Captain John Henry Winder, circa 1846. From The Library of Congress Photographic Collection.

Winder's field desk. In the possession of Carol Winder of Raleigh, North Carolina.

Winder Building, Washington, D.C., 1870. Photograph furnished by architect Richard Bergmann of New Canaan, Connecticut, the Historic Restoration Consultant for the Winder Building.

A depiction of Winder as major, 3d Artillery, 1861. This likeness has been tampered with in a number of ways. While his "Hardee" or "Jeff Davis" hat bears the insignia of the 3d Artillery, it had to have been superimposed on an earlier portrait that has been lost. Winder's mouth is badly done, and his coat buttons do not line up horizontally, a strong indication that the second row of buttons was painted on over the original likeness—a common practice of the time. Only field grade officers wore double-breasted coats, and Winder was entitled to only one row, according to regulations in 1861. The "dubbing-in" may have been done after Winder was in the Confederate Army as there is some resemblance between this image and the engraving that appeared on the "General Winder Confederate Bond" of 1862. Courtesy of the Eleanor S. Brockenbrough Library/The Museum of the Confederacy, Richmond, Virginia.

General Winder Confederate bond, issued in 1862. In the author's possession.

Brigadier General Winder, 1862, the photograph that remained in circulation long after his death. From the Library of Congress Photographic Collection.

Portrait of Winder made in Richmond in 1862. Original in the possession of Carol Winder, Raleigh, North Carolina.

Libby Prison, Richmond, shortly after the end of the war. These photographs and those that follow are from Francis Trevelyan Miller, *The Photographic History of the Civil War*, vol. 3.

Belle Isle Prison, 1862. The figure in the gray, third from the right, is Major Thomas P. Turner, commander of the camp.

Andersonville Prison, 1864. View from the stockade wall. The deadline can be clearly seen on the right.

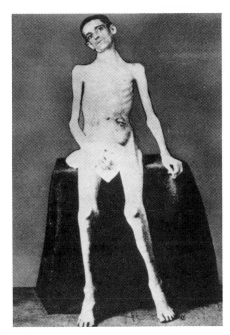
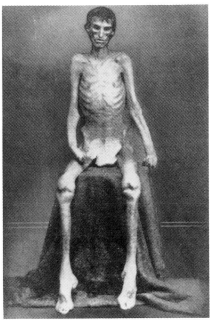

Federal prisoners who had been "Windered." Nothing inflamed northerners more than the circulation of such photographs, proof that Winder was indeed a fiend.

Colonel William Hoffman, Union Commissary General of Prisoners.

Justin Dimick, Winder's old
friend, as Brevet Brigadier
General, U.S.A.

Robert Ould, Confederate
Agent for Prisoner Exchange.

Northern prisoner of war camp, Elmira, New York.

Winder Genealogical Chart

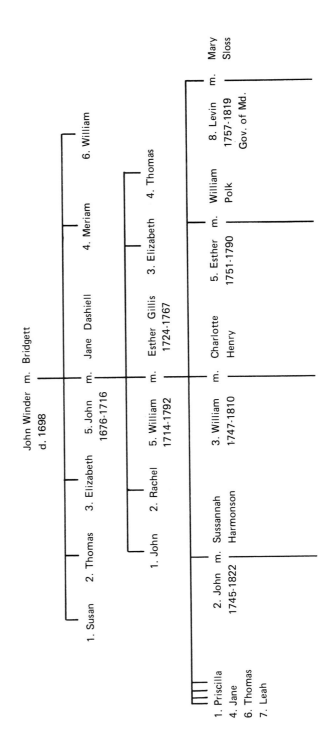

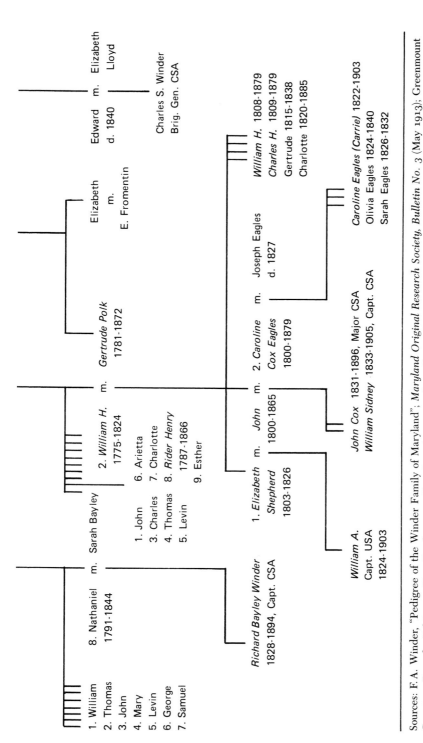

1. William
2. Thomas
3. John
4. Mary
5. Levin
6. George
7. Samuel

8. Nathaniel
1791-1844

m. Sarah Bayley

2. William H.
1775-1824

1. John
3. Charles
4. Thomas
5. Levin

6. Arietta
7. Charlotte
8. Rider Henry
   1787-1866
9. Esther

m.

Gertrude Polk
1781-1872

Elizabeth
m.
E. Fromentin

Edward
d. 1840

m.

Elizabeth
Lloyd

Charles S. Winder
Brig. Gen. CSA

1. Elizabeth
Shepherd
1803-1826

m. John
1800-1865

m.

2. Caroline
Cox Eagles
1800-1879

Joseph Eagles
d. 1827

m. Caroline Eagles (Carrie) 1822-1903
Olivia Eagles 1824-1840
Sarah Eagles 1826-1832

William H. 1808-1879
Charles H. 1809-1879
Gertrude 1815-1838
Charlotte 1820-1885

Richard Bayley Winder
1828-1894, Capt. CSA

William A.
Capt. USA
1824-1903

John Cox 1831-1896, Major CSA
William Sidney 1833-1905, Capt. CSA

Sources: F. A. Winder, "Pedigree of the Winder Family of Maryland"; *Maryland Original Research Society, Bulletin No. 3* (May 1913); Greenmount Cemetery Records, Baltimore; First Presbyterian Church, Baltimore; Polk, *Polk Family*.
Note: Names in italics are those most important in this study.

Gilbert-Hillhouse-Shepherd Genealogical Chart

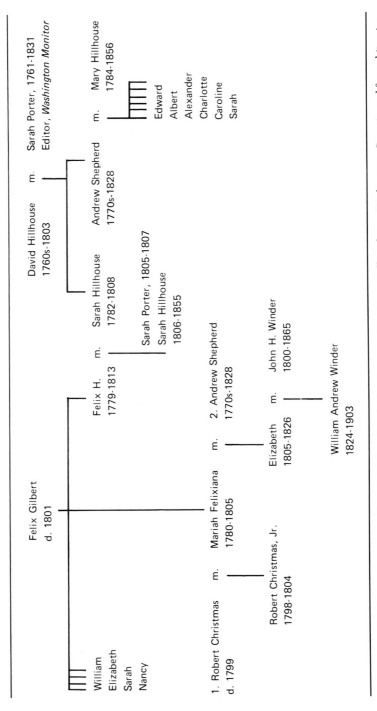

Sources: Compiled from cemetery records at the Wilkes County Courthouse and the Mary Willis Library, Washington, Georgia, and from obituaries in several newspapers.

hundred "of the most desperate set of culprits" being confined by early 1863, and life for many of the inmates became deplorable. Hardened felons beat and robbed newcomers, escape attempts multiplied, and several "wharf rats" and "plugs" attempted to blow up the building. Winder ordered Alexander to bring discipline and order to the prison and authorized the use of corporal punishment if necessary. Whippings and "buckings" became brutal and order was restored, but it came too late for some prisoners. Several soldiers, incarcerated because they had overstayed their furloughs, were broken men when their officers arranged for their release. When this became public knowledge, a congressional committee decided to investigate prison conditions. In April 1863, the committee brought charges against Alexander.[109]

Alexander was charged with killing two guards, exposing prisoners to bad weather as punishment for attempting to blow up the prison, and for brutally flogging prisoners who fought or stole. Winder informed the committee that Alexander was only following orders. "I state that in consequence of the violent proceedings of the prisoners in blowing up the building, garroting and using sling-shots upon newly arrived prisoners, robbing and endangering their lives, I gave orders to punish these ruffians severely and if necessary to resort to corporal punishment."[110] A three-member majority of the committee exonerated Alexander. They concluded that discipline was rigid but, in general, humane. Whippings were barbarous but inflicted only on "abandoned characters." Two minority reports were more critical. W. D. Simpson and Caleb C. Herbert found Alexander's actions illegal and unjust but recommended that no further action be taken, since he had not acted out of cruelty. The last report, unsigned but endorsed by Herbert, concluded that Alexander and Winder should be removed for ordering punishments that were illegal and degrading, "barbarous and cruel."[111]

Winder heeded the warning and issued a special order in September, stating that "under no circumstances" was "punishment of any kind to be inflicted on prisoners" except at his direction.[112] He returned Alexander to duty, but additional charges were brought against the superintendent in December. He was accused of extorting money from prisoners by promising to exercise his influence in their behalf and of permitting several inmates to go at large in the city. He was again exonerated, but Winder assigned him duty in Charlotte, North Carolina, and on 15 February 1864 the controversial captain departed Richmond.[113]

While Alexander was under investigation in April, Davis reduced the prison population of Castle Thunder by pardoning 500 deserters. The prison was again overflowing by October, and Winder appealed to the city council for use of the almshouse as a prison. The council, however, ruled that the needs of the poor were more important than those of Winder's charges. Balked in his request, Winder turned to a policy of redemption for some of the inmates and sent the incorrigibles to Salisbury, North Carolina. He recruited enough men from the prison to form four companies for the defense of Richmond. This force became known as the "Winder Legion" and performed well for the duration, but conditions remained poor for the inmates of Castle Thunder. On 18 May 1864, Winder ordered two trusted officers to inspect the place to determine if the food was "fit to eat."[114]

The health of all prisoners was in jeopardy long before 1864, and the same was true for all Richmond residents. Public health declined abruptly in November 1862 when smallpox became rampant. The pox ravaged the poorer sections of the city, but officials reacted promptly. Hospital wards were designated for the afflicted, a strict quarantine was effected, and inoculations were provided for everyone without regard to the ability to pay. The Richmond *Enquirer* noted that although smallpox was nothing to joke about, humorous events did sometimes occur. On 8 December an invalid soldier with a bad pox on his face appeared at Winder's office and asked for a passport. Immediately ushered into Winder's presence by the fear-stricken guards, the general took one look and ordered the unfortunate to the hospital ward. The soldier protested that he did not have the pox. "Go along, sir," said Winder, who told Cashmeyer to escort the soldier to City Hospital. Cashmeyer encountered friends along the way and ordered them to stand clear. A minor panic ensued along the route, but when the party reached the hospital, the surgeon just laughed and ordered a prescription for bedbug bites.[115] The smallpox epidemic continued until February and contributed to the overall suffering experienced by Richmonders during the winter of 1862–1863, but the number of cases was not large in regard to the total population. Winder worked with other officials to contend with the outbreak, and they were effective.[116]

Officials were not as efficient in meeting the needs of families of soldiers in the field. Winder notified Seddon on 8 November that their plight was worsening. "Daily applications for relief are made at this office and I am convinced that, unless some step is speedily taken, much suffering will insue." His forecast was accurate. By January 1863, bacon was $1.00 per pound, sugar $1.15, flour $0.13, butter $1.75, and coffee $5.00. A comparison with January 1860 prices reveals that the cost of living had increased tenfold. Sallie Putnam recorded that there was "scarcity but little want," but most residents would not have agreed. Some believed that speculators and hucksters were responsible for the shortages. Others blamed the Federal prisoners for consuming available supplies, and a few realized the truth: farmers produced sufficient foodstuffs, but the transportation system was inadequate to distribute the goods.[117]

The bleak conditions continued into spring, and a food riot broke out in April 1863. Initiated by a small group of women who decided to appeal to Governor John Letcher for relief, a large crowd soon assembled at the governor's mansion. Letcher offered sympathy but no support, and the crowd turned into a mob. Angry looters pillaged a ten-square-block area of the commercial district. They took many items besides bread and refused to listen to Letcher and Mayo when they arrived at the scene. The looters approached Main Street in full cry when a company of reserves appeared, together with President Davis. He gave the mob five minutes to disperse or he would order the troops to shoot to kill. After a few tense moments, the crowd complied and the bread riot of 2 April was over. To ensure that nothing further happened, Winder placed an artillery piece in place during the night. It was well that he did, for another crowd began gathering the following day. The presence of the cannon backed by Winder's city battalion was sufficient to prevent a recurrence; additional forces were sent for before the week was over. All of Winder's command plus two river battalions were placed at Mayo's disposal and no further demonstrations took place.

Assured that order had been established, municipal officials appropriated money to establish free-food depots in the city to relieve any actual distress, and Confederate officials tried to suppress all news of the riot. Secretary Seddon ordered that no reports of the incident should be telegraphed anywhere and asked the Richmond papers to avoid all references to the affair.[118] Most of the press complied, but the *Whig* broke the story on 6 April. Labeling the government's attempted suppression an "insane policy," the paper proclaimed that a riot had occurred but that it was not a bread riot led by hungry women. The paper asserted that the mischief was done by outcasts, deserters, and "plugs," who took little food but pillaged many stores in search of luxuries. It was, in short, a large-scale robbery committed by a mob of criminal ruffians, and the paper warned that such behavior would not be tolerated.[119]

The spring of 1863 was a busy season for Winder. In addition to ending the riot, he was ordered to require from all visiting officers their name, rank, regiment, corps, length of stay in Richmond, and a copy of their leave. Enlisted men were ordered to report to the provost marshal's office. All foreigners who claimed exemption from military service were ordered to produce their papers at Winder's office, where their names and physical descriptions were recorded. A sudden exodus of foreigners took place from March to July, and Winder and the press concluded that they feared conscription and were no longer willing to endure the hardships of living in the city. The passport office was besieged. Winder published notice of routes that had been closed to travel and arrested everyone caught without proper papers. The press of business was so great that he temporarily closed the passport office in mid-July.

Winder continued to oversee mail deliveries to and from the United States by the flag-of-truce boat, to collect the five percent duty on blockade goods, and to arrange for funerals of prominent Confederates. It was his sad duty to handle the arrangements for his kinsman, General Charles S. Winder in 1862, for "the savior of Richmond" General J. E. B. Stuart, in 1864, and for General Stonewall Jackson in 1863. He accompanied Mrs. Jackson and her husband's remains to Lexington, Virginia, in May.[120]

It was at this time that Georgia senators Benjamin H. Hill and Herschel V. Johnson recommended that President Davis promote Winder to major general. The senators stated, in their letter of 15 April, that Winder's duties had been arduous but that he had performed them "with a fidelity and efficiency that entitle him to high commendation." They noted that Davis knew Winder "too well, to require any voucher, for his sterling integrity as a man and his high and gallant bearing as a soldier and gentlemen." The request concluded, in the style and manner of the times:

It is due to General Winder to say, that this communication is made without his knowledge. Whilst we have no doubt, that his promotion would be exceedingly gratifying to him, yet such is the sensitive modesty of his nature, that it is scarcely to be expected, that he would ever make application for it. This is, therefore, rather an appeal to your generosity and justice, for a merited tribute to a good, true, and faithful officer, than the importunity of a mere seeker for promotion.[121]

Davis notified the senators that he had forwarded their recommendation to Secretary Seddon on 17 April. Hill and Johnson wrote Seddon the same day that they had a "deep interest in the matter" and requested him to consider it formally and promptly, since they were "very anxious to have the nomination sent in" before they adjourned. The nomination was not forwarded by Seddon, and the senators again petitioned Davis. On 23 April twelve senators endorsed Winder for promotion and stated that although he had not had the opportunity for distinction in the field, this had been "his misfortune and not his fault." They went on:

He has, with the modesty and patriotism of a true soldier, been ready and willing to serve, with cheerfulness and alacrity, wherever he has been ordered. He has been entrusted with more arduous and no less responsible duties than those of field service, and has discharged them with fidelity and efficiency. His patience, industry and energy have been displayed in such manner as to command the admiration and thanks of those who have been residing or sojourning in this city since he assumed his command here. He has never exhibited a prurient desire for promotion, or uttered complaints at the elevation of others above him who were his juniors in years and service. He has not sought or suggested this recommendation, and is indeed ignorant of its being made in his behalf. His unselfishness and modesty are no less admirable, and have, together with his constant, active and useful labors in office, induced us to make this recommendation.[122]

The promotion was not conferred, although both Davis and the press believed otherwise. The Richmond *Examiner* referred to Winder as "Major-General" on 10 July 1863, and Davis made the same error after the war. During his confinement at Fort Monroe in November 1866, Davis told a friend that Winder should have had even higher rank due to his long service in the army.[123] It appears that Winder's promotion was simply overlooked in the welter of events that occurred as the congressional session ended. Of the senators urging the promotion, seven were "warm party men" who supported the administration, and five, including Louis T. Wigfall, were ardent critics of Davis. Most of the senators were from the Deep South, but Allen T. Caperton was from Virginia and Landon C. Haynes represented Tennessee.[124] Winder's sponsors were fairly representative of the Senate's composition, and both Davis and Seddon supported Winder during the war and defended him afterward. The bureaucracy simply moved too slowly in this instance, and Winder never attained the coveted rank.

There is little doubt that the defeat rankled Winder. He was not the modest officer described in the petition—one who never resented the promotion of men his junior. He was as ambitious for higher rank as any, but, to his credit, he was not embittered by the setback. He never referred to the matter in any correspondence that has survived, and continued to perform his duties with as much energy as before.

In October 1863, Winder was one of the speakers at a major recruitment meeting held at Camp Lee. Several hundred guests attended a dinner held after the meeting and heard Letcher, Mayo, Winder, and others describe their respective duties in and around Richmond. This was Winder's first attempt at public speaking, and his effort was well received. Several reporters referred to his speech in favorable terms, but he never again made a public oration.[125] His father had been a masterful orator but he was not, and he reverted to written announcements and communications for the rest of his life. He might have improved his image with the press and public had he given more such performances.

Winder centralized his command post late in 1863 when he moved his headquarters into a new building on Tenth Street between Broad and Capital streets. All departments under his command were now housed in the same building, and the conduct of business improved considerably. For the first time Winder was able to have constant and instantaneous contact with his subordinates. The new facility housed Provost

Marshal Griswold, Chief of Detectives Maccubbin, Department of Henrico Quartermasters John Parkhill and Clarence Morfit, Commissary of Prisons Jackson Warner, and Medical Director William A. Carrington. The latter post was critical, since Winder was placed in command of all Richmond hospitals, military and civilian, from March to September of 1863. All wounded or sick reported to him and received assigned space in the proper hospital. He used convalescents as guards for hospitals and prisons and thus avoided hiring civilians or using fit soldiers for these duties.

The passport office was also moved to the new location in October, thereby eliminating much of that office's inefficiency. Its two entrances were separated by sex, and available routes out of the city were posted at each entry. Each applicant moved directly to a clerk in charge of the requested route. Congressmen were granted special passes early in 1864. The system as a whole remained unpopular, but it was at last possible to obtain a pass without considerable delay.[126]

Shortly after the passport office was relocated, Winder once again had cause to worry about a member of his family. In November he had a joyful reunion with his wife and daughter. Caroline and Carrie crossed the lines, but their Richmond sojourn was brief. Winder did not want them subjected to the hardships and perils of Richmond life, and they soon departed for Hillsborough, North Carolina. Caroline rented a house from her relatives (the Cheshires), and they remained there for the duration. Carrie wrote her grandmother in Baltimore of their safe arrival but did not send the letter by the flag-of-truce boat. Because of this, Winder received word on 1 December that his eighty-six-year-old mother had been arrested.[127]

After Caroline and Carrie left Baltimore, Gertrude Winder moved into the Hughes's boardinghouse. Her son Charles was visiting her on 21 November when Carrie's letter arrived. The letter had been intercepted by Federal officials, who delivered it and arrested Gertrude after she took possession. Despite her age and infirmities, she was taken to the provost marshal's office in a driving rainstorm and charged with writing and receiving unauthorized letters to Confederates. Charles explained the circumstances, and she was placed on parole and allowed to return home. The provost guard raided her rooms shortly after Christmas, searching for more evidence of disloyalty or treasonable correspondence. They found nothing and she was not molested further.[128]

The plight of his mother dampened Winder's Christmas spirit, but his mood improved with the arrival of his son John Cox and his family. They arrived in mid-December to attend the wedding of Octavia's sister Charlotte to Colonel Bryan Grimes in Orange County. Winder could not go, but he detailed Cashmeyer, "the celebrated detective," as escort. The visit was particularly welcome because Winder's wife and daughter were absent and he had recently sent Sidney to Georgia to build a prison to relieve the intolerable strain on Richmond. Federal threats against the capital made the city increasingly insecure, and Winder's days of command, like the Confederacy he served, were rapidly running out.

By May 1864, it was apparent to the Confederate leadership that a major reorganization was necessary. The Departments of Henrico and of Richmond were combined and placed under the command of Major General Robert Ransom. The Department of Richmond, created in April 1863, included parts of North Carolina and embraced the defenses of the city, including Drewry's Bluff on the James River and Manchester, south of the river. The commander, Major General Arnold Elzey, a kinsman of Winder, remained under Ransom, and Winder did, too, for a short period.[129]

On 25 May, Winder was ordered to Goldsboro, North Carolina, and placed in command of the Second District of that state. Before he left Richmond, a group of citizens raised approximately $1,200 in order to present him with a sword in recognition of his service to their city.[130] The *Examiner* reported his departure on 26 May as follows: "General Winder relinquishes . . . this Department much to the regret of officials in high quarters, who recognized his high administrative abilities in the control of his particular branch. Laborious in a remarkable degree in the discharge of the duties of his office, he has never lost a day since entering upon duty, now nearly three years ago, although above 60 years of age."[131]

Winder had labored long and arduously. He had done his best to perform his duty, and on the whole, he had succeeded. His actions were not always popular, but they were usually effective. All of his superiors praised his performance and defended him against critics, and there were many detractors. His command of the Confederate capital was controversial, and its citizens constantly berated or lauded him for his actions. The attacks and the defenses were both extreme. For example, J. J. Sloan of Goldsboro, North Carolina, wrote Seddon on 2 February 1864, that Winder was "a depraved, corrupt and drunken man" who took bribes and treated everyone but Maryland natives in an "insulting and profane" manner. Seddon was incensed and retorted that there was "not a particle of justice in the allegations against General Winder. That officer may err in being overzealous, but his honor, honesty, and loyalty are beyond all question." He added, "I wish his accusers had half his purity and devotion to our great cause."[132]

Most of the hostility created by Winder's actions occurred during his first year of command. After March 1863 he curtailed his activities to some extent and directed his forces to attempt to better their performance in fewer areas. He was more successful in rendering Richmond peaceful during the first year than later, but also caused greater dismay and unrest during the early period. He cooperated with Governor Letcher and Mayor Mayo most cordially and had few controversies with them or any other state or local official. He mended relations with Governor Vance and managed to placate North Carolina representatives and senators in the capital. His quarrels were usually with other Confederate officials— Northrop, Benjamin, Lane, Johnston, Hill, even the War clerk Jones— and happened when Winder felt they were attempting to impede his official duty.

All high-ranking Confederate officials endured carping editorials and constant criticism. Davis was a continuous target, Postmaster John H. Reagan received endless chastisement about the slowness of the mails, and other cabinet members were also severely reprimanded. Criticism was not limited to the home front; commanders in the field were also rebuked. It was part of the war. Winder fared worse than many officials because of his position and personality. He was a tactless martinet charged with an unpopular duty, overzealous and arbitrary in enforcing the law in some areas, apparently helpless to remedy evils in others. His strong defense of his "plugs" was a major mistake, one that tainted his rule long after the detective force had been abolished. His willingness to experiment with price controls and his handling of the passport system created widespread distress and resentment. The restrictions imposed by martial law were tolerable to the Richmond residents only in times of extreme emergency. If they were not actually in imminent danger of invasion by Federal forces or by outcasts and outlaws from other areas, they chafed under the suppression of their basic civil rights.

Some of the criticism of Winder was valid, but most was not. Perhaps the most unfair attacks concerned his treatment of Federal prisoners in Richmond. The local press accused him of excessive leniency in this area from 1861 on. The papers continually lamented the hardships imposed on the capital by the presence of Union captives and complained mightily if Winder appeared to be favoring the inmates in any way. During the latter months of 1863 as conditions in Richmond deteriorated, there was an increased and ultimately irresistible demand that the prisoners be removed from the capital, and Winder's responsibility in dealing with the issue increased. By 1864, he was once again in a position similar to that of late 1861, encumbered by vast numbers of Federal captives and with little or no hope of any immediate relief. It was in this area, not in his role as the "dictator" of Richmond, that his name and character were blackened beyond redemption.

CHAPTER 8

Warden of Richmond

1862–1864

Lincoln realized early in 1862 that the public would no longer support his position on the prisoner issue. The New York *Times* demanded unequivocally, "Our prisoners must be exchanged," and many other newspapers concurred, including those regarded as the staunchest supporters of the administration.[1] In addition, Congress had jointly resolved in December 1861 that a cartel be negotiated, and Lincoln was forced to yield. He designated General John E. Wool to conduct the talks but stressed that the terms of any agreement should not result in the official recognition of the Confederacy in any way. He was quite willing for the discussions to be of long duration in the hope that he might yet end the rebellion before a cartel was necessary.

Wool met with his Confederate counterpart, General Benjamin Huger, early in February 1862. Huger proposed that all captives, including those held as hostages, be exchanged immediately. The surplus prisoners would be discharged under parole and placed in a noncombat role until formally exchanged. Since the South had the majority of prisoners at that time, the terms were advantageous to the North. Federal parolees could be exchanged and returned to the ranks, while the South would have to place a large number of their returnees in a nonbelligerent position. Wool agreed to the proposal. Winder named Aiken's Landing as the rendezvous and issued orders for the transfer of captives to that point. The tentative agreement collapsed when Secretary of War Edwin M. Stanton rejected some of the terms. The new Confederate agent, General Howell Cobb, advised Winder to stop his preparations until a formal cartel was signed.

Discussions resumed on 23 February, and Wool and Cobb agreed that the Winder cartel of 1814 would form the basis for any new document.

The major obstacle to any agreement concerned the disposition of surplus captives, for the situation had reversed while the talks were going on. Grant captured 15,000 Confederates at Fort Donelson, and Burnside's expedition against Roanoke Island yielded 2,500 more. Exchange now favored the South, since the North would have the surplus who could not immediately be returned to the ranks.

Lincoln balked at this and urged a return to the status quo, the continuation of special exchanges that had previously prevailed. The South refused and remained adamant for a cartel. A stalemate resulted and the negotiations were broken off, but results on the battlefield soon changed official policy. Stonewall Jackson's actions in the Shenandoah Valley, the battle of Shiloh, and the failure of McClellan's campaign resulted in thousands of Federal captives pouring into Richmond. Lincoln, forced to reconsider, named General John A. Dix to replace Wool. The Confederates sent General D. H. Hill, Cobb being ill, and the talks resumed in July. The two men came to an agreement on the 22nd, and a formal cartel was at last in place.

The provisions closely resembled the Winder cartel. The salient features included the discharge on parole of all soldiers within ten days of their capture, and the requirement that surplus prisoners claimed by either side be placed in a noncombatant status until formally exchanged. Both sides pledged in Article 9 to continue the exchange even if disputes over the exact meaning of any of the terms occurred in the future (see Appendix).[2]

The long-awaited cartel brought much-needed relief to the Confederacy in general, but not to Richmond or Winder. On the contrary, conditions worsened for both. Prisoner congestion increased because Richmond became the place of exchange for both Federals and Confederates in the East. Union prisoners from Georgia, Alabama, and both Carolinas were concentrated in the capital, and returning Confederates were also held there until exchanged. The prison population remained high for most of the war, cartel or no, and Winder's responsibilities and work load grew. Unfortunately, so did his reputation. When prison conditions worsened, Winder was excoriated in the northern press. Maligned at an accelerating rate, his name was an anathema in the North within a year. The image of Winder as a brutal, inhuman fiend rapidly took shape; and by the time the war ended in 1865, the name Winder was indelibly imprinted in northern minds as a fit companion for that of the assassin John Wilkes Booth.

Northern criticism of southern prisons in 1861 was not directed at Winder specifically, and most of the allegations by Federal captives were trivial in nature. Conditions changed during the winter of 1861–1862, and their denouncements acquired more validity. Before the cartel was signed, Union prisoners had just cause for serious complaints. Rations were insufficient and irregular, their clothes were in tatters, and over-crowding had become critical.

Winder's difficulties with Northrop hampered his ability to furnish ade-quate food supplies, but he backed the efforts of Captain Jackson Warner, commissary general of prisons, to insure that the prisoners received the same rations as Confederates in the field, and he was generally successful. The recently released Congressman Ely reported in January 1862 that while the basic rations were army issue, he and others were able to buy all they needed from the marketplace. Further confirmation came from one of the 240 prisoners exchanged on 4 January. He wrote, "To all reasonable men our treatment while confined in Richmond has been as good as could be expected. Some cannot be satisfied. The treatment we received at the hands of Capt. Warner and Capt. Gibbs could not be better under the circumstances. They are both officers and gentle-men."[3]

Winder was powerless to correct the clothing issue. Confederate law required that all prisoners be furnished clothing, but nothing was ever done in this area. Except for North Carolina, no other Confederate state was ever able to clothe its own men. Temporary relief for some captives came in November 1861, when the Union sent some two thousand uni-forms and other garments through the lines and the Confederates distrib-uted them. A few northern states also sent outfits for their soldiers impris-oned in the South, but no long-term solution was found. Thousands were condemned to wear rags for the duration of their captivity.[4]

Overcrowding was also a problem that defied solution. Winder rented additional buildings as prisons, but the number of inmates exceeded prison capacity. In March 1862, he moved all Federal officers from the Liggons tobacco building to a former ship chandler and grocer's ware-house near the corner of Cary and 21st streets. Owned by L. Libby and Son and facetiously christened Hotel de Libby by the initial inmates, Libby prison metamorphosed into the Bastille of the Confederacy within a short time.[5]

Libby was strained to capacity from the beginning. To relieve the ex-cess, the fairgrounds at Lynchburg, Virginia, were pressed into use as a prison. Colonel George Gibbs notified Winder on 18 June that the premises were entirely unsuited for the purpose. The sleeping quarters were open stalls or "such tents" as the men could "construct with their blankets," there was no hospital or surgeon, no lumber to repair sheds, fences, and gates, and "no fuel nor well nor water buckets." It was impos-sible to guard the captives, and continual misunderstandings between the quartermaster and commissary departments resulted in "no food being provided for over 24 hours." Gibbs concluded his gloomy appraisal by reporting that in addition to all of his other problems, he had a rival who claimed to be in charge of the prison.[6]

An even more ominous omen for the future appeared in June 1862 when the decision was made to confine the excess enlisted men on Belle Isle, a small island in the James River. By this action, the leadership became vulnerable to later accusations that it was official policy to slowly exterminate Union prisoners, for Belle Isle offered no shelter whatever. If the capacity of the island were exceeded, or if adequate rations, tents, and fuel were not provided, Belle Isle was a miniature Andersonville in the making. The cartel postponed but did not prevent this ultimate tragedy. Yet the plan seemed sound in 1862. The captives were, after all, soldiers used to the outdoor life. They could prepare their food, swim daily, and wash their clothes with ease. The Richmond press reported in July that many of the 5,300 inmates at Libby were headed for Belle Isle, "a very pleasant spot. Their friends in the North may be perfectly satisfied that they will pass a pleasant summer in Richmond." The *Enquirer* declared that the prisoners were playing and wrestling in the summer breezes and that they had excellent tents and plenty to eat. "Their condition is certainly more enviable than that of several thousand of their comrades now in city prisons."[7]

This was an accurate summation of prison conditions in the summer of 1862. Libby remained overcrowded, and Winder rented two warehouses on 18th Street in July. These became known as Scott's and Pemberton's prisons, and both were soon overflowing as the battlefield captives poured in.[8] A Union prisoner, A. J. McClussy, noted that hardships had increased since the spring of the year. Until March 1862, he and other prisoners were permitted to go to the markets under guard and buy what they wanted. This was stopped because the citizens of Richmond hated to see prisoners "buying up food and articles they themselves wanted and could not afford."[9] A special guard detachment was established to purchase items requested by the prisoners, and the system worked well until Winder's ill-fated attempt to control prices resulted in the markets nearly closing down. The prisoners suffered from scarcities then, as did all Richmond residents.

Winder secured a millhouse from the company of Warwick and Barksdale on 1 July to confine captives from McClellan's campaign. This structure soon housed 4,000 men, yet the congestion was not abated. Winder was forced to parole General George McCall and other high-ranking officers to the Spotswood Hotel until he acquired Smith and McCurdy's tobacco factory for prison use. McCall and the others were held there until exchanged.[10]

Winder's resources were stretched to the limit by the time the cartel went into effect. He still faced the problem of serious overcrowding and insufficient food supplies. He wrote Lee in July that he was not receiving enough bread for his charges, that they were restless, and that his force might not be able to quell a possible uprising. Lee, busy with his campaign against McClellan, cautioned Winder to secure flour in adequate amounts and asked for a report detailing the strength of Winder's guards.[11] The bread shortage was relieved by the execution of the cartel, not by Confederate efforts; this boded ill for the future if the prisoner exchange discontinued.

In spite of the increased hardships, Federal officers remained favorably impressed with Winder's efforts. Michael Corcoran, so valuable to the Confederacy in obtaining the cartel, and several other officers told the Richmond press upon their release that they had all received decent treatment from Winder and his staff.[12] Had they been confined for much longer, they would undoubtedly have changed their minds, but fortunately for all, exchange began immediately upon the signing of the cartel.

Colonel Robert Ould was appointed agent of exchange for the Confederacy and proved to be a formidable defender of southern rights under the agreement. Ould made all arrangements for parole and exchange, and Winder carried them out. They worked well together, though the task was time consuming and tedious. Ould notified Winder of the names of the exchangees, and the general collected them from their respective places of confinement. In addition, Winder was responsible for paroled Confederates. He received the officers at his headquarters and assigned them quarters in various hotels. The enlisted men were sent to Camp Lee, the old Hermitage Fair Grounds. They were given their back pay, returned to their regiments when exchanged, or reorganized into new units for service. While awaiting exchange, Winder attempted to restrict them to the limits of the camp.[13]

The first exchange occurred on 3 August at Aiken's Landing. Winder forwarded 3,021 Federals and received 3,000 Confederates from General Lorenzo Thomas, the new Union exchange agent. Agreement was soon reached for a number of special exchanges including civilians, and the process of delivery went forward smoothly and fairly rapidly. Winder emptied the prisons at Macon, Atlanta, Mobile, Tuscaloosa, Salisbury, Charleston, and Lynchburg, but still had over 3,000 men confined at Belle Isle by late August. Sick and wounded Federals also remained in Richmond until they were pronounced fit to travel.[14]

Winder reorganized his staff to better handle the changed circumstances. Sergeant Henry Wirz, previously the popular commander at Tuscaloosa, was promoted to captain and given command of all Richmond prisons. Wirz told Captain Norris Montgomery, commander of Belle Isle, to expect 2,000 more prisoners on 31 August and to expand his lines accordingly. He also informed him that only special commissioners could trade with the prisoners and that he was to stop all other sources of exchange, especially the Richmond ladies who were selling fruits and pies to the inmates.

Winder replaced Montgomery with Captain Thomas P. Turner in October and ordered that he end all trade with the prisoners. No sutlers were to be permitted on Belle Isle and no contact with Confederate civilians would be allowed. There was too much danger of disloyal southerners conveying vital military intelligence to the prisoners awaiting exchange. Turner tried, but reported that the guards could be bribed. He concluded that he and his three employees, a druggist, steward, and clerk, could not police the guard and that some trade could not be stopped.[15]

Winder retained his son Sidney as adjutant general and added Richard Bayley Winder to his command in August. This second cousin came from Accomac County, Virginia. A wealthy thirty-three-year-old planter in 1860, he joined the Thirty-ninth Virginia Regiment in July of the following year. Notified in 1862 that the unit would be disbanded, Captain Winder called on his kinsman that summer. The general was delighted to obtain the services of this able officer and appointed him assistant quartermaster.

Before the war, Richard Winder and his family were frequent visitors at Green Mount, the plantation home of Benjamin Fleet. Fourteen-year-old Benny Fleet was in Richmond in 1862 and wrote his mother in November that he had been a guest of the Winders at the American hotel. He "had a pleasant chat" and "enjoyed some good music on the piano." The party reminded him "of the good old days at the 'Mount.'" He noted, "Mr. Winder has obtained quite a good position in Gen. Winder's Department, and is going to keeping house."[16] Benny's assessment was incorrect. The coming years would prove that any position with Winder was not good, and all of the staff would suffer because of the association.

Winder's attempt to establish an efficient prison system while the cartel was in effect was severely hampered because he was not the sole commander of all Confederate prisons. He had general supervision of the Richmond prisons and of the Salisbury complex, but he found that several commanders in various departments viewed him as a rival and would not recognize his authority over prisons in their areas. His designated prison commanders frequently informed him that the generals in the field would not recognize their authority and were not hesitant to issue orders countermanding their instructions from Winder. The War Department recognized the validity of Winder's complaints and authorized him to issue a special order on 16 October 1862, which stated that no prisoner could be transferred, paroled, or sent away from any prison without Winder's written permission.[17]

The matter of rations remained a contested point, and Winder frequently collided with Northrop. When shortages became acute in late 1862, Winder told his subordinates to make prison purchases on their own. Ordered to end this practice on 19 December, he decreed that henceforth all purchases could be made only by his direct order.[18] He was overruled in this instance and frequently in the future, when he attempted to create a central commissary command for the system. The prisoners suffered because of his failures. The Confederacy needed a commissary general for all prisoners, as the Union was quick to realize, but the leadership was slow to concede this point. In the meantime, Winder's attempts to create an effective organization were constantly frustrated.

Winder wanted his command to run by the book. For example, in January 1863, a surgeon, A. W. Thompson, asked Captain Turner to exchange two wounded Union officers. Gangrene had developed, and it was obvious that their military careers were over. Turner approached Winder and was subjected to the following philippic: "Sir: You will call the attention of Surgeon Thompson to the fact that all communications must be sent through the proper channel. You will call his attention to the Army Regulation on the subject of correspondence. Also the orders of the Adjutant General upon the same subject."[19] He issued reprimands and instructions of this nature repeatedly in his attempt to create a workable bureaucracy, but he really never attained his goal.

Exchange under the cartel created a myriad of duties for Winder. He furnished Ould with the name, rank, unit, and physical description of each soldier to be exchanged, notified the commander of each prison to deliver those prisoners, and assembled all parolees for exchange on schedule. In addition, he ordered the release of all Federals who had taken an oath to serve the Confederacy or to remain neutral. In the latter cases, he directed them to their place of employment. Finally, he oversaw the treatment of the wounded and sick, and determined when convalescents could be exchanged after consultation with the prison doctors. He was soon confronted with the delicate problem presented by the capture of black Union soldiers. His orders to his staff were to "please issue rations to the negroes confined . . . and keep the account so as to have it charged to the proper Department."[20]

The presence of blacks in uniform was one of the major reasons that exchange under the cartel ceased in 1863. The Confederacy viewed the Emancipation Proclamation as an attempt by Lincoln to incite servile insurrection, the worst form of treason, and declared that white officers of black troops would not be treated as prisoners of war. They would be executed if captured, and black soldiers would be returned as slaves to the states from which they had escaped. Further, any officers who obeyed Stanton's orders, issued on the same day the cartel was signed, to seize any "personal or real property belonging to disloyal persons" would not qualify for exchange. They would be treated as robbers and murderers.[21]

The Union rejected this interpretation of the cartel and declared that blockade runners, guerrillas, and bushwhackers would not merit exchange. Another dispute arose over men who had been captured while engaged in raising companies but who had not yet been formally mustered into service. By the winter of 1862, the quarrel reached such proportions that the exchange of officers ceased, and each side designated hostages for possible retaliation. Exchange of noncommissioned officers and enlisted men continued, but each side paused to weigh the pros and cons of obeying even that provision of the agreement.

The South had a great deal to lose if the cartel ended. Its much-needed parolees were declared exchanged and were returned to the ranks in short order; Confederate leaders were also well aware of the burden that the large group of Federal captives constituted. Still, there was the matter of principle and honor. They had already proved that they would not compromise in this area. Had they been willing to do so, the war would have been averted. They felt that it was outrageous that a former slave could become the equivalent of a white Confederate under the cartel, and that Federal officers could steal at will without reprisal.

Conversely, Union experience under the cartel had not been fortunate. Burdened by the surplus, Lincoln found the cartel to be an impediment in the conduct of the war. It was true that the exchange ended the hardships for Federal captives, and it was patently obvious that enlistment would suffer if the agreement was abrogated. But holding the surplus men in a noncombat role presented a vexatious problem; paroled Federals expected to return home until exchanged and refused to engage in any military duty that they believed violated their word under the terms of the cartel. Many expected to be mustered out permanently, and some threatened mutiny when this did not happen. As Lincoln viewed it, he was forced to house, clothe, feed, and guard his returnees as if they were captured Confederates. In addition, Federal commanders reported that too many of their men were quite willing to be captured so as to take a vacation from the rigors of war. Stanton admitted, "There is reason to fear, that many voluntarily surrender for the sake of getting home."[22]

Lincoln had been forced into the agreement and the public still demanded that he honor it, but the longer the cartel remained in effect, the more he became convinced that the evils outweighed the benefits. He was receptive to arguments that the South was violating the terms and that he could with justice end the exchange. By the summer of 1863, when the twin Confederate disasters at Vicksburg and Gettysburg immeasurably strengthened his position, he directed that regular exchange cease. By May of the following year, he and Grant prohibited all exchange regardless of the cost. He could not do this in 1862, but doubtless knew then that he had made a bad, if necessary, bargain.

The retention of all officers in late 1862 marked the beginning of Winder's ordeal. At first he had adequate resources, since all but the sick and wounded had been exchanged before the cessation. He also expected the issue to be resolved, and he sent Wirz south in September to oversee the return of all Federal officers to Richmond.[23] At the same time, he allowed the Federal commander of the Old Capitol prison, William P. Wood, to visit Castle Thunder to determine if any of the disloyal civilians confined there wanted to go North as "Lincoln's Ragged Recruits." Escorted by Alexander, who had once been his prisoner at Fort McHenry, Wood reported that conditions were good and agreed with a recently exchanged Union captain that Libby was clean and well administered.[24]

Conditions were deteriorating by the time Wirz returned with the captives in October 1862. Both governments had begun deviating from regular exchange, and when the battle of Fredericksburg in mid-December resulted in another Union defeat, Davis seized the opportunity to make a change in the interpretation of the cartel and to strike a blow against the most hated man in Federal uniform, General Benjamin F. Butler. Davis proclaimed Butler to be a felon and an outlaw—Butler, the author of the phrase "contraband of war," which he coined to describe runaway slaves who sought sanctuary behind his lines early in the war and which he used to justify their retention; Butler, the "Beast" who threatened to treat the women of New Orleans as prostitutes if they insulted his men; Butler, whose name roused Confederates to a fury unequaled until Sherman ravaged Georgia. Davis further stated that until Butler was punished, no Union officers would be released on parole before exchange, and he ordered that any officer who could capture the "Beast" was to hang him on the spot. He also proclaimed that none of Butler's officers would be considered prisoners of war.[25]

In January 1863, Davis went further and formally proclaimed a policy of retaliation. He announced that he would turn over all Union officers in Confederate hands to state authorities, who would then try them under the laws of the several states for exciting slaves to rebel against their owners. This was clearly a violation of the cartel, but Lieutenant Colonel W. H. Ludlow, an aide to General Dix who had been conducting the business of exchange, believed the Confederate threat and asked for a meeting with Ould. The two met at City Point, the new exchange place in the East, and agreed to exchange all officers captured before 12 January, the date of Davis's proclamation.[26]

The partial resumption of exchanged officers in 1863 afforded no relief for Winder or for the capital. The arrival of a large contingent of captives in January doubled the prices at the marketplace overnight. The further arrival in March of some 6,000 additional prisoners forced Winder to impress large amounts of flour destined for the Richmond markets, an act of "insane tyranny" according to the press.[27] The next month witnessed the "bread riot" and offered convincing proof that there was a scarcity of immense proportions in Richmond. Ludlow convinced Stanton that Union officers in Libby were suffering a horrible fate and received authorization to exchange all officers, man for man, without reference to the cartel. This was done on 1 April, and Winder's burdens were temporarily relieved.

A part of this exchange caused controversy after the war. Ould wrote Winder on 17 March 1863, "The arrangement I have made works largely in our favor. We get rid of a set of miserable wretches and receive some of the best material I ever saw." This was in reference to political prisoners, but someone changed the date to 1 August 1864, took it out of context, and cited it as evidence during the Wirz trial that Ould and Winder both attempted to kill or physically wreck Union captives.[28] This was not the only example of forgery that was used against Winder.

The records clearly prove that both Winder and Ould scrupulously honored the cartel, even when it was not favorable to the South to do so. For example, Winder was asked by Brigadier General W. H. Fitzhugh Lee not to permit the exchange of G. G. Otto. Otto had "been in [Confederate] lines a number of times" and could give valuable information to the enemy. Winder forwarded the request to Ould and stated that there was no evidence that the man was a spy. Ould agreed that Otto would have to be exchanged, and Winder issued the order.[29]

The special exchange of 1 April was not an indicator that either side was ready to return to the cartel. Davis remained committed to retaliation, and Lincoln refused all exchange until his counterpart revoked his hostile proclamation. Two other events further poisoned the atmosphere. In Kentucky, two Confederate officers were caught and executed for recruiting behind the Union lines. Ould informed Ludlow that two Federal officers would be selected by lot and suffer the same fate. The second case concerned the capture of Colonel A. D. Streight in Georgia. He and his officers were accused of inciting slave insurrections. Davis ordered that they be tried in Confederate courts, where a verdict of guilty and a sentence of death were a certainty. They were sent to Libby to await trial.

Lincoln's response surprised the Confederates. He had yielded to the threat of retaliation in 1862 and agreed to the cartel, but he now threatened to raise the black flag himself. The capture of General W. H. Fitzhugh Lee, son of the most famous general in the Confederacy, ended all southern threats of retaliation. Lincoln declared that Lee was to be held as hostage and would be shot if any Union officer was executed by the Confederacy. On 25 May the exchange of officers was again canceled, and on 13 July, Stanton ordered all exchange stopped until both sides agreed on exactly what the cartel meant.[30]

Agreement between Ould and Ludlow was out of the question. Each was so bitter that the only type of exchange possible was that of vituperative insults. Ludlow was replaced by General Samuel A. Meredith on 26 July, but productive talks were not forthcoming. Meredith proposed a daily exchange of prisoner correspondence, but Ould hotly replied:

"It is of far more importance that the thousands of prisoners who are languishing in your prisons, should be sent. The best and most satisfactory message from them will be communicated with their own lips. If you intend to keep them in your horrible prisons, it will be but a poor satisfaction that they have the privilege of telling their loved ones the story of their anguish."[31]

Ould's exasperation with what he regarded as Union perfidy led him to try almost anything to force a return to the Confederate interpretation of the cartel. When Provost Marshal Isaac H. Carrington recommended the transfer of Charles W. Webster, a civilian, to Libby for exchange, Ould refused and responded on 21 September as follows: "Castle Thunder is the very place for Webster. I do most sincerely hope he will not be sent to the United States. How are we to secure the release of our own people in confinement at the North, except by taking and holding Northern citizens. I hope the day is not far distant, when four or five hundred like Webster will be sent here. Then and only then will our citizens languishing in Northern prisons be released."[32]

One week later, Winder questioned the transfer of two civilians from Castle Thunder to Libby for exchange in light of Ould's treatment of Webster. Ould replied that only he had the authority to decide who would be released, that he knew what he was doing, and that if Winder refused to let them go, the responsibility would be his.[33] Winder complied. The two men were in constant correspondence, and the above example is one of a very few messages that were not cordial and cooperative.

Winder received thousands of letters from relatives and friends of both Union and Confederate captives, all anxious to determine the status of their loved ones. He gathered the requested information and forwarded it to Ould, who responded to the inquirers. Winder and Meredith also wrote frequently and without the bitterness common in Ould's epistles. Winder asked Meredith about the status of Confederate captives and forwarded the requests to Commissary General Hoffman, who supplied the information if he could. The whole business was time consuming and tiresome. In addition, Winder regularly asked Ould to see Union officers who requested special exchange. He also wanted to know how he could be sure that a paroled Confederate was telling the truth when he asserted he was not liable for service. Ould replied that anyone claiming he was captured after 1 September 1863 was probably lying, since as of that date all were declared exchanged and must return to duty.

Winder continued to promote special exchanges, but he was most desirous of a return to the cartel. He asked Ould on 12 November if he saw "any possibility of a speedy resumption of exchanges" and was not cheered by the agent's gloomy assessment. One special exchange, which would ultimately damage Winder's reputation immeasurably, occurred on 21 November. Winder asked Ould if Colonel Daniel T. Chandler was the Confederate wanted in exchange for Andrew Johnson's nephew. Ould affirmed this and Chandler returned to the Confederacy.[34] In less than a year, Chandler reported on conditions at Andersonville prison, blaming Winder for that "hell on earth." Chandler's conclusions were used with devastating effect to blacken Winder's reputation during the trial of Henry Wirz.

Winder's reputation was savaged in the Union long before the Andersonville tragedy, and the sole reason for this was the failure to resume the cartel. Winder could not provide the necessities, and Union captives suffered and died at an alarming rate. This in turn convinced the northern public that retaliation was necessary, and Commissary General Hoffman ordered a drastic curtailment of provisions for Confederate prisoners. The war hardened the hearts of both sides, and each accused the other of deliberately murdering helpless captives. The alleged atrocities required an identifiable villain, and the northern press provided one for their readers as early as November 1863. One vitriolic attack after another was levied against Winder. The following castigations printed in the New York *Times* were typical. On November 15, 1863:

> The rebel General John H. Winder was one of the well known characters in the old United States Army, and it has frequently been remarked by officers of the army and navy that never did Jefferson Davis display more knowledge of human nature than when he made him jailer of Richmond. Winder is a born turnkey, a natural spy, a ruffian of the old school, capable of any meanness and any cruelty. At the outbreak of the war, he was on duty at Pensacola, but fortunately for the cause of the Union, was temporarily absent from his post. Had he been in command instead of Lieut. Slemmer, Fort Pickens would have been immediately surrendered to the rebels. Winder had no friends among his associates in the army. He was commonly called the Old Pig, as he seemed to possess all the qualities of that dirty animal except its usefulness. As a military man he is notoriously ignorant and incapable, but his hard-hearted cruelty and rancor against his old companions in arms have eminently fitted him for the position he holds under the rebel Government, the willing jailor of thousands of suffering heroes, the fit instrument of the horrible schemes of the rebel Confederacy for undoubtedly their intention is to operate upon our Government by allowing our soldiers to rot and starve in the Richmond prisons. General Winder is just the man to carry out this plan.
>
> He is perfectly capable of stealing the money sent to the relief of our prisoners. There can be no doubt that this old thief has systematically abstracted the contents of letters sent from the North to Union soldiers in the South. An incident in his personal history will

show that he has not been proof against temptation in times past. Winder married for his second wife a Virginia lady named Eagles, a widow with one child. This child, a daughter, was possessed of property in her own right to the amount of $20,000. While this young lady was still a minor Winder got the property into his hands, appropriated it to his own use, and deliberately defrauded her of the greater part of it, for which he could never be made to account.

This hoary old villain is really primarily responsible for all the inhumanities practiced upon our soldiers in Richmond. He has been selected for his peculiar fitness to the ignoble office of chief turnkey of Richmond, and in his particular duties he is never interfered with.

To those who knew him when he was in the United States service there needs no proof of Winder's special and general villainies. His known character for meanness and dishonesty would convict him before any jury of army officers, and if it could be believed that any man would steal the pennies from a dead man's eyes, Winder is the man to do it.

On 11 December 1864:

The manner in which the Union prisoners have been treated by the rebel authorities is so different from anything in modern, or even in ancient times, that no word has yet been found to characterize it.

General Winder was not perhaps the author of this system of treatment, but he is a man of education and ability who has devoted three years of his mature life to the exercise of it, and it appears to be therefore an act of simple justice to give his name to the system . . . to say that a man has been *Windered* would convey at once a clear and definite idea, or rather a train of ideas, to thousands of mourning families, and so long as the history of this rebellion is remembered, the infamous name of WINDER should be connected with the part he has taken in it.

On 18 December 1864:

WINDER (who will be immortalized in the roll of infamy and cruelty) is said to have offered a thirty days' furlough to any guard who will shoot a prisoner walking over the "deadline."

At the same time that he was being vilified by the Union press, Winder was chastised by the Richmond papers for his continued "kindnesses" to his wards. When 500 Confederates returned from confinement at Point Lookout in wretched condition, southerners demanded that Winder cut the prison rations in retaliation.[35] The recently opened Richmond *Sentinel* reported that eleven Federal officers had been given breakfast at Linwood

House and complained, "This style of entertaining prisoners of war has gone too far." The journal listed several instances of Winder's excessive generosity and was openly jubilant when an injunction was brought against him for impressing William Grant's warehouse for use as a hospital for free Negro captives.[36]

In the summer of 1863, when the prison population was relatively low, Winder ordered a thorough cleaning of Libby prison. The floors were scrubbed, water closets hosed down, and walls and ceilings whitewashed. The improvement was obvious but temporary. When exchange ceased and the overcrowding resumed, Libby soon became an infamous name in the Union.

As late as September, when several Union reporters for the *Christian Observer* were permitted to visit, conditions in Libby were satisfactory. The officers held prayer meetings each evening and appeared in good spirits. The enlisted men on Belle Isle also had adequate shelter and supplies. This was the last time the captives experienced an acceptable situation. Conditions rapidly deteriorated as autumn yielded to winter. Both prisons would soon be labeled death camps, and the 10,000 captives there by mid-October faced an ugly ordeal.[37]

Winder received a complaint from one of Libby's most famous prisoners at this time. Colonel Streight declared that the issue of a quarter pound of poor quality beef, half a pound of bread, and half a gill of rice or beans was criminally inadequate. He asserted that the officers had to spend $1,000 per day on vegetables to eke out even a starvation diet. Winder replied that Confederate prisoners at Point Lookout and Fort Delaware were being subjected to worse conditions, but he told the colonel that he would conduct an investigation to determine if any rations were not being delivered. Winder ordered the prison commissary Warner to address the issue, and he did so promptly. He interviewed the Federals serving as mess sergeants on each floor and concluded that all rations issued were delivered and that Streight's figures were incorrect. Each man received half a pound of beef, a pound of bread, and varying amounts of rice and peas. And the Union officers charged with food distribution claimed that they served soup daily. Streight and other officers contested their colleagues' statistics, and there is little doubt that their accusations had come true by October.[38]

Lieutenant Louis R. Fortescue had another complaint. Captured at Gettysburg, he was sent to Richmond under intolerable conditions. The trip took two weeks and commenced each day at 5:00 A.M. and ended at 2:00 A.M. the following morning. He and his group of 250 men were allowed only three hours' sleep and were fed "something like dough" at 10:00 A.M. They walked the 130 miles to Stanton under these conditions, and from there they took a train to Richmond. Most were sick by the time they reached Libby. Fortescue recovered and noted after one month's confinement, "The redoubtable General Winder in consequence of having several drinks on board this morning took it into his head to allow the Yankees some reading matter—he kindly sent up one copy of the New York *World* to be read by nearly 600 officers." On 26 August he recorded that after two months' confinement, he had finally received a letter from home. By the first week of September, he, too, was concerned about rations. "The latest rumor," he wrote, "is that General Winder has concluded to allow the officers more rations and also some of the money taken from them when brought here." Conditions worsened, and on 23 November he confided to his diary that for three days they had "not a particle of meat," just rice and corn bread, and that the guards had "threatened bread and water."[39]

Winder's prison commanders confirmed that a crisis existed by late October. Sidney informed his father on 28 October that no beef had been delivered that day. Captain Alexander feared that a violent outbreak at Castle Thunder would result, and begged Winder to see that meat was issued. Captain Turner reported that the prison hospital was without meat and that Sergeant Samuel Burnham of the commissary department saw no relief in sight. Winder immediately complained to Seddon. He stated that this was the fourth time the deprivation had occurred and warned, "No force under my command can prove adequate to the control of 13,000 hungry prisoners." Quartermaster General A. R. Lawton endorsed Winder's letter and told Seddon, "This matter seems to cause great trouble and confusion. The Commissary Department and General Winder never seem to agree, and I respectively ask the interposition of the Secretary of War."[40]

Winder countered that in this issue he did "not know the Commissary General" and looked "to the Quartermaster General for any failure" that might take place. Seddon informed Winder that Northrop, not Lawton, was responsible for feeding the prisoners, and ordered Winder to stop buying additional supplies.[41] Winder complied but notified Seddon on 9 November that his charges were still without adequate rations. Two days later he reported that "not 1 *pound* of meat for 13,000 men" was available and enclosed a report from his subordinates delineating their impossible situation. In it, Sergeant Burnham asked Northrup's office for the prisoner allotment and was told that only 70 head of cattle were on hand and that this beef was to be distributed to the hospitals. The commissary could furnish 2,500 pounds on 10 November, but it was doubtful if any more would be available soon. Burnham lamented the impossibility of feeding 14,000 men on 2,500 pounds of beef, or a quarter of the required amount. "I have no substitute for beef and only a limited quantity of bread, not enough for double rations . . . thus leaving 3/4 of the prisoners in a hungry condition." Winder ended the communication with a second warning: "If these prisoners are not fed, there is great danger of an outbreak."[42]

To relieve the crisis, it was decided to send the prisoners to Danville. Winder ordered Turner to start the move on 11 November and appealed to Seddon for help: "I beg that the responsibility resting on the officers in charge of the prisoners be remembered and that a sufficient supply of provisions be insured for their maintenance."[43] Seddon tried, but Northrop ignored the appeal for rations. He was unable to provision the army, much less the prisoners, at that time. Help came from the United States in time to prevent a major catastrophe. General Ethan Allen Hitchcock, the new commissioner of exchange, ordered that 24,000 rations be sent through the lines on 12 November. Two months previously, Ould had agreed to distribute a Union issue of clothing, blankets, and medical supplies, as well as additional money and gifts, to the Union prisoners. He chose General Neal Dow, the senior captive, to oversee the operation. Dow, placed on parole, accompanied the articles to Belle Isle. The plight of the enlisted men horrified him; he predicted that one hundred deaths per day would soon occur if they did not receive immediate relief. To this end, he asked that Meredith smuggle $100,000 in Confederate money to him.

Hitchcock and Meredith rejected this suggestion but determined to find out what the actual condition of the Union prisoners was. On the day the rations were forwarded, Meredith informed Ould that all Confederate captives were comfortably housed and clad and were fed nourishing meals, including meat, three times daily. If the Union prisoners were not receiving equal treatment, he suggested that they be released and promised that all would be placed on parole in a noncombat capacity.[44]

The Confederate leadership decided to respond to this challenge by submitting a detailed report of their prison system. Isaac Carrington completed the task on 18 November and reported the presence of 11,650 prisoners dispersed as follows: Libby, 1,044; Belle Isle, 6,300; hospital, 728; and 3,578 in the various warehouses. Conditions were crowded at Scott's and Pemberton's, but no undue suffering was noted. Rations were again adequate after the earlier crisis, and the shortage of tents and medical supplies at Belle Isle was being corrected. Carrington concluded that the condition of the prisoners was roughly equal to that of the Confederate soldiers. All experienced shortages because of the blockade, but prison officials were obeying the Confederate law that their captives receive the same issue as their own soldiers. He admitted that there were complaints of beatings at Belle Isle, administered by a gang of prisoners against their fellow inmates.[45]

Winder and Ould verified the accuracy of the report and sent it to Hitchcock. At the same time, the new commissioner received a report from a group of Union surgeons recently released from prison which flatly rejected Carrington's assertions. They charged that the officers imprisoned at Libby suffered mightily from the cold and that the enlisted men were freezing to death at Belle Isle. The Libby water closets were actually filthy privies that polluted the whole building, and the Belle Isle compound resembled an animal stockade. Rations were inadequate at all prisons, and the Belle Isle inmates had no blankets or bedding, and many had no shelter at all.

In addition to this Union report, there were widespread rumors that some of the relief articles had been diverted to Lee's army while others had been stolen by rebel guards. In light of this, Hitchcock suspended further actions until he was convinced that the provisions were actually being distributed to the prisoners. Meredith soon persuaded Hitchcock that the rumors were false and resumed deliveries, but Ould informed him on 12 December that the issue had generated such adverse and malicious publicity that the South would receive no further provisions.[46]

If Hitchcock and Meredith believed the Confederates properly dispersed all provisions, the prisoners did not. They were certain the rebels stole from them, and many believed that the official policy of the Confederate government was to kill or cripple them through slow starvation and exposure to the elements. They were equally convinced that Winder, Turner, and others were involved in both criminal activities.[47]

The Confederate policy on currency permitted all prisoners to keep any gold coins in their possession, but Federal paper money was not allowed. Seddon ordered Winder on 15 September 1863 to exchange Union bills for Confederate ones at "the current rate." The prisoners could then buy what they would with Confederate money. If a prisoner refused to comply, the Federal notes were held in his name and no money would be issued to him. This policy also applied to all money the prisoners received through the mail. Winder issued the necessary orders and told his staff to deliver all articles received, but any charges on them must then be paid and a receipt issued.[48]

The prisoners' complaints of theft reached Winder, and he ordered Maccubbin's detectives to place under close surveillance all guards and civilians who had any opportunity to steal from his charges. Several arrests soon followed. Clothes, blankets, shoes, and other articles marked "U.S." had been offered for sale by guards to the detectives, but they all claimed they had purchased the goods from the prisoners.[49] It was difficult to prove otherwise because prisoners did sell government issue to the guards and used the money to buy food.

The detectives reduced but did not eliminate thefts of articles addressed to inmates. One system of petty theft was never hampered. Ever since mail delivery by flag-of-truce boats had been initiated in 1861, letters marked "money for postage inside" invariably turned up empty.

Winder complained of this annoyance to Ould, and the agent responded that he had long been aware of this "systematic robbery" and assured the general, "There is no fault in this matter in your office." Richmond postmaster John O. Stegar reported to Winder that the letters had been rifled when he received them from the boat and that he doubted it would be possible to stop it.[50]

The records prove that the prisoners were correct when they asserted that robberies took place, but wrong in their belief that Winder and his staff were participants. They were also in error in their conviction that he intended to kill or cripple them through neglect. Winder was concerned about the sudden increase in mortality rates at Belle Isle. Beginning in October 1863 and continuing through the winter, over one hundred prisoners died each month. This was a tenfold increase over the average for all previous months, and he told the medical director, William A. Carrington, no relation to the provost marshal, to conduct another investigation.[51] He believed the first report to be accurate, but something had obviously changed in the interim, and he wanted an explanation.

The surgeon reported that the essence of the problem was overcrowding. In the hospital, prisoners received the same medicines and care provided Confederate sick and wounded, but they were allotted only half of the space. The same was true for Belle Isle, where prison density was too high and the congestion resulted in increased suffering and death. Besides lack of space, there were shortages of everything else necessary for good health. There were not enough tents, bedding, blankets, or shoes, despite the Federal issue. Too many prisoners sold these items to the guards to obtain food. The bread was made of unbolted flour, and this increased the number of cases of dysentery and diarrhea. The guard detail was too small to permit the inmates to use the latrines at night, and the island was covered with putrid filth.

Carrington concluded that several other factors were unique to any prisoners who faced long confinement. With no exchange in sight, many became despondent and died of homesickness. Their woes increased when imprisoned Union doctors administered an impure substance to prevent a threat of smallpox. The supply of the substance had been obtained from a subject with secondary syphilis. The victims, who feared the hospital was staffed by Confederates who had no interest in aiding their recovery, usually suffered in silence until it was too late. Carrington closed his remarks by verifying what Isaac Carrington had mentioned in the first report: strong inmates preyed on the weak in ruthless fashion. A gang of "raiders," ruffians from New York, assaulted, maimed, killed, and robbed at will. The guards failed to maintain discipline, and the result was akin to anarchy. The only solution was to move the prisoners

and reduce the congestion. Carrington hoped that as many as possible
would immediately be moved to a "more Southern climate."[52]

Winder questioned the accuracy of Carrington's basic conclusion. He
agreed that overcrowding was a problem but believed that the virulence
of the smallpox epidemic and the attendant conditions of prison life ac-
counted for the increase in mortality rates. In any event, he could not
prevent the congestion. An insufficient number of guards forced him to
concentrate the inmates, and that situation would not change unless exchange was resumed. He did support Carrington's recommendation to
send the prisoners south. That fateful decision had been made before
Carrington finished the report. Winder sent his son Sidney to Georgia
on 24 November to locate a new site for the prisoners.[53]

There were both humanitarian and military reasons for this decision.
Northrop could not furnish sufficient supplies for the army and the increasing numbers of prisoners. Shortages had been critical even when
the Federal issue was allowed, and would certainly worsen in the near
future. With regard to maintaining security, it was increasingly dangerous
to keep so many inmates in the capital. Escape attempts were more frequent, and a general uprising or massive outbreak was probable as the
ratio of guards to prisoners assumed critical proportions. Espionage
agents would be more active, and their attempts to pass vital intelligence
would be enhanced, since many captives knew the disposition and conditions of Lee's army. Another fear was that Union cavalry raids might
result in the release of the prisoners, who would certainly terrorize the
city.[54]

One final consideration was the propaganda factor. The charge of deliberate extermination was deeply offensive to Confederate leaders, yet the
actual conditions at Belle Isle had deteriorated to the extent that even
the grotesque exaggerations of the sensation-seeking northern press attained some credibility. It was Confederate policy to send to the North
the worst cases of the sick and wounded prisoners who could still travel
through the lines; photographs of these starved and mutilated skeletons
inflamed the North as did no other issue. The pictures were appalling
and substantiated the chilling charge of widespread murder. The Confederate assertion that the suffering was caused by the blockade and Lincoln's refusal to resume exchange under the cartel became increasingly
unsatisfactory. There was a demand in the North for a resumption of
the cartel. Many believed the administration was stalling, but moderates
and even southern sympathizers could not deny the evidence before their
eyes. That many Union prisoners were suffering and dying was fact, not
propaganda, and a day of reckoning would come.

To counter the poison of northern propaganda, the South had to devise
some way to ameliorate the conditions of their prisons. The creation of

a new prison in the Deep South was viable only if certain obstacles could be overcome. The mild winter weather was an important factor, but what about the blazing summer months? The transportation facilities had to be independent of Richmond to ease the strain on Lee's army and the capital, but they had to have connections to an industrial center. The availability of food would not be sufficient in itself; there had to be a source of manufactured goods lest the prisoners be subjected to even greater hardships. In short, a system was needed. The Confederacy would have to create a central command center with an adequate staff, ensure that the various bureaucracies cooperated, and detail sufficient personnel to guard, house, feed, and provide the necessary medical care. An effective commissary general for all prisoners was essential to divert disaster.

The Confederate inability to accomplish this was one of the most tragic events of the war. For Winder, it was the tragedy of his lifetime. He worked ceaselessly to improve matters. Whether anyone could have accomplished more is a moot point. It was his responsibility and the task was too much for him. His failure meant that thousands of prisoners would die and thousands more would experience barbarous and inhuman conditions.

The first month of 1864 gave Winder a preview of what was to come. Lieutenant John Latrouche, adjutant of Libby prison, stated that another hospital *had* to be opened and that he needed at least eighteen additional guards. Surgeon T. G. Richardson reported that none of the prisons were secure. He "lived in fear of a breakout every night" and insisted that more guards and buildings had to be provided or a calamity would occur. Winder responded that the manpower was not available. He told his staff he had tried to hire civilian guards and had even attempted to get disabled soldiers to serve in that capacity but that he had "failed in every attempt." He had begged Arnold Elzey, commander of the Department of Richmond, for extra guards to relieve the crowded condition of the prisons, which condition was owing to his inability to "obtain a guard to send the prisoners off." Jones provided 240 men. Winder needed at least 1,000, and conditions continued to deteriorate.[55]

By 12 January the officers at Libby had not received meat for four consecutive days; the 8,000 enlisted men at Belle Isle had been without for eleven days, except for the few prisoners who captured the pet poodle of prison commander Virginius Bossieux and ate it. The Libby inmates were "jammed into every nook and corner." At night the floor of every room was covered, "every square inch of it by uneasy slumberers lying side by side and head to head."[56] Conditions at Belle Isle defied description.

Confederate fears of a breakout and of a Union raid became reality in February of 1864. On the 9th, Colonel A. W. Rose led 108 other officers through a tunnel under Libby in the most successful escape attempted in Richmond; forty-eight were recaptured and two drowned, but fifty-nine eventually made it to the Union lines. Among those successful was the notorious Colonel Streight. He was hidden by Elizabeth Van Lew, whom Winder had permitted to visit Libby, in her Richmond home for over a week. He arrived safely in mid-February and gave an exaggerated report of his sufferings to the press.[57]

The Richmond press blistered Winder for allowing the escape. He reported that the guard was not to blame, but the editors were not convinced. The *Whig* editorialized that a "big odoriferous rat" had been present, and Winder's "nose must have been clogged up not to have smelled it."[58] Had the press learned that Van Lew had manipulated Winder, the criticism would have been worse.

The second event that Richmonders feared lasted from 28 February to 4 March. Two columns of Federal cavalry, commanded by General Justin Kilpatrick and Colonel Ulric Dahlgren converged on the capital in an attempt to release the prisoners. Dahlgren was killed and his body mutilated, but the raid was frustrated more by bad luck than by the Confederate defense. Richmond panicked, and to some extent, so did Winder. As the Federals advanced, Seddon ordered Winder to secure the prisoners by every possible means. Winder authorized Turner to mine Libby prison, and he promptly placed two hundred pounds of gunpowder in the cellar floor. The prisoners were warned that if any attempted to escape, the charge would be set off. After the raid had failed, Winder and others reported that the action had only been a threat to keep the inmates quiet, that they had no intention of blowing up the place.[59]

The denials were no doubt true, but the affair did not speak well for Winder's character. It was a desperate measure and hinted that he might act similarly if placed in a perilous position in the future. He did not, but of all the charges leveled against him by his accusers after the war, this one was undeniably true; it strengthened the belief that if he would condone this measure, then he was probably guilty of others even more damning. On the other hand, what he did was mild compared to what Dahlgren had proposed to do. Instructions bearing his signature called for the release of the prisoners who were to take the city and hold it while his men murdered Jefferson Davis and his cabinet. Richmond was then to be burned. The Richmond press declared Dahlgren a war criminal and demanded reprisal. Seddon favored executing some of the raiders, and Josiah Gorgas, chief of ordnance, suggested that all of the prisoners should be killed.[60] But the escape and the attempted release convinced the Confederate leadership that the evacuation of the prisoners must commence at once. Other prisons, ready or not, would have to be pressed into service immediately. Regulars were detached to guard the prisoners in transit, and Winder promised to send the captives south at the rate of 400 per day. He was as good as his word. The *Enquirer* reported on 18 March that over 10,000 captives had been sent from the "Boa Constrictor of Libby" to the "more luxuriant" and "crowded granaries of Georgia."[61] A more percipient observer might have questioned this statement, but one would have to have been omniscient to foresee what actually awaited. Before the war, slaves had an abiding fear of being sent to the Deep South, for they might not know exactly what the future held, but they knew it would be bad. The prisoners were slated to face an even worse fate. Their destination was Andersonville.

CHAPTER 9

The Abyss

Southern Prisons, 1864–1865

The passage of more than a century has not lessened the horror of the name. Andersonville. The greatest tragedy of a tragic era. Nothing like it has ever been seen on the North American continent before or since. Americans can liken it only to other, more recent words, foreign words, like Auschwitz, Treblinka, or Dachau. Andersonville, graveyard for 13,000 helpless Union captives, the shame of the South, a stain on the honor of the entire Confederacy, a name inescapably linked to John Henry Winder.

How could it have happened? Unlike the Nazis, whose intent was extermination, the Confederates' aim was to relieve the suffering of their prisoners. The scale was vastly different and the intentions opposite, yet the results were all too similar. Andersonville, Florence, Salisbury, and other southern prisons were death camps for thousands. What went wrong? More specifically, who or what was to blame? Many explanations, both conflicting and diverse, have been offered for over twelve decades. None has received universal acceptance; it is unlikely that one ever will.

The series of events that would prove calamitous to the Confederacy and to the Winder name began when Sidney left Richmond on 24 November 1863. Charged with locating a prison site in Georgia, he consulted Governor Joseph Brown and Howell Cobb, general of the reserve forces of that state and soon to be the commander of the Military District of Georgia, and selected a spot about one mile east of the hamlet known as Anderson. This was his third choice. He had previously designated the more desirable locations of Blue Springs, near Albany, and Mineral Springs, between Plains and Americus, but local opposition had overruled his selections.[1]

Anderson residents also opposed his plan. That group of corn- and cotton-producing Georgians were no more anxious to have a prison in their midst than the others had been, and their opposition looms large in the list of episodes that ultimately determined the fate of the Union captives. When Captain Richard Winder arrived in December and assumed the post of quartermaster, he found that the locals would not work for him. He was finally authorized to impress the necessary labor and materials, but construction was delayed until mid-January. This was a critical and ultimately fatal delay.

The Winder cousins labored under extreme disadvantages. They encountered frustrations, delays, and shortages daily, and found that their needs ranked at the absolute bottom of both Confederate and Georgia priorities. Sidney wired his father on 24 January 1864: "A surgeon is much needed here. I am compelled to send four miles for a physician."[2] His quartermaster cousin was in an even worse predicament. Forced to rely on Columbus, fifty miles distant, for all tools and other equipment, Richard found the shipments irregular and inadequate from the beginning. He also informed Winder of his troubles.

He notified the general that he had concluded agreements with local mill owners to grind corn for prison use but warned that other foodstuffs and indispensable items could not be had. The meat supply was especially critical. He planned to secure beef in Quincy, Florida, but it proved "absolutely impossible to hire exempts to drive cattle." The available manpower was "physically unable" to make the drive, and he feared he would never be able to obtain a sufficiency of beef. In the unlikely event that he could, he lacked the necessary supply of pots and pans to prepare and serve the rations. He begged Winder to send a cook, baking pans, platform scales, and a supply of nails, padlocks, and window glass. Finally, he despaired of even finishing the prison. He had the impressed slaves for only sixty days and doubted he could complete the compound in that time. He concluded with the dire observation that Colonel Alexander W. Persons had just notified Sidney that the guard force would consist of only one hundred men, all of them "presently without firearms" of any sort.[3]

This bleak and accurate appraisal did not totally discourage the Winders, and they pushed ahead with the project as rapidly as they could. They made considerable progress despite delays caused by the intense cold and shortages of every description. The slaves and the small detail of reserves felled the lofty Georgia pines and cut them into twenty-foot logs. Placed upright and impaled five feet in the earth, the logs formed a nearly impregnable barrier. By mid-February a double stockade had begun to emerge. The outer wall covered some sixteen acres and enclosed an inner stockade of slightly smaller dimensions. Sentry boxes were placed at intervals along the top of the inner walls, and plans were made for barracks, a hospital, and a bake house. A branch of Sweetwater Creek about five feet wide bisected the compound, and Richard believed that 10,000 inmates could be comfortably housed in the finished structure if sufficient rations could be procured.[4]

Whether he was correct in his judgment must forever remain unanswered, for the compound was never completed. For all of its existence, Andersonville was a truncated mixture of prison and hospital. Massive in size, chaotic in organization, it was deficient in the very essentials for life. Pressed into use by the alarming conditions existing in Richmond, the prison was not half-finished when the first inmates arrived. As congestion increased to over three times that planned for the completed compound, Andersonville became a hell on earth for everyone there.

The urgency to send the prisoners out of Richmond was generated by the failure to continue the limited exchange initiated in December 1863 by, of all people, Benjamin Butler. About 1,000 were exchanged, but none were sent after February 1864 except the sick and wounded. Each side refused to make the necessary compromises, and exchange ceased for the better part of a year. Even before the tunnel breakout and the Union raid, Winder was ordered to make the necessary arrangements for the immediate removal of the captives.[5] He reported on 7 February to Adjutant General Cooper that, in compliance with orders, he was finalizing preparations for the removal. Officers were in place at Charlotte and Augusta to feed the prisoners, and regulars were being detached to guard them in transit. He informed Sidney at the same time that he planned to start the first group within ten days and to expect them at the rate of about three thousand per week.

This news was extremely depressing to the Winder cousins. In spite of their best efforts, the stockade was only three-fourths completed when the first arrivals reached them on 27 February. No barracks, bake house, or hospital existed; even the house for the post commander was not finished. The quartermaster's office had just been started. Richard lived at the local church, vacating it when services were held. This was the scene when Camp Sumter, the official designation, came into being.

The first arrivals were herded into the stockade, issued bake pans and uncooked rations, and left to fend for themselves. The guard, buttressed by several pieces of artillery, protected the open end until the stockade could be closed. From the first, prison officials could do little except confine the inmates and try to prevent escapes.[6] Before the prison was one month old, all of the ingredients for a first-class disaster were in place. The prisoners fashioned rude huts at random, and no internal discipline was ever established. The sick were laid out in selected areas of the stockade, ministered to by an inadequate staff of surgeons, and nursed by fellow inmates who were usually indifferent to their sufferings. Lacking sufficient food, shelter, and medical care, men began to die. The constant arrival of additional prisoners, "fresh fish" as they were called by those already incarcerated, compounded the misery. Andersonville began to resemble Belle Isle by April; 283 out of 7,500 prisoners were dead by that time.

Many of these men were near death when they reached the camp. Weakened from prolonged confinement, their strength further depleted by the arduous ten-day transport, they were no match for the hostility of their new environment. Richard became desperate. He sent appeal after appeal for help; on 11 April he reported he was "forced to bury the dead without coffins" and that he had no lumber even for the living. His cousin was no longer present to share the responsibility. Adjutant General Cooper wanted a native Georgian as post commander and recalled Sidney to Richmond on 26 February. Lieutenant Colonel Persons of the Fifty-fifth Georgia Regiment assumed the position but fared no better than Sidney in placating the irascible and uncooperative Governor Brown. Persons took charge on 1 March and immediately informed Cooper that Richard had no tools whatever, not even a spade to bury the dead. The next month he reported that Richard was bedridden with inflammatory rheumatism and that he had himself been compelled to leave his post to secure the necessary items. He returned on 17 April and found that his troops had engaged in a near mutiny during his absence.[7]

The riot of the undisciplined Georgia reserves accentuated the fatal weakness of Andersonville. Providing a sufficient guard was Cobb's responsibility, but Governor Brown ruled that no regulars could be used. All fighting men were needed at the front. Militia and reserves would have to suffice, and these groups consisted primarily of old men, young boys, and convalescents. The guards were exposed to the same shortages as the prisoners and they, too, sickened and died. Desertions increased with each passing day, and discipline virtually ceased. Underfed and insufficient in numbers, the guards became increasingly unreliable and unpredictable in their actions, and the officers could not control them. In sum, the security forces were incomplete and inadequate, just like the rest of the compound, and this made any improvement of the whole system impossible.

As chaotic as things were at Andersonville, conditions were not much better in Richmond. Winder received Sidney's report in person and became even more convinced that a central command had to be established. He informed Seddon on 12 March that a clear chain of command was not extant. His subordinates at Danville and Andersonville were under the command of Elzey and Persons, respectively, yet he still had the responsibility for both prisons. He feared that conflicting or even contradictory orders would result and asked Seddon to clarify his position. The secretary responded that he saw no problem but that if Winder objected to either commander, he had but to submit candidates as successors. Winder replied that he did not object to either officer; his concern was that the current command structure was unclear and inadequate.

Winder's letter went to the heart of the problem, but he refused to nominate himself as commissary general of prisons. That was the duty and prerogative of his superiors. All he could do was suggest that the position was necessary. He followed up his query by reporting that the recent replacement of Captain Warner as commissary of subsistence had been a mistake. He liked and respected the new commissary, but the shift caused confusion in the system and the result was that his prisoners were not being fed. The specter of starvation again faced his charges, even though the majority had been removed. Rations were sporadic and insufficient even for the remainder, and he concluded that it was the lack of a system, not the officers in charge, that was at fault.[8]

When Winder wrote Seddon, he had just been informed of the alarming rise in mortality rates at the Belle Isle hospitals. The medical director Carrington told Winder on 8 March that 590 out of 2,260 patients had died because of space, food, and medical shortages. Six days later, the surgeon T. G. Richardson and Assistant Adjutant General George W. Brent told him that the three prison hospitals could accommodate 500 patients; on that day there were 1,127 present and "in some instances two patients were found on a single bunk." The congestion was due to the paucity of guards, they concluded, for there were only three officers and 105 enlisted men guarding the whole compound.[9]

On 23 March, Carrington wrote Winder a long letter reminding him that he had previously offered Winder the use of vacant hospital beds for prisoners during the winter crisis and that he had refused the offer with the explanation that "there were not guards enough to go around." He noted that a congressional committee had reported favorably concerning conditions at the hospitals, and so had a committee of Confederate escapees headed by General John Hunt Morgan. Still, the rate of sickness and death was appalling, and while he personally did not subscribe to the idea that overcrowding was the cause of the high mortality, the fact remained that the "best hospitals in the city were empty at that time and they were *offered and refused!*" Carrington concluded that he knew Winder could not guard the additional buildings but suggested that an investigation was in order.[10]

That investigation had already taken place. Richardson and Brent were convinced that overcrowding was the basic cause of the high mortality and presented their conclusions to Braxton Bragg, special advisor to Davis. Bragg forwarded the report to Winder for his response. On 26 March, Winder responded that he was not totally convinced that overcrowding was the problem. He pointed out that the mortality rates for the 1863–1864 winter were about equal to those of the previous year, "yet the total number in hospital during the first period were very small." He continued:

> The increase of mortality for the month of February, 1864, may be fairly attributed to the virulence of smallpox—the ascription of the mortality to the crowded state of the hospital was perhaps precipitate. . . . All the facts show that the mortality is incident to prison life, and cannot reasonably be attributed to the want of space in the hospitals. I do not contend that the hospital accommodations have been such as were the most conducive to their health and comfort. The best disposition of them has been made which the guard and the means at my disposal would allow. With insufficient guard I have been compelled to concentrate them.[11]

Why Winder rejected overcrowding as a major cause of the high death rate is puzzling. He had built hospitals during his old army career, had observed their operations during the Mexican War, and had presided over them during the current war. He was certainly cognizant of the space requirements. Yet "the facts" he referred to as proof that death was incident to long-term incarceration were correct. Mortality rates were comparable for the two periods in question. In 1862 and 1863, 112 deaths occurred out of 593 cases, or about 19 percent; Carrington reported 590 out of 2,260, or about 26 percent, for 1863 and 1864. The worst cases were sent north in both instances, about 35 percent in 1862 and 1863, and 48 percent the following year. The difference could be explained by the smallpox outbreak plus the deprivations of prison life. The cartel was operative for the first period and not for the second, and the longer confinement certainly contributed to the escalating rates. Winder acknowledged that hospital conditions were bad but concluded that nothing could be done to improve the situation; the commissary officials were to blame for the food shortages, and he was so short of guards that many of his men remained on duty for over 48 hours without relief. He could not prevent the congestion without additional troops.[12]

The Richmond medical officers, including Surgeon General Moore, disagreed with Winder but offered no proof that his figures were incorrect, and all acknowledged that the shortage of guards precluded any dispersement of the inmates. Later critics asserted that Winder intentionally increased prisoner congestion at Richmond and especially at Andersonville as a part of his deliberate process of extermination.[13] What was overlooked by these accusers is that Winder was not responsible for exceeding the capacity of Andersonville. Cooper was. And while Winder was never convinced that overcrowding was the major cause of mortality, he worked to reduce congestion at Andersonville as soon as he was given command.

In all fairness, Cooper had no choice either. He knew Winder could not provide for the prisoners then in Richmond, and on 2 May he ordered that all prisoners captured south of Richmond proceed directly to Andersonville. By that date, there were 12,000 men in the stockade, and over 1,000 had already died. A surgeon, Isaiah H. White, reported from the scene that the deaths were the result of long confinement at Belle Isle and disease contracted during transit. He urged the abandonment of the makeshift hospital inside the stockade and the construction of a better facility outside the prison walls. This recommendation was shared by Cobb and by Walter Bowie, inspector general of Lee's army, who submitted a detailed report to one of his staff, R. H. Chilton, on 10 May. Winder saw the Bowie report and ordered the immediate removal of the hospital to the outside of the stockade.[14]

The lack of lumber delayed the hospital relocation for a time, and the staff ultimately resorted to providing tents. Richard was able to complete the bake house in early May. From that time on, at least some of the prisoners received the same fare as the guards, but others continued to be issued uncooked rations that they had to prepare as best they could. By his own admission, Richard had placed the bake house in a bad location. The kitchen refuse soon polluted the stream flowing through the stockade, and the inmates were forced to dig wells to obtain drinking water.

The refuse from the bake house was the least of the sanitation problems facing Captain Henry Wirz. Winder detailed him for stockade duty on 27 March, and he attacked the abysmal sanitation conditions with characteristic zest and energy. Shortly after his arrival Wirz determined to build two dams on the stockade stream. The upper area would be used for drinking water and cooking purposes, the lower for bathing. In May he began to build sinks along both banks further downstream, and he intended to flush the whole system by periodically opening both dams. Lumber scarcity halted the project, and it was never completed.

That lumber was unobtainable in a heavily timbered area underscores again the importance of a command system with the power to act. Richard was forbidden to pay more than $50 per 1,000 lineal feet of lumber, and the market rate was double that figure. He was finally authorized to impress sawmills not required by the railroads, but railroad officials told him that they had none to spare. They insisted that a complete breakdown in transportation would occur. The result was that no lumber for the Andersonville compound could be obtained. The power to impress was no power at all for a mere captain, even if he was the quartermaster of the largest Confederate prison. All Richard could do was parole prisoners who possessed carpentry and other needed skills, and this he did. They worked on the bake house, hospital, tannery, various other buildings, and the stockade proper. Others were permitted to leave the premises under guard to secure firewood for the compound.

Wirz, too, faced problems that defied solution. His duties in the inner stockade included feeding, clothing, and housing the prisoners, instilling internal discipline, and policing the prison grounds. He was fortunate even to be able to furnish rations on a regular basis. He was dependent upon Persons to provide the necessary manpower for his needs, as he had no authority over the guard detail, but Persons was unable to comply. By 9 May, when Wirz wanted to build the sinks, Persons had 1,193 guards in camp, but almost one-third were too ill for duty. With the remnant, Persons had to attempt to contain 13,000 prisoners and to prevent any breach in security that might occur from Federal cavalry raids. His force had to man the stockade, guard prisoners detailed for outside work, and man the outer fortifications in case of attack.

Near the Florida line, which was but one hundred miles distant, there were sufficient Union forces to easily overcome Persons's garrison. The Federal defeat at Olustee (near present-day Lake City, Florida) in February did not mean an end to Union raids. Persons had little to spare for Wirz, and conditions continued to worsen. In desperation, Wirz asked for a promotion, hoping that additional rank might help him in dealing with other prison officials. Even though Winder endorsed this request in the strongest language, stating that no other officer equaled him in diligence, energy, and efficiency, Wirz was not promoted. The lack of a system continued.[15]

As bad as conditions were in May, that was the last month that Andersonville resembled Belle Isle or any other previous prison. During the first three months of its existence (27 February–31 May), 1,567 prisoners died; for the next three months, the figure was 6,011. The horror had begun, and there was no end in sight. Beginning in September, Winder began transferring the inmates from Andersonville, but 2,677 more captives were in mass graves before the month ended, and 1,595 more died in October. Only after this time, when all of the prisoners except the hospital cases were relocated, did the abomination end.

The month of May, then, was the critical month. Until then, exchange had continued "in an informal way," but Grant urged an end to this practice. He meant to destroy Lee's army and wanted no Confederate reinforcements from exchange, as there had been after he paroled his Vicksburg captives. He had been outraged when Ould declared these parolees exchanged, even though no exchange took place, and he had to fight them again at Chattanooga. Lincoln supported this recommendation, hard and cruel though it was. Both men knew that Union captives would have to pay the price, but both agreed that it was worth it. To continue to exchange would mean that Grant's armies would eventually have to kill every soldier in the Confederate armies. Better to keep rebel prisoners captive; it was cheaper in every way to feed them than to fight them, even if it meant that Federal prisoners would have to undergo unimaginable sufferings.

It was the correct decision, but it was a tough one, as tough as any that were made during the whole conflict. As Grant moved south and the slaughter began, thousands of Federal captives poured into Richmond. Within weeks, over 2,000 were confined at Libby. Belle Isle was packed, and the Danville warehouses were again overflowing, as were the miserable facilities at Cahaba and Tuscaloosa, Alabama, and the stables at Lynchburg. A new prison for officers made its appearance at Macon, Georgia, and the number of prisoners at Andersonville exceeded 15,000 by the end of May.[16]

It was obvious to Wirz and Richard that the stockade had to be expanded, and Cobb agreed. He was busy constructing the Macon facility but did add two companies of reserves to the Andersonville forces. He also informed Richard that the time had long since passed when a senior officer of ability was needed at the Camp Sumter complex. Inspector General Chilton at Richmond concurred but was convinced that Cobb's recommendation to expand was not sufficient. He penned a letter to Cooper on 26 May.

> General Winder controls directly all prisoners arriving here, at Danville, and at Andersonville, Ga., and now at Macon, Ga., but has no general control over the subject. . . . With the multiplicity of duties performed by General Winder it could not be expected that he could give that strict personal supervision to duties which of themselves are sufficient to occupy the best energies of a man of intelligence, energy, and industry, and no one can examine the records and character of service relating to the department of prisoners without being convinced of the absolute necessity for a commissary-general of prisoners.[17]

Cooper forwarded the message to Davis, but the besieged president rejected the advice. He did decide to appoint a senior commander for Andersonville and recommended Winder as the "best qualified" of the available officers. Cooper notified Winder of his new orders on 3 June, and the general promptly asked if it would be possible to establish his headquarters at Americus so his family could be with him. He also wanted to know if the Macon complex was part of his command. Cooper replied that Macon was included but that he would have to live at Camp Sumter. Winder would again be apart from Caroline and Carrie.

Assured by Winder that he would depart for Andersonville on 10 June, Cooper wrote Seddon a very naive letter three days later. He recorded that Winder's "presence alone will have a beneficial effect upon the guard and the prisoners. He can inspect frequently the prisons and see that subordinate officers discharge their duties fully, and in the event of any *emente* [sic] to take prompt measures for quelling it."[18] For Winder to correct the defects of Andersonville by his mere presence was indeed a large assumption. The truth was that it would take herculean efforts to remedy the situation, and any commander would have to possess the authority to utilize all resources of the area to avert an even worse tragedy.

It took Winder seven days to make the 600-mile trip, following the same route taken by the prisoners. He arrived at Andersonville on 17 June, coincidentally the seventeenth consecutive day of unrelenting rain, to find that the command was an indescribable quagmire. There were close to 24,000 prisoners and an effective guard of 1,462 men, effective in name only, as he soon deduced. Over 2,200 Federals had died, and thirteen surgeons ministered to some 2,000 current patients, assisted by uncaring prisoners on parole. The hospital latrines had polluted the water supply, and the stockade was a frightful scene. The constant movement of men using the sinks on the creek banks had created a putrid swamp covering three and one-half acres in the center of the prison, and the swamp then became the latrine. Fecal matter from thousands of men suffering from dysentery polluted the entire area; maggots bred in the slime to a depth of fifteen inches; a small scratch might become a raging infection overnight with gangrene sure to follow. The command was truly a hell on earth, and the horror mounted with the passage of each day.

Winder's staff included his son Sidney as assistant adjutant general; Lieutenant R. W. Brown, aide-de-camp; and Lieutenant S. B. Davis, assistant adjutant general and inspector general, as well as Richard Winder, Wirz, and other officers already in place. Winder was alarmed by the meagerness of his security force and instantly realized that nothing could be accomplished until this deficiency was rectified.

The day after his arrival he informed Seddon that he had to be reinforced, that another prison was essential, and that Andersonville had to be enlarged. Three days later he endorsed a report made by his staff that rations were insufficient and of low quality, that the prisoners were destitute and in a filthy condition, and that at least 1,500 guards, 150 hospital tents, and additional surgeons were needed immediately.[19] He also issued a stern warning to the guards to increase their vigilance and properly police their camps. He threatened slackers with severe punishments if they did not instantly obey, and this had an unintentional side effect: some of the reserves became fearful of Winder's wrath and summarily shot prisoners who crossed the deadline without first warning them as required by orders. The deadline consisted of a row of posts with boards nailed to the top which ran about fifteen feet inside of the inner stockade wall. Within a short time, the prisoners became convinced that Winder had promised a thirty-day furlough to any guard who killed an inmate for crossing the deadline.[20]

Winder subjected Cooper and Seddon to a constant barrage of requests and demands from his first day of command. On 22 June he asked Cooper to permit him to retain Private William Butler, one of the escorts in transit who was due back in Richmond, as an assistant quartermaster to Richard Winder. Since the quartermaster was also responsible for the Macon prisoners, Richard needed someone he could "trust with money." Winder continued his plea:

> When the magnitude of the responsibility resting on me is considered, I hope I may have such assistance as I may deem necessary, and I hope it is unnecessary for me to say that I shall ask nothing that is not necessary. We have this morning 24,193 prisoners of war and increasing daily, larger than an army corps, and only 1,178 reserves (as raw as troops can be) for guard for all purposes. We have this morning discovered a tunnel under the pickets fourteen feet deep and from 90 to 100 feet long. This work will show the desperation of the prisoners, and the breaking out of these prisoners would be more disastrous than a defeat of the army. . . . I earnestly request that an additional force of at least 2,000 men may be immediately sent me. The Government has placed upon me a fearful responsibility, and I trust there is confidence enough in me to accord me all I ask for the proper performance of my duties.[21]

Later that day he informed Cooper that he had dispatched Lieutenant Davis to Richmond to personally convey to the high command just how perilous the situation was. Besides requesting regular reinforcements, he also asked for counterespionage agents. He feared that agents from Sherman's army had penetrated the compound and that local Georgians were guilty of treason. He had information that they had corresponded with the inmates, sympathized with them, and "ought to be looked after." He asked that Captain D. W. Vowles and three detectives from the Richmond police force be dispatched posthaste, and warned that an uprising in conjunction with a Federal raid would create havoc of unfathomable dimensions. He concluded that this could easily be prevented with a "little timely prudent preparation" and that such action must be taken.

He set about organizing courts-martial for his troops and also had to devise some system to bring internal discipline to the inmates of the stockade. The lack of discipline in both areas resulted in the cold-blooded murder of some prisoners, and both the guards and the inmates were guilty. On 23 June Private James E. Anderson notified President Davis directly: "Murder is being committed." Many of the guards were young boys who believed the killing of a Yankee "would mark them as a man."

He cautioned that an official inspection would not suffice, and he offered an alternative suggestion. "Let a good man come here as a private citizen and mix with the privates and stay one week, and if he don't find out things revolting to humanity then I am deceived."

Anderson was correct. Some of the guards were guilty as charged. One of the worst mistakes that can be made is to give power to immature and undisciplined young men, especially the power of life or death. A type of mentality often results that leads to an unaccustomed feeling of great, even omnipotent authority over individuals who are perceived to be inferior specimens of humanity as well as enemies. This tragedy has happened numerous times in history, and it happened in Civil War prisons, most notably in the southern ones during the last year of the war. Prisoners were shot for attempting to escape, for crossing the deadline, and simply "for sport." Anderson was not exaggerating, either; "things revolting to humanity" occurred far too frequently, even after Winder's attempts to impose discipline. There were some guards who defied the small provost guard headed by Captain W. S. Reed, the newly appointed provost marshal, and the "mere presence" of Winder was not sufficient to overcome this outrage. The guards were never effectively disciplined, and random shootings continued, although at a much reduced level after Winder took command.[22]

The murder of inmates by inmates increased with the arrival of the infamous "raiders" from Belle Isle during the early days of April. Beginning with clandestine robberies under the cover of darkness, these "scourings of the New York slums" graduated to openly beating, robbing, and killing their fellows around the clock. They grew in numbers and power to the extent that they controlled the stockade by early June. Wirz was powerless to suppress the marauders, and the prisoners appealed to Winder for help shortly after he arrived. His forces were too weak to end the rampage, but he granted permission to the prisoners to form a resistance organization known as the "regulators" with the authority to arrest and bring the culprits to trial. He reserved the right of final review but agreed that the rest of the operation rested with the prisoners. He gave his approval on 30 June, and by 10 July the regulators had arrested twenty-four raider leaders, convened a jury, and sentenced six to death. Winder reviewed the evidence, agreed that justice had been served, and ordered the erection of a gallows within the stockade. The next day, in full sight of all the prisoners, the six were hanged.[23] The action was effective; there were no more raiders at Andersonville, but it pained Winder that his position was so weak that the prisoners had to police themselves. This was true for the duration; the Confederate forces never were in control of the inner stockade. The only effective group on hand was the regulators, and all Winder could do was coöperate with them and attempt to strengthen his own force.

The day before he authorized the executions, Winder bluntly told Cobb that matters had arrived at the point at which he "*must* have reinforcements." This was in response to a message from Lieutenant Colonel Hugh L. Clay of the adjutant general's office, saying that, while Cooper appreciated Winder's need for reinforcements, he would have to obtain them from Cobb. "Troops cannot be drawn from any other source," concluded Clay, who also reminded Winder that he had been ordered to prepare new prisons at Cahaba or Union Springs to relieve the congestion at Andersonville. Concerning his request for Vowles and the detectives, Clay stated that the matter was still under consideration.

Winder understood the Richmond bureaucracy very well and concluded that only the most dire warning would prove effective. He dispatched the following to Cooper on 9 July, the same day he contacted Cobb:

> Send me the officers I have asked for. I have not officers enough for the duty. The guard is raw and dissatisfied. I must have the assistance of more officers. Send me the detectives I have asked for. There is treason going on around us, even to depositing arms in the adjacent counties to arm the prisoners. I am obliged to commit the investigation to incompetent hands and I fear it will fail. We are in a critical situation. Do send me the assistance I ask. Believe me there is very great danger here. Twelve of the reserves deserted last night with arms, and I cannot depend upon them.

Winder followed up this panicky plea with a detailed report of the conditions at Andersonville as of 1 July. He stated that on the first day of June there were 18,454 prisoners present: 17,415 in camp and 1,039 in hospital. He had received 9,143 prisoners during June and recaptured 44 for a total of 27,641. Of that number, 1,203 had died, 47 had escaped, and 23 had been sent to other prisons, leaving a total of 26,367 in his charge—25,012 in the stockade and 1,355 in hospital—and he had fewer than 2,000 guards to control this vast horde.[24]

He also responded to several letters of complaint sent by locals to Cooper, claiming that he had been careless in paroling so many prisoners. He admitted that, at any given time, upwards of three hundred prisoners were outside the compound cutting wood, burying the dead, or working as carpenters, bakers, teamsters, and clerks, but he insisted that it was absolutely necessary. It was also true that some captives were working for local residents and others were buying vegetables with his permission, but he denied that any were simply going about the countryside, spying on Confederate troop movements, as the complainants alleged.[25]

Winder also reported that he had finished enlarging the compound during the last week of June and the stockade now exceeded twenty-six acres in size, but he complained that the constant arrival of new prisoners rendered even the additional space inadequate and requested that no more prisoners be sent. He ended the communication by stating that he had heard that Johnston, attempting to stem Sherman's advance, had strongly recommended that the prisoners at Andersonville be dispersed, and that he agreed with that assessment.

Four days later, on 13 July, Winder traveled to Macon to consult with Cobb and to inspect the prison facilities there. He immediately dispatched three telegrams to Cooper in the most urgent manner. In the first he asked, "Please get authority for me to impress labor and teams to establish the prison at Silver Run, Alabama. The people prefer impressment. Please answer at once." He followed this up with the notification that he had been "absolutely compelled to detain" the Virginia and North Carolina regulars who had accompanied the most recent prisoner transfer. And finally, he stated that it was imperative to move the officers from the unhealthful and insecure Macon facility. "Charleston is the only place where accommodations can be had."

Three days later he wired that the move to Silver Run could not be accomplished because no guards could be found for the transfer and asked if the move to Charleston could commence without delay. The next day Seddon authorized him to distribute the prisoners and obtain guards "in the best manner and with the least delay" possible. Winder was to act on his own authority. Richmond had no information upon which to issue instructions. Seddon's telegram placed Winder in a quandary. Cobb could not furnish guards and neither could anyone else. A second wire from Seddon ordered Winder to confer with Bragg at Montgomery and to follow his instructions. Winder complied and learned that the Federals had raided Opelika and destroyed the railroad facilities. He informed Seddon that the raid "for the present puts an end to all ideas of a prison in Alabama." Winder had no choice but to leave all prisoners in place, regardless of how many suffered and died.[26]

If it was impossible to secure transport and guards in July, conditions were not much better the previous month, when the prison population was about 10,000 men less. Edward Clifford Anderson, who cooperated with Winder and left an extensive and accurate account of their activities for the latter half of 1864, noted on 11 June that all Union officers, from brigadier generals to lieutenants, had to be shipped from Macon to Charleston in boxcars. Every effort was made to secure passenger cars, but it was not possible. Even captured Brigadier General Thomas Seymore, who had a note from Davis asking that Seymore receive preferential treatment, was shipped to Charleston in a cattle car.[27]

By the middle of July, Sherman's inexorable advance had forced Johnston back to the outskirts of Atlanta, and reports of a Federal raid to free the prisoners intensified. Winder and other prison officials could only hope that any attempt would fail. Crisis followed crisis on a daily basis, but not all of the fear was the result of the Federal presence. The home front was crumbling as rapidly as the military position, and Richard Winder at Andersonville was in a state of total desperation. On 18 July he pleaded with Treasury official William L. Bailey for immediate relief. "I am so seriously in need of funds that I do not know what I shall do. For God's sake send me $100,000 for prisoners of war and $75,000 for pay of officers and troops stationed here." He had received only $75,000 for all purposes since 1 April and feared the worst.[28]

While the quartermaster begged, Winder demanded reinforcements. He could do absolutely nothing without additional troops and sent Cooper a rather blunt message on 21 July. He had on hand 29,201 prisoners, he stated, and an aggregate total of 2,421 guards. Fully one-third of his force was too ill for duty, many on duty were not reliable, and none had been paid for two months. Cooper had previously been sympathetic to Winder's pleas and had agreed that the guard was "alarmingly small," but his opinion changed as the Confederate defenses deteriorated. All available troops were needed at the front, none could be spared to guard prisoners, and he told Winder so in no uncertain language. Winder regarded this "very severe censure" as undeserved, and in reference to Cooper's order to "enlarge the stockade—place the prisoners properly," he replied, perhaps with unconscious sarcastic humor, "You speak of placing the prisoners properly. I do not comprehend what is intended by it. I know of but one way to place them, and that is to put them in the stockade where they have between four and five square yards to the man."

Winder's estimate of space was on the generous side, even if one counted the uninhabitable swamp and the area precluded by the dead-line. In any event, whatever space they had was all they had, and Winder made that clear to Cooper on 25 July. "There are 29,400 prisoners, 2,650 troops, 500 negroes and other laborers and not a ration at the post." He pointed out the obvious danger of the situation and stated that he had ordered "that at least ten days' rations should be kept on hand," but that it had never been done.[29]

When Winder's report was shown to Northrop, the commissary general exploded in justifiable outrage. The fighting troops of the Confederacy were restricted to one day's ration and Winder must be crazy if he expected anything more for the prisoners. He proclaimed that he would have countermanded Winder's order if he had been aware of it. Winder was unrepentant. The "ratio of mortality was very great" among the prisoners, and insufficient rations contributed mightily to this deplorable state of affairs. Congestion was also a factor, and he again stressed that another prison was imperative and proposed to build one near Andersonville if it could not be located in a better area. About the only satisfaction Winder gained was Cooper's announcement that his 24 June request that no more captives be sent to Andersonville had at last been honored.

Cooper had finally been stirred by Winder's communications and again took up the matter of the prisons with Davis. The president agreed that a change must take place, and they made plans to impose a system of sorts in mid-July. On the 26th, they announced that Winder would command all prisons in Georgia and Alabama, and General William M. Gardner would control all other prisons east of the Mississippi River. In all matters relating to prisons and prisoners, both officers were to report directly to and receive orders from the ranking Confederate general, Samuel Cooper.[30]

The change failed to improve the situation. The chain of command remained almost nonexistent and totally ineffective. Winder might have command on paper, but over three months later he still did not have full knowledge of what Richmond proposed to do about confining the prisoners in his command. Clearly, no system was yet in place. Equally obvious, this endeavor to improve the lot of the prisoners was not welcomed by the southern press. The Richmond *Whig* accused Grant of "trying to starve" the South into submission and reproached Davis for being too soft on the prisoners. The editor maintained that the captives would have to bear the hardship, because "the army and the people must not suffer. Self-preservation is the first law of nature." The paper also quoted the Eufaula (Georgia) *Spirit,* that from a distant hill, the huts and tents of the Andersonville prisoners looked like anthills, and the inmates looked "like a host of monkeys."[31]

The Georgia reporter was at least partially accurate. Andersonville did resemble a filthy zoo not even fit for animals, and it was at this time that Cooper ordered the aforementioned Colonel Daniel Chandler to inspect the compound. Before Chandler's arrival, Winder appealed to all citizens in a ten-county area to furnish 2,000 slaves with tools, teams, wagons, provisions, and forage to complete the complex. This was in response to a Federal raid led by General George Stoneman, whose orders were to liberate the prisoners at Macon and Andersonville. Confederate cavalry defeated Stoneman, but Winder urged that the Macon prisoners be moved immediately to a safer place. He told Cooper that the people "responded so promptly" to his appeal that it was not yet necessary to move the inmates from Andersonville.

In the midst of Winder's frantic preparations to finally bring the bake house and hospital up to an acceptable standard, Chandler arrived during the first week of August to inspect the facility. He had previously talked to local people, including the "Andersonville Unionist," Ambrose Spencer, and seemed predisposed to issue a negative report. By all accounts, his inspection was cursory, and he was not attentive to reports given by Winder or any other officer. He reported that very little had been done to provide for the basic needs of the prisoners since the prison had opened, but he commended the efforts of Wirz, Richard Winder, and Lieutenant Colonel Henry Forno, then in command of the guard. He condemned the work of Captain J. W. Armstrong, assistant commissary, and Captain Samuel T. Bailey, assistant adjutant general, but saved his special venom for Winder, as follows:

> My duty requires me respectfully to recommend a change in the officer in command of the post, Brig. Gen. J. H. Winder, and the substitution in his place of some one who unites both energy and good judgment with some feelings of humanity and consideration for the welfare and comfort (so far as is consistent with their safe-keeping) of the vast number of unfortunates placed under his control; some one who at least will not advocate deliberately and in cold blood the propriety of leaving them in their present condition until their number has been sufficiently reduced by death to make the present arrangements suffice for their accommodation, and who will not consider it a matter of self-laudation and boasting that he has never been inside the stockade, a place of horrors of which it is difficult to describe, and which is a disgrace to civilization, the condition of which he might by the exercise of a little energy and judgment, even with the limited means at his command, have considerably improved.[32]

The report caused great consternation in the Richmond command structure. Colonel Chilton, the newly appointed inspector general and commander of the Office of Inspection, endorsed his subordinate's findings, but neither Cooper or Seddon believed the report, and it does not appear that Davis ever saw it. Chandler's report was later used during the Wirz trial to prove that the top leadership had conspired to murder the captives, though the portions praising Wirz and others were conveniently omitted.

When the overall assessment of Chandler's observations were submitted to Winder for an explanation, he branded the charges as false and sent reports compiled by his staff to support his position. He did not know of Chandler's charges against him personally and never saw that portion of the report, but he strongly denied that any of the accusations were valid. He complained that Chandler had already made up his mind before the inspection and that he had refused to listen to anyone who attempted to enlighten him as to the actual conditions.

Yet the rebuttal by Winder and his officers really did not alter Chandler's conclusion that Andersonville was truly "a place of horrors" and a "disgrace to civilization." That was an accurate description of the prison in the summer of 1864, although the awful conditions were not created deliberately as Chandler charged. Confederate attempts to finish the prison had been herculean before the arrival of the prisoners, and Winder

and his staff worked desperately to improve the conditions during that
unforgettable summer; but their own records and reports made for horri-
fying reading. There were 31,678 prisoners in the stockade on 1 August,
over 1,800 having died in July. The prison population peaked at over
33,000 in August, but so did the number of deaths—2,993—and 97 men
died on the single day of 23 August.

These figures made Confederate accomplishments pale into insignifi-
cance, but perhaps even more impressive than the mortality rates were
the number of patients treated by the understaffed medical team. During
the first six months of Andersonville's existence (March through August),
42,686 prisoners were treated and 7,578 died, a rate of less than 18 percent mortality.[33] This was better than the Belle Isle rates during the worst
of times and about equal to the percentage during the winter months
of 1862 and 1863 when the cartel was in effect. Confederate efforts at
Andersonville were commendable and stupendous; the results were not.

Why Chandler attacked Winder in such a vicious manner is not clear.
He was prejudiced against the general, as the records indisputably prove,
but his reasons were not explained. Hesseltine, in his *Civil War Prisons*,
believed that the best explanation for Chandler's action was contained
in one of his letters to Stanton, asking for his release from prison after
the war was over. Chandler stated then that after he was exchanged and
returned to the Confederacy in 1863, he wanted to avoid conscription
and availed himself of the opportunity to become an inspector of a quarantine camp, but that he had always intended to return to the service of
the United States at the first favorable opportunity.

If Hesseltine's assessment is correct, it explains why Chandler ignored
Winder's extensive report of the camp's history, which detailed the insur-
mountable problems prison officials had faced since the prison's inception, and why he sped through the entire complex in a few short hours
on 4 August. Yet it does not explain his brutal description of the general.
Chandler characterized Bailey as "physically and mentally incapacitated,"
and Armstrong as incompetent. He urged their removal but did not vilify
their basic character. It is probable that Winder became abrasive when
he concluded that Chandler was not really interested in an objective
inspection, but he most probably admitted that he had never set foot
inside the stockade. Winder's last visit with any inmate was at Libby
in August 1863.[34] So far as is known, he never inspected Belle Isle at
close range after 1862, and he never ventured inside the stockade at
Andersonville, Florence, or any of the later prisons. He viewed the
prison conditions from the stockade wall and well knew the situation
without exposing himself to the dangers of entering the compound.

Chandler was not the only one who accused Winder of murdering
the prisoners in a deliberate manner. Two former prisoners, Captain
B. L. G. Reed and Lieutenant T. B. Stevenson, made the following accusa-

tion after their successful escape on 6 August, two days after Chandler visited Andersonville. Their account is so strikingly similar to Chandler's that one wonders if these men had not talked to him when he inspected their camp at Macon and before he wrote the controversial report: "General J. H. Winder has been in command of the prisoners in Georgia. He is a regular brute. His treatment of the men is infamous. They are robbed, they have no shelter, and die hundreds in a day. When told that the Yankee prisoners were dying at Andersonville one hundred a day he said 'God damn them, let them die. They don't die half fast enough; that's just what we want.'"[35]

In like manner, Ambrose Spencer, the Andersonville Unionist, testified at the Wirz trial that Sidney had declared when he built the stockade that he would not provide shelter so that he could kill "more damned Yankees" than could be "destroyed" at the front.[36] That these charges were ludicrous fabrications is fully documented by the thousands of messages contained in the official records, but these materials were used with deadly effectiveness to blacken the names of both Winders, father and son.

Even as he responded to Chandler's report, Winder was diligently seeking a site for another prison. Sidney reported on 5 August that Millen, Georgia, was a likely spot and asked Winder for permission to impress the necessary labor and supplies. Before anything could be done, a torrential rain hit Andersonville on 9 August and washed away two sides of the stockade. Winder urged that the Millen camp be finished at all costs and reported that his existing force might not be able to salvage the stockade. Three days later he informed Cooper that by keeping his whole force at constant duty for three days and nights, the situation had been brought to a level of "comparative safety," but he urged that the Millen complex be rushed to completion and begged that no more prisoners be sent to Andersonville.

The next day, Winder reported, "Never in my life have I spent so anxious a time. If we had not had a large negro force working on the defenses I think it would have been impossible to have saved the place." He added that the regulators maintained discipline among the prisoners; that, coupled with his entire force plus sixteen artillery pieces, made it possible to retain control.

The storm may have given Winder a severe fright, but it was a tremendous blessing for the prisoners. Nature did what the Confederates could not. The compound was cleansed of excrement and other filth, and a spring of pure fresh water suddenly appeared just inside the deadline. Promptly christened "Providence Spring" by the grateful inmates, it provided a better supply of water than had ever existed previously.[37] Conditions also improved because Winder insisted on the immediate removal of some of the prisoners to Millen. He was motivated by both humanitar-

ian and security concerns and refused to allow Cobb's objections to sway
him. Cobb opposed the camp at Millen, or at any other place in Georgia
for that matter, but Winder repeatedly asked for and finally obtained
Cooper's permission to start the transfer on 5 September. The Millen
post was not quite ready, so Winder ordered the initial shipments to
Savannah and Charleston over the vehement protests of the commanders
at those places, Lafayette McLaws and Samuel Jones.

McLaws notified Edward Anderson on 7 September to make preparations at Savannah to receive a large number of prisoners the following
morning. McLaws's engineers had been working on the project for six
weeks, but the stockade was far from finished. Anderson showed what
an energetic commander with sufficient force could achieve. He assembled a large force of slaves and carpenters, worked them straight through
the night, and before sunset the next day the first arrival of 1,500 prisoners had been fed and securely confined. Anderson described the inmates
as a "beggarly set of vagabonds" and informed Winder that his facility
would hold 4,500 men. Winder told him to expect between 5,000 and
10,000 arrivals within the week. The Federal capture of Atlanta made
it mandatory to transport the prisoners to more secure areas.

Anderson visited the stockade on 9 September and was shocked at
the condition of the 3,300 inmates. "They were dirty and half clad and
altogether the most squalid gathering of humanity it has ever been my
lot to look upon. The stockade is entirely without shelter and the burning
sun bakes down on them from daylight 'til dark." He was also dismayed
at the callousness of the prisoners. The "dead were side by side with
the live ones" and the living "took no notice of the corpses." Anderson
tripled the size of the prison, even though Savannah was just a holding
area, and the transfer to Charleston began on 11 September. Seddon
ordered the guards back to Andersonville on the 18th, and Anderson
began to experience the shortages that plagued all prison officials. He
was also a witness that the new prison organization was not yet a reliable
system. He noted on 21 September: "Gen. Winder arrived in the city
today. Accompanied McLaws and myself to the stockade and looked at
the prisoners. He had not heard of the intention to bring down an additional number from Andersonville nor had McLaws and I was sent for
. . . to convey the information."[38]

Winder departed for Millen the next day and told Anderson to send
him fifty mechanics selected from the prisoners to help finish the Millen
camp. Anderson complied but soon recorded that his Savannah facility
had fallen on dire times; the quartermaster failed to provide fuel, and
from 28 September to 1 October, the prisoners and the guards had to
eat their rations raw. Anderson was an influential man in Savannah but
found that he could not even secure the necessary firewood.

Within a short while, he, too, labeled the guards as "entirely worthless" and did not doubt that the prisoners were "probably running at large in the city at night." He heard that several guards had been bribed to free inmates but had no reliable force to correct the practice. By 4 October, over 10,000 men filled the stockade, and he wired Winder not to send any more. The hospital was deficient, the guard inadequate, and the prisoners were suffering fearfully. A complete reversal had occurred in less than one month.

It was very cold on 9 October, when Anderson recorded that

26 Yankee prisoners died in the stockade last night— the cold weather has been fatal to all those cases of diarrhea which have been lingering for the past fortnight, thus accounting for the large increase of mortality among the prisoners. Poor devils. It is pitiful to think that it is not in our power to succor them better—yet their Govt refused to exchange them & by blockading our ports prevents us from receiving those supplies from abroad which would enable us to clothe & care for our own men & their prisoners as well. Such is war. It was a sickening sight to see those wretched strangers— stretched off stark & stiff in the death line awaiting transportation to their place of burial. The flies were swarming over their faces & a crowd of prisoners had gathered nearby looking on in callous indifference & jesting among themselves as though there had never existed a feeling of pity in their hearts. I am told that a large number of the prisoners are afflicted with nostalgia, or homesickness—which is proving fatal in many cases among them.[39]

Anderson's ordeal ended in mid-October. The Savannah captives were sent to Millen, and McLaws ordered him to destroy the stockade and restore the grounds so that prisoners could never again be sent to his city. Anderson recorded his disgust with McLaws, a "worthless incubus upon the country . . . who has risen to prominence as a Major General as scum rises in a cauldron." He continued to oversee the hospital operation until an exchange of wounded took place on 11 November. The exchanged Confederates were "well clad" and "looked good." The Savannah residents gave them a "big feed," but they were forced to sleep on the bare ground. There were no blankets, straw, or fuel.

This account by a humane, influential, and energetic Georgian graphically illustrates the Confederate condition by late 1864. The provisions for 10,000 prisoners for one month was too much for Savannah to furnish. Anderson's experience with the prisoner issue was brief and under the best of conditions. Yet he was disgusted with McLaws, who refused to do anything much except get the prisoners out of the city as rapidly as possible. He found the guards execrable and agreed with Ira B. Simpson, a captured Federal, who branded the First Georgia Volunteers as "conscripts, mean looking, and contemptible." Anderson was ashamed that such conditions could exist and was very much aware of the contrast between his charges and recently exchanged Confederates.[40]

General Sam Jones at Charleston was even more determined than McLaws to rid his city of captives. The Federals were confined at a race-track outside of town, and though the food was superior, the grounds rapidly became contaminated and various diseases quickly took a savage toll. Jones dispatched Major F. F. Warley to build a prison at Florence and also prevailed on Seddon to order Winder not to send any more captives to Charleston. He began sending off all prisoners as soon as they arrived, even though the Florence stockade was not finished. Warley was appalled on 17 September to find that over 6,000 captives had arrived at Florence. He placed them in an open field under a loose guard, and herded them into the partially finished stockade the next day.[41] The story of Andersonville was about to be repeated. Winder himself would soon admit that conditions at Florence were worse than at Andersonville.

Winder spent much of his time during the latter months of 1864 trying to complete the Millen complex, the largest prison the Confederacy would build. Progress was slowed by lack of money (the right of impressment was not granted), but the stockade was finished by the first week of October. Winder moved his headquarters to Camp Lawton, as the complex was officially known, and left Colonel George Gibbs in charge of the sick and wounded at Andersonville.

The Millen complex was "the largest prison in the world," according to Winder. The stockade enclosed forty-two acres, water was plentiful, and there was a sufficient amount of wood for huts and fuel. The prison was divided into sections, the better to maintain internal discipline, but the rations, medicines, and hospital facilities were no improvement over those at Andersonville. Still, the death rate fell sharply, and only about four percent of the prisoners died during the camp's brief existence, but this was no better than the mortality rate at Andersonville during the early months of that prison's history.

The Millen complex was the most ambitious of Winder's projects, but a Federal raid forced the evacuation of the prison after only six weeks. Beginning in mid-November, Winder was forced to send the Millen prisoners to temporary holding areas in Thomasville and Blackshear, Georgia, before returning them to Andersonville, Florence, Salisbury, and Columbia. He moved his headquarters to the latter place shortly after he was notified that he had been appointed commissary general of prisons.

This long-delayed and much-needed position was created on 21 November, and Cooper's proclamation was specific as to Winder's powers: "All officers and men on duty at the several military prisons are placed under his command. He is charged with the custody and care of all prisoners of war and with the discipline and general administration of all prisons east of the Mississippi River. All commandants are subordinated.

All officers warned not to interfere with prisons and prisoners."[42] The
fatal flaw in the appointment was that it came far too late for anyone
to be effective in the new command. Federal raids in the diminished
Confederacy made it virtually impossible to place prisoners in secure
areas not already in use, and conditions in the existing prisons in these
regions were deplorable. Additional space for more prisons in Richmond,
Danville, and Lynchburg, or even in Charleston or Columbia, did not
exist, and Winder was forced to rely for the most part on the continued
use of Andersonville, Florence, and Salisbury during the winter of
1864–1865. Andersonville was in large measure a hospital during most
of this time, although about 3,500 prisoners from Thomasville were sent
there around Christmas of 1864, and Florence and Salisbury became
the new death camps.[43]

The stockade at Florence covered about twenty-six acres, but fully six
acres was a swamp. Winder inspected the facility early in December
and recommended that the camp be closed. He reported that the site
was unhealthy, it was vulnerable to Federal raids, the guard was worthless, and escapes were frequent. A Florence resident, Louisa Jane Harlbee, confirmed part of Winder's assessment in a letter to her cousin:
"Our part of the country has been overrun by the Yankee prisoners. From
five to eight thousand have been brought to Florence, and as they are
[secured] by a very poor guard, of course they are making their escape
in great numbers."[44] Most of the escapees were recaptured without difficulty; they were too weak to travel far, and many were apprehended
while begging for food. Winder estimated in December that the mortality
rate exceeded that of Andersonville and he was correct; 2,802 out of
12,000 died there during the five months of the camp's existence.[45]

Salisbury was even worse. This complex had been used as a prison
since 1861 and had housed political prisoners, deserters, and ordinary
criminals, along with Federal captives. The fall of Atlanta resulted in
a huge increase in the prison's population, and by early November over
8,700 Federals were in confinement. The maximum capacity of the prison
was only 2,500. A Federal who had been confined in Richmond observed
that "Libby was a palace" compared to Salisbury. The awful conditions
coupled with the lack of guards resulted in numerous escape attempts,
including an attempted mass breakout on 25 November. This revolt was
barely contained; the prisoners killed three guards and wounded ten,
while suffering sixteen deaths and sixty wounded from their ranks.[46]

Winder inspected the camp on 13 December and reported that the
prison was even worse than Florence. The six-acre compound lacked
sufficient wood and water, the ground was sticky mud, and the sinks
produced a stench "insupportable both to the prisoners and the people
in the vicinity." There was a conflict in the command system, and he
feared he might have to assume command himself. He remedied the

administrative malfunction four days later by giving General Bradley
Johnson the post, but urged the government to sell the facility and build
a new one between Columbia and Charlotte.[47]

Andersonville was the most infamous of the southern prisons, but
though it housed the largest number of captives, it was not the worst.
The mortality rate at Salisbury was the highest in the Confederacy. From
October 1864 to the following February, the scene resembled a charnel
house. During those four months, 3,479 out of 10,321 inmates died, almost 34 percent, and a visiting southern minister noted, "They throw
them in the graves like dogs." Winder told Cooper that the Salisbury
prisoners must be dispersed, but soon admitted that he could not find
any place that was safe. It was at this time that Winder first urged that
the government parole the Union captives and send them home without
benefit of exchange.[48] This was also the position of the Federal exchange
agent Hitchcock. If the Confederacy could not provision the captives,
they should send them home. It was equally obvious that Richmond
would not comply, and as conditions worsened and the death toll skyrock-
eted, the Union commissary general Hoffman retaliated, as he had previously done, by again reducing the rations for Confederate prisoners.

The plight of captives held by both sections moved William Winder,
then in New York, to propose that all prisoners be given everything they
needed and that the South be permitted to pay in cotton. Stanton rejected
the suggestion, but the idea contained merit, and on 31 October both
sides agreed to a mutual issue of provisions, the South being allowed
to sell cotton in New York to pay its share. This was done in January
1865, and agents distributed much-needed articles to all prisoners; but
Stanton and Halleck soon concluded that the South had not honored
the agreement. They believed that the articles went to resupply the ragged Confederate armies, not to relieve the Union captives, and the plan
was aborted after the first issue.[49]

The failure to follow through on his brother's idea was just one more
burden for Winder to bear. He was not able to improve the issue of
rations—indeed, that problem retrogressed—but he hoped to better the
medical care at the facilities and named Isaiah White to the top command.
White was directly accountable to Winder and Surgeon General Moore,
and Winder backed White's efforts with all the resources of his debilitated
command.

White's liaison with Moore brought results. Medical care at the prisons
improved, despite crippling shortages. Winder engaged private doctors
on contract when he could not have the use of Confederate surgeons,
and White brought some order to the system. Yet the problems were
overwhelming. In December 1864, for example, the Salisbury surgeon
informed Winder that prior to October, his 45-bed hospital was sufficient

for the 900 prisoners. But, beginning on the 10th of that month, the "sudden transfer of 9,000 prisoners" had created a "nightmare," as, the surgeon noted, Winder well knew from his recent visit. As of January 1865, the medical staff at Salisbury, including private doctors on contract, consisted of one surgeon, four assistant surgeons, and four acting assistant surgeons, to minister to the needs of about 9,000 prisoners.

At the same time, the Florence medical staff was composed of one surgeon and nine assistants, seven of whom were ill. Andersonville hospital, with a patient load of about 2,000, was staffed by three surgeons, six assistants, seven acting assistants, one steward, one matron, twenty-one ward masters, and two foragers. At Columbia, where Winder had his headquarters, there were four assistant surgeons, two acting assistant surgeons, and four privates for the wards.[50]

Columbia was the third location of Winder's headquarters in as many months. He was initially at Millen, then Augusta, and finally at Columbia; the frequent moves illustrate the general collapse following the fall of Atlanta. As commissary general, he spent much of his time personally inspecting prisons and attempting to secure new ones. In addition, he ordered that all prison commanders in the Confederacy report to him twice a month. For the first time in the war, one authority now had access to all information necessary to obtain an accurate overview of the whole situation. Yet the more efficient the bureaucratic system became, the more Winder became depressed. All of the prisons were overflowing, including Belle Isle and Danville. Every report confirmed what Winder already knew. The situation could not be saved. From Virginia to Georgia, there was not a secure area for prisons anywhere in the remnants of the Confederacy.

On 6 January, Colonel Robert C. Smith at Danville threatened to resign unless regular troops could be provided to guard his captives. In a long letter to Gardner, Smith's superior, Winder addressed the matter and expressed himself in a patient, resigned, even fatalistic manner, very much atypical of all of his previous communications. "I fear it will be impossible to get what he calls old regular troops. The same difficulty occurs at all the prisons, and if we can get reserves, or any other troops, we must be satisfied and do the best we can with them." As for Smith, "He must do as other commanders of prisons have done and are still doing; that is, to make the best use of the means at his command. Relieving him would not remedy the evil; it would only throw it on somebody else."[51]

About the same time, Northrop demanded that Salisbury be evacuated so that all rations could go to Lee's army. Winder replied that he had wanted to move the prisoners for months and had thought they might be relocated in Alabama or southwestern Georgia, but military reversals had since precluded that possibility and the Salisbury prison could not yet be phased out.

As awful as things were at Salisbury, the prison facilities near Winder's headquarters in Columbia were about as bad as any in Dixie. Beginning in October, captured officers were assembled on the west side of the Saluda River, several miles northwest of the capital. Winder dismissed the location as "nothing but an open field" that was "entirely unfit" for human habitation. The 1,200 officers, guarded by about 350 "very raw recruits" commanded by Lieutenant Colonel R. Stark Means of the "Invalid Corps," were asked to give their parole that they would not attempt to escape. They refused, wisely as it turned out, and set about constructing barracks for the winter. Rations were extremely meager, almost nonexistent, except for sorghum molasses; and with the guard so weak, escapes from "Camp Sorghum" occurred so frequently that Governor M. T. Bonham allowed Winder the use of the state insane asylum. The prisoners huddled in "Camp Asylum" until a permanent prison could be built, but the new facility, about fourteen miles north of Columbia, was never finished, and the captives were finally moved to Charlotte in early February.[52]

Winder very seldom received any message from anyone offering to take prisoners off of his hands, but he did receive an offer from Beauregard on 9 January. Beauregard wanted to use thirty prisoners to remove shells and torpedoes from a railroad siding and judged the job to be too dangerous to use his own troops. Winder refused, stating, "I don't think this is legitimate work for prisoners of war." Beauregard responded that he made the request because the Federals were using Confederate prisoners in hazardous undertakings, but the inmates were not delivered.[53]

Winder might protect his charges from perilous work details, but he could not end the illegal trading that regularly occurred between guards and prisoners. Captain Clarence Morfit at Richmond asked that this be stopped, since the trade was usually to the prisoner's detriment; but Winder replied, "The troops guarding the various prisons are so utterly worthless that it is impossible to prevent outsiders and even the soldiers from trading with the prisoners." However, he did authorize all inmates to draw on their funds without limit in hopes that they might be able to buy needed foodstuffs.

Starvation haunted almost everyone in his command by this time. Winder paroled some Union officers who had friends in Columbia, and pleaded that commissaries exclusively for prison use be established. He reported that the Florence prison was finally in decent condition except for the lack of food, but Northrop responded that unless more money was funded, prison rations could not even be continued, much less ensured by the creation of a separate commissary system for the prisons.

This news increased Winder's despondency, and on 20 January he wrote Cooper, urging for the second time that the prisoners be freed. "I am at a loss to know where to send prisoners from Florence. In one direction the enemy are in the way. In the other the question of supplies presents an insuperable barrier. I again urge paroling the prisoners and sending them home. I have consulted the Governor and General Chesnut, who both urge that they be paroled." The Richmond authorities again refused. Ould remained adamant that exchange be resumed before any prisoner be paroled, and Cooper agreed, but both changed their minds in a matter of days.[54]

In the meantime, for the few days left to him, Winder had to make the best of this deplorable decision. The situation at Florence was critical by this time. Sherman's advance moved Beauregard to demand that the prisoners be removed. Seddon agreed and asked Winder if they could be relocated in southwestern Georgia. Winder replied that it would be desirable in terms of supplies, but he was uncertain if the area was secure. He contacted Beauregard on 6 February and asked if the proposed area was safe and, if so, whether he had soldiers to spare for guard duty; "I have not sufficient troops to guard them."[55]

Winder was at Kingsville when he sent this last message, an old man on his last trip. He was completely used up. He never saw Cooper's communication of 8 February to forward all prisoners to Richmond "with a view to their delivery." Shortly after sending that message, Cooper was handed a telegram from Lieutenant Colonel Henry Forno, dated 7 February, from Florence: "Genl. Winder died suddenly, on arriving here, last night. Have assumed command and shall endeavor to carry out the Dept. views, expressed to me, by Genl. Winder."[56]

CHAPTER 10

The Aftermath

The news of Winder's death was greeted with jubilation by the prisoners. Joseph Ferguson at Camp Asylum in Columbia queried, "Is it wrong to feel elated on the death of a fellow man and foe? Every face in the prison beamed with joy, and every heart rejoiced in the thought that this demon was no more. We had all suffered from his diabolical plans to systematically starve us, and felt that God had taken the breath from this rude man as punishment for his awful crimes."[1] Rumors circulated among the Federal captives that Winder's last words were, "My faith is in Christ; I expect to be saved. Be sure and cut down the prisoner's rations."[2]

The Confederate press also reacted predictably. The Wilmington *Journal* gave an extensive and accurate account of Winder's antebellum life and Confederate career. It concluded: "In every position in which he has been placed his official conduct has been marked by strict probity, energy, and promptness, and that kind consideration towards all whose official relations made them subordinate to him, which unmistakably attested a noble and genial nature; while in private life, as husband, father, and true friend, his memory can never cease to be sincerely cherished."[3]

It was soon apparent that the North cherished nothing about Winder but his death. During the trial of his subordinate Henry Wirz, Colonel N. P. Chipman, judge advocate, summed up the charges as follows: "Chief among the conspirators and actual participators in the crime [of murder], the immediate tool first and last of the rebel government, was General Winder." The chief conspirator was dead, and the unfortunate Wirz soon joined him. Others on Winder's staff, including his cousin Richard Winder, were jailed but never brought to trial. His son Sidney was also a wanted man but managed to escape to Canada, where he remained until he learned it was safe to return to Baltimore. Major Thomas P. Turner also sought refuge in Canada.

Richard was arrested in August and placed in the Old Capitol prison with Wirz in September. He later wrote Jefferson Davis that two days before Wirz was executed on 10 November 1865, the condemned man was offered a reprieve by three men who served a "high cabinet official" of the United States. Wirz was supposedly told he would not die if he would confess that there had been a conspiracy to murder Union prisoners and that Davis was the author of that crime. Wirz indignantly refused, according to Richard, and marched to the gallows in the full knowledge of his innocence.[4]

After the execution of Wirz, Grant ordered Richard released; he was instead sent to Libby prison to face charges being prepared against him by the Andersonville Unionist, Ambrose Spencer. No trial occurred, and though there is no record of his release, he was probably able to return home by May or June of 1866. He took up the study of dentistry and twenty years later became the dean of the Baltimore Dental College.[5]

F. E. Boyle, Wirz's confessor, supported Richard's claim that Wirz was offered amnesty; but Captain George R. Walbridge, the jailer who would have had to admit the secret emissaries, claimed that he did not recall the incident. Walbridge never denied that it might have happened, and he did admit that three of the former Union prisoners who testified against Wirz had never been to Andersonville; but he refused to confirm Richard's testimony.[6] Richard Winder was indisputably an upright and honorable man, and his story must be given some credence. The same can be said of Winder's youngest son, Sidney, who tried desperately to reverse the public image of his father.

The last few months of the war were memorable ones for Sidney. The death of his father depressed him severely, and in late March 1865 he went to Richmond with the intention of resigning. He soon changed his mind and shortly became one of the nine officers charged with guarding the Confederate treasury and archives after the fall of Richmond. This small group of "the most trusted men in the Confederacy" reached the David Levy Yulee plantation in Florida on 22 May; Sidney almost died during the trip. There they learned that Davis had been captured and the Confederacy was no more. The group decided to bury the archives on the Yulee grounds and voted to allot about one-fourth of the gold to the support of Mrs. Davis and her children; the rest they divided equally among themselves.

Each officer received gold sovereigns in the amount of $1,995 and set out to seek a parole. Sidney and his longtime friend and fellow officer Tench F. Tilghman took the oath and were paroled on 10 June at Hilton Head, South Carolina. Sidney took ship for New York, sold the gold for slightly over $3,000 in United States currency, and arrived in Baltimore on 22 June. Shortly after his arrival he learned that his arrest had been ordered, and he hurriedly departed for Canada.[7]

Sidney's uncle, William Winder, promptly asked Albert Sidney Johnston if his nephew was not entitled to the benefits of the convention signed by Sherman when Johnston surrendered. Johnston replied that he was. After taking the oath, Sidney was entitled to be a free man with no fear of arrest.[8] Until the petty reign of terror instituted by Stanton subsided, however, Sidney remained in exile. He did not return to Baltimore until after March 1866. Reunited with his mother and Carrie, who were again caring for the aged Gertrude Winder, he returned to the practice of law. He and his uncle became the sole economic support for the remnants of the Winder family, and they also undertook the considerable task of attempting to clear the besmirched reputation of their beloved kinsman.

William, having begun the task prior to Sidney's return, was much experienced in this type of forlorn endeavor. Having spent most of his life trying to exonerate his father from the humiliation of Bladensburg, he now had the more demanding job of refuting the accusations that his elder brother had been a cold-blooded mass murderer. Still as defiant as when he had been released from prison in 1862, William notified Jefferson Davis that he was writing a history of Andersonville prison. He was convinced that the official records would completely vindicate the top Confederate leadership. He also thanked Davis for his comments, made to Jackson Warner in September 1865, that his brother had been "unfailingly kind" to the prisoners in his charge.[9]

William and Sidney discovered that they could expect no cooperation from the Union officials in charge of the captured Confederate archives. Without access to the documents, their undertaking became impossible. It would have been immensely difficult even if they had obtained unlimited cooperation from Federal officials, for the North was frequently inflamed by the purple prose of the press, the vivid accounts of former captives, and the expert "waving of the bloody shirt" by politicians. Even respected historians were completely biased. Benson Lossing's massive *Pictorial History of the Civil War*, published from 1866 through 1868, was regarded as the gospel in the North. Lossing had been more than fair to General William Winder in his account of the War of 1812, but he branded the son as an inhuman fiend. Winder was, at best, "an exceedingly bad man; cruel in his nature; repulsive in features; rude in manners; and foul and profane in speech," a man who after many experiments, constructed a deliberate and effective method "of destroying prisoners" by starving them to death.[10]

Much publicity was also given to Chandler's charges and to a report made by Confederate surgeon Joseph Jones. This doctor had been ordered to Andersonville in the summer of 1864 to study the causes and treatment of gangrene, malarial fevers, diarrhea, and dysentery in order to combat these maladies, then afflicting Confederate soldiers. In the hands of vindictive northern officials, this report was cited as evidence that Winder had condoned medical experiments by Jones designed to infect and kill the helpless captives. Since Chandler and Jones were Confederate officers, their reports were widely believed in the North.[11]

Sidney was also dismayed to learn in 1874 that a revised edition of George Cullum's *Biographical Register of the Officers and Graduates of the United States Military Academy* now included the comment under his father's name that he "became the inhuman jailer of Libby and other Southern prisons." He wrote Cullum that even the incomplete official records then available proved this charge to be "utterly false" and asked that the offending remark be deleted. Cullum replied that he had no personal animosity toward Winder but that he must refuse the request because the statement was based on authentic charges by former captives. Sidney responded that Winder had exceeded or even ignored his orders numerous times in response to the suffering of his charges by ordering the prison commissary to secure foodstuffs on the open market. This had caused conflict with Northrop and others, but Winder had acted anyway.

Sidney also enclosed a letter written by the former adjutant general Cooper, who stated that he had known Winder for upwards of fifty years and that "his private character was that of an upright & humane gentleman, and . . . he had the reputation in the Southern Confederacy of treating the prisoners confined to his general supervision with kindness and consideration." Cooper continued, "I do not believe that there was exercised in the military prisons of the southern Confederacy, harsh treatment of prisoners, or such treatment as violate the usages of civilized warfare."[12]

Sidney next sent Cullum a long letter from Davis with the remark that while the North might reject his political views, the former president was esteemed everywhere in the country as a man of honor and veracity. Davis's letter to Sidney, dated 18 July 1874, included the following comments:

I have no hesitation in saying that I consider the statement of Gen. Cullum . . . utterly false. My acquaintance with your Father . . . commenced when I was a cadet in the U.S. Mil. Acad., and he an assistant instructor of tactics. That acquaintance continued, though without much personal intercourse until we met in Richmond during the late war. I then saw much of him, and was confirmed in the opinion I had previously formed of him that he was a gallant soldier, and an honorable gentleman, too gallant to be cruel to any one in his power, too honorable to flatter those above him, or to oppress those below him. I could much more easily believe that he would be swerved from the strict line of duty by a generous sympathy for the suffering, than that he would be harsh in his treatment to any not in condition to resist. I knew much of the manner in which he discharged his duty while in Richmond, and there was

surely nothing in his conduct to suggest that he would be inhuman
to the prisoners under his command when he was put in charge
at Andersonville.[13]

Sidney solicited additional testimony from Seddon, Bragg, Beauregard,
Jubal Early, and others, and all repeatedly asserted that Winder was
an honorable, humane, and energetic officer and gentleman. Many of
these testimonials appeared in the 5 February 1876 issue of the *Baltimorean* in response to hostile comments made recently in Congress by James
G. Blaine. Blaine and other Republicans were opposed to granting par-
dons to former top Confederates as proposed by leaders of the Demo-
cratic party. Blaine asserted that Davis was "the author, knowingly, deliberately, guiltily and willfully of the gigantic murders and crimes at
Andersonville," that he sent "Winder to Andersonville with a full knowledge of his previous atrocities" in Richmond. "We in the North knew
from the returning skeletons what he had accomplished at Belle Isle and
Libby, and fresh from these accomplishments he was sent by Mr. Davis
. . . to construct this den of horrors at Andersonville." Blaine concluded
his attack by referring to a written order issued by Winder to his artillery
on 27 July 1864, to open fire on the prisoners if Federal cavalry came
within seven miles of Andersonville.[14]

This order was a forgery and was known to be so as early as the 1870s
to everyone in the War Department, from the secretary down through
the ranks of his subordinates, including those officials who had custody
of the archival collection that would ultimately be published as *The War
of the Rebellion: A Compilation of the Official Records of the Union
and Confederate Armies.* Sidney made repeated requests to President
Grant and Secretary of War William W. Belknap to permit him to use
the archives to refute Blaine's charges, but he never received permission.
Sidney and his kinsmen could but produce testimonials denying the existence of such an order, and this they repeatedly did. The rebuttal was
included in the *Baltimorean* referred to, as were long accounts favorable
to Winder written by Early, Cooper, Seddon, Bragg, and George W.
Brent.[15]

William and his brother Charles both died in 1879, embittered by
their ineffectiveness, and Sidney continued to struggle alone. He wrote
Davis in January 1888 that the forged order was still being cited by Union
veterans despite the pronouncement by Secretary of War William Endi-
cott that no such order could be found.[16] In desperation, Sidney sent
all of the materials he had accumulated to the War Department in 1888
and asked that copies be inserted in the official records. He included
letters-sent books, telegram books, special-order books, an endorsement
book, a registry book, and a general-order book of his father's for 1864
through 1865, as well as special orders issued by others on Winder's

staff. The records offered incontrovertible proof that he, his cousin Richard, and his father had never been cruel to prisoners in their custody after the ending of the cartel. When he asked the War Department to return his materials, he was told they had disappeared; presumably, copies were made and placed in various files, but the originals were never found.[17]

Sidney's health deteriorated during the 1870s as did his grandmother's, his mother's, and his sister's, but all were alive (except Gertrude, who died in 1872 at age ninety) when Winder's body was returned to Baltimore in 1878. Caroline died the next year and was interred beside her husband, and Sidney and Carrie withdrew into a world of their own. Neither ever married, and they shared a comfortable house at 2117 St. Paul Street until Carrie died on 3 April 1903. She left all of her possessions to her "dear brother," whom she appointed as her sole executor.

Old and alone, almost blind, and in ill health, Sidney saw few people after Carrie's death. As far as can be determined, he did not have any contact with his half-brother, William Andrew. The children of his brother John Cox Winder were welcome, if infrequent, visitors but were not a significant enough part of his life to sustain his will to live. He drew up his will, bequeathing the house and its contents plus $39,500 to his nephew and nieces, and then killed himself on 25 February 1905.[18]

Sidney's suicide was not the result of his failure to reverse the image of his father, but his was not a happy life. Winder's other sons were more fortunate. John Cox became a prominent man in the North Carolina railroad business. When he died on 22 March 1896, he was the vice-president of the Seaboard Airline Railroad. The eldest son, William Andrew, resigned from the army in 1867, became a medical doctor, and spent much of the rest of his life attempting to improve reservation life for the Indians. He died on the job on 5 March 1903, at the Rosebud Indian Reservation near Omaha, Nebraska, and was buried in Portsmouth, New Hampshire.[19]

What of their father's proper place in history? Clearly, he does not deserve the defamation enunciated by northerners, nor does he merit all of the glowing tributes he received from southern leaders during and after the war. Judged by the standards of his time, the only proper measurement, he was not a benevolent man, but neither was he cruel or vindictive. Winder was overzealous and somewhat contentious as provost marshal general, and he certainly caused resentment and controversy as commander of Richmond during 1862. It was axiomatic that he would make enemies in this command. He accepted this, and public criticism never swayed him in the execution of his duties.

True to his training as a professional soldier, he always attempted to go by the book, although he modified or revoked orders that proved unworkable. When he deviated and became innovative, he invariably got into trouble. His price-fixing policy was a disaster; and when he ordered that Federal prisoners share the dwindling supplies of the Richmond marketplace, he enraged almost every resident in the city. Still, the Richmond accusation that he was a dictator is nonsense. So too is the lament that he pampered Union prisoners and thereby subjected Richmonders to increased hardships. Equally ludicrous is the charge that he was a profane drunkard who dealt fairly only with fellow Marylanders. Winder swore and he drank, but he was excessive in neither; and the bias of southerners, especially Virginians, against natives of Maryland has been well documented.

Winder was not a lovable figure. He was abrupt and abrasive in speech, and arrogant, vain, and short tempered in demeanor. He also regarded himself as an excellent, almost unimpeachable judge of men, and this made him appear foolish and incompetent at times. He struck most Richmonders, in 1862 at least, as an unfeeling martinet, a man who did not hesitate to trample on their most cherished beliefs. In this respect, they were not totally in error, for Winder did not shun power. When he had it, he used it; but he never had enough to truly accomplish his task.

No matter what policy he attempted to enact, he never succeeded in imposing it in a permanent fashion. He certainly reduced the level of violence in Richmond caused by the consumption of alcohol, but even his modified prohibition policy failed in the long run. The passport system caused widespread distress and anger among both the military and civilian populations, but it was successful in controlling the movements of both and was fairly efficient after 1863.

Winder had less success in dealing with spies and disloyalists, though not all of his work in this area was in vain either. Some of his men did apprehend and bring to trial several important spies, but others operated with impunity throughout the war. Conversely, overzealousness on the part of Winder and his men resulted in many unwise arrests. For example, George R. Clark Todd, the brother of Mary Todd Lincoln, got drunk, damned Davis for not granting the appointment he wanted, and was immediately arrested. He was released the next day, received the appointment, and served the Confederacy for the duration. Others, William H. Hurlburt, for instance, were not originally disloyal but became so after being arbitrarily arrested and confined in one of Winder's jails. Hurlburt obtained a false passport and fled, an avowed enemy of the Confederacy.[20]

In sum, Winder never succeeded in imposing law and order in the capital, but he came close in 1862, and his overall record compares favorably with those of all other southern commanders charged with a similar mission. He was a loyal and energetic officer, totally committed to the cause he served, and the Confederacy could have used more like him. His zeal and devotion to duty gained the respect if not the affection of most in Richmond before he was reassigned in 1864.

In his role as prison commander, Winder betrayed few signs of a humanitarian nature after 1863. Until then, he was a humane jailor, far more so than his Union counterpart, Colonel William H. Hoffman. He visited his prisoners frequently, heeded their complaints, and made strenuous efforts to improve the conditions for officers and enlisted men alike. Still, his orders were to securely confine the prisoners, and this was his top priority even if the captives suffered unduly from excessive congestion and inadequate food, shelter, and clothing. Security was his paramount concern, in Richmond and elsewhere, from beginning to end, and this was as it should have been.

The war changed in 1863, and so did Winder. After the enactment of the Emancipation Proclamation and the abrogation of the cartel, he became more distant and businesslike in his actions. His personal visits to the Richmond prisons ceased. By the winter of 1863–1864, he had persuaded himself that the increased mortality at Belle Isle was simply a part of long-term incarceration and that congestion was not an important factor. The facts he assembled to support this view had merit but did not convince either his colleagues or later authorities. One factor he knew of but did not cite also supported his contention. He was no doubt influenced and sustained in his view by the knowledge that the mortality rate of Confederates in Union prisons at that time was higher than that of his charges in Confederate prisons. Unlike Federal captives, southern inmates in the North were adequately housed in most instances and never experienced the congestion that he was increasingly forced to contend with, yet they still died, and the numbers were such that he could make a convincing case that simply being confined for a long time without the hope of release was going to lead to a great deal of death.[21]

Like almost all prison commanders in both the North and the South, Winder became more hardened to the suffering of all his captives, Confederate and Union alike. He authorized brutal punishment against Confederate prisoners at Castle Thunder, a necessary but scarcely benevolent action, and he ordered the mining of Libby to forestall a possible uprising, an unsavory act. Yet the northern vilification of Winder as a murderous beast is even less warranted than the southern charge that he coddled Union captives. He was an early and earnest advocate of exchange, and he did instruct his subordinates to secure necessary provisions for his captives on the open marketplace. He also paroled hundreds of prisoners on his own responsibility, some of whom escaped, and defended his action by stating that it was absolutely necessary to take this action, since his force could not provide for the needs of the inmates or even properly secure them.

Until he left Richmond in May 1864, there is no doubt that he had done everything possible, given the force at his command and the restrictions under which he labored, to comply with Confederate law respecting prisoners of war. Much suffering and death had occurred, but everyone in the Confederate capital was aware that he had worked diligently to improve conditions—too diligently in the opinion of many—and they were also aware that his failings were not intentional or the result of indifference, malice, or neglect.

When Winder arrived at Andersonville, he inherited a situation that was destined for monstrous ignominy. He had been informed by his kinsmen and other officers for five months that the prison was truly becoming a hell on earth. As Ovid Futch later noted, there is something heartbreaking in reading the hundreds of messages that Richard Winder sent begging for help.[22] One cannot read these communications without concluding that Richard was an honorable man being torn asunder by the awful scene daily passing before his eyes. One can also read the cold-blooded assessments forwarded to Winder by Major Thomas P. Turner. After inspecting Andersonville on 25 May 1864, he notified Winder that unless tents or barracks were provided, the captives "will die off by the hundreds, and will be a dead loss to us in the way of exchange."[23] [Other reports can be found in sympathy with both Richard and Turner, and many others whose views were in between, those of Wirz for example.]

Winder's communications reflected his concern for security, but he also repeatedly informed his government of the atrocious circumstances existing at the prisons. He stated on more than one occasion during the last year of the war that he would be glad to accept rations and clothing for his charges from the Federal government, and scarcely a day passed that he did not point out that he was powerless to mitigate the ongoing catastrophe without reinforcements.

Catastrophe is not too strong a word for what took place during the last year of his life; fully two-thirds of all Union prison deaths occurred from February of 1864 to February of 1865. By far the largest number of these died during the summer and fall of 1864, after he was placed in charge of Andersonville and other prisons in Georgia and Alabama but before he was appointed commissary general.

Was there anything he could have done to prevent this tragedy? Would he have been able to prevent the succession of horrors if he had been appointed commissary general in the spring of 1864? Even with the benefit of hindsight, it is difficult to see what he could have done that would have rendered the situation acceptable. From the time he took command at Andersonville, he attempted to disperse the prisoners and made determined efforts to build additional prisons, but he was hamstrung by the insufficiency of the guard, unreliability of the commissary system, lack of a central prison command, and the rapid deterioration of the Confederacy. He paroled hundreds of prisoners, hired out others, and refused to permit southern commanders to use his charges in dangerous occupations.

Yet his efforts did not slow, much less stop or reverse, the abomination that was Andersonville. He must have known shortly after his arrival that the situation was hopeless, and he knew better than anyone that there was no penal system in the offing which could possibly cope with the awful reality he faced. When he accepted the command, he did inform his superiors that he expected them to furnish all necessary resources commensurate with his "awesome responsibilities," but he should have known that he would fare less well, cut off from the power center of Richmond, than when he had been at the capital.

If he had refused the command, would it have made any difference—to his reputation and above all to the ultimate fate of the prisoners? His name was already odious in the Union, but even if he had been remembered as master of the "boa constrictor" that was Libby, he would at least have escaped linkage with Andersonville, the most notorious prison in American history. Clearly, he erred in accepting the command, as far as his reputation is concerned, and the question of why he did it must be addressed.

Critics have charged that he accepted the position so he could "kill as many Yankees as possible." Defenders have asserted that he was the best-qualified officer available for the job. Winder's correspondence indicates that he felt it was his duty to serve, and duty was all important to him. His country required that he do this duty, honor permitting, but where could there be any honor in this posting? He seems to have found an answer, a self-serving one: only an extraordinary man, a decent, extremely efficient senior officer, could rectify the situation. He was arrogant enough to believe that he was that man, and he may have been correct. There was no one in the Confederacy who possessed both his experience and the respect of Davis and Cooper, and this was of paramount importance. These two men, along with Robert Ould, would determine the fate of the Union captives, and Winder had the ear of all three.

The summer of 1864 must have disabused him of the idea that honor could coexist with duty at Andersonville. Richmond ordered him to confine and succor the captives and he in turn issued orders to that effect, but the death rate soared to the point where almost one hundred men died every day, about four every hour. Clearly, while the orders received and given were benign, the results were lethal.

At what point should he have concluded that these orders could not be obeyed any longer? When should his hubris have yielded to reality, forced him to admit defeat, and induced him to resign his command and even his commission? Probably during July or August, certainly no later than September. By that time it was obvious to all but the most obtuse that Confederate prisons were truly death camps. If Winder ever contemplated resignation, he never recorded it in any correspondence

that has survived. Why he clung to this unenviable command he never
explained, and his reports to Cooper and others indicate that he was
pessimistic about the future even if he were to be empowered to take
control of the entire penal system.

When he was finally given the position of commissary general in November, he did make improvements. The death rate dropped markedly
during the last winter of the war, despite the imminent collapse of the
Confederacy, and this suggests that he might have been able to at least
ameliorate some of the worst conditions if he had attained the position
earlier. Still, he recommended within a month of his appointment that
the Federal captives be paroled and sent home without benefit of exchange.

This was the proper conclusion. By today's ethics, he was some four
or five months late in making the decision, yet he was ahead of his superiors, who adamantly refused to consider anything short of a resumption
of the cartel. The inescapable conclusion seems to be that the fate of
the Federal captives would have been just as horrible, no matter who
was in command, and could have been even worse.

When Winder finally recognized that his world was ending, he was
not apologetic in any way. He was just as unrepentant about his actions
during the war as he had been when he owned over fifty people as slaves.
He had never been intentionally cruel to his slaves and had never condoned cruelty in regard to the prisoners, who were, to some extent,
in a position similar to chattels.

It was apparent to him by December of 1864 that there would be
no Confederate States of America. He was convinced that he had done
his best for the prisoners up to that time, but he was also convinced
that the only possible solution was to parole them immediately. He apparently felt no personal guilt about the number of prisoners who had died,
never made any statement that indicated any feelings of personal remorse, yet he had himself overseen the compilation of the awesome totals
as they were reported from the various prisons.

The total number of prison deaths has been a matter of dispute ever
since the war ended, but the generally accepted figure is that 30,218
out of 194,743 captured Federals died in captivity.[24] This casualty rate
is too low, since reports from at least thirteen southern prisons and holding areas were never found (see table of Confederate military prisons,
1861–1865). On the other hand, as virtually all historians of the twentieth
century have pointed out, this 15.5 percent mortality rate compares favorably with the 12 percent fatality that Confederates experienced in Union
prisons; the fact that 25,976 out of 214,865 rebel captives died in the
North, where no shortages of any kind existed, is much more inexcusable.
Had the fates been different and the Confederacy victorious, Commissary

Confederate Military Prisons, 1861–1865

Location	Prison
Richmond, Virginia	Liggons
	Atkison's tobacco factory
	Scott's tobacco factory
	Pemberton's tobacco factory
	Mayo's tobacco factory
	Grant's tobacco factory
	Smith & McCurdy's tobacco factory
	Yarborough's tobacco factory
	Ross's tobacco factory
	Crew's tobacco factory
	Royster's tobacco factory
	Barrett's tobacco factory
	Libby's ship chandlers
	Belle Isle
Danville, Virginia	Six tobacco warehouses
Petersburg, Virginia	Barracks
*Lynchburg, Virginia	Fairgrounds stables
Salisbury, North Carolina	Tobacco factory, five adjacent buildings
Charlotte, North Carolina	Jail, before 1865 exchange
Charleston, South Carolina	Castle Pinckney
	Charleston city jail
	Fairgrounds
Columbia, South Carolina	City jail
	Fairgrounds
	Camp Sorghum
	Camp Asylum
	Killian's mills (unfinished)
Florence, South Carolina	Florence Stockade
Cahaba, Alabama	Cotton shed
	Cahaba Stockade
*Tuscaloosa, Alabama	Papermill
*Savannah, Georgia	Camp Davidson
*Blackshear, Georgia	Open field
*Macon, Georgia	Camp Oglethorpe
*Thomasville, Georgia	Open field
*Millen, Georgia	Camp Lawton stockade
*Atlanta, Georgia	Slave pen
Andersonville, Georgia	Camp Sumter stockade
Tyler, Texas	Camp Ford
Hempstead, Texas	Camp Groce

*No records found.

Note: There were also holding compounds of short duration at Raleigh, North Carolina; Shreveport, Louisiana; Mobile, Alabama; and at Marietta and Augusta, Georgia, for which no records were found.

General Hoffman would have gone down in history as the mass murderer of helpless captives, not John Henry Winder.

As historians such as Hesseltine, Futch, and others have noted, war was the great villain in this tragedy, but some of the suffering and death could have been prevented if each side had adhered to the cartel. This would have eliminated the huge toll of prison deaths, although the exchanged men might have been crippled or killed in battle, or died simply because they were returned to the ranks. As Bruce Catton has observed, just being in the army killed more than twice the number of men who died in battle, and they died in large measure for the same reasons the prisoners died: poor food, lack of shelter, improper hygiene, and a total ignorance of microbic diseases.[25] Even so, adherence to the cartel would have eliminated the most poisonous aspect of the war, the vituperation and recrimination that each side manifested against the other for the alleged mistreatment of thousands of helpless prisoners of war.

The responsibility for the termination of the exchange rests primarily on Lincoln, and perhaps the termination was necessary if the war were to be won, but Davis also must share the blame for the ending of the cartel. Davis might proclaim, as he did to the Confederate Congress in May of 1864, that he was unable to comprehend Lincoln's policy on the issue. He lamented, "Prisoners held by us, in spite of humane care, are perishing from the inevitable effects of imprisonment [and this] spectacle of their suffering augments our longing desire to relieve from similar trials our own brave men who have spent so many weary months in a cruel and useless imprisonment." But he clearly violated the cartel when he declared Butler beyond the pale.[26] In addition, his refusal to recognize black soldiers as anything but runaway slaves reflected his inability to come to terms with the reality of the times, to concede that the war had become total and revolutionary, to understand that slavery could not have continued in the old way even if the Confederacy had won. His position allowed Lincoln and Grant to claim the high ground, to end the exchange for idealistic and moral reasons as well as for more pragmatic ones.[27]

Yet the breakdown of the cartel should not have resulted in the high prison death rate that both sides endured. That it did is the fault of Lincoln and Davis; neither executive insisted that a more determined effort be made to improve the condition of their captives, and the result was that over 56,000 men died in captivity, a stain on the honor of all America, Confederate and Union. Against this it must be noted that neither man gave way to the considerable pressures to raise the black flag, to intentionally maim and murder their captives. If they had responded to the desires of many of their respective constituencies and heeded the popular clamor from otherwise respectable and respected people, the whole issue certainly would have become far more heinous.

As for Winder, he could have resigned in protest and enhanced his reputation to some degree. He did not. Some might regard this as a fundamental flaw in his character. Not he. He believed that his resignation would not remedy the evil; quitting would only make it worse. So he persisted, as doomed as the cause he served. He viewed his duty to his country as a matter of honor, but there was no honor in it. He was neither saint nor sinner, martyr nor fiend. He was a man of above-average qualities caught up in an extraordinary situation. He performed his duty to the best of his ability to the bitter end, and the end was bitter. The final tragedy is that, given the same set of circumstances, no one could have done any better.

APPENDIX

The Cartel of July 22, 1862

Haxall's Landing, on James River, Va., July 22, 1862

The undersigned, having been commissioned by the authorities they respectively represent to make arrangements for a general exchange of prisoners of war, have agreed to the following articles:

Article 1. It is hereby agreed and stipulated that all prisoners of war held by either party, including those taken on private armed vessels known as privateers, shall be discharged upon the conditions and terms following:

Prisoners to be exchanged man for man and officer for officer; privateers to be placed upon the footing of officers and men of the navy.

Men and officers of lower grades may be exchanged for officers of a higher grade, and men and officers of different services may be exchanged according to the following scale of equivalents:

A general commanding-in-chief or an admiral shall be exchanged for officers of equal rank, or for sixty privates or common seamen.

A flag-officer or major-general shall be exchanged for officers of equal rank, or for forty privates or common seamen.

A commodore carrying a broad pennant or a brigadier-general shall be exchanged for officers of equal rank, or for twenty privates or common seamen.

A captain in the navy or a colonel shall be exchanged for officers of equal rank, or for fifteen privates or common seamen.

A lieutenant-colonel or a commander in the navy shall be exchanged for officers of equal rank, or for ten privates or common seamen.

A lieutenant-commander or a major shall be exchanged for officers of equal rank, or eight privates or common seamen.

A lieutenant or a master in the navy or a captain in army or marines shall be exchanged for officers of equal rank, or four privates or common seamen.

Masters' mates in the navy or lieutenants and ensigns in the army shall be exchanged for officers of equal rank, or four privates or common seamen.

Midshipmen, warrant-officers in the navy, masters of merchant vessels, and commander of privateers shall be exchanged for officers of equal rank, or three privates or common seamen.

Second captains, lieutenants, or mates of merchant vessels or privateers, and all petty officers in the navy, and all non-commissioned officers in the army or marines shall be severally exchanged for persons of equal rank, or for two privates or common seamen, and private soldiers or common seamen shall be exchanged for each other, man for man.

Article 2. Local, State, civil, and militia rank held by persons not in actual military service will not be recognized, the basis of exchange being the grade actually held in the naval and military service of the respective parties.

Article 3. If citizens held by either party on charges of disloyalty or any alleged civil offense are exchanged, it shall only be for citizens. Captured sutlers, teamsters, and all civilians in the actual service of either party to be exchanged for persons in similar position.

Article 4. All prisoners of war to be discharged on parole in ten days after their capture, and the prisoners now held and those thereafter taken to be transported to the points mutually agreed upon at the expense of the capturing party. The surplus prisoners not exchanged shall not be permitted to take up arms again, nor to serve as military police or constabulary force in any fort, garrison, or field-work held by either of the respective parties, nor as guards of prisons, depots, or stores, nor to discharge any duty usually performed by soldiers, until exchanged under the provisions of this cartel. The exchange is not to be considered complete until the officer or soldier exchanged for has been actually restored to the lines to which he belongs.

Article 5. Each party, upon the discharge of prisoners of the other party, is authorized to discharge an equal number of their own officers or men from parole, furnishing at the same time to the other party a list of their prisoners discharged and of their own officers and men relieved from parole, thus enabling each party to relieve from parole such of their own officers and men as the party may choose. The lists thus mutually furnished will keep both parties advised of the true condition of the exchange of prisoners.

Article 6. The stipulations and provisions above mentioned to be of binding obligation during the continuance of the war, it matters not which party may have the surplus of prisoners, the great principles involved being, first, an equitable exchange of prisoners, man for man, officer for officer, or officers of higher grade exchanged for officers of lower grade or for privates, according to the scale of equivalents; second, that privateers and officers and men of different services may be exchanged according to the same scale of equivalents; third, that all prisoners, of whatever arm of service, are to be exchanged or paroled in ten days from the time of their capture, if it be practicable to transfer them to their own lines in that time; if not, as soon thereafter as practicable; fourth, that no officer soldier, or employee, in the service of either party, is to be considered as exchanged and absolved from his parole until his equivalent has actually reached the lines of his friends; fifth, that the parole forbids the performance of field, garrison, police, or guard, or constabulary duty.

JOHN A. DIX, Major-General
D. H. HILL, Major-General, C.S. Army

Source: Miller, ed., *The Photographic History of the Civil War*, 7:345–46.

NOTES

Abbreviations

ASPFR *American State Papers: Foreign Relations.* Vol. 3. Washington, D.C., 1832.

ASPMA *American State papers: Military Affairs.* 7 vols. Washington, D.C.: Gales & Seaton, 1832–1860.

LC Library of Congress

NA National Archives

OR United States War Department. *The War of the Rebellion: A Compilation of the Official Records of the Union and Confederate Armies,* 127 vols. Washington, D.C., 1880–1901.

RG Record Group. Used in citing material in the National Archives.

SHC Southern Historical Collection, Wilson Library, University of North Carolina, Chapel Hill.

USMA United States Military Academy, West Point, N.Y.

Introduction

1. For a current listing of the most important Civil War accounts, consult the bibliography provided by James M. McPherson in his *Battle Cry of Freedom* and the extensive reading list offered by J. G. Randall and David Donald in their classic study *The Civil War and Reconstruction.* One must also mention a few other classic accounts, beginning with the multivolume works *Ordeal of the Union* and *War for the Union* by Allan Nevins, the superb accounts of the Army of the Potomac in Bruce Catton's *Centennial History of the Civil War, R. E. Lee, A Biography,* by Douglas Southall Freemen, and Lincoln's own writings, edited by Roy Basler et al. and entitled *The Collected Works of Abraham Lincoln.* The prisoner-of-war issue has not been examined in depth since 1930, when William B. Hesseltine's *Civil War Prisons: A Study in War Psychology* was published, and a true accounting of the experiences of over 400,000 prisoners was not possible until the day of the computer ar-

rived. For a lively defense of the case study, see "The Case for the Case Study" by Suzanne Goldsmith and Katherine Boo.

2. Hesseltine, *Civil War Prisons*, offers an extensive listing of accounts by former Union prisoners who condemned Winder as their warden. In addition, nearly all newspapers in the North called him the "inhuman fiend of Andersonville" and similar appellations at the end of the war. Perhaps the best-known defense of Winder and other prison officials is R. Randolph Stevenson, *The Southern Side; or, Andersonville Prison;* but also see J. William Jones, *Confederate View of the Treatment of Prisoners, Compiled from Official Records and Other Documents*, and the memoirs of all high Confederate officials, beginning with Jefferson Davis.

3. Rhodes, *History of the United States from the Compromise of 1850*, 3:602–3; Miller, ed., *Photographic History*, 7:172.

4. Kantor, *Andersonville*, 328.

5. McElroy, *This Was Andersonville*, xv, xxi.

6. Hesseltine, comp., *Prisons*; Thomas, *Richmond*; Futch, *Andersonville*, 119.

7. Duffy, "Military Administrator."

8. *Niles Weekly Register*, 36:262, obituary of William Henry Winder, 25 May 1824.

9. Hesseltine, *Civil War Prisons*, 254–56; Futch, *Andersonville*, 119.

10. For example, see McPherson, *Battle Cry of Freedom*, 434, 442.

Chapter 1

1. Wilmington (N.C.) *Journal*, 9 February 1865.

2. New York *Times*, 6 November 1863; Dowdey, *Experiment in Rebellion*, 126, quoting William C. Harris.

3. Ely, *Journal*, 24, 96; Page, *True Story of Andersonville Prison*, 74–75.

4. *OR*, 8:96. All references are to Series 2 unless otherwise stated.

5. Winder urged Adjutant General Samuel Cooper to release the Union captives without exchange on 20 January 1865, and referred to his previous recommendation to free the captives in this communication. His first message has not been found, but he may have sent it late in December 1864, since it was at that time that he expressed great despair at the situation at the Florence and Salisbury prisons. See *OR*, 7:96, 97, 1127–29, 1151, 1219–21.

6. Ibid.; King, "Epilogue to Andersonville," 37. I would like to thank Professor G. Wayne King of the history department at Francis Marion College in Florence for his many courtesies and for giving me an extensive tour through the remains of the Florence prison.

7. *OR*, 8:135, 160–61, 168.

8. Ibid., 172, 184, 191, 451–53, 754, 765–66.

9. Ibid., 7:1219–21; King, "Epilogue to Andersonville," 38–39; Brown, *Salisbury Prison*, 162–66; Futch, *Andersonville*, 106–7.

10. King, "Epilogue to Andersonville," 39; Florence (S.C.) *Morning News*, 3 February 1959.

11. *OR*, 8:766.
12. Charleston *Daily Courier*, 11 February 1865; Woodward and Muhlenfeld, eds., *The Private Mary Chesnut*, 227.
13. Greenmount Cemetery Records, Baltimore. Winder's stepdaughter, Caroline "Carrie" Eagles, requested the return of the remains on 26 March 1878. The inscription was originally meant to read "Blessed Are The Pure In Heart." I have been unable to determine why the change was made. The Baltimore press announced the reinterment on 28 March (see the *Sun* of that date) but did not give many details. Winder, his wife, Caroline, Carrie, and Sidney are all buried next to each other in Beach Area 1, lot 13.

Chapter 2

1. RG 94, Register of Letters Received by the Office of the Adjutant General, Main Series, 1812–1889, Microcopy 711, Roll 62, Item W-185. This is the "index" to the main collection, and it contains brief summaries in most instances of letters received and indicates if the full transmission is recorded in the main collection. Cited hereafter as RG 94, Register of Letters.
2. Haskin, *History of the First Artillery*, 500.
3. Tebeau, *History of Florida*, 204–5.
4. RG 94, Register of Letters, Roll 61, Item W-144.
5. Ibid., Roll 62, Item W-185.
6. Ibid., Roll 62, Item W-300.
7. Freeman, *Lee*, 431–37; McKinney, *Education in Violence*, 89. Although West Point did not adopt "Honor, Duty, Country" as the official motto until 1898, the committee at that time announced that those words summed up the mission of the academy since its creation. It is therefore proper to use this symbol of the academy in antebellum times. This information was provided by Wendy A. Whitfield, Military Affairs Librarian, USMA Library.
8. Tolbert, ed., *Ellis Papers*, 768.
9. John Henry Winder Papers, SHC, M-915. Cited hereafter as J. H. Winder Papers. Colonel Lorenzo Thomas informed Winder that his resignation was official as of 21 April 1861.
10. Torrence, *Old Somerset*, 332–33; Laird, [ed.], "Some Records of the Winder Family," 5–19; F. A. Winder, "Pedigree of the Winder Family," Maryland Original Research Society, Baltimore.
11. Laird, [ed.], "Some Records of the Winder Family," 3.
12. Ibid.; Mahon, *War of 1812*, 103, 112, 291.
13. Winder, "Pedigree of the Winder Family," Maryland Original Research Society, Baltimore; Laird, [ed.], "Some Records of the Winder Family," 5; Johnson, *Winders of America*, 86–89; Duffy, "Military Administrator," 2–3.
14. Eaton Papers, SHC, 234, Folder G-234; Lossing, *War of 1812*, 918n. Lossing obtained Winder's papers from his daughter, Charlotte Aurelia Winder Townsend of Oyster Bay, New York, and used them extensively and accurately. I have also made a thorough examination of the Winder collections

and will cite certain documents and letters that Lossing did not have access to. I have relied on Lossing primarily for little-known details concerning Winder's actions, and on more recent scholars for overall accuracy.

15. Barnes, *Maryland Marriages, 1778–1800,* 253; Polk, *Polk Family,* 54–58, 211.

16. Second Census of the United States, 1800, Reel 12, Somerset County, p. 39 for William Henry and p. 43 for his father, William Winder. At this time, Levin had 43 slaves and one free Negro on his plantation. The largest slaveholder in the county had 128 slaves, and only five families owned 50 or more. There were 9,340 whites, 7,432 slaves, and 586 free Negroes there in 1800. It was a land of small farms and medium plantations. Most slaveholders owned from one to five slaves, but a sizable percentage owned from 10 to 30; tobacco was the major crop.

17. J. Thomas Scharf's *Chronicles of Baltimore* is old but still valuable. More recent histories are Hamilton Owens, *Baltimore on the Chesapeake,* and Gary Lawson Browne, *Baltimore in the Nation.*

18. Laird, "Some Records of the Winder Family," 18.

19. Baltimore *American and Commercial Advertiser,* 4 September 1802.

20. Duffy, "Military Administrator," 5.

21. Greenmount Cemetery Records, Baltimore; Third Census of the United States, 1810, Reel 13, Baltimore, 135; Polk, *Polk Family,* 211; Duffy, "Military Administrator," 6; Register of the First Presbyterian Church, Baltimore, 101, 122, 174, 176, 198.

22. Laird, "Some Records of the Winder Family," 17–18; Scharf, *Chronicles of Baltimore,* 240–41, 286–89.

23. Scharf, *Chronicles of Baltimore,* 290.

24. Laird, "Some Records of the Winder Family," 18–19; Hard information on Winder's classroom abilities before he went to West Point is scarce, but it is doubtful that he excelled during his younger days in Baltimore, since he remained an indifferent scholar all of his life.

25. *ASPMA,* 1:493–94.

26. *Niles Weekly Register,* 4:100. A random sampling of newspapers indicates that Winder was widely regarded in 1813 as an able and efficient officer. See *Maryland Gazette and Political Intelligencer,* Baltimore *Federal Gazette, National Intelligencer,* New York *Gazette,* and New York *Spectator;* even the Washington (Ga.) *Monitor* voiced approval on 8 May 1813. Scott's more accurate appraisal is quoted in Tucker, *Poltroons and Patriots,* 2:496.

27. Washington *Monitor,* 20 March 1813; Lossing, *War of 1812,* 294.

28. *ASPMA* 1:507. Winder made the application for his son's admission to West Point in January 1814.

29. Lossing, *War of 1812,* 600–602.

30. Ibid., 603–35; Mahon, *War of 1812,* 137–58; Leckie, *Wars of America,* 260.

31. Standard accounts on this topic are William E. V. S. Flory, *Prisoners of War: A Study in the Development of International Law,* Herbert C. Fooks, *Prisoners of War,* and *ASPFR,* 3:598–728. The only detailed examination of the actual cartel is Basdevant, "Deux conventions peu connues sur le droit de la guerre," 5–29.

32. A thorough account of the hostage issue can be found in Tucker, *Poltroons and Patriots*, 2:491–500; Lossing, *War of 1812*, 408–9, 788–89; ASPFR, 3:634–35; and Robinson, "Retaliation," 65–70.

33. Miscellaneous MS Collection, Box 199, LC, letter from William H. Winder to Henry B. Dawson, 3 March 1860; *Niles Weekly Register*, 5:365; ASPFR, 3:637–38.

34. Quoted in Robinson, "Retaliation," 68.

35. *Niles Weekly Register*, 6:11; Tucker, *Poltroons and Patriots*, 2:724.

36. Lossing, *War of 1812*, 789; ASPFR, 3:728; Robinson, "Retaliation," 68–69.

37. *Niles Weekly Register*, 6:146, 427; *Dictionary of American Biography*, 10:382. Winder was adjutant inspector general from 19 May to 2 July 1814.

38. Mahon, *War of 1812*, 111–22.

39. Lossing, *War of 1812*, 917.

40. ASPMA, 1:552.

41. W. H. Winder Papers and Correspondence, MS 919, Box 4, Museum and Library of Maryland History, Baltimore. Cited hereafter as W. H. Winder Correspondence.

42. Ibid.; ASPMA, 1:543.

43. Ibid.; Lossing, *War of 1812*, 919–20; *Niles Weekly Register*, 6:427.

44. ASPMA, 1:554, 560, 568.

45. Ibid., 536, 556; Lossing, *War of 1812*, 922–24.

46. Mahon, *War of 1812*, 298; ASPMA, 1:538, 556.

47. ASPMA, 1:548.

48. Mahon, *War of 1812*, 298–300.

49. Tucker, *Poltroons and Patriots*, 2:532.

50. Mahon, *War of 1812*, 298–300; Lossing, *War of 1812*, 927–32; ASPMA, 1:558, 565.

51. Mahon, *War of 1812*, 310–15.

52. ASPMA, 1:559.

53. Ibid., 524–99.

54. *Maryland Gazette and Political Intelligencer*, 2 March 1815.

55. W. H. Winder Correspondence, MS 919. This quotation is from a letter to W. H. Winder, Jr., from Paul Cameron, 27 June 1855. Cameron stated that he heard Jackson so express himself when he visited the president in August 1829.

56. *Niles Weekly Register*, 36:262; RG 92, Quarter Masters Consolidated File, Entry 225, Box 1250 (cited hereafter as RG 92, QM File), letter from Roger B. Taney to Joel Poinsett, 3 July 1838, characterizing Winder as that "most unfortunate general."

57. Hunt, ed., *Writings of James Madison*, 8:292–95, 542–44; Ammon, *James Monroe*, 328–36; Swisher, *Roger B. Taney*, 67; Miscellaneous MS Collection, Box 199, LC.

58. Alvarez, *Travel*, 34–35.

59. Ela, *Sights and Secrets*, 21–22.

60. J. H. Winder Papers, SHC, M-915, John Ellis to Winder, 9 May 1861. I found no reference listing Winder as a passenger on any ships departing during the first week of May. The Union blockade existed only on paper

at this time, traffic was heavy, and the newspaper coverage of normal events was disrupted. Since he could not go by train (the Annapolis-to-Washington branch of the Baltimore and Ohio was in the hands of General Benjamin Butler's troops), and travel overland by any other means was slow and laborious, it is inconceivable that he did not go by water.

Chapter 3

1. J. H. Winder Papers, SHC, M-915, Ellis to Winder, 9 May 1861.
2. Ibid.; Russell, *My Diary*, 87–98.
3. Tolbert, ed., *Ellis Papers*, 768–69.
4. Ibid., 641.
5. Winder's life from 1814 to 1828 is explored in chapters 5 and 6 herein. He was ordered to Smithville on 2 September and reported on 5 November that he was at the post. See RG 94; Letters Received by the Office of the Adjutant General (Main Series), 1822–1860, Microcopy 567, Roll 40, Items W-77 and W-104. These letters are on 636 rolls of microfilm and will be cited hereafter as RG 94 with the appropriate roll and item numbers, or by roll and date if no item number was assigned.
6. Bentley, *Fort Johnston in the History of the Lower Cape Fear*, 11–13.
7. Lee, *History of Brunswick County*, 130–37.
8. Greenmount Cemetery, Baltimore, tombstone of Caroline Cox Winder. On her marriage to Eagles, see the Edenton (N.C.) *Gazette*, 8 February 1820. The Raleigh *Register*, Cape Fear *Recorder*, and *North Carolina Gazette* erroneously reported the date of the marriage as 8 February; see the 18 February 1820 issue of each paper.
9. McKay, *Early Wilmington*, 1; Waddell, *History of New Hanover County*, 47; Lee, *Lower Cape Fear*, 126.
10. Deed Book C, 296, Brunswick County Courthouse, Bolivia, N.C.
11. Brunswick Estate Records, Book K, 242–43, Brunswick County Courthouse, Bolivia, N.C. This is a plat of the division of the estate of Joseph Eagles in 1833.
12. Last Will and Testament of Joseph Eagles, 19 June 1827. This will was proved on 11 December 1827 in court and is recorded in Book C, 97, of New Hanover County Wills, North Carolina Archives, Raleigh; Fourth Census of the United States, 1820, Reel 84, Wilmington, 237.
13. Greenmount Cemetery, Baltimore, tombstone of Caroline Ann Eagles; Cemetery Records, Brunswick County, N.C., Archives, Raleigh; Deed Book S, 215, New Hanover County Courthouse, Wilmington, N.C. The property was purchased from William MacKay for $1,830. I have not been able to find the exact dates of Sarah's birth and death, but several references indicate that she had been born by March 1826 and that she died in April 1832. See Brunswick Estate Records, Book K, 242–43, Brunswick County Courthouse, Bolivia, N.C.
14. Not only was George Davis Caroline's nephew by marriage; he was also

a distant relative of Winder's through his wife, Mary Polk, who was a descendant of Winder's great aunt. For a biographical sketch of Davis, see *Dictionary of American Biography*, 5:114.

15. Last Will and Testament of Joseph Eagles, in New Hanover County Wills, Book C, 97, North Carolina Archives, Raleigh. I am indebted to the staff of the Search Room, North Carolina Archives, for their help in explaining the operation of the Sixth Rule of Descents.

16. Ibid.

17. Cape Fear (N.C.) *Recorder*, 1 October 1828, 23 September and 28 October 1829.

18. New Hanover County Court Minutes, 1827–1832, 2:126, 10:91, 136, 148, North Carolina Archives, Raleigh. Eagles owed the Bank of Cape Fear $4,903.02.

19. J. H. Winder Papers, SHC, M-915.

20. Deed Book U, 106, New Hanover County Records, Microfilm 39, State Archives, Raleigh.

21. Cape Fear (N.C.) *Recorder*, 17 November 1830; *St. James Church, Wilmington, North Carolina, Historical Records 1737–1852*, compiled by Ida B. Kellam and Elizabeth F. McKey, notes the marriage on 55, and a pamphlet entitled *St. James Church*, 2, identifies Cairns as the minister. Both works were published by, and are available at, the church.

22. Caroline's wedding ring, a portrait of her, and one silk dress are in the possession of a descendant, Mrs. Caroline D. Ashford of New Bern, North Carolina. John Winder Hughes, interview by the author, December 1986. For a description of Elizabeth, see Bowen, *Wilkes County, Georgia* 1–5.

23. Wilkes County Wills, 1819–1836, Book HH, 267–69, Wilkes County Courthouse, Washington, Ga.

24. Wilkes County Papers, 1773–1833, Microfilm Reel 242-11, Item 1613, p. 18, Georgia State Archives, Atlanta. It appears that Winder took possession of two couples and eight young single slaves of both sexes. Some of these were the children of the adults, but it does not appear that this was true in each case. The 1820 census did not list all of Shepherd's slaves, since many of them had been leased. This makes it impossible to compare names with those that appear in the 1830 census. It does appear that every attempt was made to keep families together, based on the final disposition as compared to the 1830 census data, but the final settlement did not give a breakdown by name or any other description.

25. General Winder had left Gertrude the house and one male slave, age eighteen, two female slaves, ages nineteen and twenty, and one free Negro woman, the mother of the slaves, when he died in 1824. In 1830, Gertrude still had the slaves, but the free Negro was not listed. By 1840, she had freed the two females, but the male, then thirty-eight years old, and two other females, ages twenty-five and twenty-seven, were still slaves. The latter two slaves were almost certainly the two young slaves Winder sent ten years before. See reports for Baltimore in the Census of 1820, Reel 42, p. 278; Census of 1830, Reel 54, p. 279; and Census of 1840, Reel 158, under Charles H. Winder, p. 131.

26. Record of Deeds, Book K, 202, Brunswick County Courthouse, Bolivia, N.C.
In 1838, while serving in Florida during the Second Seminole War, Winder
joined six other officers who asked Adjutant General Roger Jones for compen-
sation for the travel costs of their servants, a request that was denied but
that indicates that Jack was with Winder then. See RG 94, Roll 178, Item
W-44, Winder to Jones, 24 June 1838. Jack also accompanied Winder from
1846 to 1848 in Mexico. See RG 134, "Accounts of Fund of Lieut. Governor's
Court by Capt. John H. Winder," Entry 152. Cited hereafter as RG 134,
Winder Fund.

27. Fifth Census of the United States, 1830, Reel 118, Wilmington, 333.

28. Haskin, *History of the First Regiment*, 41–42.

29. Brunswick Estate Records, Book K, 242–43, Brunswick County Courthouse,
Bolivia, N.C.; Deed Book V, 254–56, New Hanover County Courthouse,
Wilmington, N.C. Sarah Moore received the acreage containing the mill,
and Caroline sold the house to Isaac Northrop on 6 February 1834.

30. Cape Fear (N.C.) *Recorder*, 21 December 1831.

31. Ibid., 1–15 February, 25 April 1832.

32. Duffy, "Military Administrator," 36–37; Marshall, *American Bastille*, 268.
William continued to list himself as a merchant long after he became a contractor. In Philadelphia his firm was located at 37 South Wharves until 1842,
when he relocated to 125 South Front. He apparently lived at his place
of business until 1843, when he bought a house at 36 Walnut Street. The
city directory lists him at 76 ½ Walnut Street after 1850. He traveled extensively and was not in Philadelphia when the the federal census was taken
in 1840, 1850, or 1860, and I have not been able to determine where he
was or what his net worth was for any of those years.

33. RG 94, Roll 77, Item W-54; Roll 90, Item W-251; Roll 102, Item W-17.

34. Deed Book L, 19, 375, Brunswick County Courthouse, Bolivia, N.C.

35. New Hanover County Court Records, 1832–1838, 2:137–38, North Carolina
Archives, Raleigh.

36. Deed Book L, 380, Brunswick County Courthouse, Bolivia, N.C.

37. J. H. Winder Papers, SHC, M-915, an account of the Eagles-Winder Estate
from 1830 to 1849; Cape Fear (N.C.) *Recorder*, 23 November 1831.

38. RG 94, Roll 77, Item W-54; Brunswick Estate Records, 1783 to 1920, "Report
of Commissioners to Divide Land, 1833" [of Joseph Eagles], North Carolina
Archives, Raleigh. Sarah's death necessitated a trip to Edenton to take care
of the legal arrangements with guardian John Cox.

39. RG 94, Roll 77, Item W-54.

40. Duffy, "Military Administrator," 27; RG 94, Roll 199, Item W-178; Roll 221,
Item W-301. The Winders gave each of their children an engraved silver
spoon at birth, but only Sidney's has been located. It was in the possession
of John Winder Hughes of Wilmington at the time of his death.

41. Cullum, *Biographical Register*, 1:253, gives the date as 30 November 1833,
but this is incorrect. Winder received the commission one year later, filled
in the form, and appeared before a justice of the peace to take the required
oath of allegiance. He neglected to sign the oath, and it was returned on

29 November 1834. He signed it on 24 December 1834, so it was not really finalized until that date. See RG 94, Roll 102, Item W-205.

42. Cape Fear (N.C.) *Recorder,* 25 January, 8 February 1832. The slaves were hired for six- or eight-week intervals and were issued regular army rations.

43. RG 94, Roll 115, Item W-124.

44. See Laumer, *Massacre,* on the beginning of the war.

45. The standard account of the war is Mahon, *Second Seminole War.*

46. RG 94, Roll 115, Item W-124.

47. Ibid., Roll 155, Items W-281, W-311, W-338, W-399.

48. RG 94, Engineer Department Records Relating to the U.S. Military Academy, Microcopy 91, Roll 8, 247, Roll 9, 530 (cited hereafter as RG 94, Engineer Records); RG 94, Roll 221, Item W-256.

49. RG 94, Roll 221, Item W-301. His infant daughter, whose name was not recorded, was buried on 24 July 1840, at St. James Episcopal Church in Wilmington. See Kellam and McKey, comps., *Historical Records,* 70.

50. Cemetery Records, Brunswick County, North Carolina Archives, Raleigh; Wilmington (N.C.) *Weekly Chronicle,* 30 September 1840.

51. RG 92, QM File, letters from Winder to Thomas Jesup, 3 September and 9 November 1841; Duffy, "Military Administrator," 29. The Winder silverware ended up in Sidney's possession, and he bequeathed it to his niece, Caroline Winder Hughes, of New Bern, North Carolina. Her descendants still own it. The field desk was also left by Sidney to a nephew, John Henry Winder of Columbus, Ohio, and is now in the possession of Mrs. Carol Winder of Winston-Salem, North Carolina.

52. J. H. Winder Papers, SHC, M-915, letter from William to John, 16 November 1846; RG 94, Engineer Records, Roll 8, 247, Roll 9, 530.

53. RG 94, Roll 221, Items W-404, W-417, W-434.

54. J. H. Winder Papers, SHC, M-915, "The Estate of Joseph Eagles in account current with J. H. Winder, 1830–48."

55. Marshall, *American Bastille,* 268; Duffy, "Military Administrator," 36–37; Topham, "Winder Building," 37:169–71. In 1846, shortly before he began the project, William was arrested in Philadelphia and charged with a shortage of $80,000 in the loan account of the LeHeigh Coal and Navigation Co. with the Northampton Bank of Allentown, which was in bankruptcy. He paid the money but was so angered by the arrest that he challenged the bank's attorney to a duel at Allentown and then failed to appear; this resulted in new accusations of cowardice as well as fraud. However that may be, in November 1850 he agreed to rebuild the National Theater in Washington, D.C., which had burned in 1845 and was in complete ruin, in the incredible time of six weeks. Even more amazing, he did it; Jenny Lind, the "Swedish Nightingale," made her debut there on 20 December. William was not much when it came to dueling, but he was a first-class builder. See Bergmann and Lehman, "The Winder Building," 10–11.

56. A transcript of this letter, prepared by Winder's sister Charlotte Townsend in 1885, was provided by John Winder Hughes of Wilmington. The original has long since been lost.

57. Register of the First Presbyterian Church, Baltimore, 101, 122, 174, 176; Augusta (Ga.) *Chronicle*, 18 February 1823; First Marriage Book, 1806–1834, 84, Georgia State Archives, Atlanta.

58. Winder, "These Notes on the American Branch of the Winder Family," 15 March 1945, 3—4 (MS in possession of Winder family). The author, John Henry Winder, was a grandson of the general, and it is for him that the town of Winder, Georgia, is named. See also the obituary of William Andrew Winder, San Diego *Sun*, 6 March 1903.

59. RG 94, Roll 398, Item W-748; Roll 419, Items W-64, W-131; RG 94, Register of Letters, Roll 21, Item 252. William Andrew was sworn in on 17 March 1848 but did not serve in Mexico.

60. Wilmington (N.C.) *Weekly Chronicle*, 20 January 1848; Deed Book HH, 736, New Hanover County Records, Wilmington Courthouse, Wilmington, N.C.

61. Inventories, Accounts of Sales, Guardian Accounts, 1847–1857, 394, New Hanover County Records, North Carolina Archives, Raleigh; New Hanover County Court Records, 1852–1854, 19:182, North Carolina Archives, Raleigh; Record of Deed Book P, 640, Brunswick County Courthouse, Bolivia, N.C.

62. J. H. Winder Papers, SHC, M-915, letter from George Davis to Winder, 13 May 1854.

63. *Niles Weekly Register*, 20:56. Winder had the use of one of his father's slaves after he joined the army, possibly the same servant who accompanied him during his cadet years. I deduce this from the fact that William Winder listed two male and three female slaves in 1810 and one male and two females in 1820. I cannot account for the absence of one of the female slaves. She must have died, for she was over forty-five years old in 1810. It is almost certain that Winder would not have sold her, since there is no record that he ever sold any of his chattels. The same was true of his wife, Gertrude. Even after William's death, when she was in severe economic straits, she never sold any of the slaves. See Third Census of the United States, 1810, Reel 13, Baltimore, 135, and Fourth Census of the United States, 1820, Reel 42, Baltimore, 278. There is no reference to a servant while he was in Mexico, but I think it likely that he had one, since the practice was so common among southern officers.

64. Between 1810 and 1820, Winder's father freed one female slave and employed her in his household; his widow, Gertrude, freed one male and two female slaves between 1830 and 1840 and emancipated the remainder by 1850. By that year, all of Winder's family had ceased to own slaves, and he himself would have been out of the business by then except for the legal problem of guardianship, which delayed the transaction until 1853. See Second Census of the United States, 1800, Reel 12, Somerset County, 39, and the reports for Baltimore in the Census of 1820, Reel 42, 278; Census of 1830, Reel 54, 279; Census of 1840, Reel 158, under Charles Henry Winder, 131; and Census of 1850, Reel 102, Washington, D.C., under Charles H. Winder, 195; Laird, "Some Records of the Winder Family," 18; Last Will and Testament of William Henry Winder, Folio 27, Book 12, Baltimore City Register of Wills, Hall of Records, Annapolis, Md.

65. Inventories, Accounts of Sales, 394, New Hanover County Records, North Carolina Archives, Raleigh.
66. Ibid. There is a total absence of any humanitarian feeling in this document, which lists all the slaves by name and age and includes Winder's comments about the sale. It is a straightforward, dispassionate business agreement.
67. Potter, *Impending Crisis*, 90–120. Potter entitled this chapter "The Armistice of 1850," reflecting a viewpoint that I endorse.
68. RG 94, Roll 475, Item W-438.
69. J. H. Winder Papers, SHC, M-915, Cooper to Winder, 21 June 1861; *OR*, Ser. 1, Vol. 41, Pt. 2, p. 146; Ser. 2, Vol. 3:683.

Chapter 4

1. Thomas, *Richmond*, 15–31.
2. Richmond *Enquirer*, 17 September 1861.
3. Putnam, *Richmond*, 76.
4. *OR*, 3:694–95.
5. Jones, *War Clerk's Diary*, 1:59–60.
6. RG 109; Quartermaster General's Office and the Quartermaster General's Department, requisition for fodder signed by Winder of the Maryland Flying Artillery, 11 July 1861. This record group, the War Department Collection of Confederate Records, will be cited hereafter as RG 109 with the appropriate departmental identification, i.e., RG 109, Adjutant General, RG 109, Richmond Military Prisons, RG 109, Headquarters of the Forces, etc.
7. RG 109, Headquarters of the Forces, Special Orders No. 223 and No. 225, dated 16 July and 18 July, respectively.
8. Woodward, ed., *Mary Chesnut's Civil War*, 118. Mary Stark wrote to Mary Chesnut on 28 July 1861 that Gertrude Winder was in Columbia with her daughter Emma and that it was feared she might die of consumption. Gertrude did not have a daughter, daughter-in-law, niece, or sister of that name. I suspect that "Emma" was actually Alma Townsend Winder, Gertrude's sister-in-law, but find no proof other than the census report to support this contention.
9. Ibid.; Tolbert, ed., *Ellis Papers*, 641; Sprunt, *Chronicles of Cape Fear*, 281, 308; *OR*, Ser. 1, Vol. 51, Pt. 2, p. 193; 67:1156, 1289.
10. Richmond *Whig*, 29 December 1863; Duffy, "Military Administrator," 102; interview by the author with John Winder Hughes, December 1986.
11. J. H. Winder Papers, SHC, M-915; U.S. Congress, Senate Doc. 234, *Journal of the Congress of the Confederate States*, 1:515; John Winder Hughes interview by the author, 17 December 1986.
12. *OR*, Ser. 1, Vol. 50, Pt. 2, pp. 108–9, 505, 920, 925, 929, 1006–7.
13. Ibid., 1082–83, 1109.
14. William Andrew's antebellum army career was above average but not outstanding. He was primarily assigned to mediate differences between Indians and whites in California, and he became convinced that the Indians had

been treated unjustly in almost every instance involving a controversy with whites. This was not a popular position, but it became a lifelong obsession with him. Phillips, *Chiefs and Challengers,* 133–34, 144; San Diego *Sun,* 6 March 1903.

15. Eighth Census of the United States, 1860, Reel 105, District of Columbia Slave Schedules, 3.

16. *OR,* 2:721; New York *Herald,* 19 November 1862. The continuing allegations against Charles were due solely to the fact that his brother was continuously described by the northern press as the "beast" in charge of the Richmond prisons.

17. Marshall, *American Bastille,* 268.

18. Ibid., 269; *OR,* 2:730; Davis, *Breckinridge,* 284.

19. *OR,* 2:730.

20. Ibid., 730–31, 736–38.

21. Marshall, *American Bastille,* 269–77; Haskin, *History of the First Artillery,* 41–42.

22. The Winder papers housed in the Southern Historical Collection and the letter from Winder to his son John Cox, previously cited, were saved in this manner.

23. The Richmond papers reported the arrest and detention of both of Winder's brothers. See the Richmond *Examiner,* 16, 25 September 1861 and 29 November 1862. There was a brief stir in the northern press in December 1862 when it was erroneously reported that William Sidney Winder, the general's son, had been captured aboard the schooner *Exchange* on the Rappahannock River by forces from the USS *Anacostia.* This may have been an uncle of Winder's, but it was not his son. See U.S. Navy Department, *Official Records of the Union and Confederate Navies in the War of the Rebellion,* Ser. 1, 5:209, and Winder, "Pedigree of the Winder Family," Maryland Original Research Society, Baltimore.

24. Richmond *Enquirer,* 17 September 1861, 20 November 1863.

25. Ibid., 16 July, 24 December 1861.

26. Richmond *Examiner,* 1–31 October, 1–26 November 1861.

27. Richmond *Enquirer,* 25 November 1861.

28. Ibid., 1–25 November 1861; Richmond *Examiner,* 1–31 October 1861.

29. Jones, *War Clerk's Diary,* 1:70–71.

30. *OR,* 2:1361–62, 1368–70, 1397–98, 1409–10. 1424–27, 1490, 1502–8.

31. Duffy, "Military Administrator," 65; Andrews, *History of Maryland,* 480–81; Estvan, *War Pictures,* 104–5; Lonn, *Foreigners,* 89.

32. Richmond *Examiner,* 18 July 1861, 2–24 May 1862.

33. Estvan, *War Pictures,* 104. The War Department clerk Jones, for example, was a notorious anti-Semite, and this fueled his biased coverage of Winder's men.

34. *OR* 2:1373.

35. Ibid., 1371–74, 1398; Duffy, "Military Administrator," 63; Jones, *War Clerk's Diary,* 1:82, 96; Richmond *Enquirer,* 24 September 1861.

36. Duffy, "Military Administrator," 63; *OR* 2:1315–18.

37. Kane, *Spies,* 236.

38. Richmond *Whig*, 9 August 1861.

39. Younger, ed., *Inside the Confederate Government*, xxv–xxvi; Jones, *War Clerk's Diary*, 1:83–85, 87–88, 90–91, 93, 98–99. No concrete evidence was ever produced, but this is one of the reasons Winder later fired the whole force.

40. Jones, *War Clerk's Diary*, 1:84–85. The Richmond press was quick to criticize Winder, but this allegation by Jones was not supported by any of the newspapers or by any other contemporary source.

41. *OR*, Ser. 1, 5:825; 2:350–51.

42. Richmond *Enquirer*, 3, 6 September, 4 October 1861, 11 February 1862; Jones, *War Clerk's Diary*, 1:72–88.

43. Duffy, "Military Administrator," 45; Richmond *Examiner*, 19 November 1861.

44. Richmond *Examiner*, 30, 31 October 1861; Trexler, "Davis Administration." None of the other papers endorsed Pollard's charge against Winder, and he, too, dropped it immediately.

45. Ely, *Journal*, 53.

46. Richmond *Dispatch*, 2, 3 July 1861; Richmond *Examiner*, 30, 31 July 1862.

47. See Ely, *Journal*; Corcoran, *Captivity*; Jeffrey, *Richmond Prisons*.

48. *OR*, 3:680; C.S.A. War Department, *Regulations for the Army*, 726–27. The Provisional Confederate Congress passed the law on 21 May 1861.

49. Hesseltine, *Civil War Prisons*, 1–13.

50. Ibid., 55–68; Hesseltine, comp., *Prisons*, 8–9.

51. Ibid. Hoffman intentionally reduced rations and failed to provide other needed services for Confederate prisoners at this time. There was no acceptable reason for his malicious action. His excuse, and that of higher authorities, was that the deprivations occurred in retaliation for alleged Confederate atrocities. The hardships inflicted on Union captives were basically due to inadequate management of resources, not malicious intent; but Union mistreatment of southern captives can only be explained by hate and a desire for revenge. In this matter, Lincoln's hands were as black as anyone's.

52. Walker wrote to Governor Ellis in June, but Ellis had died and Clark assumed the office. *OR* 3:681–82, 690–93.

53. Richmond *Enquirer*, 30 July 1861; Jeffrey, *Richmond Prisons*, 89–98.

54. Ely, *Journal*, 24, 53, 96.

55. Corcoran, *Captivity*, 29; Miller, ed., *Photographic History*, 7:176–77; *OR*, 3:768–70.

56. Gray Diary, SHC, 2569, p. 37.

57. Ibid.

58. Harris, *Prison Life*, 21, 126–27.

59. *OR*, 3:698–700, 726. The reprimand from Walker, dated 7 August 1861, is in the Letterbook of Leroy Pope Walker, Secretary of War, in the Manuscript Collection, LC.

60. Jeffrey, *Richmond Prisons*, 89.

61. Ibid., 21–22; Hesseltine, *Civil War Prisons*, 61; *OR*, 3:700, 703–4, 711.

62. Richmond *Enquirer*, 6–10 September 1861; *OR*, 3:718–19.

63. Ely, *Journal*, 101.

64. Hesseltine, *Civil War Prisons*, 58–59. The quote is from T. C. DeLeon, *Four Years*, 114.
65. *OR*, 3:710–11, 749–50.
66. Ibid., 689–90, 704; Hesseltine, *Civil War Prisons*, 8–9; Richmond *Enquirer*, 10 September 1861.
67. Richmond *Enquirer*, 8 October 1861; *OR*, 3:704, 713. All of the evidence indicates that Winder followed his orders to the letter but did not at any time urge that harsh treatment be directed against his charges. The extensive correspondence between Winder and Colonel Robert Ould, commissioner of exchange, was clear concerning the prisoners as a whole and certain captives as individuals. None of Winder's letters advocated increased punishment in order to gain concessions from the Union. This is true for the period prior to the cartel, during the cartel, and after the cartel was abandoned. See also Davis, *Rise and Fall*, 2:585.
68. *OR*, 3:738–39.
69. Ely, *Journal*, 211–17.
70. A mass meeting took place at Faneuil Hall in Boston on 5 February 1862, and Corcoran's supporters demanded that Lincoln secure his release. See New York *Times*, 6 February 1862.
71. All of the prison mail was censored, and Winder and his staff knew better than any other government officials that public opinion in the Union was dismayed with the status quo and desirous of a general exchange of prisoners. It is not possible to reveal in detail exactly what advice Winder gave to Davis or how much impact it had in the formation of official policy, but it is inconceivable that it was not given a great deal of credence, for the position that Davis took was exactly that taken by Winder's father during the War of 1812. Davis wrote Sidney, William, and their cousin Richard Winder after the war that Winder had been a wise choice for the controversial position and that he had always advocated that the prisoners be treated with the utmost kindness. This is not really that significant, since Davis tended to praise and exaggerate the worth of most Confederate officials in his postwar writings, but it is significant that during the war he never overruled Winder or questioned his judgment on anything relating to the prisoner controversy. See Rowland, ed., *Jefferson Davis*, 7:277, 475–77, 497–98; 10:24–25.
72. Ely, *Journal*, 262; Thomas, *Richmond*, 62–63; Jones, *War Clerk's Diary*, 1:101–2. Charles J. Faulkner was the Confederate exchanged for Ely.
73. Richmond *Enquirer*, 17, 20 September 1861.
74. Ibid., 25 October, 23 November 1861.
75. *OR*, 3:720, 733, 736, 751.
76. Richmond *Enquirer*, 19 November 1861.

Chapter 5

1. U.S. Congress, House Doc. 789, 58th Cong., 2d sess., *Centennial* 1:229; Reed, *Cadet Life*, 28; Croffut, ed., *Fifty Years in Camp and Field*, 40–42;

Dupuy, *Where They Have Trod*, 100–104; Baumer, Jr., *West Point*, 13–15; Ambrose, *Duty, Honor, Country*, 24–37; Fleming, *West Point*, 1–3; Coffman, *Old Army*, 11.

2. *ASPMA*, 2:75–80.

3. Dupuy, *Where They Have Trod*, 22; Fleming, *West Point*, 4; Webb, *Alden Partridge*, 17–29; *Niles Weekly Register*, 3:151–52; Ambrose, *Duty, Honor, Country*, 51.

4. RG 688, List of Applications for West Point, 3.

5. RG 94, Class Rolls of the Cadets of the Military Academy, Merit Roll as a Result of the General Examination in December, 1817, with Remarks Showing the State of Each Class on May 1, 1818, Entry 230, Box 129. There are some inconsistencies in these records, but it appears that Winder's application was received in January and approved on 9 May 1814.

6. Cadet uniforms, except for the color change, remained standard and consisted of gray coats, gray vest, and gray pants (winter), white vest and white pants (summer), underclothes, a black stock, round hat, cockade with eagle and hoops, Jefferson shoes, a cut-and-thrust sword, and a musket slightly lighter than the regular army issue. The cost of a winter uniform was about $50, not including the sword and musket, and summer clothing cost about $35 in 1815. The cadet's pay increased but slightly during the antebellum years, from $15 to $30 per month. See Ambrose, *Duty, Honor, Country*, 70, 149; Reed, *Cadet Life*, xiv; U.S. Congress, House Doc. 789, *Centennial*, 1:510–11; *ASPMA*, 2:79–80.

7. Webb, *Alden Partridge*, 31, 38–50; *Niles Weekly Register*, 8:151–52.

8. Ibid.; Fleming, *West Point*, 5–10; Dupuy, *Where They Have Trod*, 93; Ambrose, *Duty, Honor, Country*, 44–55.

9. New York *Commercial Advertiser*, 27 August, 7 September 1814.

10. Very few records for the years 1814–1817 survived the fire of 1838. There is nothing regarding Winder's academic standing for those years and little else of any consequence. Although Samuel Cooper knew Winder when the news of Bladensburg arrived, he never referred to this period when he later discussed Winder's character. There is no mention of Winder in George D. Ramsey's recollections about this period of academy history either, but his observations about cadet life from 1814 to 1820 offer some suggestion that Winder's classmates, especially the upperclassmen, probably made life difficult for the cadet whose father had allowed the enemy to burn the national capital. Ramsey's "Recollections of the United States Military Academy at West Point, 1814–1820" (Miscellaneous MS, USMA Library), was partially included in Cullum's *Biographical Register*, 3:596–648.

11. The attorneys included his father; John and Nathaniel Winder; Ephraim K. Wilson; and Josiah Polk. The medical doctors were Thomas, Samuel, and George H. Winder; Thomas, Washington, Gordon, and William Winder Handy. The planters, all of whom had extensive holdings, were Major Ephraim King Wilson, Hugh Gamil, and Major Nehemiah King. Levin and John Winder were aged and ill men in 1815 and did not have sons ready or able to take over their holdings at that time. See Laird, ed., "Some Records of the Winder Family," 8–16, and the genealogical chart "Pedigree

of the Winder Family," prepared by Frederick Winder, at the Maryland Original Research Society, Baltimore.

12. Scharf, *Chronicles of Baltimore*, 296, 375–80; Lossing, *War of 1812*, 918n; Owens, *Baltimore*, 218–20; Swisher, *Roger B. Taney*, 27; Steiner, *Life of Roger Brooke Taney*, 71–78, 81–82; Hemphill, *Papers of Calhoun*, 7:58–59, 432, 8:8, 134. The newspaper coverage of William Henry Winder was national and extensive from 1814 to 1824. Issues that demonstrate both the high esteem accorded him by the preeminent men of his time and the popularity he enjoyed as the "orator of the day" at mass patriotic rallies are the *Maryland Gazette and Political Intelligencer*, 13 July, 24 August, and 14 December 1815, 19 December 1816, 9 January 1817, 5 July 1820, and 25 May 1824; Baltimore *American and Commercial Advertiser*, 6–8 July 1820; *Niles Weekly Register*, 36:262. The *National Intelligencer* (Washington, D.C.) carried his 4 July 1820 oration in full, and newspapers all over the nation quoted from the *Intelligencer*. That organ estimated the crowd at over 30,000 and announced that Winder's voice was so penetrating that everyone clearly heard his words. See the 8 July 1820 issue.

13. As will be shown repeatedly, Winder had a total disdain for physical danger. His strength and basic constitution carried him through many bouts of illness that would have killed a lesser man, and he was never physically intimidated by anyone at any time during his long army career. It is most improbable that he behaved differently at this time of his life. His attitude toward Partridge is evident in that he was one of the cadets who signed a circular supporting him during the 1816 investigation. See Office of the Judge Advocate General, Majority of Corps of Cadets, NA.

14. *Niles Weekly Register*, 9:17–18.

15. Ibid., 12:303–4; Webb, *Alden Partridge*, 39.

16. Fleming, *West Point*, 5–7; Croffut, *Fifty Years in Camp and Field*, 40–41; Webb, *Alden Partridge*, 28–29.

17. Webb, *Alden Partridge*, 62–63; Ambrose, *Duty, Honor, Country*, 44.

18. Webb, *Alden Partridge*, 76–90.

19. Duffy, "Military Administrator," 17–18; RG 94, Adjutant General's Office, United States Military Academy Semi-Annual Muster Roll of Cadets, 1816–1828, Entry 226. Cited hereafter as RG 94, Adjutant General's Office. In this folder there is a checklist, and on p. 17, Winder is listed as "on vacation" for August and September of 1816, and his name does not reappear until the following January.

20. Ambrose, *Duty, Honor, Country*, 62–86.

21. Ibid.; *Niles Weekly Register*, 8:31, 48; Dupuy, *Where They Have Trod*, 130. Rider Henry Winder was the youngest brother of Winder's father and served in the army during the War of 1812 and again from 1816 to 1819. He held various government positions, federal and state, and might have made more of an impact had it not been for his extreme bashfulness. He was born on 9 May 1787 and died 29 April 1866. He provided all of the information supplied in Laird, "Some Records of the Winder Family." A survey of his military experiences is in Heitman, *Historical Register*, 1:1049. Although

Partridge was ordered cashiered, President Monroe did allow him to resign, an act of clemency common at the time.

22. Ambrose, *Duty, Honor, Country,* 67, 77–79.
23. RG 94, Miscellaneous Rolls, 1818–1828, Entry 227. The extant records indicate that Winder was the only one of his class without a demerit. Casting doubt on this evidence is the fact that no mention of it was ever made in any official publication by the academy, and it was indeed rare for a cadet to accomplish this feat at any time throughout the long history of West Point.
24. RG 94, Class Rolls of the Cadets of the Military Academy, Entry 230, Box 129. Many if not most of the military writings of the day were written in French, and mathematics was deemed essential for training in the engineering profession. See Ambrose, *Duty, Honor, Country,* 90–92.
25. Ibid.
26. Ibid.; RG 94, Miscellaneous Rolls, 1818–1828, Entry 227; RG 94, Consolidated Weekly Class Reports, 1819–1831, Entry 226; Cullum, *Biographical Register,* 1:252.
27. Cullum, *Biographical Register,* Vol. 1, classes of 1814–1821.
28. Just, *Military Men,* 42–43.
29. Ibid.; Ambrose, *Duty, Honor, Country,* 97–98.
30. Most graduates of the academy did not remain in the military. They became the civil engineers of America and had an enormous impact on the technology of their day. They built roads and bridges, became presidents of railroads, and generally succeeded quite well in civilian life; but many of them did record their belief that the academy had ruined them for anything but the military life. The quote is from Eaton, *Jefferson Davis,* 15.
31. John Winder Hughes, interview with author, 27 December 1986. Mr. Hughes informed me that his mother vividly recalled meeting Winder in 1864 and found him to be a kind and gentle man, but his voice and even his accent were harsh to her young ears.
32. Thayer's rules were designed to measure the totality of the cadet's conduct, not just classroom performance. Demerits were routinely assigned for literally hundreds of minor violations including the use of alcohol and the odor of tobacco in a cadet's room. Winder was never cited for these or any other violation of the puritanical rules of the superintendent. Regular army officers who were drunks were cashiered or forced to resign from the service during the days of the old army, but most of the others did drink moderately. It was a hard-drinking society, and Winder experienced problems in imposing prohibition on his company during the antebellum years, and he found it an impossible task in Richmond.
33. RG 94, Roll 7, letters of 8 July and 23 July 1820, to and from Adjutant General Jones. Summer encampment for that year was at the national capital, but Winder was notified that he would not be expected to make the trip. He accepted the commission on 8 July, visited Washington briefly, and then proceeded to Baltimore.
34. Register of the First Presbyterian Church, Baltimore, 122. In the surviving correspondence between John and William, Charlotte is mentioned fre-

quently. Both were concerned when she married James Townsend of New York in 1846. Townsend was fifteen years older than Charlotte and only moderately successful in business, but the marriage was a happy one. See J. H. Winder Papers, SHC, M-915, letter from William to John, 16 November 1846, and W. A. Townsend, *A Memorial of John, Henry, and Richard Townsend*, 164.

35. *Maryland Gazette and Political Intelligencer*, 19 December 1816, 24 May 1824; Swisher, *Roger B. Taney*, 27; Hemphill, *Papers of Calhoun*, 8:8, 134. The noted attorney Reverdy Johnson recorded that Winder was one of the most outstanding attorneys of his generation. See Owens, *Baltimore*, 375–80.

36. The Third Audit revealed that Winder owed the money because the government had disallowed that amount for the raising and equipping of the Fifth Regiment during 1812 and 1813. A copy of the Third Audit was made available to the author by William F. Sherman, Judicial and Fiscal Branch, Civil Archives Division, National Archives and Records Service, Washington, D.C. The case is also cited in White, *Jeffersonians*, 181.

37. The HARP (Historical Archeological Restoration Project) Collection at Fort McHenry in Baltimore is a treasure. This extensive project, undertaken during the 1950s, resulted in this fort being the best-documented in America, perhaps in the world. It does not appear that anything or anyone of consequence connected with the fort has been overlooked. There is not much information on John Henry Winder, since his stay was so brief, but there is more material on William Henry Winder here than in any other single repository. A biographer of Winder, Sr., would find this holding indispensable. The materials are alphabetically organized by topic but do not lend themselves to any understandable citation and will be referred to hereafter simply as HARP Collection. See Thompson and Newcomb, eds., *Historic Structure Report*, for a concise but excellent history of the fort.

38. HARP Collection, Baltimore. The muster rolls and information about Winder's transfer were found by the HARP team in the estate papers of George Armistead. Hindman's command consisted of one captain, three second lieutenants (including Winder), a surgeon, quartermaster, adjutant, and sixty-three enlisted men.

39. *Niles Weekly Register*, 19:283–87, 298; 20:111; 23:267–69. For an early account of the army, see Ganoe, *History of the U.S. Army*. This sprightly written book has been superseded by Coffman's definitive history, *Old Army*, but both are a joy to read. I obtained the Houston quote and many insights from an unpublished manuscript, "Basic Military Problems, 1792–1860," written by my colleague John Mahon of the University of Florida, who generously shared his vast knowledge of this topic with me.

40. *Niles Weekly Register*, 20:198, 21:8–9; Baltimore *American and Commercial Advertiser*, 20 August 1821. Cullum, *Biographical Register*, 1:252, states that Winder was assigned to the Fourth Artillery on 1 June, but he was ordered to that corps on 26 May 1821.

41. Since I am a native Floridian and have lived all over the state and teach its history, I do not feel the need to document these paragraphs. For those

readers who wish more detail, a good start would be Charlton Tebeau, *A History of Florida.* This standard textbook also has an adequate bibliography.

42. *Maryland Gazette and Political Intelligencer,* 17 June 1824, quoting the Baltimore *Federal Gazette.*

43. Winder's beliefs regarding Indians and alcohol are developed in chapters 6 and 10 herein.

44. RG 94, Roll 8, Item W-4, Winder to Jones, 19 January 1822.

45. *Niles Weekly Register,* 20:56. Winder apparently had the use of one of his father's slaves after he joined the army. He may have had this servant while a cadet, but I have found no evidence to support that view. See note 63, chapter 3, for my explanation. On Winder's allowance as a second lieutenant see U.S. Congress, House Doc. 209, 29th Cong., 1st sess., "Pay for Officers."

46. Cullum, *Biographical Register,* 1:252.

47. Willingham, *We Have This Heritage,* 30–31; Bowen, *Wilkes County, Georgia,* 1–5.

48. Will Book DD, 234, Wilkes County Courthouse, Washington, Ga.

49. Augusta *Herald,* 17 October 1805.

50. Cemetery Records, Mary Willis Library, Washington, Ga. This daughter, Sarah Porter Gilbert, died in 1807 at age two.

51. Augusta *Herald,* 26 April 1807.

52. Fourth Census of the United States, 1820, Reel 9, Wilkes County, Georgia, 199. The four Shepherd children, three girls and a boy, were all between the age of ten and fifteen in 1820, with Elizabeth being the eldest by three years.

53. Willingham, *We Have This Heritage,* 133–36; Washington (Ga.) *Monitor,* 9 February 1813.

54. Bowen, *Wilkes County, Georgia,* 170.

55. Deed from James Alexander to Andrew Shepherd, dated 26 January 1816, Mary Willis Library, Washington, Ga.

56. Ibid.; Fourth Census of the United States, 1820, Reel 9, Wilkes County, Georgia, 199. Shepherd paid $1,800 for the house and land in 1816.

57. Willingham, *We Have This Heritage,* 137, 185.

58. Washington (Ga.) *Monitor,* 10 July 1813. General Winder appeared frequently in subsequent issues, from 1815 until his death in 1824.

59. Willingham, *We Have This Heritage,* 31; Laird, ed., "Some Records of the Winder Family," 18–19; Fourth Census of the United States, 1820, Reel 9, Wilkes County, Georgia, 199.

60. Will Book HH, 84, Wilkes County Courthouse, Washington, Ga.; Wilkes County Papers 1773–1833, Item 1613, Reel 242-11, p. 18, Georgia State Archives, Atlanta.

61. Augusta *Chronicle,* 18 February 1823; recorded in First Marriage Book, 1806–1834, 249, Georgia State Archives, Atlanta; Will Book HH, 84, and Returns of Administrators and Guardians, Book I, 193, both in Wilkes County Courthouse, Washington, Ga.

62. RG 94, Roll 31, Item W-12. Cullum, *Biographical Register,* 1:252, notes that Winder was on ordnance duty from February to 20 August 1822 and was on leave from that time until he resigned on 31 August of the following

year. Winder certified that this was correct. However, in January of that year, a summary of his resignation appeared in RG 94, Register of Letters, Roll 4, Vol. 2, Winder to Jones, 19 January 1823.

63. The Tax Digest for 1826 reveals that Winder never owned any real estate in Wilkes County but that he had defaulted on his taxes for that year to the sum of $0.26. See Drawer 45, Box 9, Georgia State Archives. Although the historical record is silent on this point, I strongly suspect that Elizabeth became pregnant and lost a child prior to this pregnancy, since over seventeen months passed before their first child was born. In Winder's second marriage, his firstborn came within eleven months of the nuptials, and this more accurately reflects the birth practices of the times.

64. *Maryland Gazette and Political Intelligencer,* 26 May 1824; Miscellaneous MS Collection, Box 199, LC, letter from W. H. Winder, son of the general, to Henry Dawson, 3 March 1860.

65. Miscellaneous MS Collection, Box 199, LC.

66. *Niles Weekly Register,* 36:262.

67. *Maryland Gazette and Political Intelligencer,* 25 May 1824.

68. Hemphill, *Papers of Calhoun,* 9:115.

69. Ibid., 118, 126, 141; RG 94, Adjutant General's Office, Entry 227. William had also suffered a childhood accident and had partial vision in one eye.

70. RG 94, Adjutant General's Office.

71. Baltimore City Register of Wills, Microfilm CR 10699-1, Folio 37, Book 12, Hall of Records, Annapolis, Md.; *Maryland Gazette and Political Intelligencer,* 1 June and 1 September 1824. The will was proven by Roger B. Taney, Jonathan B. Davidge, and John Meredith.

72. Hopkins, ed., *Papers of Henry Clay,* 897–98, 902–3; *Maryland Gazette and Political Intelligencer,* June– December 1824.

73. I have not been able to determine the exact date that William Andrew Winder was born, but his Military Service Record indicates that he was born in Maryland in 1824, and his Bounty-Land Warrant File makes it apparent that he was born after 23 June of that year (both documents in NA). None of the Maryland newspapers carried the announcement, probably because the family was so preoccupied with the death of the general, and neither the cemetery records nor the obituary notices in the California and New Hampshire newspapers gave the date of his birth.

74. For example, in addition to his immediate family, Winder was supporting two female relatives in his household in 1820. The records are not complete, but these women were probably Levin Winder's widow, Mary, and her niece Mary H. Winder. See Fourth Census, Baltimore, Reel 42, p. 279; Laird, ed., "Some Records of the Winder Family," 18. Winder also employed one free Negro to help with the entertaining.

75. Baltimore City Register of Wills, Folio 37, Book 12; RG 94, Adjutant General's Office.

76. Fourth Census of the United States, Baltimore, Reel 42, p. 278.

77. Hopkins, *Papers of Henry Clay,* 5:807–8. The family made an agreement with George Shaw of Annapolis to sell oil portraits of General Winder for $1.00 each in late 1824 and early 1825, but it is doubtful that this enterprise

generated much income. See *Maryland Gazette and State Register,* December 1824 and January 1825.

78. Cullum, *Biographical Register,* 1:252; John H. Winder File, Special Collections Division, USMA Library, Winder to Cullum, 10 July 1855 and 6 September 1859. Cited hereafter as J. H. Winder File, USMA.

79. Andrew Shepherd's last will and testament, 31 October 1825, clearly shows that his illness was severe by that date. See Will Book HH, 1819–1836, Wilkes County Courthouse, Washington, Ga.

80. The date of Elizabeth's death is unknown. There was no obituary for her or her sister Sarah, who died in 1828, in either the local or any other Georgia newspaper. All of the Shepherds were buried in the family cemetery, and all markers have disappeared. Because of this, none of the family are mentioned in any later compilations of cemetery records for Wilkes County. There is a bill for the coffins of Andrew and Sarah in the Wilkes County records, but no mention of Elizabeth. See Wilkes County Papers, 1773–1833, Item 1613, Reel 242-11, p. 18, Georgia State Archives, Atlanta. Duffy, "Military Administrator," 23, speculates that Elizabeth died in childbirth but gives no documentation. This could be true, but I suspect she was one of the victims of yellow fever, which was raging in the area during that summer. See the Washington (Ga.) *Monitor,* July, August, and September 1826.

81. Tax Digest, 1826, Wilkes County, Drawer 45, Box 9, Georgia State Archives, Atlanta; Wilkes County Papers, 1773–1833, Item 1613, Reel 242-11, p. 18.

82. Ambrose, *Duty, Honor, Country,* 117. A little less than one-half of Winder's class (14 of 30) resigned within a short time after receiving commissions, but none of them ever reentered the army and made it their career, as Winder did. Most became engineers, but some became planters and lawyers.

83. RG 94, Roll 31, Item W-12.

84. Ibid., Items W-12, W-26.

85. Ibid., Item W-30.

86. Ibid. I found no mention of either William or Charles Winder in Jones's correspondence to Barbour. Thayer made the request for Winder's service on 25 September 1827. See RG 94, Roll 39, Thayer to Jones of that date.

87. Croffut, *Fifty Years in Camp and Field,* 50–53.

88. Ibid., 49; Atlanta *Constitution,* 12 June 1827; Ambrose, *Duty, Honor, Country,* 73–75.

89. Rowland, ed., *Jefferson Davis,* 7:495.

90. Duffy, "Military Administrator," 25. The letter from the board was sent to the adjutant general's office on 17 June 1828.

91. Ibid., 25–26.

92. Croffut, *Fifty Years in Camp and Field,* 53; RG 94, Roll 40, Items W-69, W-77.

Chapter 6

1. RG 94, Roll 134, Item W-343, Winder to Jones, 30 November 1836; Coffman, *Old Army,* 54.

2. RG 94, Roll 154, Items W-169, W-207, W-216; Roll 155, Item W-399.

3. J. H. Winder Papers, SHC, M-915, materials relating to the Third Audit, 1839.

4. For a history of this region of Florida, see Blakey, *Parade of Memories*. The suffering at Fort Heileman is detailed on pp. 41–46.

5. RG 92, QM File, Winder to Gibson and Winder to Jesup, 14 April 1838.

6. RG 94, Roll 178, Winder to Jones, 5 March 1838.

7. Ibid., Stewart to Poinsett, 6 July 1838.

8. Ibid., Taney to Poinsett, 3 July 1838.

9. RG 92, QM File, Winder to Gibson, 29 April 1838, Eustis to Jones, 4 August 1838; RG 94, Roll 178, Items W-208, W-209, W-277, W-278, W-318; Roll 179, Item W-343.

10. RG 94, Roll 440, Item W-635; RG 94, Register of Letters, Roll 22, Item W-131; Winder, "Pedigree of the Winder Family," genealogical chart, Maryland Original Research Society, Baltimore; Proprietors Cemetery Records, Portsmouth, New Hampshire, Library. I should like to thank John Griffin of that city for providing me with this information. For the obituary of William Andrew Winder, see the Portsmouth (N.J.) *Herald*, 9 March 1903.

11. RG 94, Register of Letters, Roll 13, Vol. 15, Item 178; J. H. Winder Papers, SHC, M-915, materials relating to the Third Auditor's office, 1839.

12. E. D. Keyes, *Fifty Years' Observation*, 16.

13. RG 94, Roll 200, Item W-390; J. H. Winder Papers, SHC, M-915, Winder to Jesup, 1 November 1839; Account of the Third Auditor, Account No. 7235, pp. 1–18. A copy of the audit may be obtained from the National Archives and Records Service, Judicial and Fiscal Branch, Civil Archives Division, Washington, D.C.

14. RG 94, Engineer Records, Microcopy 91, Roll 8, 247. There was ample opportunity to acquire an Indian mistress, and some officers did, but I have not found any indication that Winder did. See Coffman, *Old Army*, 107.

15. RG 94, Roll 279, Item W-141. Winder was promoted to captain in October and ordered to take command of Fort Sullivan on the twenty-second of that month. He reached the post on 7 November 1842.

16. Ibid., Roll 279, Item W-141.

17. Ibid., Items W-200, W-256; RG 94, Register of Letters, Roll 17, Items 20, 115.

18. RG 94, Roll 292, Item W-127.

19. Ibid., Roll 283, Item C-12. Winder recommended Smith for the position in a letter to Colonel Ira B. Crane on 10 January 1844.

20. Ibid., Roll 307, Item W-506.

21. Ibid.

22. Ganoe, *History of the U.S. Army*, 53, 183, 193–94. For the classic account of the enlisted man, see Coffman's *Old Army*, 137–211. Before 1833, floggings of up to 100 lashes were fairly common, but after that they could not exceed 50 lashes and were given only to deserters. See Coffman, *Old Army*, 197.

23. RG 94, Roll 307, Item W-506. The record does not indicate whether Winder resorted to flogging, but I suspect that he did. He was willing to do anything necessary to maintain discipline throughout his career, in war or peace, and he probably found flogging necessary here at Fort Kent.

24. Ibid., Roll 307, Items W-481, W-528, W-534.
25. Ibid., Item W-534.
26. Ibid., Roll 329, Items W-11, W-33, W-44.
27. Ibid., Items W-33, W-292.
28. Ibid., Roll 312, Item C-150.
29. Ibid., Roll 330, Item W-385.
30. Ibid., Item W-614.
31. Ibid., Roll 324, Item W-313; J. H. Winder Papers, SHC, M-915, William to John Winder, 16 November 1846.
32. Anderson, *Artillery Officer,* 71.
33. Haskin, *History of the First Artillery,* 333. Winder's orders were issued on 23 January 1847.
34. RG 94, Roll 364, Item W-313.
35. Anderson, *Artillery Officer,* 131.
36. Ibid., 133-70; Haskin, *History of the First Artillery,* 95; J. H. Winder File, USMA Library, letters from Winder to Cullum, 10 July 1855 and 6 September 1859.
37. Haskin, *History of the First Artillery,* 99–100.
38. Ibid.; J. H. Winder File, USMA Library, letter of 6 September 1859, from Winder to Cullum.
39. Anderson, *Artillery Officer,* 192.
40. Haskin, *History of the First Artillery,* 106.
41. Ibid.
42. Ibid., 107.
43. Ibid., 107–8.
44. Ibid., 108–9; Cullum, *Biographical Register,* 1:253.
45. Ibid. Winder had eleven total casualties, seven of whom died. This was the second highest rate of the five companies engaged.
46. J. H. Winder File, USMA Library, letter of 6 September 1859, from Winder to Cullum.
47. Haskin, *History of the First Artillery,* 332; Anderson, *Artillery Officer,* 312.
48. J. H. Winder File, USMA Library, letter of 6 September 1859, Winder to Cullum.
49. Anderson, *Artillery Officer,* 312.
50. Haskin, *History of the First Artillery,* 333.
51. Ibid., 116; J. H. Winder File, USMA Library, letter of 6 September 1859, Winder to Cullum.
52. RG 134, Winder Fund, Entry 152.
53. RG 140, Field Report of the First Brigade, Second Division, Commanded by Persifor F. Smith; RG 137, Register of Officers at Post, Vera Cruz, 1–4; and RG 134, Orders AQ.
54. RG 137, Register of Officers, 3–4; J. H. Winder Papers, SHC, M-915, order dated 24 May 1848. The register of officers cited above does not cover all of Winder's activities, but it does provide an example of his manifold duties, including the return of runaway slaves. He returned a man named Abraham to his New Orleans owner, Joseph Grillier. There is mention of other actions of this type, but no details were given.

55. RG 134, Orders AQ, Nos. 22, 23, and 25.

56. RG 94, Roll 398, Item W-748; Roll 419, Items W-64, W-131; RG 94, Register of Letters, Roll 21, Item 252. William Andrew saw no combat and only limited duty in Mexico, but he did qualify for bounty land made available by Congress in 1850 to veterans of that conflict. His application for 160 acres is included in his personal file, available at the National Archives.

57. Seventh Census of the United States, 1850, Reel 534, New York City, Ward 1, p. 214. The women were Margaret Riley and Ann Daly, aged twenty and twenty-five. Winder also employed twelve-year-old Sarah Webster from Maine, but her duties were not specified in the census.

58. Frisbie, *Peace River Pioneers*, 15–16; Covington, *Billy Bowlegs War*, 19–22. In 1842, the Seminoles were temporarily assigned to the lands between Charlotte Harbor and the Peace River on the west, and the Kissimmee River and Lake Okeechobee on the east, Lake Istokpoga being the northern, and Shark River the southern, limit.

59. Grismer, *Tampa*, 105–19; Mormino and Pizzo, *Tampa*, 46.

60. RG 94, Roll 440, Item W-635; Godown and Rawchuck, *Yesterday's Fort Myers*, 19–20; Grismer, *Fort Myers*, 65–66. The quotation is from a report by Captain F. A. Hendry in 1854 and appears in Grismer, *Fort Myers*, 65. Twiggs's son-in-law was Colonel Abraham Charles Myers.

61. RG 94, Roll 475, Item W-453.

62. Cooper's defense of Winder is quoted in detail in the last two chapters of this work. For a summary of Cooper's career, see Heitman, *Historical Register*, 1:326. Twiggs turned the command over to Justin Dimick in September 1850, and Childs took command from Dimick in November. See Heitman, 1:374, for the change of command.

63. RG 94, Roll 475, Item W-438; Covington, *Billy Bowlegs War*, 19. For a description of the Peace River, see Blakey, *The Florida Phosphate Industry*, 40–41.

64. Covington, *Billy Bowlegs War*, 19; RG 94, Roll 456, Item W-255.

65. RG 94, Roll 456, Item W-255.

66. Covington, *Billy Bowlegs War*, 21–26; Tebeau, *History of Florida*, 169.

67. RG 94, Roll 474, Item W-151.

68. Ibid., Item W-172.

69. Ibid., Roll 475, Item W-438.

70. The exact location of Fort Winder cannot be determined, as the area is now a subdivision, but it was approximately one-half mile from the Peace River in DeSoto Peace River Heights. For a map of the Peace River area in 1891 that shows Fort Winder, see Shrader, *Hidden Treasures*. A good description of the probable location is in De Vane's *Early Florida History*, Vol. 2, no pagination.

71. RG 94, Roll 475, Item W-438.

72. Ibid.

73. Ibid.

74. Godown and Rawchuck, *Yesterday's Fort Myers*, 19–20.

75. In my article published in the October 1984 issue of the *Florida Historical Quarterly*, 166, I inadvertently omitted part of a sentence that resulted in

Colonel Ira B. Crane, not Major French, being identified as the officer responsible for bringing Winder's violation of Special Order No. 4 to Childs's attention. I regret this error.

76. RG 94, Register of Letters, Roll 21. Crane made the request on 8 June 1848 and later had extremely harsh words to say about Winder. See John D. Hayes, ed., *Samuel Francis DuPont,* 2:289–90.

77. RG 94, Roll 475, Item W-438.

78. U.S. Congress, House Doc. 209, 29th Cong., 1st sess., a report to the Senate by the secretary of war, giving the pay and allowances for officers of various grades for the years 1812, 1824, 1838, and 1846. The pay scale for 1846 was still in effect in 1852.

79. Cullum, *Biographical Register,* 1:117.

80. Heitman, *Historical Register,* 1:374. Unlike Winder, Justin Dimick was an extremely religious man. When a church was not available, he held services in his tent, and both officers and enlisted men were welcome. See Coffman, *Old Army,* 81.

81. Charleston *Daily Courier,* 25 April 1853, quoting the Jacksonville *Florida Republican.*

82. Ibid., 29 April 1853, quoting the *Florida Mirror.*

83. RG 94, Register of Letters, Roll 25, letters of 20 January, 2 August, 21 August, and 30 September 1853, from Winder to Cooper; William Andrew Winder File, Bounty Land Application, NA.

84. RG 94, Register of Letters, Roll 26, letter of 19 April 1854, from Winder to Cooper, reporting his arrival and the results of the artillery practice that he had just conducted.

85. RG 94, Roll 508, Item W-369.

86. Charleston *Daily Courier,* 9 February 1865.

87. Duffy, "Military Administrator," 36–37. The Richmond *Enquirer* of 25 September 1861 contains a brief biographical sketch of William Winder, and the Winder File at the Museum and Library of Maryland History in Baltimore is also useful. I have not been able to determine why a man of such prominence escaped each census from 1840 to 1860, except to note that he traveled extensively each summer and most probably was not in residence when the census taker made the tally.

88. RG 94, Register of Letters, Roll 28, Item 544. See Marriage Bonds for Wake County, Vol. 3, North Carolina Archives, Raleigh. After 1856, when Winder was on leave, he gave his address as 55 Lexington Street, Baltimore, his mother's home.

89. RG 94, Roll 573, Item W-414.

90. Ibid., Roll 594, Items W-202, W-291; RG 94, Register of Letters, Roll 30, Items 106, 127; Roll 31, Items 55, 56. Winder made several errors in his reports at this time. For example, on 3 March 1859, he corrected a mistake he had made the previous month about the death of one of his men. He originally reported that John Malley had died instead of John Meanley, and although the names are similar, he knew his men intimately and had never made an error of this type before. At the least, it is obvious that his mind was not on his work.

Chapter 7

1. Thomas, *Confederate Nation*, 125–28, 143–45, 190–214.
2. Richardson, ed., *Messages and Papers of the Confederacy*, 1:220; *OR* Ser. 1, Vol. 51, Pt. 2, p. 482.
3. Richmond *Examiner*, 28 February 1862; Richmond *Enquirer*, 4 March 1862; Richmond *Whig*, 3 March 1862.
4. Owsley, *State Rights*, 157–61. See Roland, *Confederacy*, 76, on the unpopularity of Mansfield Lovell's actions in New Orleans. On the unpopularity of the whole provost system in the Confederacy, see Radley, *Rebel Watchdog*.
5. Owsley, *State Rights*, 154–55.
6. Richmond *Examiner*, 8 March, 19 April 1862.
7. Ibid., 12, 24 May 1862; Richmond *Whig*, 6 March 1862; Richmond *Enquirer*, 2 May 1862.
8. Thomas, *Richmond*, 82–83.
9. Richmond *Examiner*, 26 March 1862.
10. Richmond *Dispatch*, 5 March 1862; Richmond *Enquirer*, 2, 5–6 March 1862; Richmond *Whig*, 11 March 1862. The *Whig* did not approve of Winder's firearm ordinance from the beginning.
11. Richmond *Enquirer*, 14 March 1862; Richmond *Dispatch*, 5 March 1862.
12. Richmond *Whig*, 14 March 1862; Richmond *Enquirer*, 14 March 1862.
13. Richmond *Examiner*, 24 March 1862.
14. Ibid., 18 April 1862.
15. Ibid., 24 March 1862.
16. Jones, *War Clerk's Diary*, 1:178. Winder fired the detectives on 24 October 1862. See the Richmond *Dispatch* of 9 June for his statement concerning identification.
17. Richmond *Enquirer*, 13 June 1862.
18. RG 109, Secretary of War, Letters Rec'd, Winder to Randolph, 28 October 1862.
19. Thomas, *Richmond*, 106–7; Richmond *Whig*, 9 August 1862.
20. Richmond *Dispatch*, 6 March 1862; Richmond *Enquirer*, 11 March 1862.
21. Jones, *War Clerk's Diary*, 1:113; Richmond *Examiner*, 10 March 1862.
22. Richmond *Enquirer*, 17 March 1862.
23. Jones, *War Clerk's Diary*, 1:121; Richmond *Enquirer*, 20 March 1862.
24. Richmond *Examiner*, 5 October 1862.
25. Jones, *War Clerk's Diary*, 1:133.
26. Ibid., 146.
27. RG 109, Secretary of War, Letters Rec'd, Griswold to Winder, 15 January 1863.
28. Hamilton, ed., *Papers of Randolph Abbott Shotwell*, 367.
29. Ibid., 368, 383.
30. Richmond *Dispatch*, 1 July 1861. Fortress Monroe was officially renamed Fort Monroe during Jackson's first administration, but the newspapers and the population at large still referred to it as fortress thirty years later.
31. Richmond *Enquirer*, 2 May 1862.

32. Jones, *War Clerk's Diary*, 1:115–16.
33. Ibid., 120.
34. Richmond *Whig*, 20 March 1862.
35. Duffy, "Military Administrator," 81.
36. Richmond *Whig*, 25 March 1862.
37. Ibid., 27 March 1862.
38. Richmond *Dispatch*, 12 March, 4 April 1862.
39. Richmond *Whig*, 16 July 1862.
40. Richmond *Enquirer*, 28 July 1863.
41. Eaton, *History of the Southern Confederacy*, 231.
42. Sterling, ed., *A Belle of the Fifties*, 178–79.
43. Richmond *Examiner*, 2, 9 April 1862.
44. Thomas, *Richmond*, 87.
45. Richmond *Whig*, 13 April 1862.
46. Thomas, *Richmond*, 87; Duffy, "Military Administrator," 79.
47. Quoted in Thomas, *Richmond*, 87.
48. Richmond *Whig*, 19, 25 July, 1, 8 August 1862; Thomas, *Richmond*, 106.
49. RG 109, General and Staff Office Files, Northrop to Randolph, 3 November 1862.
50. Thomas, *Confederate Nation*, 198.
51. Richmond *Enquirer*, 14 March, 22 April 1862.
52. Ibid., 18 April 1862; Richmond *Whig*, 18 April 1862.
53. Duffy, "Military Administrator," 77–78; Richmond *Enquirer*, 11 April 1862; Richmond *Examiner*, 11 June 1862.
54. Thomas, *Richmond*, 84–85, 90.
55. Richmond *Whig*, 22 April 1862.
56. Coulter, *Confederate States*, 89–92.
57. Duffy, "Military Administrator," 62; Thomas, *Richmond*, 82, 90; Richmond *Whig*, 3, 10, March 1862; Botts, *Great Rebellion*, 279–94. Winder's letter to Botts (28 April 1862) notifying him of the terms of his release was official but courteous in tone.
58. Richmond *Whig*, 3 April 1862; RG 109, Register of Letters and Telegrams Rec'd, Various Commands, 1861–1865, 236, 330. This register contains records for the Department of Richmond and Winder's office for the years 1862–1865, and the materials are so varied that it should be labeled "Miscellaneous Records."
59. Johnston, ed., *Zebulon Baird Vance*, 1:444–51. The editor of the *Enquirer*, Obediah Wise, sent the two accusatory letters to Winder.
60. Tucker, *Zeb Vance*, 279–82; Fayetteville *Observer*, 15 December 1862; Williams and Hamilton, eds., *William A. Graham*, 5:433–35. See the Raleigh *Standard*, 17 December 1862, for a detailed account of the arrest of Robert Graves.
61. The Fayetteville *Observer* and the Raleigh *Standard* led the attack during the first half of January 1863.
62. North Carolina Historical Commission, *Calendars of Manuscript Collections*, 1:258.
63. Ibid., 258–59.

64. Williams and Hamilton, eds., *William A. Graham*, 5:453.

65. Vance Collection, 233, 260, 265, Perkins Library, Duke University.

66. Marks, *Peninsular Campaign*, 430.

67. Hayes, ed., *Samuel Francis DuPont*, 2:289–90. John M. Brannan, West Point class of 1837, was a captain in 1854 when he served with Winder, and Charles M. Crane from Massachusetts was a surgeon, promoted to major in 1861. See Heitman, *Historical Register*, 1:241, 335.

68. John Henry Winder Letters, 1862–1865, MS Collection, Perkins Library, Duke University. Scholfield asked for Winder's help on 22 December 1862.

69. Richmond *Whig*, 4 March 1862; Richmond *Examiner*, 3 April 1862; Cunningham, *Doctors in Gray*, 52; Brewer, *Confederate Negro*, 101–2.

70. Richmond *Examiner*, 2 March 1862.

71. Richmond *Whig*, 21 March, 2 September 1862.

72. *OR*, Ser. 1, Vol. 2, Pt. 3, p. 506.

73. Ibid., 542; Ser. 1, Vol. 11, Pt. 3, pp. 516, 527, 577, 643; Duffy, "Military Administrator," 76; RG 109: Letters and Orders Issued, Confederate Military Prisons, Richmond, Virginia, January 1862–December 1863, Vol. 199 1/2, Chap. 9, cited hereafter as Confederate Prisons. Lee issued the order to Winder on 23 May 1862.

74. RG 109, Secretary of War, Letters Rec'd, No. W439, Winder to Randolph, 22, 28 May 1862; *OR*, 1:1139.

75. Richmond *Examiner*, 30 May 1862; Duffy, "Military Administrator," 73–74. On 31 December 1862, Winder had 85 officers and 1,486 men present for duty out of an aggregate of 2,017. See *OR*, 6:278. For most of his time in Richmond, Winder's force averaged about 1,400, and it is doubtful if 1,000 were present for duty at any time. The story of Thomas Murphy appears in the 9 August 1862 issue of the Richmond *Whig*.

76. *OR*, 4:774.

77. For specific examples, consult Freeman, *Lee's Lieutenants* and *R. E. Lee*.

78. Sterling, ed., *Belle of the Fifties*, 187.

79. Thomas, *Richmond*, 97; Richmond *Enquirer*, 13 June 1862; Richmond *Whig*, 6 June 1862; Putnam, *Richmond*, 151, 154.

80. Thomas, *Richmond*, 99–100; Cunningham, *Doctors in Gray*, 45–48.

81. Jones, *War Clerk's Diary*, 1:142; Richmond *Dispatch*, 8 July 1862. Winder reported on 16 July that there were 7,847 Federals in the Richmond prisons. See *OR*, 4:821.

82. Harrison Collection, Box 8, LC, letter from Harrison to Professor Quinche of Oxford, Miss., 21 March 1862.

83. On 29 July, Winder set the prices for the following articles at a fixed rate: corn, $1.40 per 50 lb. bushel; cornmeal, $1.50 per 50 lb. bushel; seed oats, $.80 per 32 lb. bushel; he also established a maximum price for clover, hay, fodder, straw, and shucks. See Richmond *Enquirer*, 12, 29 July 1862.

84. Jones, *War Clerk's Diary*, 1:148–50.

85. RG 109, Southern Historical Society Papers, 45:248–50. These are copies of original records housed in the SHC, and will be cited hereafter as RG 109, SHS. Richmond *Enquirer*, 26 August 1862.

86. Thomas, *Confederate Nation*, 150–52.

87. Richmond *Dispatch*, 4 October 1862.

88. RG 109, SHS, 45:242–47; 46:102–4, 187–88; 47:77, 112.

89. Jones, *War Clerk's Diary*, 1:159–60, 169.

90. RG 109, A & IGO Office, Letters Rec'd, No. W2044, Winder to Randolph, 12 November 1862.

91. Richmond *Enquirer*, 18 September, 21 October 1862.

92. *OR* 4:877.

93. Richmond *Enquirer*, 1 August, 30 September, 21 October 1862; RG 109, SHS, 46:209–10.

94. Richmond *Dispatch*, 9 October 1862.

95. Richmond *Enquirer*, 27, 31 October 1862; Richmond *Whig*, 5 November 1862; Richmond *Examiner*, 31 October 1862; Richmond *Dispatch*, 1 November 1862; Jones, *War Clerk's Diary*, 1:178.

96. Richmond *Whig*, 5, 10 November 1862; Richmond *Enquirer*, 14 November 1862, Richmond *Examiner*, 5–8, 17 November 1862.

97. RG 109, Register of Letters and Telegrams Rec'd, Various Commands, 236:135–36.

98. Richmond *Examiner*, 28 November 1862.

99. Richmond *Whig*, 22 February 1863.

100. Ibid., 10 November 1862; Duffy "Military Administrator," 85; Richmond *Whig*, 1 May, 17 November 1863.

101. Richmond *Enquirer*, 20 November 1863; Duffy, "Military Administrator," 85. The gold watch, custom-made in Scotland in 1813 for William H. Winder, went to his son when the general died in 1824. It is now in the possession of James B. Hughes, Jr., of Jacksonville, Florida.

102. Copies of both letters were made available to the author by James B. Hughes, who obtained them from John Winder Hughes, of Wilmington, North Carolina. The letter from R. B. Washington is dated 6 April 1863, and the one from G. Washington, 21 April 1863.

103. Richmond *Whig*, 29 March, 1 July 1864.

104. Richmond *Sentinel*, 17 August, 7 October 1863; Richmond *Whig*, 29 February 1864.

105. Richmond *Whig*, 9–12 March 1864. Cashmeyer was on parole and returned to work on 28 March 1864.

106. Ibid., 2 March, 23 June 1862; Richmond *Dispatch*, 6 March 1862.

107. Baltimore *Sun*, 22 February 1895.

108. Richmond *Whig*, 18, 22 October 1862; Richmond *Enquirer*, 23 October, 19 November 1862; Richmond *Sentinel*, 27 June, 30 November 1862, 18 March 1863.

109. Duffy, "Military Administrator," 96–97.

110. *OR*, 5:916.

111. Ibid., 919–24.

112. RG 109, Confederate Prisons, 199 1/2:107, 6 September 1863.

113. Richmond *Enquirer*, 18 December 1863; Baltimore *Sun*, 22 February 1895. Alexander commanded the Salisbury prison during May and June of 1864 and finished the war as an assistant adjutant general in Seth Barton's brigade in North Carolina.

114. Richmond *Sentinel*, 7 August, 1–2 October 1863; Richmond *Whig*, 19 December 1863, 22, 31 January 1864; Richmond *Dispatch*, 16 May 1864; Duffy, "Military Administrator," 97–98; RG 109, Special Orders, Department of Henrico and Richmond and Provost Marshal's Office, 1864, 250:17–18. All former prisoners in the Winder Legion were under the command of Captain D. W. Vowles and served from 20 May 1864 until the fall of Richmond. Winder ordered Captain I. M. Thompson and Lieutenant L. B. Davis to inspect the food at Castle Thunder on 18 May 1864.
115. Richmond *Enquirer*, 8 December 1862.
116. Thomas, *Richmond*, 114.
117. RG 109, Secretary of War, Letters Rec'd, No. W1125, Winder to Seddon, 8 November 1862; Thomas, *Richmond*, 113–14; Putnam, *Richmond*, 209; Richmond *Dispatch*, 29 January 1863.
118. Thomas, *Confederate Nation*, 203–4; Thomas, *Richmond*, 119-22.
119. Richmond *Whig*, 6 April 1863.
120. Duffy, "Military Administrator," 87–91.
121. John Henry Winder Folder, General Officers File, NA, B. H. Hill and H. V. Johnson to Davis, 15 April 1863.
122. Ibid., H. V. Johnson to James Seddon, 17, 23 April 1863. The twelve senators who sent the appeal to Davis were Clement C. Clay, Jr., George Davis, Thomas J. Semmes, Landon C. Haynes, James L. Orr, Augustus Maxwell, Robert W. Johnson, Robert L. Y. Peyton, John B. Clark, Allen T. Caperton, Herschel Johnson, and Louis T. Wigfall.
123. Richmond *Examiner*, 10 July 1863; Rowland, ed., *Jefferson Davis*, 7:277.
124. Yearns, *Confederate Congress*, 238–44.
125. Richmond *Whig*, 8 October 1863; Richmond *Enquirer*, 9 October 1863.
126. Duffy, "Military Administrator," 100–101; RG 109, Medical Department, Letters Sent, 1862–1863, 416:147–68.
127. Duffy, "Military Administrator," 102; Richmond *Whig*, 1, 3 December 1863; Richmond *Examiner*, 2 December 1863.
128. Richmond *Whig*, 29 December 1863.
129. RG 109, A & IGO, Letters Rec'd 1864, W1015, 6 May 1864.
130. Duffy, "Military Administrator," 142; Richmond *Examiner*, 2 June 1864.
131. Richmond *Examiner*, 26 May 1864.
132. *OR*, Ser. 1, Vol. 51, Pt. 2, pp. 815-16.

Chapter 8

1. New York *Times*, 9, 17 July 1862.
2. Hesseltine, *Civil War Prisons*, 19–33.
3. Richmond *Dispatch*, 3–4, 6 January 1862. The quote from the unidentified prisoner is in the 6 January issue.
4. Hesseltine, *Civil War Prisons*, 65–67. In addition to Hesseltine, all eight volumes of Ser. 2 of the *OR* and most of chap. 7 of Miller's *Photographic History* deal with the prisoner-of-war issue.

5. The transfer to Libby took place on 7 March 1862. See the Richmond *Dispatch* of that date.
6. *OR*, 4:779.
7. Richmond *Enquirer*, 11 July 1862.
8. Richmond *Dispatch*, 1 July 1862.
9. Ibid., 7 March 1862.
10. Ibid., 1–5 July 1862.
11. *OR*, 4:822.
12. Richmond *Dispatch*, 5 April 1862.
13. Hesseltine, *Civil War Prisons*, 68–74.
14. Ibid., 70.
15. RG 109, Confederate Prisons, 199 1/2:17, 26, 32, 37.
16. Richard Winder's assets exceeded $25,000 in real estate and $35,000 in personal property. See Eighth Census, 1860, Reel 1330, p. 156; Fleet and Fuller, eds., *Green Mount*, 181–82; *OR*, 4:873–75.
17. RG 109, Confederate Prisons, 199 1/2:13. Braxton Bragg, P. G. T. Beauregard, and James G. Martin frequently countermanded Winder's orders in their departments. See *OR*, 4:875, 6:147, and 3:795-99.
18. *OR*, 5:784–87.
19. RG 109, Confederate Prisons, 199 1/2: 10.
20. Ibid.
21. Hesseltine, *Civil War Prisons*, 71–71, 83–86.
22. Ibid., 77; *OR*, 4:499.
23. Richmond *Dispatch*, 15, 29 September 1862. Captain Thomas D. Jeffers succeeded Wirz at Libby until October when Thomas P. Turner took command.
24. Ibid., 11, 14, 23 October 1862.
25. Ibid., 24 December 1862; *OR*, 5:795–97.
26. Hesseltine, *Civil War Prisons*, 87–88.
27. Richmond *Whig*, 9, 10 March 1863.
28. Hesseltine, *Civil War Prisons*, 89, 254.
29. John Henry Winder Letters, 1862–65, MS Collection, Perkins Library, Duke University.
30. Hesseltine, *Civil War Prisons*, 93–96, 100–101.
31. RG 109, Letters Sent, Agent of Exchange of Prisons, Nov. 1862–Mar. 1865, 245 1/2:124.
32. RG 109, Endorsements on Letters Rec'd, Agent of Exchange of Prisons, 228:35–36.
33. Ibid., 44.
34. Ibid., 47–48, 57, 94, 99, 110.
35. Richmond *Whig*, 3, 7, 16 November, 7, 29 December 1862.
36. Richmond *Sentinel*, 23 April, 1 October 1863.
37. Ibid., 9, 13 May, 22, 29 July, 26 September, 19 October 1863.
38. Hesseltine, *Civil War Prisons*, 116–17.
39. Fortescue Diary, SHC, 3404. This diary is crosswritten and difficult to read, but it appears to be an accurate account of his ordeal.
40. *OR*, 6:439–40.
41. Ibid., 456.

42. Ibid., 497–99.

43. Ibid., 502.

44. Hesseltine, *Civil War Prisons*, 119–20.

45. *OR*, 6:122–23.

46. Hesseltine, *Civil War Prisons*, 122–23.

47. Boggs, *Eighteen Months*, 9–11, is representative of the prisoners' opinion of Winder.

48. *OR*, 6:273–92.

49. Richmond *Enquirer*, 18 December 1863.

50. RG 109, Endorsements on Letters Rec'd, Agent of Exchange of Prisons, 228:32–33.

51. RG 109, Statistical Reports of Hospitals in the Department of Virginia, Medical Director's Office, 151:59, 67, 102; *OR*, 6:587–88.

52. *OR*, 6:587–88; Richmond *Enquirer*, 18 March 1864.

53. *OR*, 6:558.

54. Hesseltine, *Civil War Prisons*, 129–30.

55. RG 109, A & IGO Office, Letters Rec'd, W50, Winder to Elzey, 12 January 1864; Latrouche to Turner, 2 January 1864; Richardson to Griswold, 11 January 1864.

56. Richmond *Enquirer*, 2 February 1864.

57. New York *Times*, 17 February 1864.

58. Richmond *Whig*, 12 February 1864.

59. Hesseltine, *Civil War Prisons*, 132; *OR*, 33:168–224. Dahlgren was buried in an unmarked grave in Richmond, but local Unionists unearthed his remains and he was soon reinterred in Philadelphia. This demonstrates that Winder's forces had been unable to purge the capital of a rather effective spy ring.

60. Faust et al., eds., *Historical Times Illustrated Encyclopedia*, offers and accurate and succinct account of this event.

61. Richmond *Enquirer*, 18 March 1864.

Chapter 9

1. Futch, *Andersonville*, 3. Cobb became commander of the Military District of Georgia on 28 September 1864.

2. Morgan Papers, SHC, 2842, Folder 9, telegram dated 24 January 1864, from Sidney to Winder.

3. *OR*, 6:976–77, 1000.

4. Ibid., 7:730–31; Futch, *Andersonville*, 4.

5. Hesseltine, *Civil War Prisons*, 112–14, 210–32.

6. Ibid., 135; Futch, *Andersonville*, 9; *OR*, 6:925–26.

7. Futch, *Andersonville*, 12–15; *OR*, 6:925, 993; 7:40, 63–64, 169–70; 8:731.

8. *OR*, 6:1041–43; 7:61–62.

9. Ibid., 1048–49.

10. RG 109, Letters Sent and Rec'd, Medical Director's Office, 1864–1865, 364:32–33.

11. *OR*, 7:1051.

12. RG 109, Statistical Reports of Hospitals, 59, 67, 102; *OR*, 6:1048–49. This is at variance with the conclusions of Futch and Hesseltine, who relied on the material from the *OR* cited above but did not consult RG 109. Winder offered what appeared to be indisputable facts to support his contentions about the increased mortality rates, and I have not found any evidence to dispute these figures.

13. See Hesseltine, *Civil War Prisons*, 127.

14. *OR*, 7:89–91, 103, 135.

15. Hesseltine, *Civil War Prisons*, 134, 139–40, 142; Futch, *Andersonville*, 17, 20, 25, 27.

16. Hesseltine, *Civil War Prisons*, 152; Beers, *Guide to the Archives*, 250–58. This book is indispensable for any scholar researching RG 109 and all other Confederate records.

17. *OR*, 7:172–73.

18. Ibid., 169–73, 192, 213. Like most West Point graduates of the time, Cooper felt obligated to use a French word now and again, and usually misspelled it. He wanted *emeute*, the word for disturbance.

19. Ibid., 377–78, 392–93.

20. Hesseltine, *Civil War Prisons*, 144.

21. *OR*, 7:395–96.

22. Ibid., 396–97, 403, 410–11.

23. Futch, *Andersonville*, 71.

24. *OR*, 7:438, 445–46, 451.

25. Futch, *Andersonville*, 81.

26. *OR*, 7:458, 463, 473, 476.

27. Anderson Papers, SHC, 3602, 6:91–92.

28. *OR*, 7:473.

29. Ibid., 480, 499.

30. Ibid., 490, 493, 499–500, 501.

31. Richmond *Whig*, 29 June 1864.

32. *OR*, 7:429–30, 483, 503–4, 552; Futch, *Andersonville*, 86–90; Hesseltine, *Civil War Prisons*, 148, 253.

33. Ibid.; *Andersonville Prison Park*, 2, a pamphlet available from the Quartermaster General, Department of the Army.

34. *OR*, Ser. 1, 7:25–26, 36–37; Duffy, "Military Administrator," 155; Hesseltine, *Civil War Prisons*, 253. None of the published accounts of former Union prisoners mention Winder's presence after July 1863, but Captain Louis Fortescue's diary states that Winder's last visit to Libby was on 22 August 1863.

35. *OR*, Ser. 1, 5:220.

36. Hesseltine, *Civil War Prisons*, 242.

37. *OR*, 7:565, 583–86, 588–89, 773.

38. Anderson Papers, SHC, 3602, 6:121–28, 132–33.

39. Ibid., 139–40, 143, 145–46.
40. Ibid., 147–48, 150–59; Simpson Diary, SHC, 3870, entry for 8 May 1864, from Andersonville prison. Simpson was sent to Savannah with other officers on 29 July, to Charleston on 13 September, and to Columbia, South Carolina, on 5 October. Anderson later became the mayor of Savannah and the director of the Georgia Central Railroad.
41. King, "Epilogue to Andersonville," 35; OR, 7:821.
42. Hesseltine, Civil War Prisons, 156–57; OR, 7:866–70, 1150.
43. OR, 7:1238–39, 1258.
44. Harlbee Papers, SHC, 1550, Folder 7, entry for 25 September 1864, Louisa Jane Harlbee to Ann Harlbee.
45. King, "Epilogue to Andersonville," 38–39, 41.
46. Brown, Salisbury Prison, 69. The officer quoted was B. F. Booth, who recorded his experiences in a postwar publication entitled Dark Days of the Rebellion.
47. Brown, Salisbury Prison, 12, 31, 45, 75–77; OR, 7:1169, 1219–21, 1240.
48. OR, 7:1303–4. See the Mangum Papers, SHC, 483, Ser. 3, Folder 15, entry for 8 November 1864, for the quotation cited. Brown, Salisbury Prison, 162–66, suggests that as many as 3,700 died, and he uses this figure to refute the total of 11,700 deaths claimed in 1871 by Colonel Oscar Mack, whose total was later used by Rhodes and Hesseltine. By Brown's calculations, only 11 percent of imprisoned Federals died in southern prisons, but his math is dubious.
49. Hesseltine, Civil War Prisons, 206–9.
50. OR, 8:19; RG 109, Letters Sent, Agent of Exchange of Prisons 245 1/2:502, 504, 573, and Endorsements on Letters Rec'd, Agent of Exchange of Prisons, 228:257–302; White Papers, Perkins Library, Duke University. There are nineteen communications in White's file. The ones cited are, in order of presentation in the text, nos. 11, 10, 16, 15, 12, and 17.
51. OR, 7:1193, 8:33. Sidney informed all commanders that Columbia was the new headquarters on 1 January 1865. See 8:5.
52. Ibid., 7:894–1046, 1062, 1179–80, 1184, 1196–97, 1220; 8:11–12, 83–86.
53. Ibid., 8:49.
54. Ibid., 96–97, 137–38, 160–61, 168.
55. Ibid., 111, 159, 172, 184, 191.
56. Ibid., 198. A copy of Forno's telegram conveying the news of Winder's death is in the MS Collection, Perkins Library, Duke University.

Chapter 10

1. Ferguson, Life Struggle, 174.
2. McElroy, This Was Andersonville, 264.
3. Wilmington Journal, 9, 16 February, 1865. See also the Charleston Daily Courier and the Columbia South Carolinian, 9 February 1865.
4. Rowland, ed., Jefferson Davis, 7:86–87. Richard made this claim to Varina

Davis when he met her in New York in 1866, and wrote her in confirmation of his statement on 9 January 1867. See also 10:93–95, for additional details.

5. Ibid., 10:93; *OR*, 8:796–98, 815–20, 834; Hesseltine, *Civil War Prisons*, 245–46; Richard B. Winder, General Officers File, NA. He was moved to Libby on 4 December and incarcerated there as late as March 1866. His counsel was William Linn Brown, but his trial never occurred as reported by Marks and Schatz, eds., *Between North and South*, 405. He became dean of the college in 1888.

6. Rowland, ed., *Jefferson Davis*, 10:93–95.

7. "Death of the Confederacy: The Diary of Tench Francis Tilghman," 1–67. A transcript was provided the author by a descendant of the same name, currently residing in Southport, North Carolina. Alfred J. Hanna used the diary in *Flight into Oblivion*, 108–16, and in "The Confederate Baggage and Treasure Train," 160–63. See also the *Baltimorean*, 5 February 1876, for an account of Sidney's exile in Canada with Jubal Early.

8. J. H. Winder Papers, SHC, M-915, letter from A. S. Johnston to William Winder, 12 October 1865.

9. Rowland, ed., *Jefferson Davis*, 7:275–77. Gertrude Winder, aged ninety, died in 1872 while visiting her daughter Charlotte in Oyster Bay, New York. She was buried beside her husband in Greenmount Cemetery, Baltimore.

10. Lossing, *Pictorial History*, 3:594–97.

11. *OR*, 8:588–632; Hesseltine, *Civil War Prisons*, 151, 242, 253.

12. J. H. Winder File, USMA Library, letters from Sidney to Cullum, 29 May and 4 June 1874, Cullum to Sidney, 3 June 1874.

13. Ibid., Sidney to Cullum, 18 July 1874.

14. Russell, *Blaine of Maine*, 267–70.

15. *Baltimorean*, 5 February 1876.

16. Rowland, ed., *Jefferson Davis*, 7:469–72, 491–92; 10:24–25. No authoritative refutation of this order appeared until Hesseltine published his *Civil War Prisons* in 1930.

17. Beers, *Guide to the Archives*, 249; statements to the author by archivists Charles Shaughnessy and Michael Musick, July 1980.

18. Hughes Account Book, 49, Museum and Library of Maryland, Baltimore, lists fifteen visits for Caroline from May to November, 1876, twelve visits for Carrie from May 1876 to July 1877, and eight visits for Sidney during the same time period; Last Will and Testament of Caroline Ann Eagles, Folio 527, Book 70, and Last Will and Testament of William Sidney Winder, Folio 58, Book 48, are located in the Baltimore City Register of Wills, Hall of Records, Annapolis. Sidney also left $200 to place a cross above Carrie's grave. According to John Winder Hughes, grandnephew, Sidney cut his throat with a straight razor.

19. Wake County Estate Records, 1770–1941, folder of John Cox Winder, North Carolina Archives, Raleigh; J. H. Winder, "These Notes on the American Branch of the Winder Family," (MS in possession of the Winder Family).

20. Coulter, *Confederate States of America*, 90–91.

21. As mentioned, Surgeon General Moore and other contemporaries were not convinced by Winder's reasoning, and neither were Hesseltine and other

scholars; but none of them examined the mortality rates of each side at any given time. A cursory examination of the sources reveals that Confederates died at higher rates than Federals until 1864, when Andersonville and other notorious prisons came into operation. This is surprising in view of the high death rate at Belle Isle during 1863. Hesseltine provides a fine overview of the conditions existing at various Union prisons and fully documents the harsh treatment meted out by various prison officials, but he did not conclude what his own evidence showed—that more Confederates than Federals died prior to the breakdown of exchange.

22. Futch, *Andersonville*, 4–12.
23. *OR*, 7:168–69.
24. Hesseltine, *Civil War Prisons*, 254–56, provides a good overview of the way these figures were obtained.
25. Catton, *Stillness at Appomattox*, 311–14.
26. Richardson, ed., *Messages and Papers of the Confederacy*, 1:445–46.
27. Barney, *Flawed Victory*, 89.

BIBLIOGRAPHY

Primary Sources

Manuscript Collections

Anderson, Edward Clifford. Papers. SHC.

Eaton, John Rust. Papers. SHC

Fortescue, Louis R. Diary. SHC.

Gray, Charles Carroll. Diary. SHC.

Harlbee, William Curry. Papers. SHC.

Harrison, Burton. Collection. LC.

Hughes, Addison. Account Book. The Museum and Library of Maryland History, Baltimore.

Mangum, Adolphus W. Papers. SHC.

Morgan, John Hunt. Papers. SHC.

Ramsey, George D. "Recollections of the United States Military Academy at West Point, 1814–1820." Miscellaneous Manuscripts, USMA Library.

Simpson, Ira B. Diary. SHC.

Vance, Zebulon B. Collection. William R. Perkins Library, Duke University, Durham, N.C.

Walker, Leroy Pope. Letterbook. Manuscript Collection, LC.

White, Isaiah H. Papers. William R. Perkins Library, Duke University, Durham, N.C.

Winder, John H. File. Special Collections Division, USMA Library.

Winder, John Henry. Letters, 1862–1865. William R. Perkins Library, Duke University, Durham, N.C.

Winder, John Henry. Papers. SHC.

Winder, W. H. Papers. Historical Archaeological Restoration Project. Fort McHenry, Baltimore, Maryland.

Winder, W. H. Papers. Miscellaneous Manuscript Collection, Box 199, Library of Congress.

Winder, W. H. Papers and Correspondence. Manuscript 919, Box 4, Museum and Library of Maryland History, Baltimore.

Federal Documents

Old Army and West Point Records, National Archives

Record Group 92. Quarter Masters Consolidated File. Entry 225, Box 1250.

Record Group 94. Adjutant General's Office. United States Military Academy Semi-Annual Muster Roll of Cadets, 1816–1828. Entry 226.

Record Group 94. Consolidated Weekly Class Reports, 1819–1831. Entry 226.

Record Group 94. Class Rolls of the Cadets of the Military Academy. Entry 230, Box 129.

Record Group 94. Class Rolls of the Cadets of the Military Academy. Merit Roll as a Result of the General Examination in December, 1817, with Remarks Showing the State of Each Class on May 1, 1818. Entry 230, Box 129.

Record Group 94. Letters Received by the Office of the Adjutant General (Main Series), 1822–1860. Microcopy 567.

Record Group 94. Miscellaneous Rolls, 1818–1828. Entry 227.

Record Group 94. Register of Letters Received by the Office of the Adjutant General (Main Series), 1812–1889. Microcopy 711.

Record Group 94. Engineer Department Records Relating to the U.S. Military Academy. Microcopy 91.

Record Group 134. Accounts of Fund of Lieut. Governor's Court by Capt. John H. Winder. Entry 152.

Record Group 134. Orders AQ, Vera Cruz.

Record Group 137. Register of Officers at Post, Vera Cruz.

Record Group 140. Field Report of the First Brigade, Second Division, Commanded by Persifor F. Smith.

Record Group 688. List of Applications for West Point.

Judge Advocate General, Office of. Majority of Corps of Cadets.

Register of Letters and Telegrams Received, Various Commands, 1861–1865. Vol. 236, Chap. 2.

Winder, John Henry. General Officers File.

Winder, Richard B. General Officers File.

Winder, William Andrew. File. Bounty Land Application.

Confederate Records, National Archives

Record Group 109. A & IGO Office, Letters Rec'd.

Record Group 109. Adjutant General.

Record Group 109. Endorsements, Letters Rec'd, Agent of Exchange.

Record Group 109. Endorsements on Letters Rec'd, Agent of Exchange of Prisons.

Record Group 109. General and Staff Office Files.

Record Group 109. Headquarters of the Forces.

Record Group 109. Letters and Orders Issued, Confederate Military Prisons. Richmond, Virginia, January 1862-December 1863.

Record Group 109. Letters Sent, Agent of Exchange of Prisons, Nov. [18]62–Mar. [18]65.

Record Group 109. Letters Sent and Rec'd, Medical Director's Office, 1864–1865.

Record Group 109. Medical Department, Letters Sent, 1862–1863.

Record Group 109. Orders Issued Confederate Military Prisons.

Record Group 109. Quartermaster General's Office and the Quartermaster General's Department.

Record Group 109. Register of Letters and Telegrams Rec'd, Various Commands, 1861–1865.

Record Group 109. Richmond Military Prisons.

Record Group 109. Southern Historical Society Papers.

Record Group 109. Secretary of War, Letters Rec'd.

Record Group 109. Special Orders, Department of Henrico and Richmond and Provost Marshal's Office, 1864.

Record Group 109. Statistical Reports of Hospitals in the Department of Virginia, Medical Director's Office.

Record Group 109. War Department Collection of Confederate Records.

Miscellaneous

Account of the Third Auditor. Account No. 6771, 29 March 1820. Judicial and Fiscal Branch, Civil Archives Division, NA.

Account of the Third Auditor. Account No. 7235, 11 November 1839. Judicial and Fiscal Branch, Civil Archives Division, NA.

American State Papers: Foreign Relations. Vol. 3. Washington, D.C.: Gales & Seaton, 1832.

American State Papers: Military Affairs. 7 vols. Washington, D.C.: Gales & Seaton, 1832–1860.

C.S.A. War Department. *Regulations for the Army of the Confederate States and for the Quartermaster's and Pay Departments.* New Orleans, 1861.

U.S. Congress. House. Document 789, 58th Cong., 2nd Sess. *The Centennial of the United States Military Academy at West Point, New York, 1802–1902.* Washington, D.C.: GPO, 1904.

U.S. Congress. Senate. Document 234. 58th Cong., 2d Sess., Serial Nos. 4610–16. *Journal of the Congress of the Confederate States of America, 1861–1865.*

U.S. Census (unpublished). 1800, 1810, 1820, 1830, 1840, 1850, 1860. Schedules 1 and 2, for Maryland, North Carolina, Georgia, New York, Pennsylvania, and Washington, D.C.

U.S. Navy Department. *Official Records of the Union and Confederate Navies in the War of the Rebellion.* 31 vols. Washington, D.C., 1894–1927.

U.S. War Department. *The War of the Rebellion: A Compilation of the Official Records of the Union and Confederate Armies.* 127 vols. Washington, D.C., 1880–1901.

State and County Documents

Georgia

First Marriage Book, 1806–[18]34. Georgia State Archives, Atlanta.

Returns of Administrators and Guardians. Book I. Wilkes County Courthouse, Washington, Ga.

Wilkes County Papers, 1773–1833. Microfilm Reel 242-11, Item 1613, Georgia
    State Archives, Atlanta.
Wilkes County Wills, 1819-1836. Book HH. Wilkes County Courthouse, Wash-
    ington, Ga.

Maryland

Greenmount Cemetery Records. Baltimore.
HARP (Historical Archeological Restoration Project) Collection. Fort McHenry,
    Baltimore.
Last Will and Testament of William Henry Winder. Microfilm CR 10699-1, Folio
    27, Book 12, Baltimore City Register of Wills, Hall of Records, Annapolis.
Last Will and Testament of Caroline Ann Eagles. Folio 527, Book 70, Baltimore
    City Register of Wills, Hall of Records, Annapolis.
Last Will and Testament of William Sidney Winder. Folio 58, Book 48, Baltimore
    City Register of Wills, Hall of Records, Annapolis.
Register of the First Presbyterian Church. Baltimore.
Tilghman, Tench Francis. "Death of the Confederacy: The Diary of Tench Francis
    Tilghman." The original diary is in the possession of a descendant of the same
    name, but a typescript of the document was given to me by John Winder Hughes
    and is currently in my possession.
Winder, Frederick, A. "Pedigree of the Winder Family of Maryland, and Other
    States in America." 1894. Maryland Original Research Society, Baltimore.

North Carolina

Brunswick Estate Records. Book K, Brunswick County Courthouse, Bolivia.
Brunswick Estate Records, 1783 to 1920. Report of Commissioners to Divide
    Land [of Joseph Eagles], 1833. North Carolina Archives, Raleigh.
Cemetery Records, Brunswick County. North Carolina Archives, Raleigh.
Deed Books C, K, L, and P, Brunswick County Courthouse, Bolivia.
Deed Book HH. New Hanover County Records. Wilmington Courthouse, Wil-
    mington.
Deed Book S. New Hanover County Courthouse, Wilmington.
Deed Book U. New Hanover County Records, Microfilm 39, State Archives,
    Raleigh.
Inventories, Accounts of Sales, Guardian Accounts, 1847–1857. New Hanover
    County Records, North Carolina Archives, Raleigh.
Inventories, Accounts of Sales. New Hanover County Records, North Carolina
    Archives, Raleigh.
Last Will and Testament of Joseph Eagles. Recorded in Book C of New Hanover
    County Wills, North Carolina Archives, Raleigh.
Marriage Bonds for Wake County. Vol. 3. North Carolina Archives, Raleigh.
New Hanover County Court Minutes, 1827–1832. North Carolina Archives, Ra-
    leigh.
New Hanover County Court Records, 1832–1838. North Carolina Archives, Ra-
    leigh.
New Hanover County Court Records, 1852–[18]54. North Carolina Archives,
    Raleigh.

North Carolina Historical Commission. *Calendars of Manuscript Collections.* Raleigh: Edwards and Brougton, 1926.

Wake County Estate Records, 1770–1941. Folder of John Cox Winder. North Carolina Archives, Raleigh.

New Hampshire

Proprietors Cemetery Records. Portsmouth, New Hampshire, Library.

Newspapers

Augusta (Ga.) *Chronicle,* 1823–1830.

Augusta (Ga.) *Herald,* 1805–1827.

Baltimore *American and Commercial Advertiser,* 1802–1824.

(Baltimore) *Federal Gazette,* 1813–1824.

Baltimore *Sun,* 1878, 1895.

Baltimorean, 1876.

Cape Fear (N.C.) *Recorder,* 1820–1850.

Charleston (S.C.) *Daily Courier,* 1853, 1865.

Columbia *South Carolinian,* 1865.

Edenton (N.C.) *Gazette,* 1820.

Fayetteville (N.C.) *Observer,* 1863.

Florence (S.C.) *Morning News,* 1959.

Jacksonville *Florida Mirror,* 1853.

Jacksonville *Florida Republican,* 1853.

Maryland Gazette and Political Intelligencer (Annapolis), 1815–1824.

National Intelligencer (Washington, D.C.), 1813–1824.

New York *Commercial Advertiser,* 1814.

New York *Gazette,* 1813–1814.

New York *Herald,* 1862.

New York *Spectator,* 1813–1814.

New York *Times,* 1862–1865.

Niles Weekly Register (Baltimore), 1800–1824.

North Carolina Gazette (Wilmington), 1828–1850.

Portsmouth (N.H.) *Herald,* 1903.

Raleigh *Register,* 1862–1863.

Raleigh *Standard,* 1862–1863.

Richmond *Dispatch,* 1861–1865.

Richmond *Enquirer,* 1861–1865.

Richmond *Examiner,* 1861–1865.

Richmond *Sentinel,* 1862–1865.

Richmond *Whig,* 1861–1865.

San Diego *Sun,* 1903.

Washington (Ga.) *Monitor,* 1812–1830.

Wilmington (N.C.) *Journal,* 1865.

Wilmington (N.C.) *Weekly Chronicle,* 1828–1850.

Books

Boggs, S. S. *Eighteen Months a Prisoner Under the Rebel Flag.* Lovington, Ill.: published by author, 1887.

Botts, John Minor. *The Great Rebellion: Its Secret History, Rise, Progress, and Disastrous Failure.* New York: Harper & Bros., 1866.

Corcoran, Michael. *The Captivity of General Corcoran, the Only Authentic and Reliable Narrative of the Trials and Sufferings Endured, During His Twelve Months' Imprisonment in Richmond and other Southern Cities, by Brig. General Michael Corcoran, the Hero of Bull Run.* Philadelphia: Barclay & Co., 1862.

Croffut, W. A., ed. *Fifty Years in Camp and Field: Diary of Major-General Ethan Allen Hitchcock.* New York: G. P. Putnam's Sons, 1909.

Cullum, George W. *Biographical Register of the Officers and Graduates of the United States Military Academy at West Point, New York, from its Establishment in 1802 to 1890, with the Early History of the United States Military Academy.* 2 vols. New York: Houghton Mifflin & Co., 1891.

Ela, J. B. *The Sights and Secrets of the National Capital.* New York: Harper & Bros., 1869.

Ely, Alfred. *The Journal of Alfred Ely.* New York: D. Appleton & Co., 1862.

Estvan, Bela. *War Pictures from the South.* New York: D. Appleton & Co., 1863.

Ferguson, Joseph. *Life Struggle in Rebel Prisons.* Philadelphia: James Ferguson, 1865.

Harris, William C. *Prison Life in the Tobacco Warehouse at Richmond.* Philadelphia: George W. Childs, 1862.

Jeffrey, William H. *Richmond Prisons, 1861–1862, Compiled from the Original Records Kept by the Confederate Government: Journals Kept by Union Prisoners of War, Together with the Name, Rank, Company, Regiment, and State of the Four Thousand Who Were Confined There.* St. Johnsbury, Vt. Republican Press, 1895.

Johnson, R. W. *Winders of America.* Philadelphia: J. B. Lippincott & Co., 1902.

Jones, John Beauchamp. *A Rebel War Clerk's Diary at the Confederate States Capital.* Edited by Howard Swiggett. 2 vols. New York: Old Hickory Bookshop, 1935.

Keyes, E. D. *Fifty Years' Observation of Men and Events Civil and Military.* New York: Charles Scribner's Sons, 1884.

Laird, Philip D., ed. "Some Records of the Winder Family of Maryland, Written by Rider Henry Winder of Cambridge, Md., for Philip D. Laird, in the year 1864 or 1865." *Maryland Original Research Society of Baltimore Bulletin Number Three* (May 1913).

Lossing, Benson J. *The Pictorial Field Book of the War of 1812.* New York: Harper & Bros., 1869.

———. *Pictorial History of the Civil War in the United States.* 3 vols. Philadelphia: G. W. Childs, 1866–1868.

Marks, J. J., M.D. *The Peninsular Campaign in Virginia; or, Incidents and Scenes on the Battlefields and in Richmond.* Philadelphia: J. B. Lippincott & Co., 1864.

McElroy, John. *This Was Andersonville.* Edited by Roy Meredith. New York: McDowell & Obolensky, 1957.

Page, James Madison. *The True Story of Andersonville Prison: A Defense of Major Henry Wirz*. New York: Neale Publishing Co., 1908.

Polk, W. H. *Polk Family and Kinsmen*. Louisville: Bradley & Gilbert Co., 1912.

Putnam, Sallie Brock. *Richmond During the War: Four Years of Personal Observation*. New York: G. W. Carleton & Co., 1867.

Reed, Hugh T. *Cadet Life at West Point*. Chicago: published by author, 1896.

Russell, William Howard. *My Diary North and South*. Edited by Fletcher Pratt. New York: Harper & Row, 1965.

Stevenson, R. Randolph. *The Southern Side; or Andersonville Prison*. Baltimore: Turnbull Bros., 1876.

Townsend, W. A. *A Memorial of John, Henry, and Richard Townsend, and Their Descendents*. New York: published by author, 1865.

Interviews

Hughes, John Winder. December 1986.

Shaughnessy, Charles, and Michael Musick. July 1980.

Secondary Sources

Books and Articles

Alvarez, Eugene. *Travel on Southern Antebellum Railroads, 1828–1860*. University: University of Alabama Press, 1974.

Ambrose, Stephen E. *Duty, Honor, Country: A History of West Point*. Baltimore: Johns Hopkins University Press, 1966.

Ammon, Harry. *James Monroe: The Quest For National Identity*. New York: McGraw-Hill, 1971.

Anderson, Robert. *An Artillery Officer in the Mexican War*. New York: G. P. Putnam's Sons, 1911.

Andrews, Matthew. *History of Maryland: Province and State*. New York: Doubleday Doran & Co., 1929.

Barnes, Robert W. *Maryland Marriages, 1778–1800*. Baltimore: Genealogical Publishing Co., 1978.

Barney, William L. *Flawed Victory: A New Perspective on the Civil War*. New York: University Press of America, 1980.

Basdevant, Jules. "Deux conventions peu connues sur le droit de la guerre (Etats-Unis d'Amérique et Grande-Bretagne, 12 Mai 1813: Colombie-Espagne, 26 Novembre 1820)." *Revue général de droit international publique* 21 (1914).

Baumer, William H., Jr. *West Point, Moulder of Men*. New York: D. Appleton-Century Co., 1942.

Beers, Henry Putney. *Guide to the Archives of the Government of the Confederate States of America*. Washington, D.C.: G.S.A., 1968.

Bentley, Joseph H. *Fort Johnston in the History of the Lower Cape Fear.*

Private printing, 1970. Available at the Southport, North Carolina Public Library.

Bergmann, Richard, and Donald J. Lehman. "History of the Winder Building, 1847–1988." Report prepared for Max O. Urbahn Associates, Inc., Architects and Planners, New York, N.Y., 1 November 1976.

Blakey, Arch Fredric. *The Florida Phosphate Industry: A History of the Development and Use of a Vital Mineral.* Cambridge: Wertheim Committee, Harvard University Press, 1973.

——. *Parade of Memories: A History of Clay County, Florida.* Green Cove Springs, Fla.: Clay County Bicentennial Commission, 1976.

Bowen, Eliza A. *The Story of Wilkes County, Georgia.* Marietta, Ga.: Continental Book Co., 1950.

Brewer, James H. *The Confederate Negro, Virginia Craftsmen and Military Laborers, 1861–1865.* Durham, N.C.: Duke University Press, 1969.

Brown, Louis A. *The Salisbury Prison: A Case Study of Confederate Military Prisons, 1861–1865.* Wendell, N.C.: Avera Press, Broadfoot's Bookmark, 1980.

Browne, Gary Lawson. *Baltimore in the Nation, 1789–1861.* Chapel Hill: University of North Carolina Press, 1980.

Catton, Bruce. *A Stillness at Appomattox.* New York: Doubleday & Co., 1953. Reprint. New York: Cardinal Giant, 1958.

Coffman, Edward M. *The Old Army: A Portrait of the American Army in Peacetime, 1784–1898.* New York: Oxford University Press, 1986.

Coulter, E. Merton. *The Confederate States of America, 1861–1865.* Baton Rouge: Louisiana State University Press, 1950.

Covington, James W. *The Billy Bowlegs War, 1855–1858: The Final Stand of the Seminoles Against the Whites.* Chuluota, Fla.: Mickler House Publishers, 1982.

Cunningham, H. H. *Doctors in Gray: The Confederate Medical Service.* Baton Rouge: Louisiana State University Press, 1958. Reprint. Gloucester, Mass.: Peter Smith, 1970.

Davis, Jefferson. *The Rise and Fall of the Confederate Government.* 2 vols. New York: D. Appleton & Co., 1881.

Davis, William C. *Breckinridge: Statesman, Soldier, Symbol.* Baton Rouge: Louisiana State University Press, 1974.

DeLeon, T. C. *Four Years in Rebel Capitals: An Inside View of Life in the Southern Confederacy from Birth to Death.* Mobile: Gossip Printing Co., 1890.

De Vane, Park. *De Vane's Early Florida History.* 2 vols. Sebring, Fla.: Sebring Historical Society, 1979.

Dowdey, Clifford. *Experiment in Rebellion.* New York: Doubleday & Co., 1946.

Duffy, Sarah Annette. "Military Administrator: The Controversial Life of Brigadier General John Henry Winder, C.S.A." Master's thesis, Creighton University, 1961.

Dupuy, Ernest. *Where They Have Trod: The West Point Tradition in American Life.* New York: F. A. Stikes Co., 1940.

Eaton, Clement. *A History of the Southern Confederacy.* New York: Macmillan Co., 1954.

——. *Jefferson Davis.* New York: Macmillan Co., 1977.

Fleet, Betsy, and John D. Fuller, eds. *Green Mount: A Virginia Plantation Family during the Civil War: Being the Journal of Benjamin Robert Fleet and Letters of His Family.* Lexington: University of Kentucky Press, 1962.

Fleming, Thomas J. *West Point: The Men and Times of the United States Military Academy.* New York: William Morrow & Co., 1969.

Flory, William E.V.S. *Prisoners of War: A Study in the Development of International Law.* Washington, D.C.: American Council on Public Affairs, 1924.

Fooks, Herbert C. *Prisoners of War.* Federalsburg, Md.: J. W. Stowell Printing Co., 1924.

Freeman, Douglas Southall. *Lee's Lieutenants: A Study in Command.* New York: Charles Scribner's Sons, 1945.

————. *R. E. Lee: A Biography.* New York: Charles Scribner's Sons, 1934.

Frisbie, Louise. *Peace River Pioneers.* Miami: E. A. Seemann Publishing Co., 1974.

Futch, Ovid L. *History of Andersonville Prison.* Gainesville: University of Florida Press, 1968.

Ganoe, William A. *The History of the United States Army.* New York: D. Appleton-Century Co., 1942.

Godown, M., and A. Rawchuck. *Yesterday's Fort Myers.* Miami: E. A. Seemann Publishing Co., Inc., 1975.

Goldsmith, Suzanne, and Katherine Boo. "The Case for the Case Study." *Washington Monthly* (June 1989).

Grismer, Karl. *The Story of Fort Myers.* St. Petersburg, Fla.: St. Petersburg Printing Co., 1949.

————. *Tampa: A History of the City of Tampa and the Tampa Bay Region of Florida.* St. Petersburg, Fla.: St. Petersburg Printing Co., 1950.

Hamilton, J. G. de Roulhac, ed. *The Papers of Randolph Abbott Shotwell.* Raleigh: North Carolina Historical Commission, 1925.

Hanna, Alfred J. "The Confederate Baggage and Treasure Train Ends Its Flight in Florida: A Diary of Tench Francis Tilghman." *Florida Historical Quarterly* 17 (January 1939).

————. *Flight into Oblivion.* Bloomington: University of Indiana Press, 1959.

Haskin, William L. *The History of the First Regiment of Artillery from Its Organization in 1821 to 1 January 1876.* Portland, Maine: B. Thurston & Co., 1879.

Hayes, John D., ed. *Samuel Francis Du Pont: A Selection from His Civil War Letters.* New York: Cornell University Press, 1969.

Heitman, Francis B. *Historical Register and Dictionary of the United States Army, from Its Organization, September 29, 1787, to March 2, 1903.* 2 vols. Washington, D.C.: GPO, 1903.

Hemphill, W. Edwin. *The Papers of John C. Calhoun.* Columbia: University of South Carolina Press, 1973.

Hesseltine, William B. *Civil War Prisons: A Study in War Psychology.* Columbus: Ohio State University Press, 1930.

————, comp. *Civil War Prisons.* A reprint of the contents of *Civil War History* 8, No. 2 (1962). Kent, Ohio: Kent State University Press, 1972.

Hopkins, James F., ed. *The Papers of Henry Clay.* Lexington: University of Kentucky Press, 1963.

Hunt, Gaillard, ed. *The Writings of James Madison.* 9 vols. New York: G. P.
Putnam's Sons, 1900–1910.

Johnston, Frontis W., ed. *The Papers of Zebulon Baird Vance.* Raleigh, N. C.:
State Department of Archives and History, 1963.

Jones, J. William, et al., eds. *Southern Historical Society Papers.* 52 vols.
1876–1959. Reprint, with 2 vol. index, New York, 1977–1980.

Just, Ward. *Military Men.* New York: Alfred A. Knopf, 1970.

Kane, Harnett T. *Spies for the Blue and Gray.* New York: Doubleday & Co.,
1954.

Kantor, MacKinlay. *Andersonville.* New York: World Publishing Co., 1955.

Kellam, Ida B., and Elizabeth F. McKey, comps. *St. James Church, Wilmington,
North Carolina, Historical Records 1737–1852.* Available at the church.

King, G. Wayne. "Epilogue to Andersonville: Death Camp at Florence." *Civil
War Times Illustrated* 12, No. 9 (January 1974).

Laumer, Frank. *Massacre.* Gainesville: University of Florida Press, 1968.

Leckie, Robert. *The Wars of America.* New York: Harper & Row, 1968.

Lee, Lawrence. *The Lower Cape Fear in Colonial Days.* Chapel Hill: University
of North Carolina Press, 1965.

————. *The History of Brunswick County, North Carolina.* Bolivia, N.C.: Brunswick County Heritage Press, 1980.

Lonn, Ella. *Foreigners in the Confederacy.* Chapel Hill: University of North
Carolina Press, 1940.

Mahon, John. *The Second Seminole War.* Gainesville: University of Florida Press,
1967.

————. *The War of 1812.* Gainesville: University of Florida Press, 1972.

Marks, Bayly E., and Mark N. Schatz, eds. *Between North and South: A Maryland Journalist Views the Civil War.* Rutherford, N.J.: Associated University
Presses, 1976.

Marshall, John A. *American Bastille.* Philadelphia: Thomas W. Hartley & Co.,
1884.

McKay, Elizabeth R. *Early Wilmington Block by Block from 1733 On.* Wilmington: Edwards & Broughton Co., 1967.

McKinney, Francis F. *Education in Violence: The Life of George H. Thomas
and the History of the Army of the Cumberland.* Detroit: Wayne State University
Press, 1961.

McPherson, James M. *Battle Cry of Freedom.* New York: Oxford University
Press, 1988.

Miller, Francis Trevelyan, ed. *The Photographic History of the Civil War.* 10
vols. New York: Review of Reviews Co., 1912.

Mormino, Gary, and Anthony Pizzo. *Tampa: The Treasure City.* Tulsa: Continental Heritage Press, 1983.

Owens, Hamilton. *Baltimore on the Chesapeake.* Garden City, N.Y.: Doubleday,
Doran & Co., 1941.

Owsley, Frank. *State Rights in the Confederacy.* Chicago: University of Chicago
Press, 1925.

Phillips, George H. *Chiefs and Challengers: Indian Resistance and Cooperation
in Southern California.* Los Angeles: University of California Press, 1975.

Potter, David M. *The Impending Crisis, 1848–1861*. New York: Harper & Row, 1976.

Radley, Kenneth. *Rebel Watchdog: The Confederate States Army Provost Guard*. Baton Rouge: Louisiana State University Press, 1989.

Rhodes, James Ford. *History of the United States from the Compromise of 1850 to the McKinley-Bryan Campaign of 1896*. 8 vols. New York: Macmillan Co., 1895–1917.

Richardson, James D., ed. *A Compilation of the Messages and Papers of the Confederacy, including the Diplomatic Correspondence, 1861–1863*. Nashville: United States Printing Co., 1905.

Robinson, Ralph. "Retaliation for the Treatment of Prisoners in the War of 1812." *American Historical Review* 44, no. 1 (October 1943).

Roland, Charles P. *The Confederacy*. Chicago: University of Chicago Press, 1960.

Rowland, Dunbar, ed. *Jefferson Davis, Constitutionalist: His Letters, Papers and Speeches*. 10 vols. Jackson, Miss.: Department of Archives and History, 1923.

Russell, Charles Edward. *Blaine of Maine: His Life and Times*. New York: Cosmopolitan Book Corp., 1931.

Scharf, John Thomas. *The Chronicles of Baltimore*. Baltimore: Turnbull Bros., 1874.

Shrader, Jay. *Hidden Treasures: The Pebble Phosphates of the Peace River Valley of South Florida*. Bartow, Fla.: Varn & Varn, 1891.

Sprunt, James. *Chronicles of Cape Fear, 1660–1916*. Raleigh: Edwards & Broughton Printing Co., 1916.

Steiner, Bernard C. *Life of Roger Brooke Taney, Chief Justice of the United States Supreme Court*. Baltimore: William & Wilkins Co., 1922.

Sterling, Ada, ed. *A Belle of the Fifties: Memoirs of Mrs. Clay of Alabama, Covering Social and Political Life in Washington and the South, 1853–1866*. New York: Doubleday Page Co., 1935.

Swisher, Carl Brent. *Roger B. Taney*. New York: Macmillan Co., 1931. Reprint. Camden, Conn.: Archon Books, 1961.

Tebeau, Charlton. *A History of Florida*. Coral Gables, Fla.: University of Miami Press, 1971.

Thomas, Emory M. *The Confederate Nation, 1861–1865*. New York: Harper & Row, 1979.

———. *The Confederate State of Richmond: A Biography of the Capital*. Austin: University of Texas Press, 1971.

Thompson, E. N., and R. D. Newcomb, eds. *Historic Structure Report: Fort McHenry*. Baltimore: National Park Service, 1974.

Tolbert, Noble J., ed. *The Papers of John Willis Ellis*. Raleigh, N.C.: State Department of Archives and History, 1964.

Topham, Washington. "The Winder Building." *Records of the Columbia History Society* 37.

Torrence, Clayton. *Old Somerset on the Eastern Shore of Maryland*. Richmond: Whittet and Shepperson, 1935.

Trexler, Harrison. "The Davis Administration and the Richmond Press." *Journal of Southern History* 16 (May 1955).

Tucker, Glenn. *Poltroons and Patriots*. 2 vols. New York: Bobbs-Merrill Co., 1954.

———. *Zeb Vance, Champion of Personal Freedom*. New York: Bobbs-Merrill Co., 1965.

Waddell, Alfred Moore. *A History of New Hanover County and the Lower Cape Fear Region, 1723–1800*. Wilmington, N.C.: private printing, 1909.

Webb, Lester A. *Captain Alden Partridge and the United States Military Academy, 1806–1833*. Northport, Ala.: American Southern, 1965.

White, Leonard D. *The Jeffersonians: A Study of Administrative History, 1801–1809*. New York: Macmillan Co., 1951.

Williams, Max R., and J.G. de Roulhac Hamilton, eds. *The Papers of William Alexander Graham*. Raleigh: North Carolina Office of Archives and History, 1973.

Willingham, Robert Marion, Jr. *We Have This Heritage: The History of Wilkes County, Georgia, Beginnings to 1860*. Washington, Ga.: Wilkes Publishing Co., 1969.

Woodward, C. Vann, ed. *Mary Chesnut's Civil War*. New Haven: Yale University Press, 1981.

———, and Elisabeth Muhlenfeld, eds. *The Private Mary Chesnut: The Unpublished Civil War Diaries*. New York: Oxford University Press, 1984.

Yearns, Wilfred Buck. *The Confederate Congress*. Athens: University of Georgia Press, 1960.

Younger, Edward (ed.). *Inside the Confederate Government: The Diary of Robert Garlick Hill Kean*. New York: Oxford University Press, 1957.

INDEX